AF505030

COLLEEN BROWNING

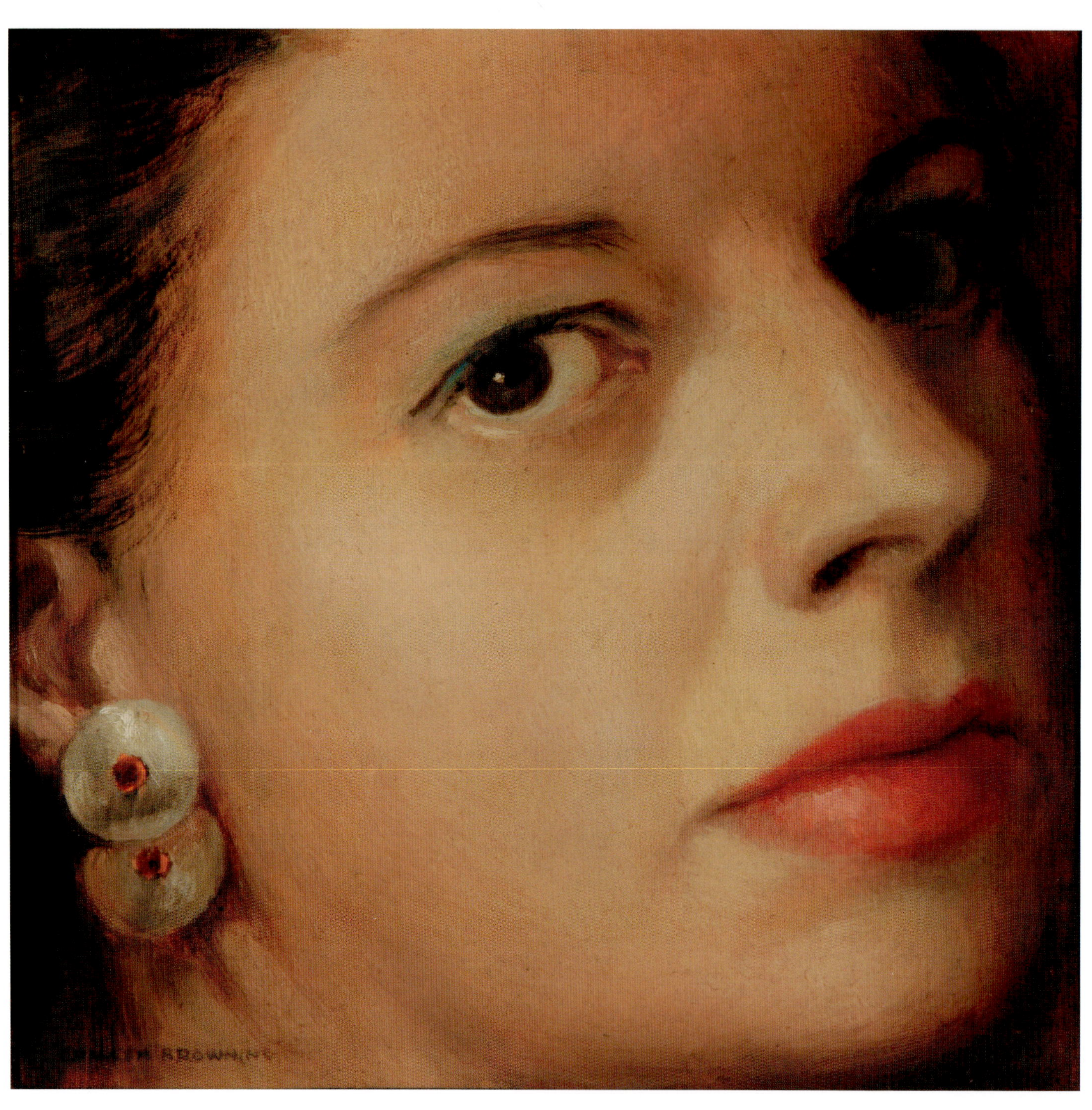
BROWNING

COLLEEN BROWNING

The Enchantment of Realism

by Philip Eliasoph

Introduction by John T. Spike

Hudson Hills Press
Manchester and New York

Exhibition Itinerary

Axis: Ballymun, Dublin, Ireland
September 12–October 28, 2011

National Academy of Design,
New York, NY
May 16–August 26, 2012

Southern Alleghenies Museum of Art
Ligonier, PA
August 22–November 3, 2012

Johnstown, PA
August 23–October 6, 2012

Altoona, PA
August 24–December 1, 2012

Loretto, PA
August 25–December 1, 2012

The Thomas J. Walsh Art Gallery,
Quick Center for the Arts and Bellarmine
Museum of Art,
Fairfield University, Fairfield, CT
January 24–March 24, 2013

The Butler Institute of American Art,
Youngstown, OH
April 21–June 16, 2013

Amarillo Museum of Art, Amarillo, TX
October 25, 2013–January 5, 2014

First Edition

Copyright © 2011 by Philip Eliasoph

All rights reserved under International and Pan-American Copyright Convention.

Published in the United States by Hudson Hills Press, LLC
P.O. Box 205, 3556 Main Street, Manchester, Vermont 05254

Distributed in the United States, its territories and possessions, and Canada by
National Book Network, Inc.
Distributed outside of North America by Antique Collectors' Club, Ltd.

Publisher and Executive Director: Leslie Pell van Breen
Production Manager: David Skolkin
Design: David Skolkin / S+C Studio, Santa Fe
Copyeditor: Linda Gustavson
Proofreader: Ted Gilley
Production Editor: Marisa Crumb
Indexer: Barbara E. Smith
Printed and bound by Toppan Leefung
Founding Publisher: Paul Anbinder

Manufactured in China

Library of Congress Cataloging-in-Publication Data

Eliasoph, Philip.
  Colleen Browning : the enchantment of realism / by Philip Eliasoph ; introduction by John T. Spike.
    p. cm.
  Includes bibliographical references and index.
  ISBN 978-1-55595-366-9
  1. Browning, Colleen--Criticism and interpretation. I. Browning, Colleen. II. Title.
  ND237.B875E45 2011
  759.13--dc22
                           2011003021

Cover: *Colleen Browning, WOW Car, 1977. Oil on canvas, 36 x 54 inches. Gift of the artist.*
Frontispiece: *Colleen Browning, Self-Portrait n.d. Oil on board, 7 x 7⅛ inches. Gift of the Estate of Geoffrey Wagner.*

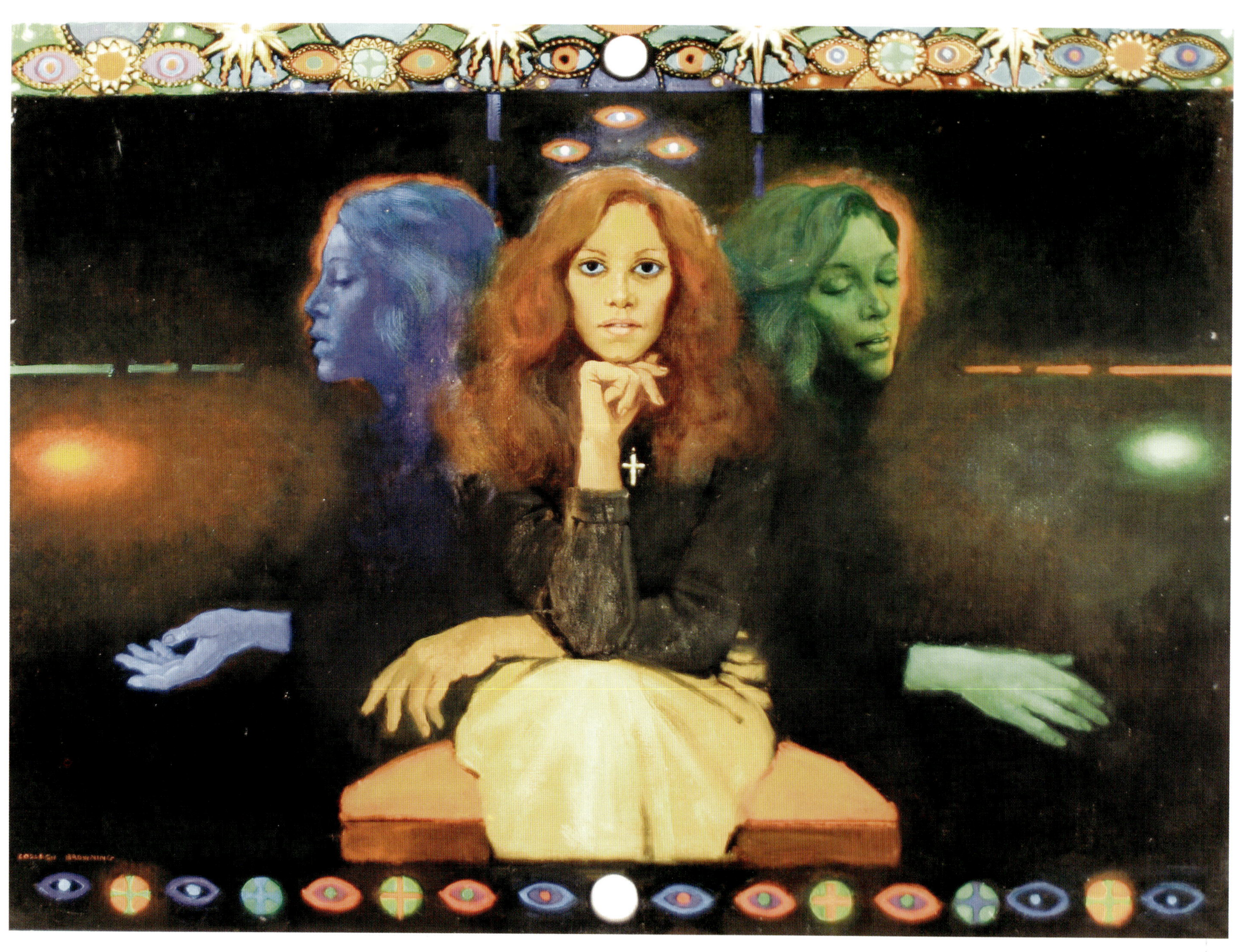

Colleen Browning, Clairvoyant, *1984.*
Oil on canvas, 31 x 41½ inches.
Gift of the artist.

AS A YOUNG BOY, I learned early on that my father was a wonderful storyteller. Although never published, he was a writer, and I think, a pretty good writer. I listened intently to his stories about magic, flying carpets, wishes, mystical places, and other tall tales. His stories were presented in such vivid detail that they sprang to life in my mind's eye.

The realist painters enchant me in a manner akin to my childhood memories. I am spellbound by the narrative style of these talented artists—Colleen Browning, Edward Hopper, George Tooker, Robert Vickrey, Andrew Wyeth, and others. They worked their magic, transforming a blank canvas and giving their work a voice. To me, these artists tell their stories so deftly in color, line, shadow, and shape.

One such voice that deserves to be heard is that of Colleen Browning, an enchantress in the world of realism and illusion. I was introduced to Browning's realist paintings early in my tenure as executive director with the Southern Alleghenies Museum of Art (SAMA). I have come to respect and admire this talented artist. SAMA featured Browning's artwork in the 1997 *Retrospective* and again in the 2009 exhibition, *Colleen Browning: Realist – Illusionist*. During her lifetime, Browning gifted many of her works to SAMA. The Museum is most fortunate to be situated as the largest repository of Browning works, as well as the source of a wealth of information on the artist's life and career.

In this regard, the Southern Alleghenies Museum of Art was identified as one of two remainder beneficiaries of the Geoffrey Wagner Estate. The late Geoffrey Wagner honored his wife's memory through his charge to rediscover and revitalize the works of Colleen Browning. SAMA's mission, as articulated in its 1976 articles of incorporation, to preserve, exhibit, and advance American art is aligned with the directive in Wagner's will to preserve, protect, and promote Browning's artwork.

Colleen Browning makes it easy for you to fall in love with her work. She is an artist who possesses God-given talent, who demonstrates remarkable skill, and whose creative spirit is comfortable in a world that is real or imagined. Each of her paintings is a beautiful vignette. We are fortunate that she left behind a robust portfolio that is diverse, rich, and wonderful. Her life's work is to be treasured and enjoyed.

Although I never met Colleen Browning, I was captivated by her persona. I have listened to the stories told to me by the Museum's founder, Father Sean Sullivan, T.O.R., SAMA's Director Emeritus, Michael Strueber, and other SAMA patrons who knew Browning. Attorney and friend Batya Levin described the Wagners (Geoffrey and Colleen) as a sophisticated and striking couple . . . Gatsbyesque. William Meek, from Harmon-Meek Gallery, represented Browning, respected her work, and remembered her fondly. They tell me that she was a charismatic and captivating personality. She was a fun person; she was a clever and skilled painter. Her pleasant disposition was infectious. Her work was admired. Her memory is revered.

Early on, Geoffrey and Colleen elected to live in New York City's East Harlem. In 1952, *Newsweek* headlined Browning's Harlem experience as "Realism without Tears." She was quoted in New York's *Daily Mirror* as saying, "Whenever I do my household shopping, I take a three-hour tour of a living gallery." Today, we look to the minimarket and the drive-thru to get in and out in short order. This was not the case with Browning, who took the time to observe and absorb the life that pulsed around her. She was a student of people and place. She transferred her mental snapshots of Harlem's people and its neighborhoods to paintings on canvas. It was in these early years of her career that Browning made an indelible mark on the art world as evidenced in the article "U.S. Praises Colleen" (*Empire News*, January 27, 1952). In 1952, Browning's paintings in a Manhattan gallery captured the attention of a *TIME* magazine art critic, who responded with unequivocal praise, launching Browning's American career: "Harlem has been painted more expertly, but seldom with more sympathy or with a quicker eye for vivid detail."

I was awestruck by SAMA's 2009 exhibition *Colleen Browning: Realist – Illusionist*. Browning offers up a myriad of images—real and imagined. The diverse subject matter, unbounded imagination, and artistic talent she displays create an unforgettable experience. Browning can take you on a *Walk to the Beach*, 1985 (see p. 195), or transport you to an adobe *Village*, 1968 (see p. 156). You stare into the eyes of the *Clairvoyant*, 1984, and you are mesmerized. *The Dream*, 1996 (see p. 207), provides an escape from the everyday hustle and bustle. You let your mind wander and hope that it comes back from the illusion of *Mindscape*, 1973 (see p. 170). Her painting entitled *Jubilee*, 1988 (see p. 177), is a crescendo of fireworks, and, to me, it could very well be a celebration of this artist's labor of love—painting.

Based on my discussion with Philip Eliasoph, PhD, who also authored *Robert Vickrey: The Magic of Realism*, I truly believe that at another time and in another place Colleen Browning would most certainly have received ongoing acclaim for her artistic talent and her rich body of work. Her realism was a brush against a strong current of abstract art—in short, Browning's story.

These pages hearken back to SAMA's commitment to Colleen Browning when she entrusted this museum with the magic of her cultural legacy. This magnificent book has been years in the making, and it is a story that we are honored to share through Philip Eliasoph's scholarly research and writing, which memorialize Browning's significant contributions to the art world and serve as a voice for her.

Appreciating her undervalued stature, SAMA was in the forefront of American museums presenting to the public Browning's remarkably rich offerings. In his introductory comments for the 1997 retrospective of her work, Michael M. Strueber, former SAMA director, wrote, "In the middle of the 20th century there were those who proclaimed that Realism was dead. Refusing to be swept away by the myriad of trends that inundated the art world, Browning refused to compromise her artistic integrity and remained true to her personal vision. She helped to re-establish Realism as a significant presence in American art. For fifty years her work has been acclaimed, and, as we enter the 21st century, it will continue to be appreciated."

G. Gary Moyer
Executive Director
Southern Alleghenies Museum of Art
January 2011

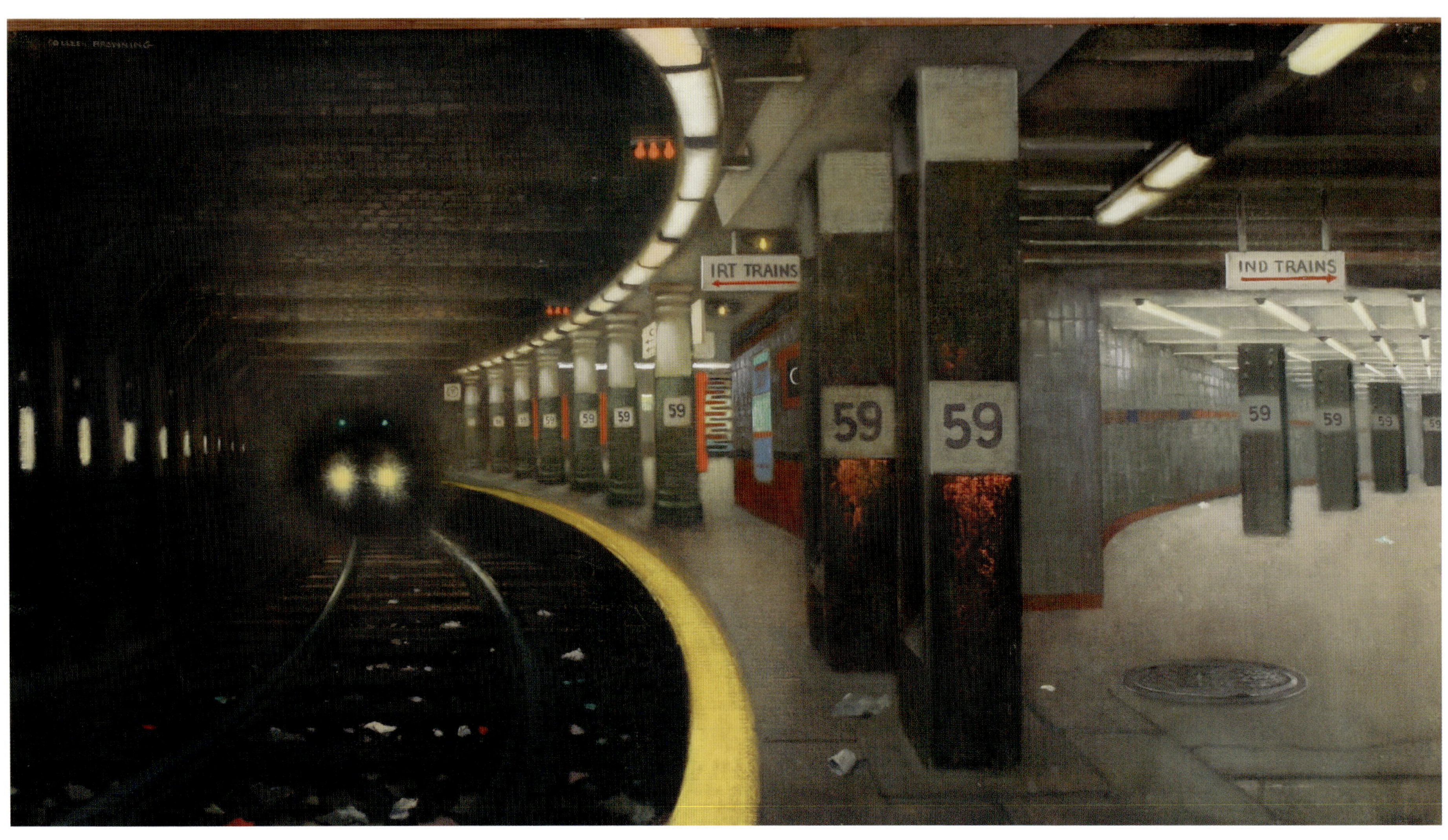

Colleen Browning, 59th Street Station, 1969. Oil on canvas, 22¾ x 40½ inches. Citi Collection of Fine Art, New York, NY.

Considering a lifelong engagement with the cyclical fates of American realist painters in the age of the avant-garde, the message on my cellular phone did not come unexpectedly in early June 2007. I was just downshifting gears into summer mode. The stack of unread bestsellers, history tomes, and biographies on my nightstand had gone untouched since the last winter break. I thought, wrongly, that I had a respite from the ongoing saga of forgotten mid-century artists whose visibility had dropped off the art world's nebulous radar screen.

Retrieving the phone message, the cacophonous static of Manhattan's taxi horns and rumbling subways pierced the air. Colleen Browning's devoted gallerist Bill Meek shouted over the deafening noise: "I've just come from a trustees meeting about Colleen Browning with a team of tip-top attorneys. Her late husband created a special trust for us to memorialize her life and art. Philip, this is right up your alley!" From that moment, the sense of being propelled into a spiraling vortex has not diminished. Appropriately in sync with the enchanted spirit and faerie land themes of Browning's art, the estate's simple book project was transformed into a dizzying odyssey of sorts. I felt like Lewis Carroll's Alice being pulled down the rabbit's hole, realizing the journey's revelations were completely unknown.

Sorting out this cryptic message, I would eventually be charged with the task of organizing a comprehensive biographical project to promote the artist's legacy. Entrusted with placing Browning's prolific career onto the map of twentieth-century art, I sensed that a revised and updated perspective on this fascinating and beguiling Magic Realism artist was imperative.

Awaiting art history's judgment, akin to Alice's appeal during the final tribunal before the King and Queen of Hearts, I got down to work. "The White Rabbit put on his spectacles. 'Where shall I begin, please your Majesty?' he asked. 'Begin at the beginning,' the King said gravely, 'and go on till you come to the end: then stop.'" At the beginning, I first encountered Browning's unique artistic voice while still a graduate student some 40 years ago. Sniffing out the trail of what I believe was then a deeply enshrouded lost generation of representational realists—Paul Cadmus, Jared French, John Koch, Henry Koerner, Edward Laning, Alton Pickens, Priscilla Roberts, and Robert Vickrey—it was logical to come across Browning within this diverse, nonconforming circle.

I had presented her works in small exhibitions I curated at our university gallery, but possessed just minimal information about her life. Only later would I lift veils of obscurity and decipher enigmatic elements within a biography embedded with intentionally fabricated blind turns and misleading clues. Little did I expect that with each leaf unturned, Colleen Browning's art and life would expand into a episodic thriller of sorts. "A man's face is his autobiography," noted Oscar Wilde. "A woman's face is her work of fiction."

Philip Eliasoph
Fairfield, Connecticut

M Y SINCERE APPRECIATION is extended to those individuals who worked tirelessly to bring this book to fruition. I offer a special thank you to the Geoffrey Wagner Estate and the Trustees of the Estate (Eleanor Jackson Piel, executor and trustee of the Estate of Geoffrey Wagner and William Meek, director-owner of Harmon-Meek Gallery in Naples, Florida, along with Batya S. Levin, Esq. and attorneys from the firm of Kramer Levin Naftalis & Frankel, as well as the accountants at Ernst & Young and financial advisors at Oppenheimer) for their commitment to the project, their passion for the arts, and their vision of the Browning legacy. Our gratitude is directed to Philip Eliasoph, PhD, whose love for the arts, investigative research, scholarly style, and sophisticated writing honor the multifaceted career and artistry of Colleen Browning. We were very pleased to work with Leslie Pell van Breen at Hudson Hills Press in the professional development of this major monograph. I would be remiss if I did not acknowledge here the noteworthy contributions made by William Meek, Michael Strueber, and Father Sean Sullivan as they recognized Colleen Browning's talent, supported her work, and created a vessel for her artistic legacy. I thank the Museum staff for their efforts on this project. The SAMA Board of Trustees also deserves to be recognized for their active involvement, timely direction, and strategic leadership. Finally, I thank the Museum's patrons and other donors who give so generously to help make our work possible.

G. GARY MOYER
Executive Director
Southern Alleghenies Museum of Art
January 2011

ACKNOWLEDGMENTS

THE SOUTHERN ALLEGHENIES MUSEUM OF ART (SAMA) merits enormous praise for its steadfast commitment to the art of Colleen Browning. Earlier visionaries such as Father Sean M. Sullivan, T.O.R. and Michael M. Strueber had laid the groundwork for the institution's sympathetic understanding of American representational art. The entire Board of Trustees of SAMA—both past and present—should receive a lifted cup of champagne to toast their enduring and sustained patronage, especially for art and artists who were not always on the front pages of art magazines or rising to instant fame. Their attention reflects a cultivated sense of enduring values against a majestic background of three centuries of American art in their handsome collection. Congratulations to the entire staff and dedicated patrons of SAMA for taking on this duty as the stewards of the Browning legacy.

No individual has given more personal attention, professional credibility, and roll-up-the-sleeves, can-do work on this project than the museum's talented Executive Director, G. Gary Moyer. Along with his charming wife Susan, we have been graciously hosted during my visits to Loretto, Pennsylvania. I consider their genuine warmth as something far beyond an obligation but more accurately as the beginning of a lifelong friendship, which my wife Yael and I will long cherish.

En route, this book benefited from the wise advice, good counsel, and warm support of countless well-wishers, colleagues, friends, and family. Though this listing is all too brief, it cannot possibly convey my indebtedness to those who have offered such unstinting encouragement and support. With humility and embarrassment, I am mentioning them here, unable to fully detail how each person nourished my efforts. This book reflects both their labors and beliefs.

I thus need to extend heartfelt thanks to Henry Adams, Coleman "Spike" Barkin, Leslie Pell van Breen, David Skolkin, Richard Camp, Louise Carcusa, Marisa Crumb, Jill Deupi, Scott Dimond, Melanie Finigan, Martha Fleishman, Tova Francus, Richard Frank, Linda Gustavson, Helen A. Harrison, Virginia M. Mecklenburg, Bill Meek, Diana Mille, Bobby Moore, Alexa Mullady, Leslie A. Norton, Adelia C. Rasines, Jason Schoen, Anthony Speiser, John T. Spike, Diana Thompson, Jerry L. Thompson, Bruce Weber, and Carey Mack Weber. Special thanks to Toby and Emil Meshberg for offering me the quiet refuge of their house, allowing me to concentrate on this project. All the Eliasoph brood—children and grandchildren—gave me the time and space to properly elicit the magic in Colleen Browning's art.

Beyond any words of gratitude, parallel to the subjects of this book who met each other on a volcanic beach on the isle of Ischia in the summer of 1948, this labor reflects the devotion to my own enchantress, Yael. Coincidentally, we also spent our first summer as newlyweds under the azure skies at the very same sublime place—Ischia's beautiful Spiaggia Maronti—more than four decades ago. "*Te valde amo ac semper amabo.*"

Philip Eliasoph
Fairfield, Connecticut
April 2011

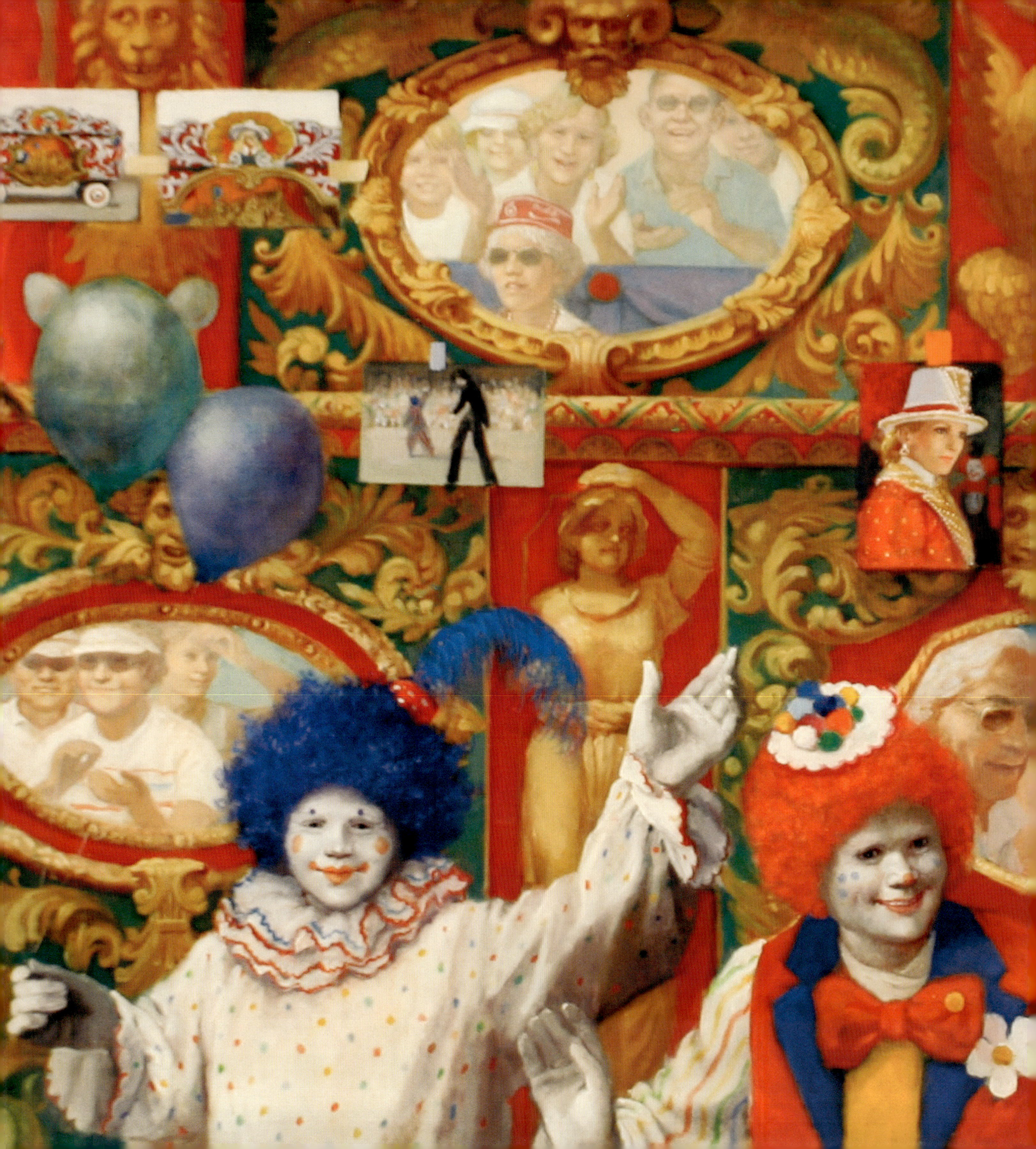

Colleen Browning loved America, the young, fresh nation where she and her husband, Geoffrey Wagner, started new lives across the ocean from their native England. Born in the last year of the War to End All Wars, Browning had gone through the pain and deprivation of its unwanted sequel, World War II. Now she resolved to dedicate the rest of her life to her husband, her art, and the pursuit of happiness. In 1949, Browning felt immediately at home in New York, responding at once to the warmth and realism of artists like Joseph Hirsch, Ben Shahn, and George Tooker. These artists, who were famous then, were inspirational to her desire to make lasting images of daily life.

Browning would live in the United States for the next 54 years, yet she never lost her fascination with the sights and sounds of her adopted country. Late in her career, she arrived at one of her most important paintings by traveling out to Milwaukee, Wisconsin, to enjoy the spectacle of the Great Circus Parade of 1988. With two cameras around her neck and loads of film, she snapped picture after picture of this quintessentially American event, which bubbles over every summer with raucously painted circus wagons pulled by teams of huge draft horses, brightly costumed riders, acrobats, clowns, brass bands, a herd of elephants walking trunk to tail, and an uproarious steam calliope. Returning to New York, she sorted out her snapshots. It took her approximately nine weeks of daily work, a process she detailed a year later in an illustrated article in *American Artist*. The result of her trip was her intricately named (because intricately composed) *Picture of a Painting of the Great Circus Parade* (see p. 198).

An ornately carved and colored circus wagon became the compositional scaffold for *Picture of a Painting of a Circus Parade*. Zooming in for a close-up, Browning covered the canvas with its three horizontal bands. The golden caryatids on red backgrounds that stand

Colleen Browning, Picture of a Painting of the Great Circus Parade*, 1988 (detail of fig. 8.16).*

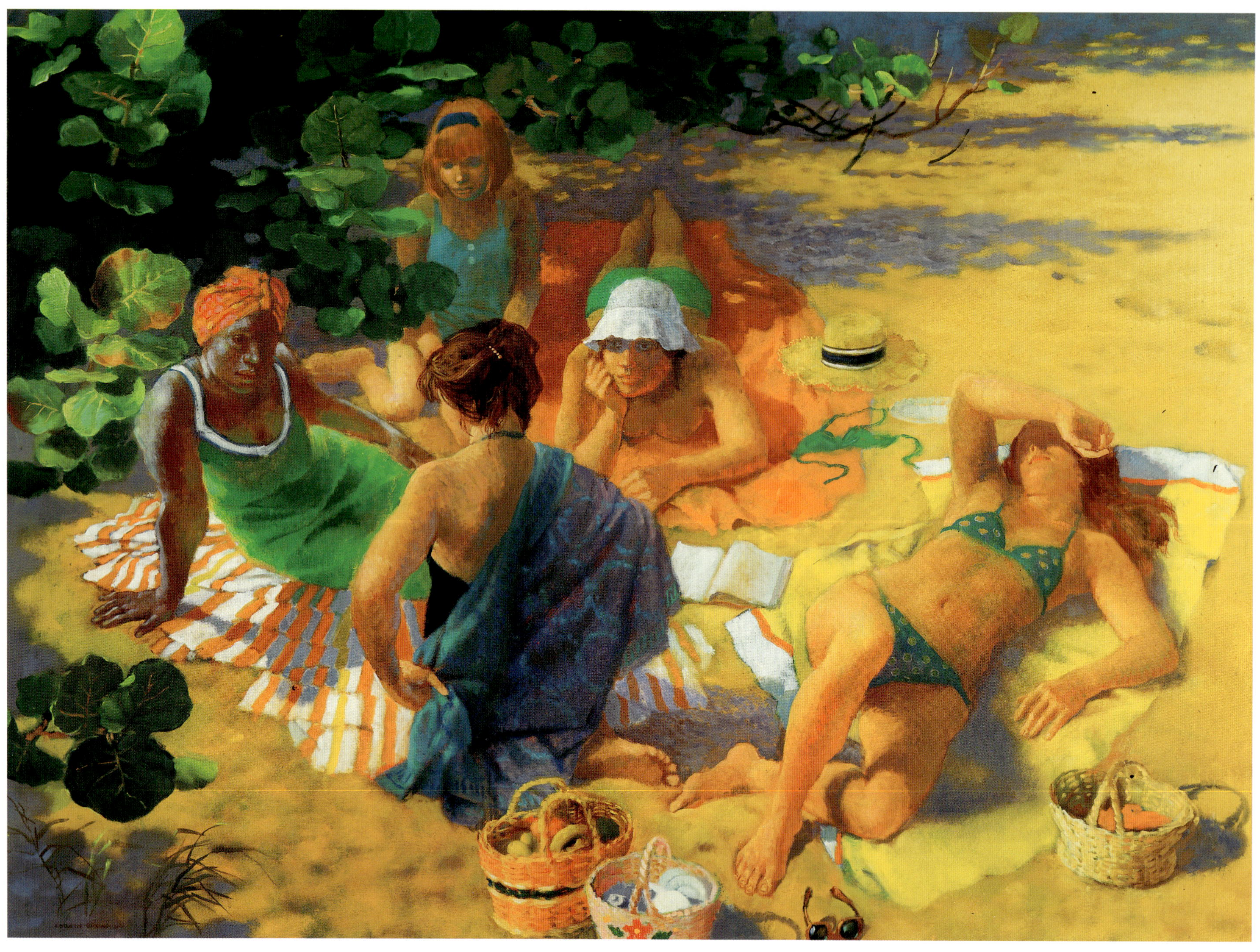

Colleen Browning, Picnic, 1982. *Oil on canvas, 56½ x 42 inches. Gift of the Estate of Geoffrey Wagner.*

between the oval mirrors reflecting faces in the crowd hold up the whole thing, as the layers rise like a wedding cake frosted red, white, and blue.

Picture of a Painting of the Great Circus Parade proceeded with meticulous care. Browning taped photographs—clowns, the crowd, a man on stilts, Pocahontas, and the ringmistress—to the painting and moved them around, looking for juxtapositions. The skinny young man on stilts proved the most problematic for Browning. Early in the process, she placed him looming over the other clowns, a black silhouette walking stiffly with arms outstretched. His white pancake makeup and leering red mouth, although not so remarkable in the snapshot, looked almost ghoulish. In fact, the man on stilts was by far the most arresting figure in the picture—until suddenly it struck her that

> "his presence was too menacing and overpowering, and the black of his clothes added a somber, sinister note that was completely at variance with my recollection of the joy and excitement of the parade on that dazzlingly sunny day…I knew that I could change the black of the clothing of the man on stilts, but that would have been untrue to the facts, so I painted the figure out."[1]

Thus the discordance was deleted. Browning repainted the man on stilts in two images at the upper right, sticking closely to the innocuous photographs. What she wanted in art, and life, was freedom from fear and a harmony between the pieces. One can see this in picture after picture. When out the window of her first apartment she paints the Harlem kids at play, she doesn't make the rickety fire escape seem desolate or glamorous, either. She uses it to give her picture a structure that has a place for everyone.

It bears pointing out that choosing to accentuate the positive is a courageous, rather than a naïve choice, as art critics sometimes claim. Browning deliberately banished nightmares from her images—not mystery. And she recognized the inescapable shadows. Her self-portrait of 1970, titled *Nine Times One (Self Portrait)* (see p. 166), shows the same view of her face in different moods determined by the colors, not all of them happy. Using a grid composition invented by Andy Warhol, she makes us think about the different faces we put on.

During the 1950s, American optimism was admired as a forward-looking alternative to the disillusionment of war-worn Europe. Beyond the escapist fads promoted on Madison Avenue—hula-hoops and fins on cars—the first full postwar decade was marked by a national commitment toward education and against religious and racial bigotry. In the arts, this current was epitomized in the activity of Edward Steichen. Born in Luxembourg in 1879, Steichen pioneered art and commercial photography in the United States and served as a photographer in both world wars and the Korean War. To educate the public about the "monstrosity" of war, Steichen organized several exhibitions of war images, "but the shock, he found, quickly wore off."[2]

Passionate about his message, Steichen tried another approach: the idea came to him leafing through Carl Sandburg's biography of Abraham Lincoln. Three words leapt out at him from a Lincoln speech: "family of man." In 1952, Steichen wrote and traveled to countries all over the world, requesting images for an exhibition that would demonstrate "the essential oneness of mankind throughout the world."[3] The *Family of Man* opened in 1955, toured the world for seven years in five different versions and was seen by nine million people, the largest audience ever for a photography exhibition.[4]

Even before the *Family of Man,* Colleen Browning was already painting scenes of lively dialogues in the huge city she now called home—for example, *Holiday*, 1952 (see

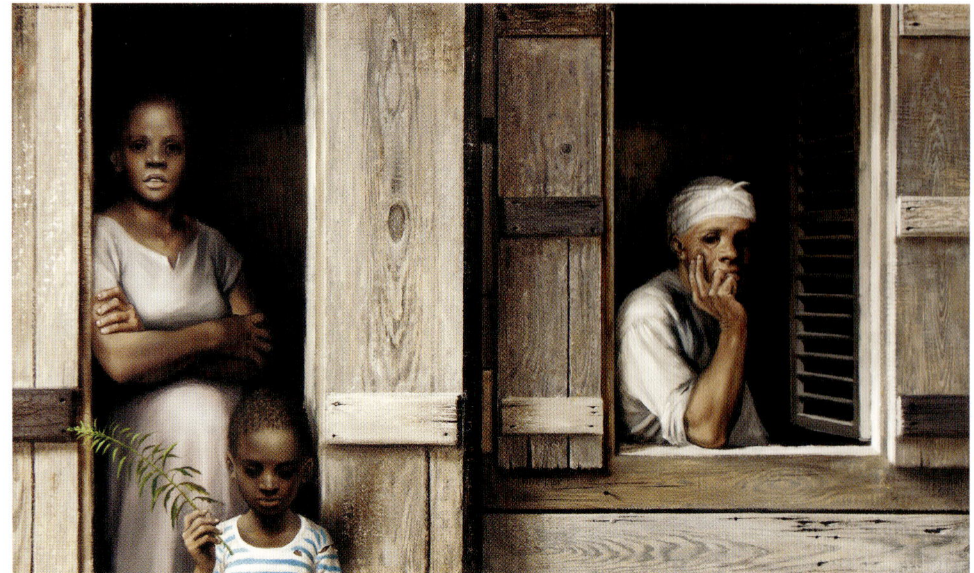

Colleen Browning, At Micaud*, 1956.*
Oil on board, 21¼ x 35½ inches.
Private collection.

p. 114), *Door Street*, circa 1953 (see p. 137), and *Telephones*, 1954 (see p. 135)—pictures that celebrate the pulse of life. After 1955, many of her large figure paintings, from *At Micaud*, 1956, to *Picnic*, 1982, share affinities with both the spirit and the images of Steichen's landmark show.

She saw art as a life-generating force.

> "The seed of every painting I do is some sudden, direct revelation, a decisive moment when some ordinary and even banal event becomes vital and significant by a momentary juxtaposition of ingredients…. All my pictures spring from visual experiences and I hope that in them I can communicate some of the surprise and fascination I have felt in sensing the unexpected relationships of man and his contemporary environment."[5]

During the next five decades she explored life around her—the streets of Harlem where she and her husband, the teacher Geoffrey Wagner first lived, the awful proliferation of subway graffiti in which she somehow discerned beauty, people peering through portholes as if spacemen, gardens, telephone booths, vegetable stands, and children at play. Drawing inspiration from movies, photographs, and old masters alike, she found the heartbeat of her subjects and reconstructed it so that viewers see themselves in her paintings.

> "The artist is like a god. He reconstructs the world the way he sees it, the way he wants to see it, and brings out the essence of what he feels about the world….[6] My interest has always been the human condition and the world around me, and the magic that can occasionally inform it; I hope that these images can sometimes touch on universal archetypes, so that there is a direct understanding between viewer and artist.[7]

Though possibly a realist, as she is usually described, or an illusionist, as she her-self suggested, Colleen Browning created a pictorial world in which freedom triumphs over fear.

John T. Spike
Florence, Italy
November 2010

NOTES

1. Colleen Browning, "The Evolution of a Painting, or, the Appearance and Disappearance of the Picture Plane," *American Artist,* July 1989, p. 57.

2. Raymond A. Schroth, *Dante to Dead Man Walking: One Reader's Journey through the Christian Classics* (Chicago: Loyola Press, 2002), p. 145.

3. *The Family of Man, The Photographic Exhibition Created by Edward Steichen for the Museum of Modern Art* (New York: Simon and Schuster for the Museum of Modern Art, 1955), p. 4.

4. Eric J. Sandeen, *Picturing an Exhibition: The Family of Man and 1950s America* (University of New Mexico Press, 1995), p. 4.

5. Norman Kent, "Colleen Browning," *American Artist*, February 1957, pp. 20–22.

6. Georgina Ellen Challis, "Colleen Browning: A Rich Tapestry of Color," *American Artist*, September 1981, p. 95.

7. *Colleen Browning: Retrospective*, exhibition brochure, Southern Alleghenies Museum of Art, 1997.

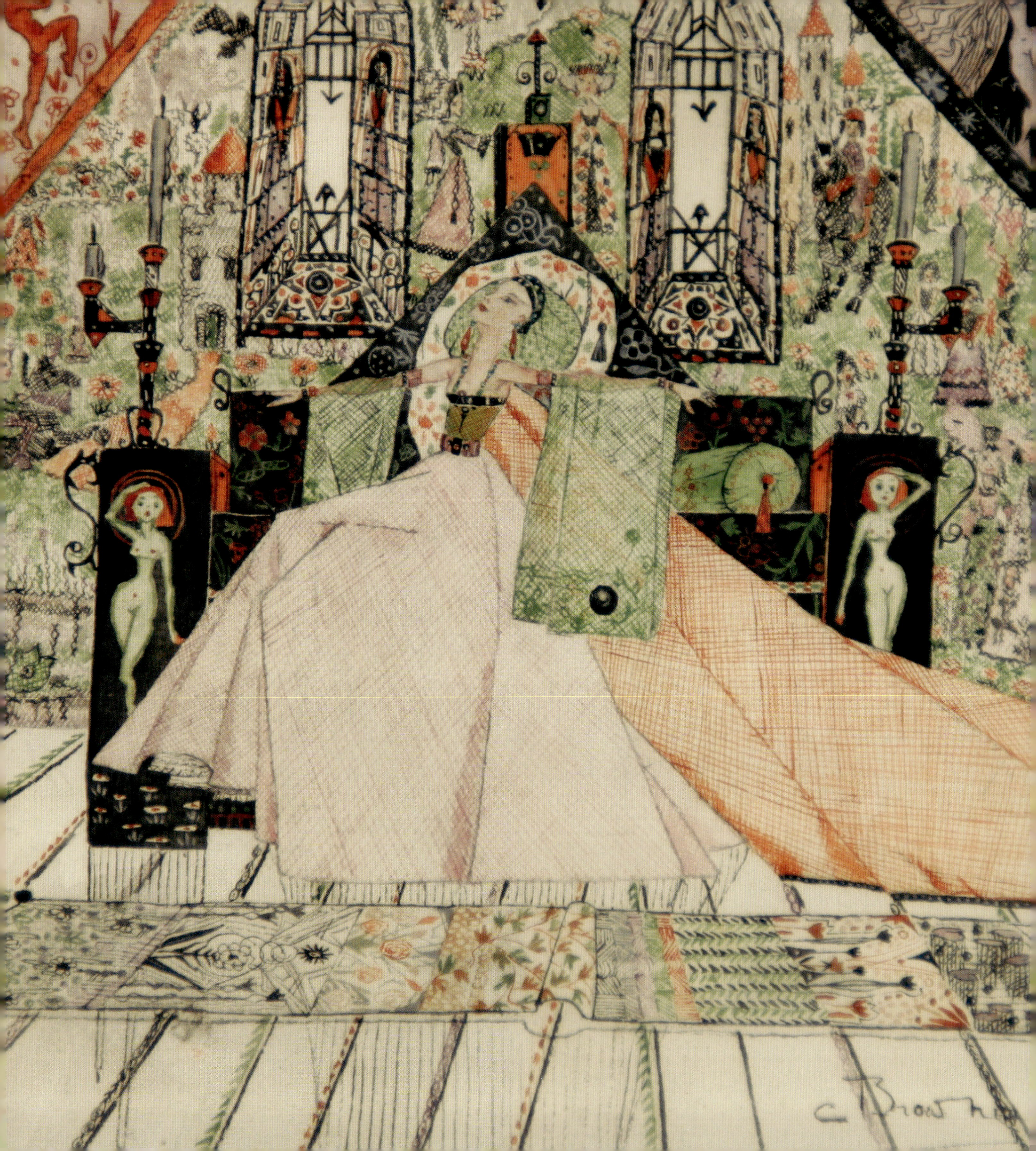

"VOYAGE TO ROMANCE" splashed across the pictorial tabloid pages of London's *Daily Mail*, morning edition of June 9, 1949. A buoyantly pleased young woman (fig. 1.1) was photographed leaning on a teak rail of the ship. Miss Colleen Browning (May 16, 1918–August 22, 2003) had boarded the *H.M.S. Queen Elizabeth* (fig. 1.2) the previous morning with considerable fanfare. Engaged to marry a dashing young scholar and veteran of the North African campaign, the newspapers were joyfully reporting a postwar-era love story.

Moments before the ship was towed from its berth in Southampton, press photographers from society news swarmed about, anxious to catch a juicy story. Here was Browning, a decorated British general's daughter of Irish ancestry, departing to America to marry a young, Oxford-educated professor, Geoffrey A. Wagner (December 27, 1920–August 21, 2006). Unexpectedly, the couple had committed themselves to a nine-month separation, in order that he might complete a fellowship to teach the King's English at an American university in upstate New York.

After their lightning love affair in Italy was sparked the previous summer on a dreamy beach on the isle of Ischia, their reunion was now only a matter of a swift transatlantic crossing. Additional photo clips with amorous taglines describing the attractive ingénue who "sails to marry" appeared in the *Evening Standard* and *Glasgow Bulletin* newspapers.

Filling up her juvenile sketchbooks and diaries years earlier with whimsical legends of elfin nymphs, Browning's boundless imagination already projected her onto this life-changing cruise. At age 15, her essay was published in *The Knoll*, a small literary magazine published by her day school in the Sussex village of Camberley. Browning's ripe imagination foretold of a "Voyage to romance" in her essay "Life":

CHAPTER 1

A Retrospective Overview:
"Sailing into the 'Sea of Life'"

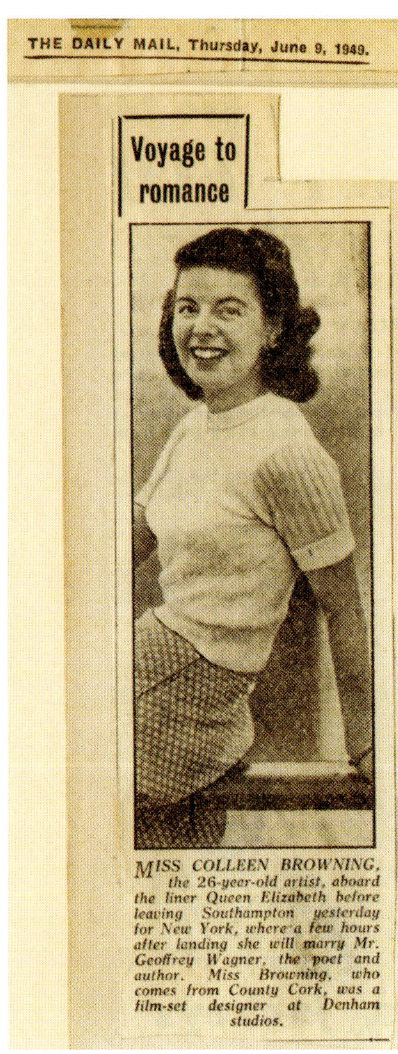

Fig. 1.1. *"Voyage to romance,"*
The Daily Mail, *June 9, 1949.*

In the early Dawn we set sail in our frail vessel from the land of Before. It was a beautiful land, a wonderful land, a blessed land—but I cannot remember it well, for the mists float across it and shut it away…High up in the clouds, small white doves mingle with the drops, and above all looms a boundless cross of whirling stars and planets. We set forth on the Sea of Life.

As if she were predestined, the headmaster of her art academy in Salisbury, England, predicted in his year-end summary report of 1937: "Miss Browning is a student of brilliant promise…Indeed, the ground work throughout is so good—having two of her figure compositions accepted for exhibition at the Royal Academy of this year—as to raise hopes for a real career in art for this young student who should one day make a name for herself."

Browning's artistic identity was forged by her ironclad purpose. She determined to master her technical skills while exhibiting a richly diversified and prolific portfolio of first-rate paintings, drawings, and prints. Since childhood, her purpose for living was dedicated to the perfection and advancement of her art. From her earliest juvenile drawings' enchanted faerie spirits, to her final paintings of mystics and clairvoyants, art was her medium of self-realization.

This overarching motivation consumed her daily pursuits in perfecting these fundamental artistic goals for most of her 85 years. In this biographical narrative we will fully appreciate how arduously she labored with paintbrush and pencil. She was equally steadfast in her desire to remain open-minded and free to render whatever struck her curiosity.

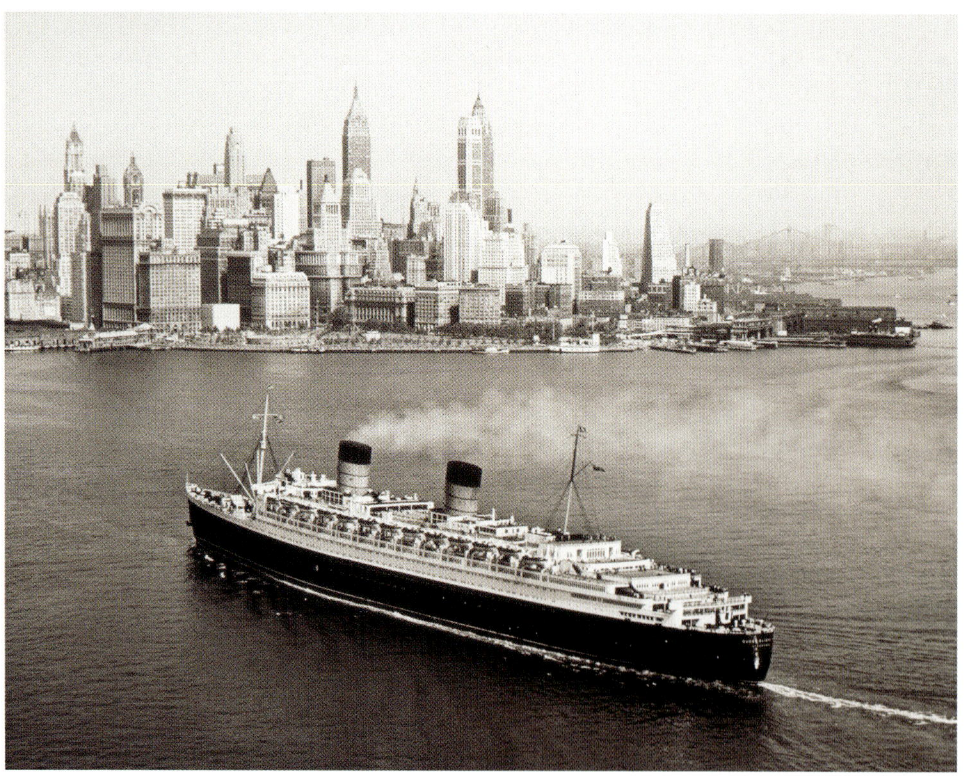

Fig. 1.2. *"Home Port,"* Queen Elizabeth *entering New York Harbor, 1946. Archive Holdings, Inc., Hulton Archive/Getty Images.*

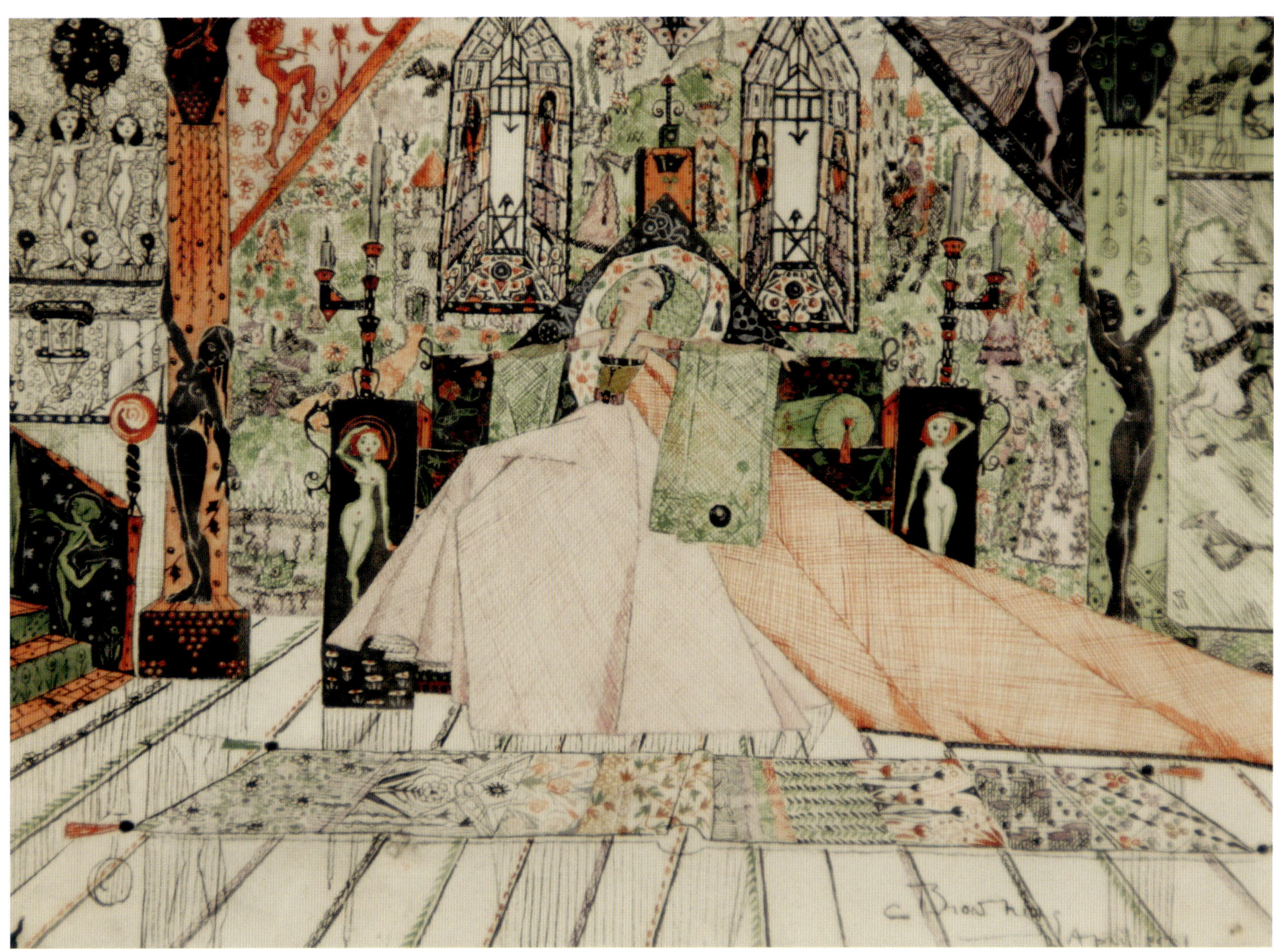

Colleen Browning, Fantasy Scene 2, 1931. Watercolor and gouache on paper, 7 x 9⅜ inches. Gift of the Estate of Geoffrey Wagner.

Seductive, with a thick mane of auburn hair, an aquiline nose, and winning smile, Browning was embarking on her "rendezvous with destiny." Virtually unknown in 1949 when she arrived in the States, this British painter possessed a marginal exhibition record with scattered appearances at the Royal Academy's open exhibits and one solo show at a London gallery.

Unexpected, but hard earned fame imminently awaited in the United States; Colleen Browning would acquire an enviable place in her new land. Her premier New York solo exhibit—which sold nearly every painting to some of the nation's most celebrated collectors—propelled her works onto the pages of *TIME* and *Newsweek* in January 1952. "All of which scared the artist half to death…. [the demand] for her Harlem pictures so paralyzed her that she was unable to continue painting such subjects with integrity for four months."[1]

The majority of struggling painters of that time would not attain coveted credentials with instant acceptance into the Whitney Museum's annual exhibition, or inclusion in competitively judged national exhibitions of the leading artists of that era. Nor could many attain representation at one of those eminent New York top-drawer galleries that featured important established artists at impressive prices. With a determined grit, spunkiness, and nervy aplomb, Browning tasted many triumphs. Adventurous and audacious, she willed herself into the forefront of American art at mid-century.

But the wheel of fortune spins with no guarantees. Although she attained sensational early success on the American art scene, her fame has almost entirely evaporated. American master Edward Hopper, himself highly skeptical about ongoing recognition for aging artists, stated: "Ninety percent of them are forgotten ten minutes after they're dead."[2]

With the incandescence of a comet's tail Browning ascended quickly. By the mid-1950s she was pushing the upper stratosphere of the American art galaxy. And like the comet hurling through time and space, she, for a time, blazed with great intensity only to have the memory of her work fade into virtual oblivion.

But the history of art is filled with names and personalities who were never fully appreciated in their day, only to be rediscovered with a more sympathetic appreciation by later audiences. What can we come to understand about this remarkably gifted woman? How did she enter, find her place, and flourish in the rapidly changing American art scene? This book is a tribute, a commemoration, and an unraveled narrative that seeks to disclose the public and private circumstances of a larger-than-life artistic personality.

This is Colleen Browning's wonderfully odd, sometimes baffling, and consistently enigmatical story that keeps her art as its primary focus. This is the story of Browning's "Voyage to Romance." An enormously prolific body of work was born out of this lifetime of meritorious artistic achievement. With the 20/20 vision of the present, we may grasp, with sharpened perspective, the relevant facts. As we lift the veil, our purposes strive to answer: "Who was Colleen Browning?"

So, in keeping with the unexpected twists and turns of this biography, we glimpse into her portentous future. Indicative of her astonishingly bright future was John Canaday's 1965 *New York Times* review of Browning's exhibition at Jacques Seligman's 57th Street gallery. Canaday wielded considerable authority as the most powerful chief art critic in the United States during his fifteen-year tenure at the *Times*.

At the zenith of her career, Browning picked up the most influential newspaper in the nation on the morning of March 27, 1965, and read its eye-opening headline: "Art: Against the Current of Fashion." Canaday had woven into the warp and weft of his review a sequence of silken threads. "Colleen Browning is an artist worth noticing because she is a painter of talent who works against the current fashion and has the technical skill to do whatever she wants, in whatever way…Miss Browning never suggests eclecticism…She is not a borrower. Rather, she adopts different styles for different subjects…the final tribute to Miss Browning is that from picture to picture she offers herself a lot of still competition. There are some diminutive still lifes where scattered fruits, lovingly painted, are designed to capitalize on the abstract beauties of their natural shapes, although they are rendered in acutely literal detail."[3]

On that early spring morning of 1965, Browning's thoughts might have wandered. Glancing out across her terrace with its sweeping panoramic vistas of the Hudson River, Browning might have paused to recall disembarking on the nearby West Side pier. Sixteen years earlier, with a suitcase full of dreams, she had been about to commence her American journey.

More impressive were Canaday's comparisons of the English import's paintings to America's most revered artists. "And finally there are some moody landscapes full of damp air and soft light that can remind you of the Hudson River School and of Andrew Wyeth simultaneously…[Miss Browning] is an excellent painter…she has put on an excellent group show."[4]

Six decades after Browning's journey from England, of inestimable value is the assessment of a distinguished professional colleague. Just a few weeks after celebrating his 90th birthday in August 2010, George Tooker (1920–2011), awarded the National Medal of Arts in 2007, spoke to this author. When asked to comment about Browning, he offered his warm remembrances:

> *I have such pleasant memories of Colleen Browning. I admired her work greatly—and I often told her so. We were certainly friends—although we did not see much of one another. But I always felt a fondness for her and enjoyed our time together at our gallery showings.*[5]

Browning came into contact with Tooker in a capricious manner. For several years in the 1950s their solo exhibitions often ran back-to-back in scheduling at the Edwin Hewitt and then Durlacher Brothers galleries. On an even larger stage, their works were also exhibited simultaneously at the Whitney Museum of American Art's *Annual Exhibition of Contemporary American Painting*. They were the vestigial tail end of the Renaissance-inspired academic painters being exhibited at that time.

Throughout the 1950s, those showcase exhibitions became the arena where traditional realists were tolerated—like antiquated, fixed bi-wing aircraft—to glide for a few more years. Inevitably it was the avant-gardist abstractionists who increasingly enjoyed the Whitney's prestigious launch pad, as the New York School achieved an explosive lift off.

Introducing Tooker's 2009 retrospective, which triumphantly toured New York, Philadelphia, and Columbus, Ohio, National Academy of Design Curator Marshall C. Price wrote: "Tooker and others who continued to work with the figure and narrative painting have often been overshadowed by the attention that critics gave to Abstract Expressionism. The dominant critical narrative of the postwar American art world had associated abstraction with innovation and considered so-called representational art as retrograde."[6]

If time and place are beyond one's control, Colleen Browning was unfurling the sails on her life's journey just as the current and headwinds were pushing against her classically inspired art. Within the clarifying lens of our revisionist perspective, we can understand how representational and figurative painting would soon be eclipsed by the surging ascendance of Abstract Expressionism. Norman Rockwell cleverly addressed this societal trend in his now iconic cover for *The Saturday Evening Post* of January 13, 1962. *The Connoisseur* (fig. 1.3) humorously captures a conservatively dressed, middle-

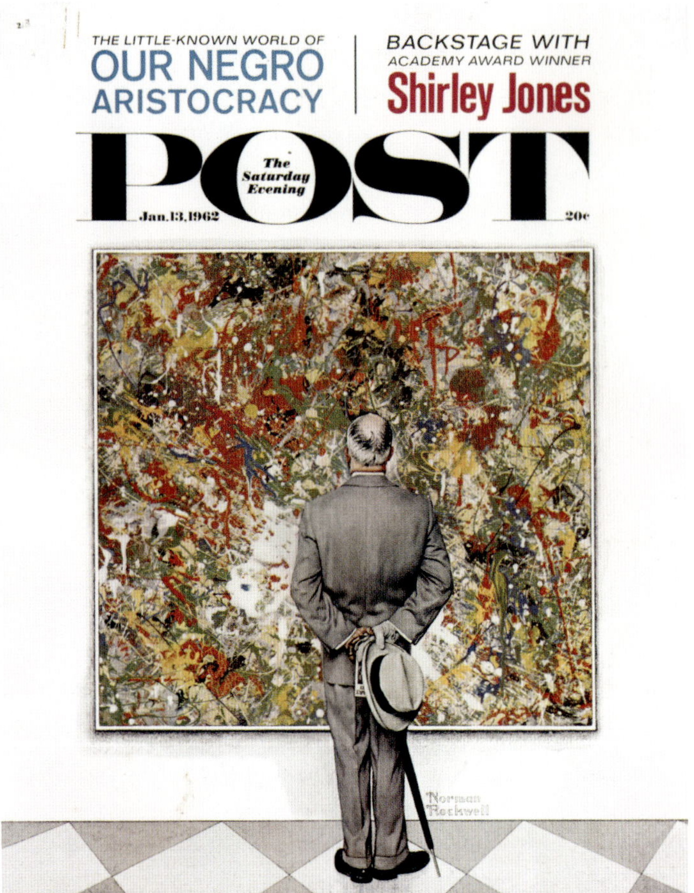

aged executive who is seriously bewildered. The well-tailored, cultured man realized his sophisticated social circle was now embracing abstractionism. The white-gloved, fedora-wearing corporate executive realized that Nelson and David Rockefeller actively promoted this befuddling painting at The Museum of Modern Art. Intuitively he felt some social pressure to comprehend the incomprehensible. The New York School had transcended popular taste as critical acclaim endorsed by what came to be known as the Triumph of American Painting.

Virginia M. Mecklenburg, senior curator at the Smithsonian American Art Museum, recently presented an exhibition to reevaluate Rockwell's legacy in a new light, especially his openness to avant-gardism:

> …*The connoisseur in this image stands silently before an erstwhile drip painting by Jackson Pollock just looking, studying the surface of the canvas on which paint was poured and splattered. Above his right shoulder, an unmistakable red 'JP' alerts the viewer to the painting's presumed author.*
>
> …*The* Post's *editors surmised that Rockwell's version of Jackson Pollock did not match reader prejudices about what 'real' art looked like, so they presented the picture as a joke about modern art: 'Is that prosperous – looking art collector about to reach for his checkbook to buy a prizewinning work titled 'The Insubstance of Infinity'? Or is he simply imagining his teen-aged daughter calling it 'Strictly from Blobsville'? They*

In this context, Browning's enormous talents were undervalued as she too suffered by this myopic narrative. "In this version of history, such artists as Tooker [and Browning] were either ignored or treated lightly as a kind of aberrant proof that people still made illusionistic paintings. In general, critics and art historians have emphasized realism and abstraction as polar opposites, pitting them against each other politically as irreconcilable styles."[8]

This retrospective exhibition and accompanying text endeavors along this revisionist path. Overcoming the limitations of the now obsolete realist versus abstractionist dichotomy, we are enabled with a wider, richer, and ultimately more artistically sophisticated depth of field lens in this process. "Much has changed in the intervening three decades in the field of American art and in our cultural climate," asserts Price in his framing of the National Academy's re-assessment of Tooker's legacy.

Wherever we go in this reevaluation of Colleen Browning's life and art, we are constantly faced with unexpectedly pleasant surprises. As archaeologists might dig for successive seasons before unearthing a significant layer of Bronze Age artifacts, the art historian sometimes uncovers—either by methodical research or serendipitous good fortune—revealing discoveries.

Easily accessible research data available about Browning is a notable reference in the Sunday magazine of *The New York Times*, February 1, 1953. Aline B. Louchheim, associate art editor, organized an imaginatively designed color spread in the magazine's pages presenting paintings by six artists under the banner: "As the Artist Sees New York." "The city is a landscape of modern painting…its people living, loving, playing in the Asphalt Jungle or in terrible isolation in the crowd." Curiously, she lifted the title of John Huston's 1950 award-winning crime caper film noir, *The Asphalt Jungle*.

Browning's painting *Lenox and Mondrian*, 1952 (fig. 1.4) is a vertiginous view of black children playing with a kite and jump rope, and marking graffiti on the sidewalk pavement with chalk. This recorded her first glimpses of East Harlem looking down from her fourth floor window. She would become famous depicting street scenes pulsating with infinite vitality, shortly after her arrival in Manhattan (fig. 1.5).

The painting was reproduced immediately to the left of the story title, and impressively alongside masterworks by John Marin, Stuart Davis, Joseph Stella, and Piet Mondrian. But it was the magical effect of this humble picture that has recently come to light. The fable is emblematic of an artist who once wielded considerable influence, but is of late virtually anonymous.

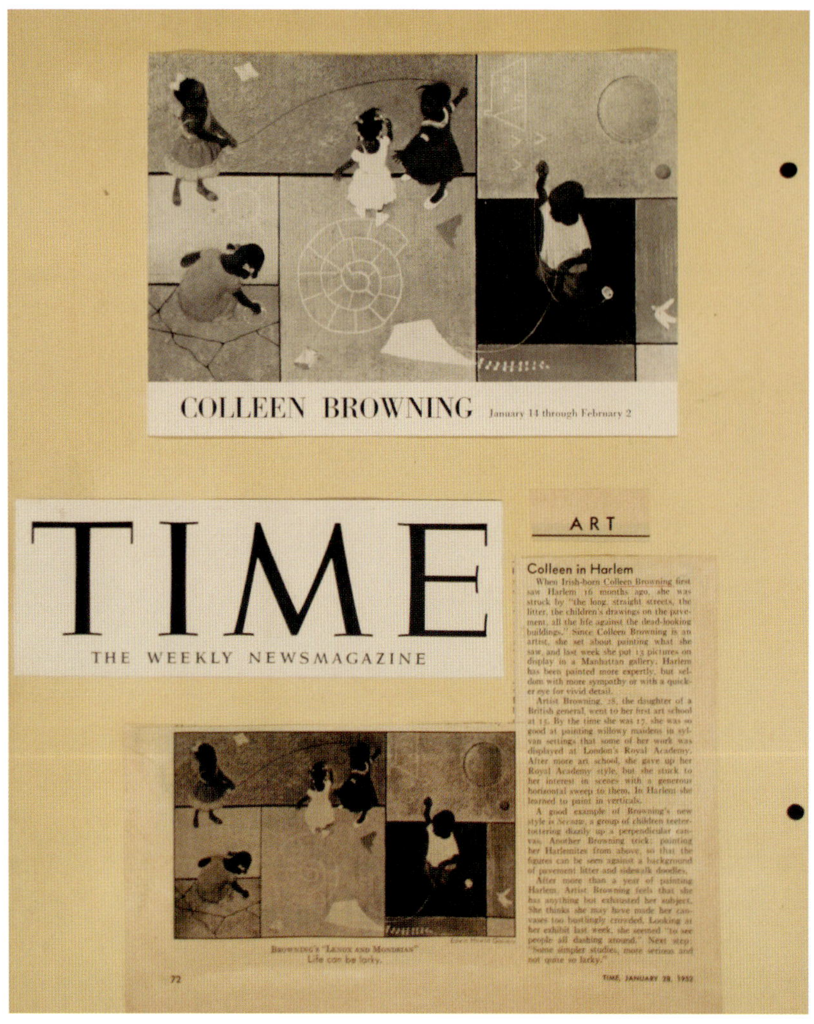

Fig. 1.4. "Art: Colleen in Harlem,"
TIME *magazine, January 28, 1952.*

Left and below: Colleen Browning,
Lenox and Mondrian, *1952.*
Collection unknown.

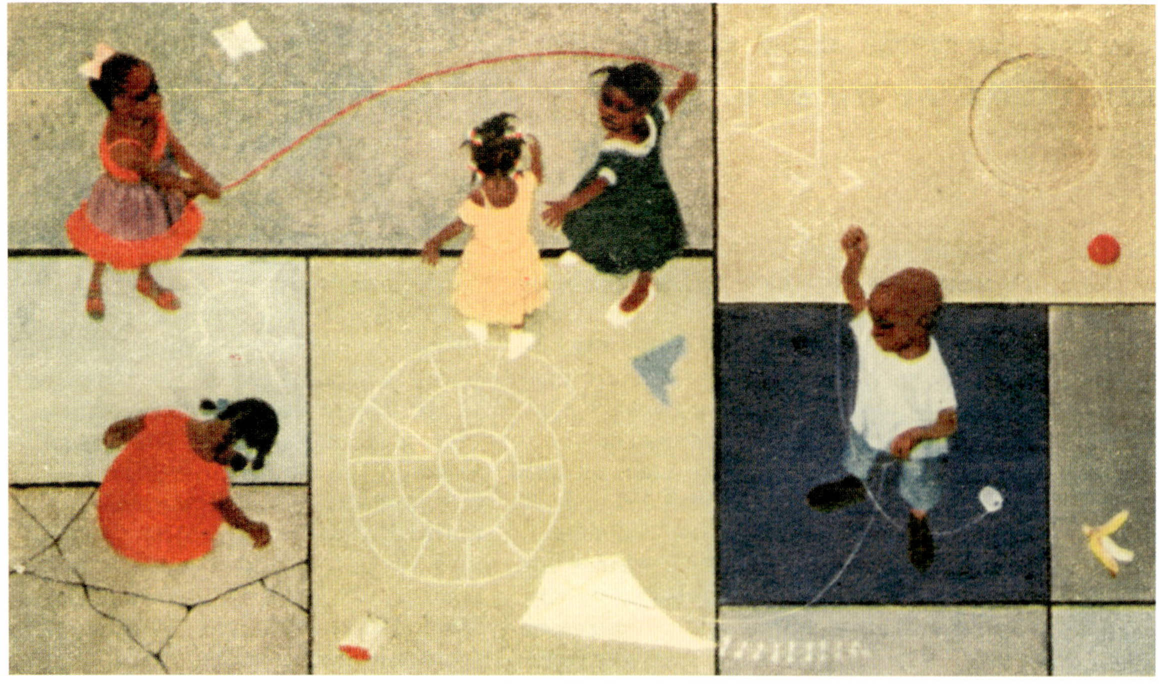

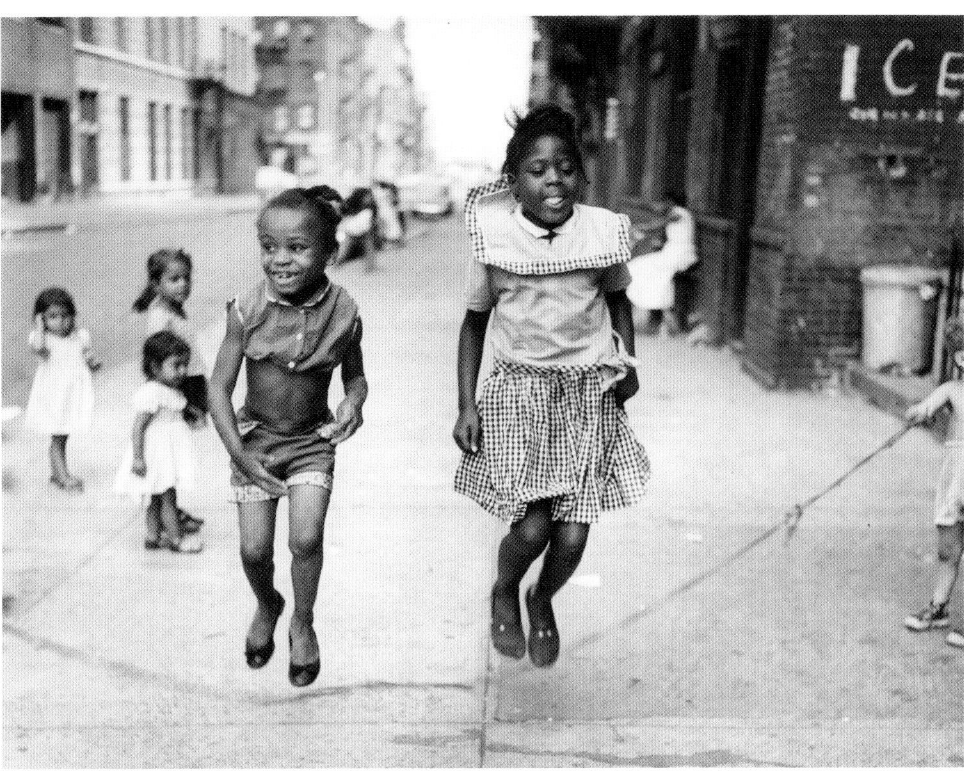

Fig. 1.5. Children jumping rope, 1956. Museum of the City of New York. Photograph © Bill Perlmutter.

A young Catholic seminarian at that time would later write, "It was love at first sight – for all five of them – the five little children…they are all the subtle suggestions of true art. There are hints of poverty and debris, of suffering and pain, both present and future. But mainly there is the loveliness and beauty of little children unaware of it all; unseeing, uncaring, just absorbed in their playing. They barely even notice each other so lost are they in their own little worlds…It is a picture of children anywhere and everywhere, but to me it just a little more sad, a little more beautiful because they were Negro children. I loved it the moment I saw it."

A young Dominican priest's "obsession…yearning and dreaming" was later told by Reverend Michael King, in the parish newsletter, "Stray Notes: From the Shrine of the Little Flower" for St. Peter Claver's Church. Writing from the heart of Brooklyn's Bedford-Stuyvesant slum, one of the nation's most devastated inner city black ghettos, the consequence made Browning's painting become both a divination and an incantation.

Father King's story began when he spotted *Lenox and Mondrian* and he "couldn't take [his] eyes off of it" as he was absorbed "in the picture and all what it said and meant to me." Returning to his seminary studies, he cut it out of the magazine. "I folded it up and put it in my wallet." Five years passed, when after "my ordination" he had lost the scrap of paper in his wallet. Now assigned to St. Peter Claver's Church, he wanted to find a reproduction of the painting to decorate the rectory. The link of St. Peter Claver (1581–1654), Jesuit apostle who declared himself "the slave of the negroes" of Cartagena, Colombia, was obvious. Cartagena was the largest slave market in the New World and St. Peter Claver's Church was established in 1922 as the first Catholic parish serving the black community of Brooklyn.

"I couldn't even remember what year it was published," he recalled. He went to the New York Public Library and spent "six hours looking through the biggest pile of newspapers you have ever seen in the your life…I went through [all the summer issues] between 1951 to 1957 looking for that picture—and I didn't find it." Weeks later he visited the *New York Times* building and asked a receptionist for assistance. The newspaper collected about 250 pictures every day—that meant between 1951 and 1957 "it would mean there were 6,000 images to sift through. It was crazy, foolish, and it would just be impossible."

But then a resourceful "Mr. Aaron" remembered that an artist named "Coleen [*sic*] Browning" had painted "Negro subjects." *The Times* saved "in individual folders under the artist's names" reproductions of artworks published. As his "heart was pounding," it turned out another characteristic Harlem painting of Colleen's slipped out of the folder. "Hope was blazing now." This lead to locating her works represented at that time at the Jacques Seligman Gallery at 5 East 57th Street. "I was getting closer and closer, but traveling further and further. This time to Miss Browning's studio-apartment on LaSalle Street. This was my one lasting disappointment…I never did get to meet my favorite artist, she was on her way to Greece. I met her husband, Mr. Geoffrey Wagner, Professor of English Literature at Columbia University [*sic*]…. He told me the painting had been purchased by Mr. and Mrs. Otto L. Spaeth and he gave me post card replicas of the painting."

At long last, Father King contacted the prominent art collectors, Otto L. and Eloise O. Spaeth who lived just off of 81st Street and Park Avenue and was invited for a visit. Trembling as the doorman walked him "down the carpeted hallway, my hand was shaking slightly as I rang the doorbell. The maid answered and let me into a very comfortable duplex apartment. There were many paintings on the walls—all, I am sure, originals. They are deeply cultured people, so well-spoken, extremely gracious, and most well-informed Catholics. They possess all the social virtues, poise, tact, finesse, taste, all those niceties which just add so much to a person."

The Spaeths were also very wealthy Wisconsin-based industrialists of that refined generation that championed American art when the market was still European oriented. He became vice president of the Whitney Museum and she led a campaign to raise money for the Archives of American Art in collaboration with Lawrence A. Fleischman, whose Kennedy Galleries would later represent Browning's art.

Father King's unlikely story concluded: "Extremely self-conscious of my own brand of broken Brooklynese, I was afraid to speak at all. I'm sure these fine people, understood my embarrassment, but I know I gave the impression of being at least uncouth, if not rude, especially when Mrs. Spaeth said so matter-of-factly, 'The painting is yours.'"[9] The present location of the painting is unknown. Perhaps another stroke of "Irish luck" will see it resurface to a new audience.

Among the multiple purposes and outcomes of this commemorative investigation into Browning's contribution, we hope to achieve a clearer understanding of her achievements. Through a judicious reassessment of her phenomenally prolific career, we will demonstrate how she earned an enviable position within the scope of American realist and figurative art in the second half of the twentieth century.

A militating circumstance for Browning's relative obscurity at present is that her most noteworthy achievements and critical successes were largely skewed toward the beginning of her American career, between the years 1950 and 1970. If she had passed away shortly after Canaday's desirable review that attested to her complete artistic sovereignty, we might be reconsidering Browning on a completely different playing field. She was a vital, throbbing presence in American painting during that era. An entirely different tombstone would have been carved. If her life had ended at around age 52 in 1970, she would have been remembered as dying at the peak of her fame. Instead, she struggled through subsequent decades, never again achieving the burst of fame when her supernova had exploded onto the art scene in the early 1950s.

Browning, living to age 85, witnessed her reputation evaporating off the map as she all but disappeared from the charts of American painting. As we shall come to understand, she consciously attempted to remain in sync and up to date by incorporating elements of contemporary styles and experimentation into the 1980s and 1990s. With some degree of futility, she put on her best game face in several frustrating attempts to be of her time.

The late paintings are combination of trend-setting reconnaissance and failed subject matter. But the innovations were too little, too late, as she simply would not or could not relinquish her innately academic principles. An underlying motif emerged in every feature story published in the art press of the 1950s–60s: her impeccable virtuosity, charismatic charm, and radiant attractiveness. That luminosity seemed to fade inexorably; her career was negatively impacted by her longevity, partially disguised by a self-propelled blurring of her actual age.

Spiking early in her New York art career, Browning graciously endured her later years in relative obscurity. Losing her representation with a major New York gallery in the 1990s, her final surge of paintings was exhibited on the periphery of the art world in Naples, Florida. Were it not for the Herculean efforts of gallerist J. William "Bill" Meek intervening to rescue her during this final decade, Browning's career might have suffered an irrevocably total collapse.

In her starkly candid biography of Alice Neel (1900–1984), revisionist author Phoebe Hoban sheds light on another enigmatic female realist painter. Neel's career trajectory was almost 180 degrees opposite from that of Browning. Oddly enough they both lived within blocks of each other in Manhattan's Upper West Side, but there is no evidence of any interaction. In contrast to Browning's almost instant fame, Neel toiled with little success as a social realist during the W.P.A. era of the 1930s.

New York Times critic Deborah Solomon surmises the struggle for female artists: "Alice Neel has never commanded the household-name status of Georgia O'Keeffe or Frida Kahlo, art heroines who have been the subject of multiple biographies…[Neel] had to await the advent of 'women's lib' as it was then called, before her career took off."[10]

Unlike Browning, whose premiere New York solo show caught media attention in *TIME* and *Newsweek*, Neel achieved only late-in-career notoriety. "In 1970, *Time* published a cover article on Kate Millett, [achieving sudden fame] with her patriarchy-bashing best seller, *Sexual Politics*. Neel was asked by *Time* to furnish the portrait… Virtually overnight, Neel became famous for her lack of fame, the long years of neglect." In one fell swoop, Solomon has entwined the perplexing lives of Browning and Neel into their shared dilemma: "One finishes Hoban's book wondering among other things, how a woman so narcissistic and needy became such an empathetic chronicler of other lives."[11]

Just as we can track Browning's rise in John Canaday's inestimable praise in 1965, so can we track the trajectory of her decline on those very same pages. The inevitable shift in styles and attitudes from easel painting toward post-modernism in the post-Pop era precipitated Browning's fall.

There is incontestable evidence of her descending into a Dante-esque purgatory, if not utter damnation under the sulfurous, scorching flames of the New York art world's own form of inferno: critical admonishment in the powerful *Times* pages. In three reviews spanning 1965 to 1972, Browning's career seems to move from an awakening, up-and-coming master with top ranking on the art world's marquee to a painter who has descended to the small credits of an "also ran" near oblivion and the end of a movie.

At the next juncture of her career—reviewing her premiere exhibit in March 1969, at Kennedy Galleries located at 20 East 56th Street just off Fifth Avenue—Canaday was less charitable. This time he shifted emphasis from "excellent" glowing praise to concern about her "degrees of conventionalization." He became impatient with her command of technique over expression, noting:

> *The application is always expert, but somewhere the artist's response to her subjects has become lost—at least it was not relayed to this observer.... Miss Browning, known as a staunch defender of figurative art, is really doing what figurative painters object to abstract painters doing: she is painting about painting at the expense of what she is nominally saying.*[12]

Hilton Kramer assumed the mantle as the *Times*'s leading-edge critic between 1965 and 1982, overlapping Canaday's term during a period of seven years when they often widely disagreed on the same pages. An intractable controversialist, author of *The Revenge of the Philistines*, Kramer once wrote: "We seem…to be at the end of a period of art criticism, if not in art itself." He was unapologetically partisan toward the modernist artists he supported. Many of the "old guard" realists were skewered with his white-hot pen.[13]

Rarely hesitating to cast an evil eye on those in his disfavor, Kramer castigated Browning with full-throttle acerbity. In a particularly harsh review published in the art page of the *Times* on January 8, 1972, he rebuked: "Miss Browning spreads her sickeningly sweet sentimental vision as if she were piling jam on soggy toast. The results give one the esthetic equivalent of a bad toothache."[14]

Browning's career as a figurative realist painter was dramatically intersected with the crossing trends of twentieth-century modernism. But she could never usurp or counteract the powerful narrative driving the triumphant ascendance of the New York School's invention of abstract expressionism. Navigating her desire to remain an artist "of her time" presented immediate challenges. Ultimately this predicament would overcome Browning, as her late years were sidetracked into a remote tributary of New York's wide harbor and flowing torrents of modernism. Much to her credit, she put up an honorable counterattack in her efforts to remain current. But a clarifying lens sharpens our focus of her strengths and weaknesses at the very moment when the history of art had shifted from Munich, London, and Paris to be irreversibly developed and centered in Manhattan. *New York Times* art critic Roberta Smith judiciously explained how "myopically" this mythology is now etched in stone:

> *When it comes to the past, the Modern stays the course as only the Modern*
> *can, which is magnificently, lavishly, intelligently, if also myopically....Alfred H. Barr,*
> *Jr., the Modern's visionary founding director, drew a well-known outline of Modern*
> *art movements and famously likened the museum's collection moving through time....*
> *But art is not amenable to outlining, and art movements are really messy, edgeless*
> *things that should only become more so with age. Maybe it is time for a new, less*
> *militant metaphor.*[15]

Observing a daily routine as an obsessively engaged artist for more than 60 years of professional productivity, she had but one other affection—a devoted commitment to her husband Geoffrey Wagner. She was in mind and spirit the embodiment of Puccini's heroine, Madame Tosca. A haunting aria declares Browning's purpose for living: "*Vissi d'arte; vissi d'amore*" — "I have lived for art, I lived for love."

NOTES

1. Frank Getlein, *Colleen Browning*, exhibition catalogue, Kennedy Galleries, NY, March 5–29, 1969, p. 9.

2. Gail Levin, *Edward Hopper: An Intimate Biography* (New York: Alfred A. Knopf, 1995), p. xiv.

3. John Canaday, "Art: Against the Current Fashion," *New York Times*, March 27, 1965, p. 23.

4. Ibid.

5. George Tooker, telephone interview with author, August 25, 2010.

6. Robert Cozzolino, Marshall N. Price, M. Melissa Wolf, *George Tooker* (New York: Merrell Publishing, 2009), p. 9.

7. Virginia M. Mecklenburg, *Telling Stories: Norman Rockwell from the Collections of George Lucas and Steven Spielberg* (New York: Harry N. Abrams, Inc., 2010), pp. 176–78.

8. Robert Cozzolino, Marshall N. Price, M. Melissa Wolf, *George Tooker* (New York: Merrell Publishing, 2009), p. 9.

9. This and the preceding seven quotations are all from "Stray Notes: From the Shrine of the Little Flower," a humble parish newsletter published for St. Peter Claver's Church. The inexpensively printed circular was miraculously uncovered, tucked into a pile of stained, unmarked files of random clippings. Inquiries from the author to the current monsignor at the church determined the parish has no records of the painting's current location.

10. Deborah Solomon, "The Nonconformist," *New York Times*, Sunday Book Review, January 2, 2011, pp. 14–15.

11. Ibid.

12. John Canaday, "Art: Wood Carvings of Puerto Rico," art review, *New York Times*, March 22, 1969, p. 29.

13. Hilton Kramer, *The Revenge of the Philistines* (New York: The Free Press, 1985), p. 305.

14. Hilton Kramer, "Avery's Mastery in Paintings on Paper," *The New York Times*, art reviews, January 8, 1972, p. 25.

15. Roberta Smith, "Artists Conversing with a Jury of their Peers," exhibition review of The Museum of Modern Art's *Abstract Expressionist New York: The Big Picture*, *The New York Times*, October 1, 2010, p. c25.

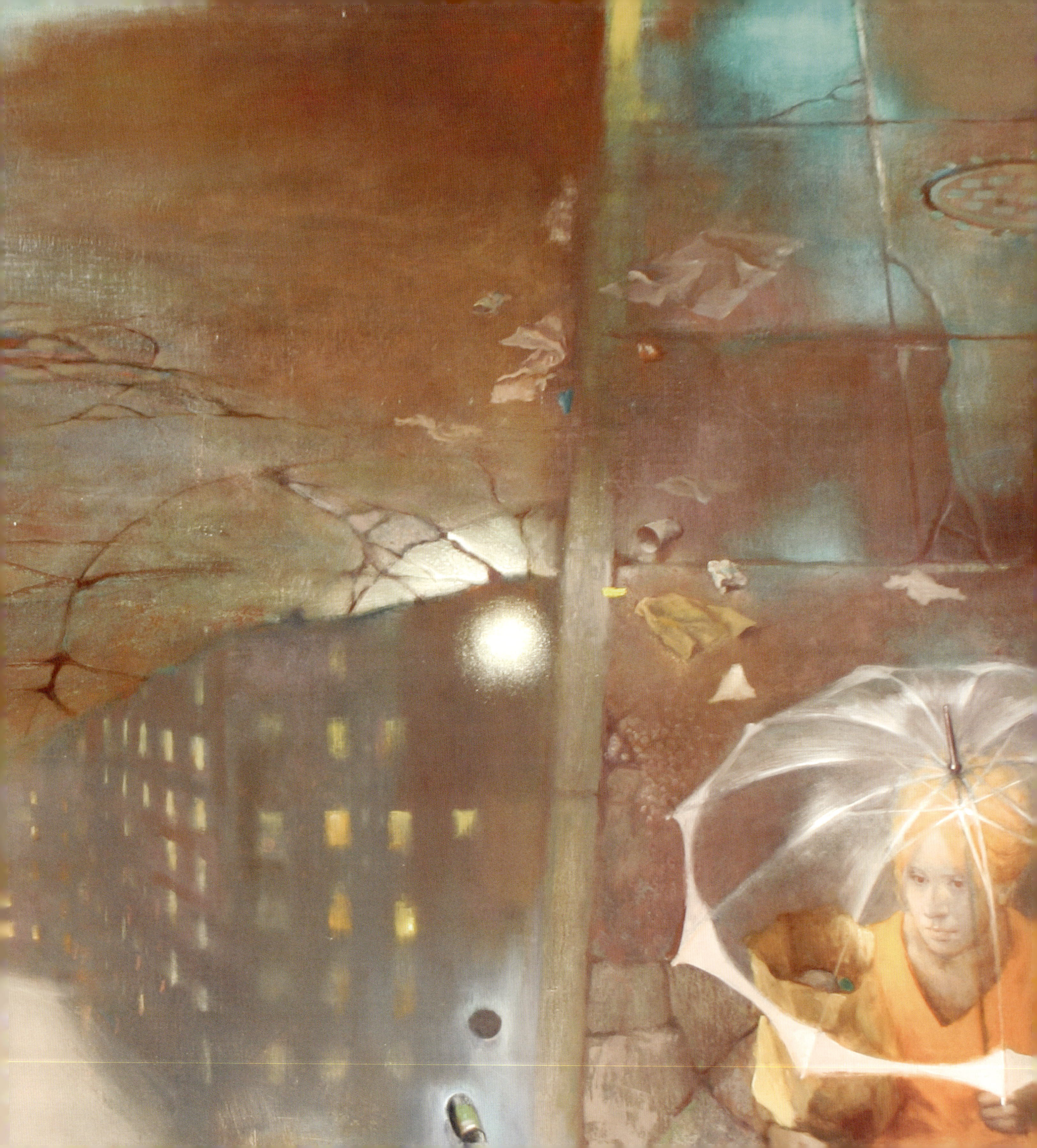

*"It is a riddle, wrapped in a mystery, inside an enigma;
but perhaps there is a key."*

—Winston Churchill, 1939

*"Like her other work, it is a personal response to an actual experience…
surely one of the most unconventional self-portraits ever painted."*

—*Journal of the American Medical Association*, April 1995

P ICTURING THE GRANDE DAME OCEAN LINER as it made its way into New York's harbor, we can only imagine, bird's eye view, the *deus ex machina* forces swirling in the currents below. An inevitable artistic squall was about to burst as Browning's artistic career would be launched in her soon-to-be adopted country of the United States.

Classically trained at England's most prestigious art academy, Slade School of Fine Art at University College London, she was about to storm ashore. Little did she realize the sands and tides of styles were shifting under her feet even as she was arriving in New York's beachhead of modern art.

Just one week after being photographed aboard the HMS *Queen Elizabeth*, Browning was married to Wagner in a civil ceremony at the Office of the City Clerk in New York City's Municipal Building before a deputy civil clerk.

Although England had been a vast global empire of dominions, protectorates, mandates, and territories, a new geo-political map was being drawn by the late 1940s. The era of British colonialism was waning as new nations in Asia and Africa were achieving independence. A collection of new flags were being raised for Burma, Ceylon, India, Israel, Jordan, and Pakistan around the world as the Union Jack was being lowered from flagpoles from Jerusalem to Singapore.

Launched in 1938 by Queen Elizabeth with Princess Elizabeth and Princess Margaret at her side, the 33,000-ton twin funneled liner steamed effortlessly at 29 knots using its quadruple screw propulsion powered by single reduction steam turbines. Paying tribute to her service ferrying three quarters of a million troops into the war theatre during the Second World War, Winston Churchill acknowledged the ship's service as "the Queens [including her sister ship, HMS *Queen Mary*] had shortened the war by a year."

CHAPTER 2

Disguises, Enigmas, and Espionage: Art & Illusion

We learn quickly about the vivacious "girl in the picture" in the *Daily Mail*'s caption: "Miss Colleen Browning, the 26 year old artist aboard the liner Queen Elizabeth before leaving Southampton yesterday for New York where a few hours after landing she will marry Mr. Geoffrey Wagner, the poet and author. [She] comes from County Cork [and] was a designer at Denham [film] studios."

Unraveling this fairytale-in-the-making, we eventually learn of two factual errors that were not the fault of the *Daily Mail* or countless news reporters or art press interviewers then, or in the future. Just 22 days earlier, she had celebrated her 31st birthday. A disconcerting degree of subterfuge seemed to surface with each turn of the page as Browning either embellished, falsified, or simply re-invented pertinent facts about her age, origins, or whereabouts prior to her arrival in the States.

Throughout her career Browning consistently misrepresented her true age with surreptitious playfulness. Possibly a foible of vanity, or more calculatingly, a strategy to advance her career, she somehow masked key elements of her identity. In constructing a plausible narrative for Browning's life and production, this author will strive to introduce relevant evidence of how her personality directly impacted her art.

A museum director in South Carolina, writing an introduction for a Browning exhibition many years later, intuitively sensed Browning's elusive persona. For her exhibition at the Columbia Museum of Art in March 1972, he commented: "Someplace there is an elusive adjective that can be applied to the paintings of Colleen Browning. Like a particle of mercury, though, it always escapes our grasp.... It is an adjective that defines confinement...and must be kin to this artist's intuitive perceptiveness of life....These are diverse, seemingly capricious ingredients that make up our artist.... Hers is a talent which opens new worlds of pleasure, sensuous beauty...a visual sharing of fugitive poesy."[1]

As the fabled transatlantic liner's smokestacks began working, Browning, too, sent out a smokescreen by deducting five years from her age. Many years later, in 1981, she was featured in *American Artist* with a laudatory overview of her abilities as a creative force of "consummate skill, imagination, and dedication."[2] But we see the fingerprints of her yarn-spinning biography ever enlarged to the unsuspecting art journalist: "Born in 1929 in Ireland to a British general and his upper-class wife, Browning had the good fortune to have parents who appreciated her talent."[3] The year and place of her birth were false, and her father was at that time a rising captain.

By the time she established residency in the U.S. in the early 1950s, she had determined that all future interviews, art books, encyclopedia listings, and self-enrolled registrations for prominent exhibits at venues, such as the Whitney Museum of American Art, Carnegie Institute, or National Academy of Design, would show she was eleven years younger.

Late in her life the Southern Alleghenies Museum of Art (SAMA) celebrated her career with a landmark retrospective that toured the United States in 1997. Museum director Michael M. Strueber had continuously championed her work. "Browning refused to compromise her artistic integrity and remained true to her personal vision... as we enter the twenty-first century, [her work] will continue to be appreciated."[4]

In a recent interview, Strueber explained: "Although we had spoken on the phone many times, sensing her charismatic vitality, I was completely shocked to finally meet a very frail, elderly woman." As the author of her most complete biography at the time for SAMA's sumptuously printed color catalogue, he was under the impression that he was "entertaining as if she were a queen," a robust woman he assumed was 68 years old. He was flabbergasted to learn recently that she was in fact 79, but could finally rectify why Browning appeared so fragile in appearance.

We might ask: what re-arrangement of one's age might be permissible as a quibbling, minor transgression? Perhaps a fudge of three or maybe even five years? But an eleven-year discrepancy is beyond the limits of being winked away. It represents a substantial falsification—indeed, it doesn't place her artistic development into a full decade earlier where it belongs. Of course, the issue of age alteration is inherently a Pandora's box of motives and apologizing rationalizations. To give females in public life "the benefit of the doubt" would explain the double standards of a society that worshiped youth, especially for females in the limelight.

Actress and comedienne Gracie Allen, wife of George Burns, published her birth date as July 1906. When questioned about the whereabouts of her birth certificate, she claimed all records were destroyed in the great San Francisco earthquake and fire. The discrepancy was discovered that her invented birth date was in fact after the April 1906 destruction. Eva Peron was born in 1919, but after becoming Argentina's first lady, had all official records changed to make her three years younger.

In Hitchcock's 1959 *North by Northwest*, actress Jessie Royce Landis played the role of Cary Grant's mother. The handsome actor was then 55 years old and his "mother" was in fact eleven months younger—another indication of the public's unwillingness to see women portrayed accurately.

Acknowledging that in her later years her artwork fell out of favor, we can then question if this falsification of her biological age actually came back to bite her. In her art she was consistently striving to modify her style to stay up to date with rapidly changing trends. By dating herself eleven years younger, this became a Sisyphean task. And we also learn that Geoffrey Wagner mirrored Browning's actions by falsifying his age in a number of published sources. They decided, together, to create new identities in the United States.

The artistic consequence of this alteration is that Browning could never really paint in a manner appropriate to her true age. She was a child of the 1920s, who trained at art academies in the 1930s while fostering the illusion that her coming of age was in the 1940s. She may therefore have been the instrument of her own decline, as later critics rejected her art as old-fashioned. By the time she was in her 50s, she made admirable attempts to stay with the trends by adopting graffiti-tag-bombing paintings on subway cars to emulate the youthful energies of street kids with Krylon spray cans. All of this is excusable, but revelatory about her artistic strategies of deception.

A curator who knew her very well was Howard DaLee Spencer from the Wichita Art Museum. In his 1994 exhibition catalogue he writes warmly of his interactions

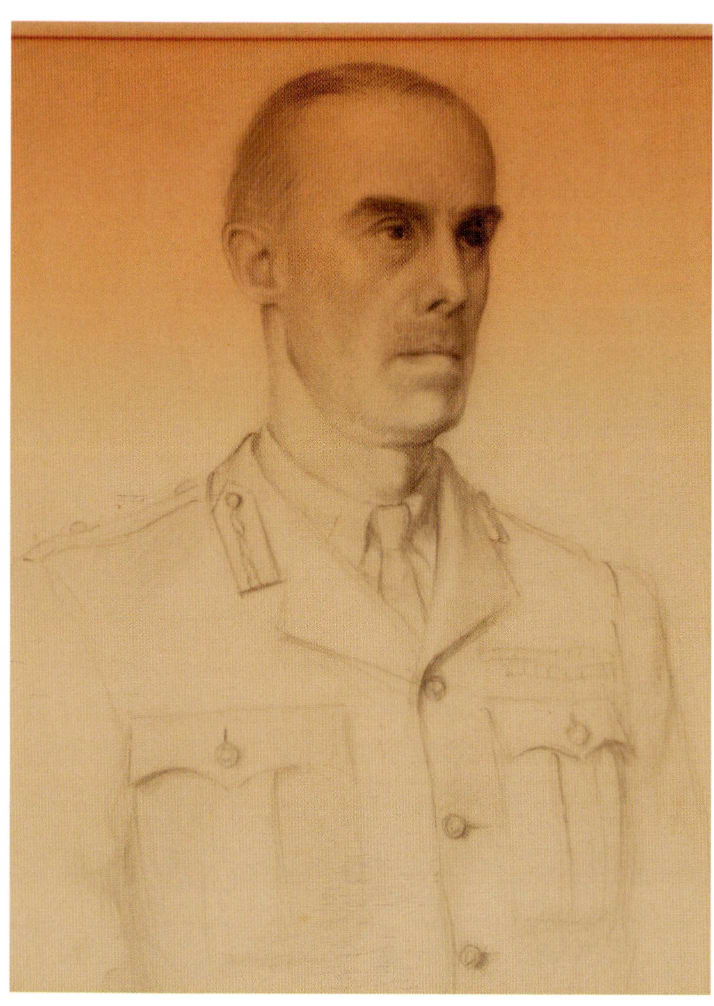

Colleen Browning,
Portrait of an Officer, *n.d. Pencil on paper, 14 x 10½ inches. Gift of the Estate of Geoffrey Wagner.*

working with Browning as a "richly rewarding and often times humorous" series of phone calls, letters, and "over lunch in New York City."

The fault line inevitably occurred when Spencer points out: "She comes from the same generation of artists as Philip Pearlstein [born 1924]; Alfred Leslie [born 1927] and William Bailey [born 1930] whose works have been grouped by some critics under the title New Realism." Spencer, knowing Browning better than any professional in the field at that time, had been hoodwinked by her age fabrication. Hence his own critical assessment was misinformed.

In the 1930s, Pablo Picasso converted into his Surrealist style, with deference to Salvador Dali's originality. But Picasso was born in 1881 and Dali in 1904; those twenty-three years were the difference between the innovator of his time versus the late-comer. Rock-a-billy's new "shake, rattle, and roll" was invented by Elvis Presley, born in 1935, but John Lennon's psychedelic "A Day in the Life" was light years away even though he was born only five years later in 1940. Basically, creative artists cannot sustain untruthful age differentials without paying the consequences of being out of sync with their time.

Although Browning was not actually from County Cork, as she said to the hungry journalists that morning in a spontaneous interview on the promenade deck of the *Queen Elizabeth*, she was of Irish descent; both of her parents were Irish by birth and her family genealogy is well documented in *Burke's Irish Family Records*. As a child she had visited her grandparents' Georgian manor house, Cregg House at Fermoy, during summer holidays. Her father's regimental duty placed him in South Ireland from 1919 to 1921. Browning's short visits to Ireland were sentimentally idealized. Unquestionably, her Irish roots were a source of considerable pride, especially after she came to America.

Major General Langley Browning (1891–1974), her adoring father, was a career servant of the Crown, spending most of his military service in England or at foreign postings across the British Empire. His father, Lt. Colonel Winthrop Benjamin Browning (1855–1934), lived the retired life of a country squire at Cregg House, at Fermoy, County Cork. Violet Muriel Cairnes, the artist's mother, was born at The Glen, Drogheda, County Louth, Ireland.

Considering her modest exhibition record prior to her arrival, Browning attained sensational media exposure. Unequivocal critical praise and genuine curiosity about this newly discovered immigrant soon appeared in the art press: *ARTnews, Art Digest, Arts*

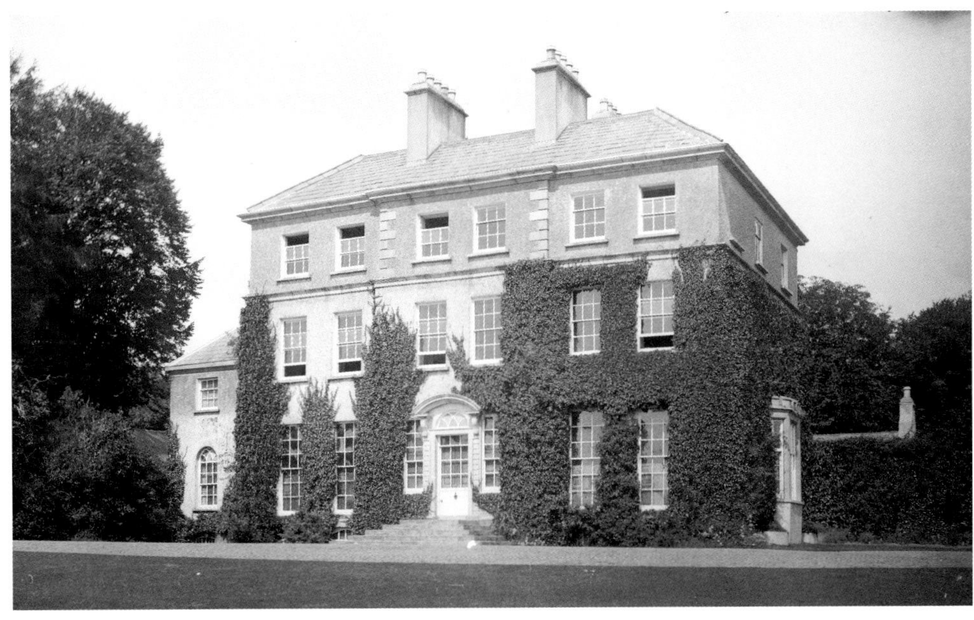

Cregg House in Fermoy, Ireland. Courtesy National Library. L_CAB_04028.

International, and *Architectural Digest*, and more generalized media: *TIME*, *Newsweek*, *The New York Times*, *Herald Tribune*, *Nation*, and *New Republic*—securing her early fame.

A human wave with thousands of immigrant stories like Browning's were indelibly etched into the nation's history in the twentieth century. Achieving the American Dream were several generations of immigrants before her—each ready to achieve success upon their debarkation. Browning's "Voyage to romance" shared archetypal elements, such as leaving loved ones and familiar surroundings for the unknown and relative youthfulness of American culture.

Fortunately, we have inherited a richly embellished visual record of those experiences, allowing us to peek over her shoulder on her American odyssey. Consistently, she was true to her bearings. She summarized her singular adherence to representationalism for her 1987 solo exhibition at the Wichita Art Museum:

> *I paint different subjects. But I am always a realist, an illusionist if you prefer. I attempt to interpret my world, the world surrounding me, as clearly as possible; and as I live in and see new places or things, it reflects itself in my work.*[5]

With her paintbox, brushes, and palette packed into her luggage, Browning traveled to America fully equipped to continue her blossoming career as a portrait painter and symbolic fantasist. Her painting tools were like a quiver filled with golden-tipped arrows used with bulls-eye accuracy. She was inexorably and unerringly a finely honed, precisely trained, realist painter.

A curious parallel is the journey of another immigrant painter, one who would move American art at mid-century in an alternative direction, Willem de Kooning. In his coming-of-age tale, de Kooning embarked from Rotterdam in 1926 to transform the nature of art in New York. "From the dark passage by ship to the eventual acclaim, de Kooning's life invoked the greatest of the classic American stories—that of the immigrant who crosses the ocean in search of a better world. His long life with roots deep in the nineteenth century, stretches across most of the twentieth, and embodies many archetypal American themes."[6]

Browning's trajectory—although more logically unfolding as a traditionalist than a rebel—had an uncanny similarity. Reclusive, always re-positioning her realist frame of reference, and caught up in the vortex of the New York art scene at the very moment of its most intensive vibrancy, her life mirrored de Kooning's in more ways than we might assume. Although she might not have attained the status of becoming a household name in the lexicon of American art, there is much evidence that she shared, in some ways, an equally impressive rise to prominence.

> *He is a loner. He reinvents himself. He becomes a star. At the same time, his emigration to America parallels another cultural passage: the coming of age of American art. Most critics believed, during the 1950s, that the center of the art world was moving from Paris to New York.… For de Kooning, the late 1940s and '50s in particular represented an extraordinary series of intoxications—in art, in love, and in fame.*[7]

Browning's story is the crest of an extended wave. Scores of transplanted Irish and English immigrants in the United States rode the same pulsating current toward new horizons for their individual and professional lives. When Frances (Fanny) Trollope arrived from London to America's shores in 1827, she remarked it's a "fine country well worth visiting for a thousand reasons, nine hundred and ninety nine of these are reasons founded on admiration and respect."[8]

Fanny's far more amiable son, Anthony, followed as another English observer of American manners, morals, and mercantilism. He noted the infinite opportunity for talented individuals and in some trades "there is no defined limit. Painting is as much open to women as to men."[9] Concluding his three volumes on America, published in 1862, he wrote: "Men and women do not beg in the States…they walk like human beings made in God's form. They know they are men and women, owing it to themselves and to the world that they should earn their bread by their labor, but feeling that when earned it is their own."[10]

By 1954, the rapidly blossoming female artist received a lovely bouquet: a coveted color spread—"Colleen Browning's Young Career"—in the smart-set's *Glamour* magazine. A refreshing article amidst the masculine dominated art world, *Glamour* heralded Browning's aplomb to its female readership. Without being cast in the defiant role of the emerging Beat generation, Browning was portrayed as a "modern woman." She managed to express herself creatively *and* care for her domestic household duties. Browning might have pushed the glass ceiling, but remained well within the paradigmatic image of a 1950s housewife.

Glamour painted an energetic portrait of a "*young wife with a career of her own as an artist. Even her marketing trips through Manhattan's Upper East Side serve her paintings. Laden like a Sicilian donkey with shopping bags in either hand, …the dark-haired, outrightly handsome young woman suddenly stops, props her burdens on the ground against either knee, and begins making surreptitious scratches on a piece of paper cupped in her hand.*

There is nothing 'La Vie Boheme' about the [conflict between keeping house and painting]. *Colleen paints in a neat white blouse and tweed skirt and stockings.…As for living in East Harlem, the Wagners consider that a stroke of real luck. Their fourth floor walk-up is inexpensive, light and airy. Second Avenue is a far cry from the County Cork* [Ireland] *house where Colleen was born.*[11]

Glamour's entrenched view of the subservient housewife reflected American popular culture stereotypes. Reinforced and amplified during the '50s Golden Age of television, mainstream women's journals like *Glamour* were unwilling to relinquish this traditionalist view. Media critic and cultural historian Eric Burns noted: "In some ways, the entertainment shows on television treated women better than they did blacks. In some ways they treated them worse."[12] For example, in *Father Knows Best*, Jim (actor Robert Young) tells Margaret (Jane Wyatt) in a manner more teasing than demanding, "C'mon, woman, let's get on with the cooking."

One quarrelsome female media observer noted television's portrayal of women's humiliation, servile nature, and helplessness. "In an article for *TV Guide*, the woman wrote that television dismissed the average American female as a 'stupid, unattractive, insecure, little household drudge, who spends her martyred, mindless, boring days dreaming of love—and plotting nasty revenge against her husband.'"[13] That writer was Betty Friedan, author of *The Feminine Mystique*, the book that ignited the women's movement in the 1970s.

Brash and persistent, Browning never quite fit into the weepy, vacuous, inconsequential, and submissive stereotypical images of dutiful housewives of the 1950s. Thoroughly prim and proper in her British demeanor, she and Wagner were more like suave, quirky oddballs. Too elegant to be disheveled beatniks or bohemians—they were cut out of good, strong, tattersall cloth, Italian silk scarves, and could dress with a *Vogue* magazine sense of flair—they were an ironclad unit in their artistic and intellectual pursuits. By nature, they were nonconformists.

Notching up into the top tier, Browning was included in *Cosmopolitan* magazine's feature on the up-and-coming role of female artists, published in October 1961. In "The Amazing Inventiveness of Women Painters," Jean Lipman, then editor of *Art in America*, and art critic Cleve Gray co-authored an upbeat, prescient look. "Women are more intuitive and are able to express their emotions with less constraint than men…. This generation of [abstract expressionist] women artists is not competing with men, it is simply saying, 'Look at my work, this is what I, a woman, feel.' The ability to express their own selves without attempting to rival the work of men has made for many successful marriages between artists.…The reader should not forget that these young women were preceded by many fine artists like Georgia O'Keeffe, and Dorothea Tanning, wife of

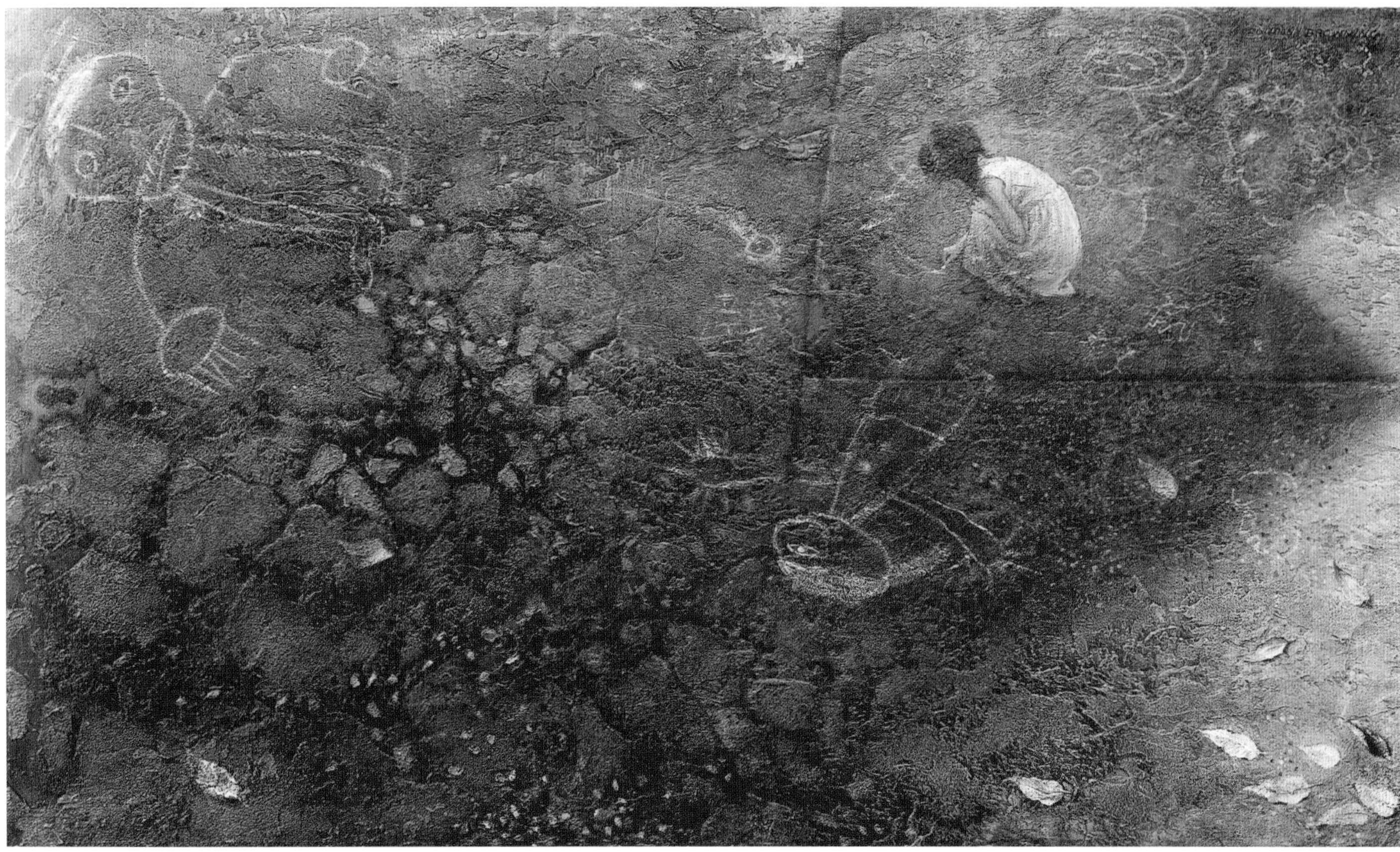

the painter Max Ernst. Moreover, there is a fine group of realistic artists such as Priscilla Roberts, Colleen Browning…and Isabel Bishop."

Reading avant-garde literature, attending New Wave French cinema at New York's Paris Theatre, Browning's and Wagner's self-image was that of international sophisticates. They detested socially "square" suburbanites like Ward and June Cleaver in *Leave It to Beaver* or Alex and Donna Stone of *The Donna Reed Show*.

The sweet taste of success and recognized achievement came quickly—almost paralyzing Browning with an instinctive premonition that it was all too good to be true.

> *Her buyers include such knowledgeable patrons of American art as Lincoln Kirstein* [he purchased *Jungle Gym*], *Nelson Rockefeller* [he purchased *Sidewalk* (fig. 2.1)], *and Mrs. James Fosburgh* [Mary Cushing, divorced from William Vincent Astor, she married artist James Whitney Fosburgh, who led Jacqueline Kennedy's redecorating campaign to restore the White House]. *Her two exhibitions at Manhattan's Edwin Hewitt Gallery have done famously and both critics and collectors speak for Colleen's paintings before they leave the easel.*[14]

When we survey the motives of Browning's career, we see an underlying motif emerging that blurs the edge of autobiography and visual strategy: concealment. Despite her allegiance to paint—along with her likeminded comrades in the "human condition" figurative movement of the 1950s—we actually discover a self-imposed hermetical posture.

Art was the perfect shield that kept her audience at bay. But pictorial illusionism became confused with a deceptive sense of self. Pretending to be more than a decade younger might seem just a bit over the line of reasonable vanity. It is unclear how far she contrived or accepted an invented persona as a considerably younger woman. Fabrication would determine much of Browning's and Wagner's external lives. Tightly confined in their small apartment, with no discernible common friendships or professional relations of note, they buried their secrets into each other's confidences. There is good reason to sense that they were truthful only to one another.

Browning seemed to favor secrecy, withdrawn seclusion, and the need to maintain impenetrable screens. This detachment became a protective barrier. To some degree the cloistered air of mystery fortified her Magical Realist image-making. But it is also possible this aloofness clouded her daily affairs, and relegated social intercourse and genuine friendships to burdensome obligations.

As if stepping off the *Queen Elizabeth* created enough of a safe distance from Great Britain, Browning established her artistic platform as a detached observer of the American scene and as a true outsider looking in. She presented a perplexing and consistently obscured view of her artistic persona. A close examination of her often-camouflaged painting themes bears witness to this process. The entire narrative of her life thus became an extended metaphor for a pictorially designed and elegantly executed form of hide and seek.

Wet (fig. 2.2), painted in 1971, demonstrates her incognito presence. At first glance it is an expertly handled oil painting of a watchful female with a transparent umbrella. Handled with virtuoso effects, Browning strains the viewer's visual resources to separate out raindrops, asphalt, and the harsh lighting effects of streetlamps. Fantastically arranged areas of tangible and ambiguous shapes and forms float across the surface. The entire mood of the painting is shadowy and eerie—with perhaps even a premonition of malevolence.

Congealed blobs of viscous color bisect the yellow painted stripe on the broken asphalt street. The textures of Browning's awe-inspiring rendering skills are plainly in evidence—there are almost seamless transitions. Delicately painted foliage shifts into the slickly painted road surface, all capped by the mushrooming design of the raindrop-spattered umbrella held by the red-tressed woman.

Does Browning's art deserve an uncomplicated, straightforward observation? On the most immediate level, we might easily dismiss the picture's metaphorical possibilities. Erring by taking this at face value would unfortunately reduce the imagery's symbolic meanings, leaving the artist's real intentions as an unlocked puzzle.

To pass this off as a rather intriguing picture of a forlorn girl in the rain would be the same as mistakenly assuming that Edward Hopper's iconic image of *Nighthawks* (fig. 2.4) is merely about some randomly observed people sipping coffee at an all-night diner. Both Browning (fig. 2.5) and Hopper demand greater depths of understanding and each detail—the individuals, coffee urns, cake, plates, unoccupied stools, and the deafening

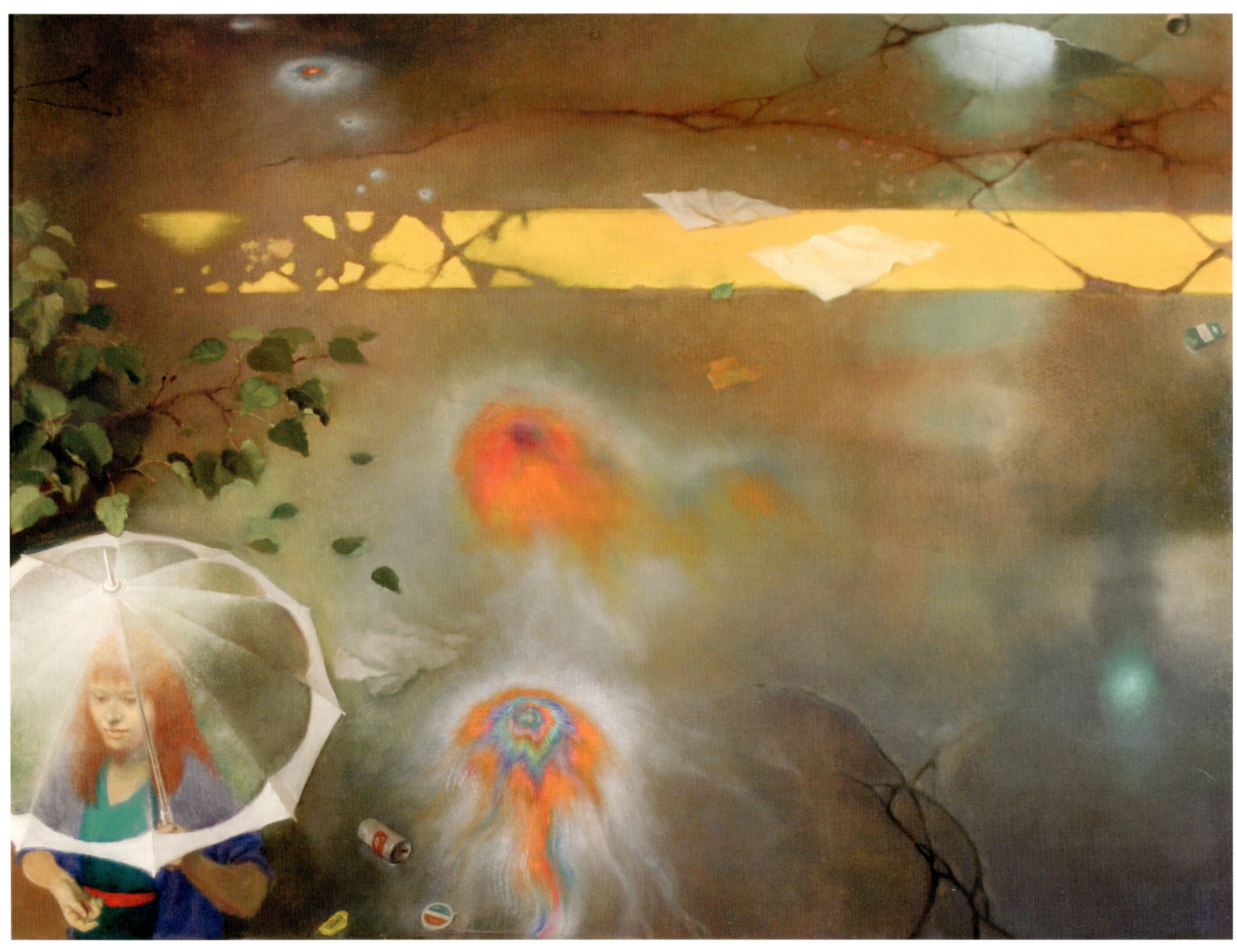

Fig. 2.2. Colleen Browning, Wet, 1971.
Oil on canvas, 35 x 46½ inches.
Gift of the artist.

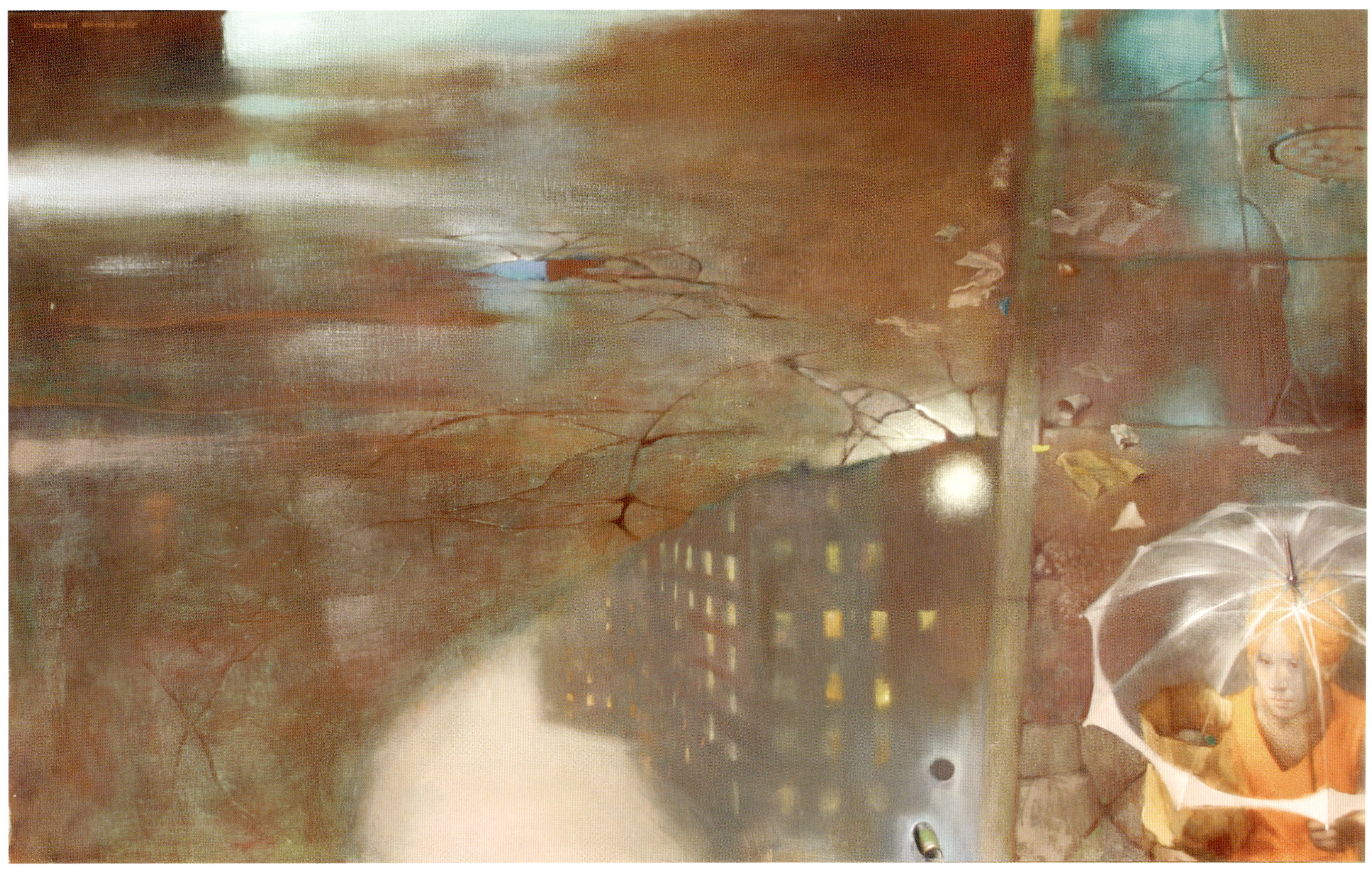

Fig. 2.3. Colleen Browning, Wet Evening, 1969. Oil on canvas, 30½ x 48 inches. Gift of the artist.

silence of the milieu—is open to interpretation. Very little is left to chance in the working method of both artists.

Hopper's sullen couple (perhaps on a one-night tryst or accepting their entrapment after years of marital torment?) is enshrouded in mystery. Browning's four African Americans in a Harlem coffee shop are also utterly enigmatic in their expressionless thoughts. The morsels of information the artists have suggested are starting points for interpretation. Realists skillfully compose, arrange, and construct the artifice of their fictitious narratives. There is little truth—it is largely a series of pictorial lies—allowing the viewer to suspend disbelief and to construct whatever narrative one wishes to invent. But in some instances, the visual narrative's hoax points directly to an astonishingly revealing reality.

In fact, *Wet* references a series of hidden meanings that transform our understanding of Browning's innermost motives. Disguised in its imagery are three distinctive

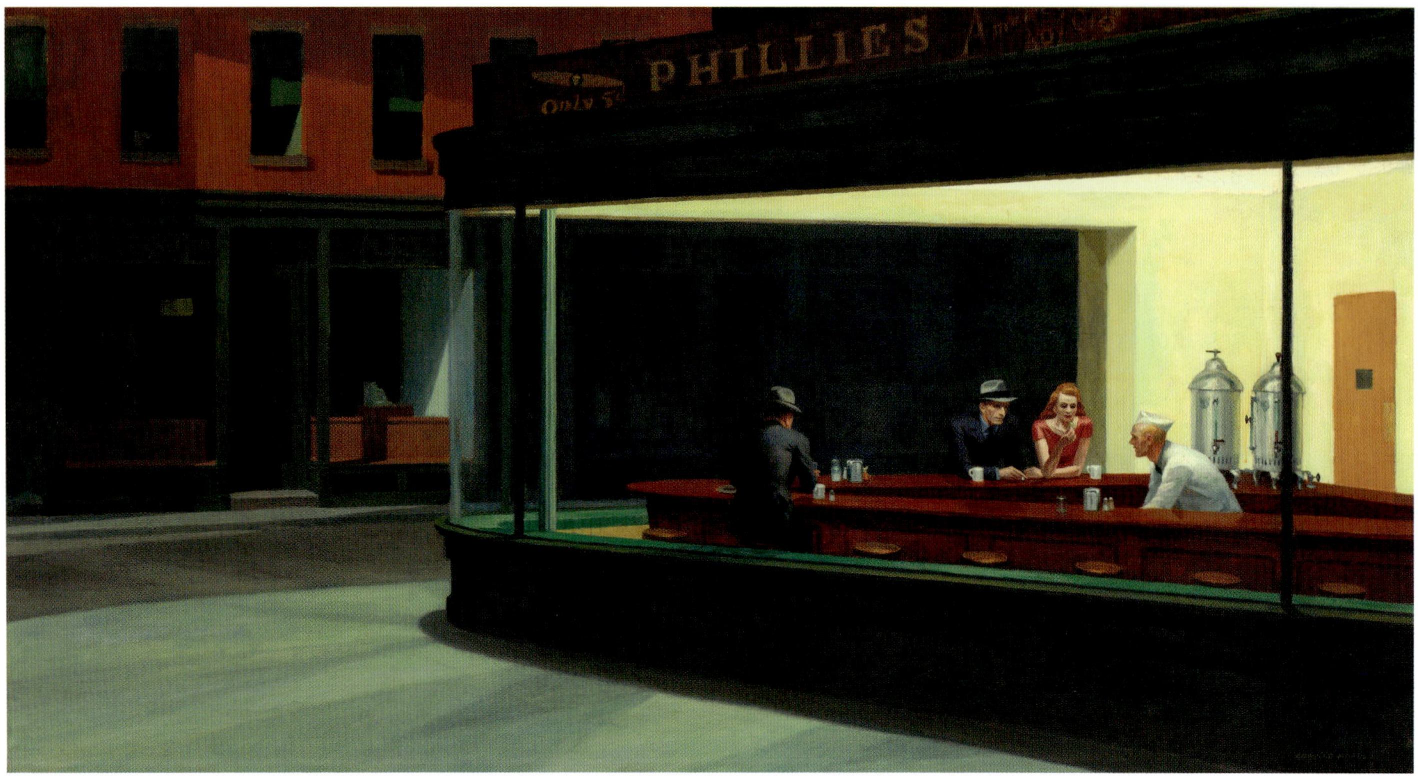

Fig. 2.4. Edward Hopper, Nighthawks, *1942. Oil on canvas, 33 x 60 inches. The Art Institute of Chicago, Friends of American Art Collection, 1942.51. Reproduction, The Art Institute of Chicago.*

features. Deconstructing the clues in an iconographic reading of *Wet* heads us in the right direction for gaining a credible "read" on Browning's art.

First, the young woman with the flowing red hair—perhaps in her early 30s?—is a psychic self-portrait of Browning. She was 51 years old at the time she completed this canvas. In this instance, and repeated in many more paintings, the somewhat obscured, indefinite features are self-portraits. Throughout her career she inserted herself—real or imagined—in successive paintings. Whether gazing in a mirror out of the corner of her eye for a close-up scrutiny of her face, or in remote and exotic locations around the world, Browning portrayed herself as model and subject.

Second, we see the sullen female beneath a transparent plastic umbrella. But this everyday object becomes more than a shield from the rain as it is repeated by Browning in a highly personalized set of images. Our sleuthing sets us on the trail of defensible conclusions.

"These symbols can provide both structure and meaning to a painting," Browning explained in her 1988 guidebook, *Working Out a Painting,* published by Watson-Guptill. This is a significantly reliable source in disassembling the artist's innermost thoughts since Watson-Guptill specialized in artist-to-artist books that combined the "heart and mind" of the master artists sharing their secrets with acolytes. When describing *Wet Evening* (fig. 2.3), a 1970 sister painting to *Wet,* done precisely in the same manner and set of elements—woman, transparent umbrella, and rain-slicked pavement—Browning notes:

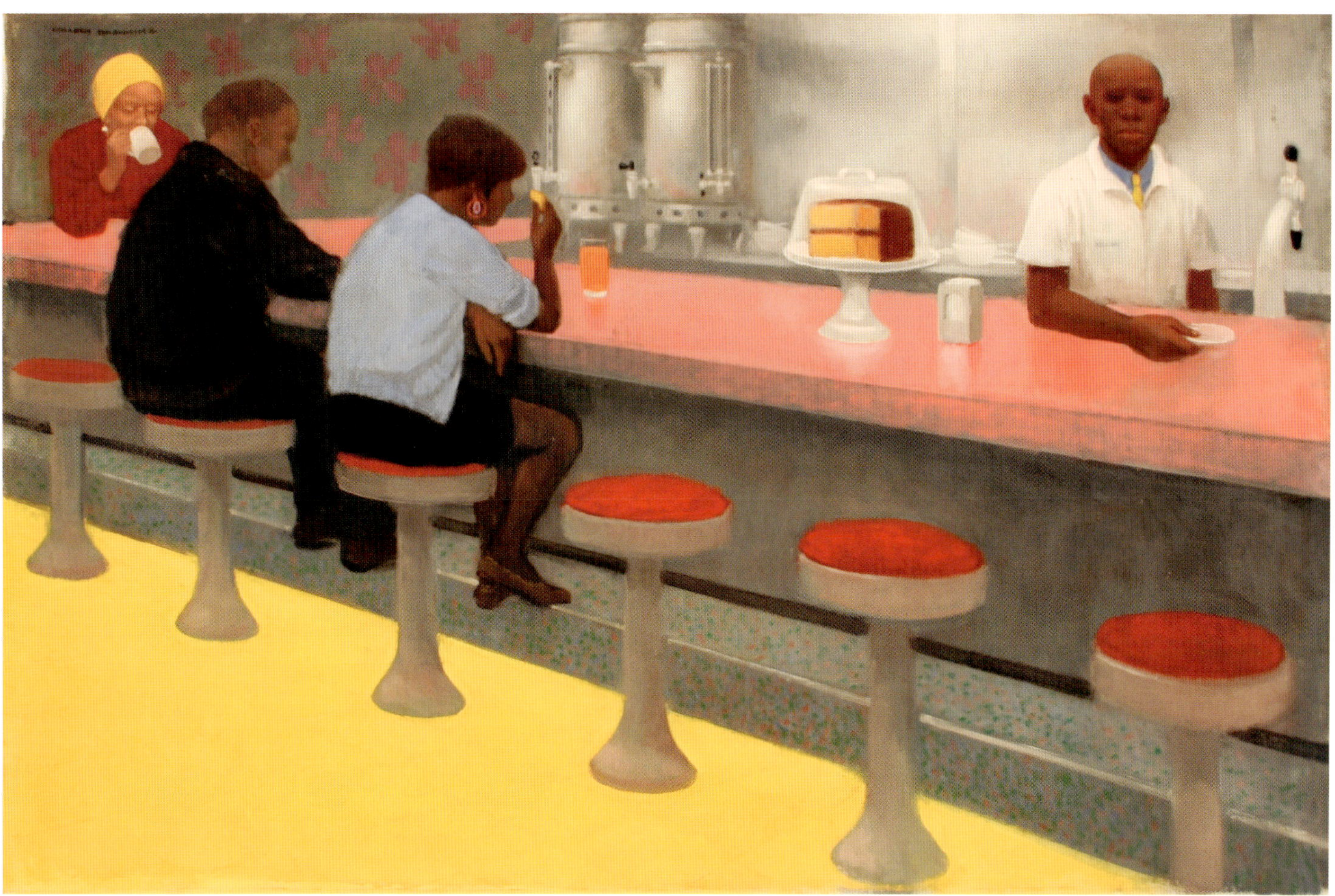

Fig. 2.5. Colleen Browning, Uptown Coffee Shop, *1967. Oil on canvas, 28½ x 43¼ inches. Gift of the Estate of Geoffrey Wagner.*

Third, and perhaps even more revealing, is knowledge of a deeply personal and traumatically violent episode. A crucial painting of this sequence is *Red Umbrella*, 1972 (fig. 2.6). Apparently, it was during this period of 1971–72 or thereabouts, while on a Caribbean vacation, Browning was assaulted in her kitchen by a knife-wielding assailant. Because of the horrifying attack, she courageously transformed this painful memory into a series known as the *Umbrella* paintings. This series is a deep mineshaft of sublimated memories, images, and symbolic painting motif. As if bubbling up from her subconscious, the savage attack was transformed into an iconic metaphor.

Browning was permanently scarred on her forehead by the attacker. This fact is corroborated by later photographs in which she disguised this disfigurement with a

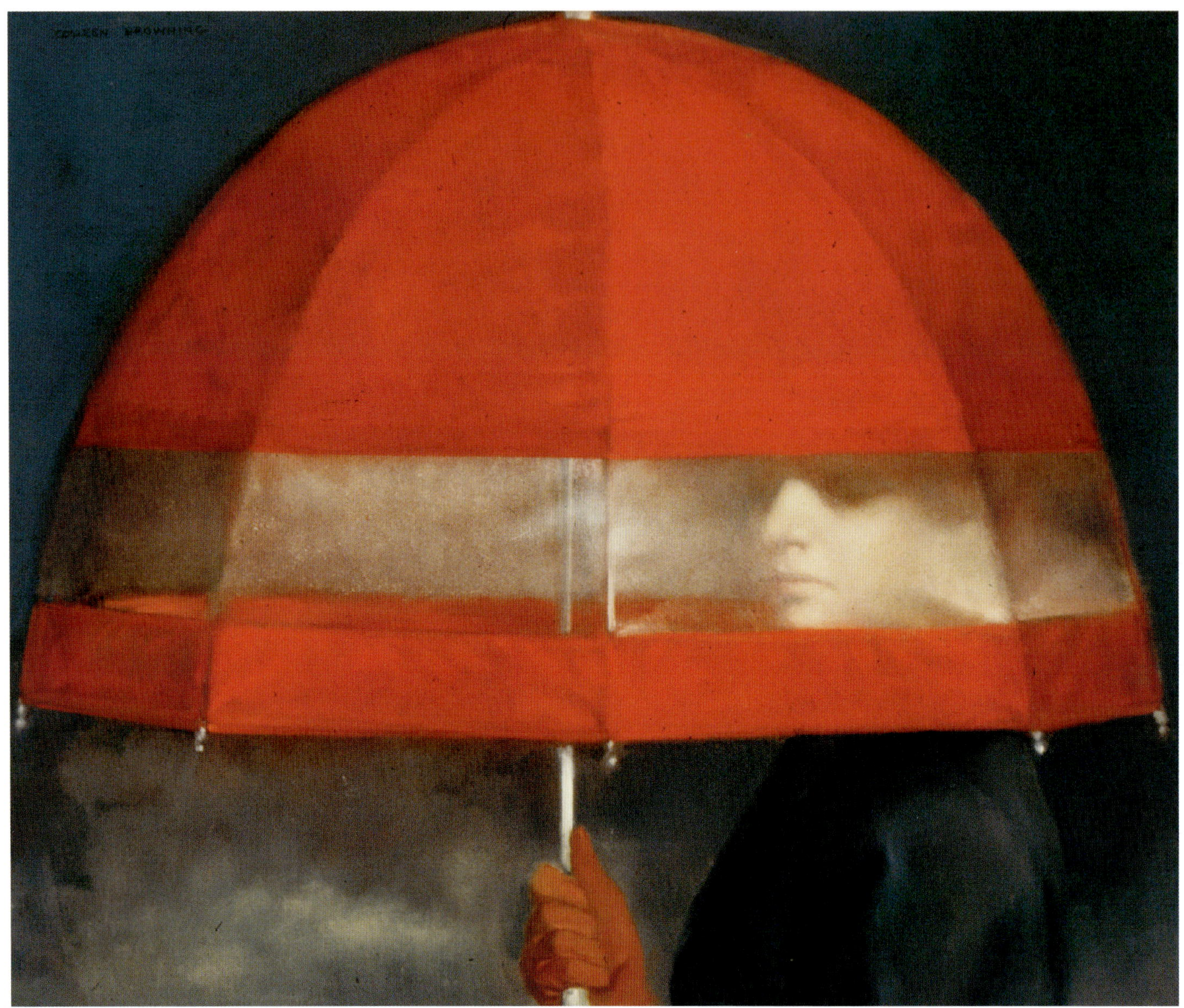

Fig. 2.6. Colleen Browning, Red Umbrella, *1972. Oil on canvas, 25 x 29¼ inches. Collection of Maier Museum of Art at Randolph College, Lynchburg, VA. Gift of the Cynthia L. Hellman Memorial Fund, 1973.*

change of hairstyle into full, forward bangs. Wagner also mentioned the attack in a letter about an *Umbrella* series painting sale in 1973.

Red Umbrella was purchased in 1973 from Kennedy Galleries by the mourning parents of Cynthia L. Hellman, a murdered college girl. It was a gift to the art collection of Randolph-Macon Women's College in Lynchburg, Virginia, as a memorial. Through a confidential source it has been determined that the Hellman family had no idea that the protective image of the umbrella was intended by the artist as a symbol of her own psychic desire to seek protection from violence. But somehow, out of the many artworks they had considered to memorialize their beloved daughter, they felt the connection with this painting.

Featured on the cover of the *Journal of the American Medical Association*, April 26, 1995 issue, *Red Umbrella* was given extensive analysis in a detailed article by JAMA art editor M. Therese Southgate, MD. Browning was interviewed in the preparation of Dr. Southgate's article, as the artist is quoted in her first-person voice, speaking about how she had escaped the "acquired blindness" of a city dweller. Aware of the urban decay and squalor around her, she hoped that her humanistic art might not become "too happy for real realism" in response.

> Red Umbrella *shows a woman* [the artist]—*her face, turned slightly, is misted and indistinct. Her hand, sheathed in a reddish brown glove, is at the lower center of the canvas. Like her other work,* Red Umbrella *is a personal response to an actual experience. Not surprisingly, it is a self-portrait. And although in itself it is surely one of the most unconventional self-portraits ever painted, its circumstances make it even more so.* Red Umbrella *was completed shortly after Browning had been knifed in the face.*[16]

Furthermore, Dr. Southgate learned from Browning that the plastic umbrella was a "sort of protective cage" that the artist felt could serve as a "shield or helmet, or even a mask." Southgate sensed that Browning relied on an artistic technique by implementing elements of camouflage. "Often, a disguise is adopted when protection is needed."[17] She extended the interpretation into a sexual-fertility metaphor: "Browning has likened the red umbrella to a placenta and suggests that her women [herself?] are awaiting a rebirth with a clear identity."[18]

In an April 1976 review of her Kennedy Galleries exhibition on 57th Street, *ARTnews* noted: "Though extremely eclectic, Browning is versatile.… The umbrella paintings—a series of works in which individual women peer out at us from beneath plastic see-through umbrellas—marvelously symbolize the relation and separation of our interior and exterior worlds.… Seen close up, the windowed faces become even more dramatic and mysterious."[19]

Browning's coming of age in the late 1930s, when disguises, deceptions, and unmasked identities were shaping the course of modern history, cannot be overlooked in the forming of her artistic persona. The young artist consciously and unconsciously infused her images with compelling pictorializations of the "interior and exterior worlds" noted in the *ARTnews* decades later.

One final take on the *Umbrella* series was late in her career. In 1993, with gallery agent Bill Meek following her around his Naples, Florida gallery with a shaky handheld video camera in advance of her opening there, he had the presence of mind to document the artist's recollections and reminiscences. Browning, rather stooped over, spoke to Meek's lens with perfect poise and dramatic flair. With paintings from almost every decade of her career, she suddenly stopped in front of *The Crossing* (fig. 2.7). Without missing a beat, she said:

> *I don't like deliberately symbolizing for painting if a symbol grows into a painting, it's very happy. I'm very happy about it. And here again is this woman inside an umbrella and it is her own private world—it is a prison and it is a womb—*

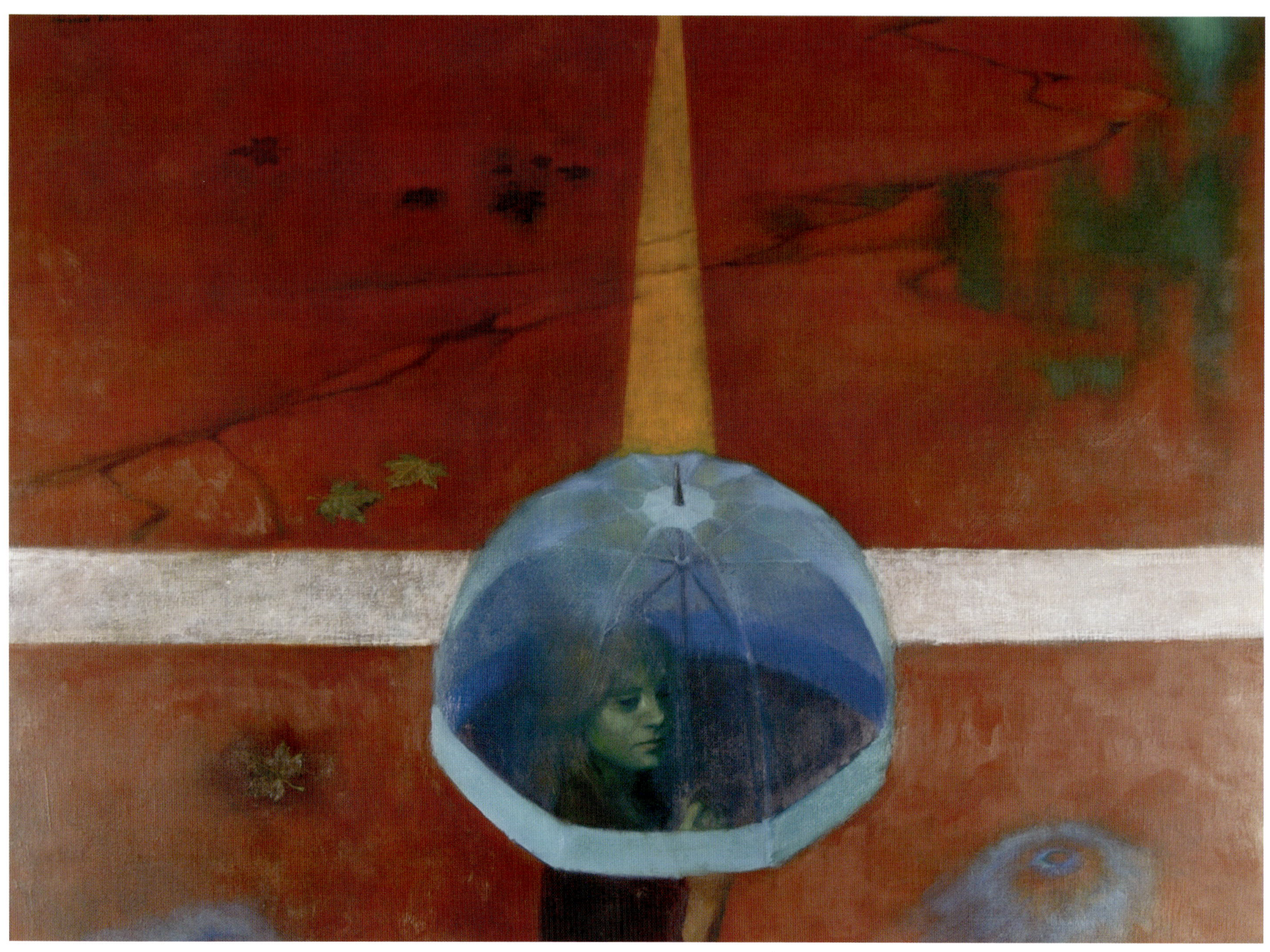

Fig. 2.7. Colleen Browning,
The Crossing, 1972. Oil on canvas,
34½ x 40 inches. Collection of Missouri
State University, Springfield, MO. Gift
of the Estate of Geoffrey Wagner, made
possible through the efforts of Sam and
June Hamra and the Harmon-Meek
Gallery, Naples, FL.

and it could be anything. It is an enclosed space and at the same time it's this crossing and shape. Is she at a crossing in her life or a crossing in her emotions?[20]

Considering her deeply connected family ties to the British military, it is perfectly understandable to view Browning's coming of age in the context of ominously evolving world events. Attending art school in the late 1930s and living in London in the early 1940s while it was being subjected to nightly blackouts, food rationing, and the ever constant threat of a land invasion from across the Channel, she had firsthand experience of how the cat-and-mouse games of diplomacy degenerated into a global apocalypse.

Browning spent a good portion of her early adulthood, between 22 and 27, with her country under aerial and naval attack. As one among the many, she knew how Britons were thrust into inescapable danger. England was caught off guard by Neville Chamberlain's 1938 appeasement strategy at Munich. It quickly dissolved into a monumental deception as the Werhmacht seized Czechoslovakia's Sudeten region. The price of deception began to be understood as storm clouds formed over an isolated Britain. Her generation never forgot the bitterness of the Blitz, a nightmarish scenario, as they crouched in London's Underground station shelters. These times are now remembered as England's "finest hour."

Winston Churchill aptly described the deceptive mood of that era. Citing the Soviet Union's duplicity in his 1939 radio broadcast, he said, "It is a riddle, wrapped in a mystery, inside an enigma; but perhaps there is a key." The blatantly deceptive context of the Molotov-Ribbentrop treaty (August 23, 1939) stunned the world; it was the tripwire that inevitably launched the war.

Little information exists that documents Browning's early war years, especially during the Battle of Britain. We have published confirmation of Browning living with her parents, along with her younger brother Shane, at Winterbourne Dauntsey for some period of time. This is a charming hamlet just a few kilometers north of the famous Neolithic Stonehenge monument in Wiltshire County, about a two-hour drive from Central London. Fortunately she was at a safe distance from the 76 consecutive nights of Luftwaffe bombings in London during the Blitz.

Between July 1940 and May 1941, England was attacked by waves of German bombers, resulting in the loss of more than 43,000 lives, approximately half within the city of London. Even more unimaginable horror came toward the end of the war when Nazi scientists perfected the jet-propelled V-1 and V-2 rockets. From early June 1944 through the end of the war, the English were vulnerable to the unpredictable destruction that took more than 16,000 innocent civilian lives.

Undoubtedly, Browning learned to maintain her poise despite any number of nightmarish outcomes, even the possibility of a full-scale land assault from the continent. Knowing that her father would soon be called back into active service, she was probably living with her mother near Salisbury as they worried about a possible German attack. With 141 Werhmacht divisions comprising 3.3 million troops stationed just across the Channel after the collapse of France in May 1940, Browning was right in the thick of it.

During this time, Browning created aerial bombing maps for the Royal Air Force, working as a cartographer. She later told an interviewer about the demanding skills needed to "draw the fjords of Norway—even irrelevant work can be a help" to England's defense. It was a thin line between her finely drawn maps of Nazi-occupied Europe and the realities of ground-zero targets. She must have appreciated how her visual references were essential guidance tools for the pilots of four-engine Lancaster bombers carrying their ten-ton payloads.

Writing an essay years later, Browning reflected about how her art was manipulated from vagueness into her illusory patterns. She admitted to the depiction of a camouflaged riddle. Is it invisible ink or a secret code? "I mean, what am I doing? Because unless I know what I am painting, I feel like I am just making a mess. Paint plops are like a Rorschach test blot in which you have a blot and the person makes something of it and the psychiatrist can identify whatever is troubling you from your blots. I am doing this sending a mixture of an unconscious impulse."[21]

Indeed, one might argue that professional deception is widely associated with fiction, film, or historical facts as one of Great Britain's most intriguing national characteristics. Perfectly in step with this theory was the "life is stranger than fiction" saga of the distinguished art historian and keeper of the Queen's pictures, Sir Anthony Blunt. As a pillar of England's cultural elite, he had unimaginable political access to support his betrayal of England as an active Soviet spy for more than 40 years.

With deceptively depicted images floating to the surface of Browning's paintings, we are reminded of Sir E.H. Gombrich's principles set forth in his classic work, *Art and Illusion: A Study in the Psychology of Pictorial Representation* (1960). Gombrich brilliantly propels us through the frailties of human perception, gullibility, and the delights of visual chicanery.

In the long run, many painters—as Browning surely understood—incorporated the language of deception into their work as a powerful tool. Realists constantly perpetrated visual skullduggery with their depicted falsehoods. A revelatory "unconscious impulse" became Browning's most effective artistic tool and signatory trademark. She not only understood illusion, but reveled in its psychological effects.

This exquisitely fine-tuned approach to deception did not go unnoticed by Browning's alert observers. In his uncannily perceptive introduction for Browning's first showing at New York's prestigious Kennedy Galleries exhibition (March 1969), art critic Frank Getlein noted her disguised patterns in the flowing Golo River on the island of Corsica and other subjects: "Separately or together, what the pictures of the Golo [river] seen from a bridge really represent is the sustained effort to see the world clearly and to discern its usually hidden order on the part of a remarkable young painter, Colleen Browning of Ireland, England, New York."[22] Aside from being two months short of turning 51 at the time, Getlein was probably charmed by Browning's appearance, deceived that she was "young" at age 40.

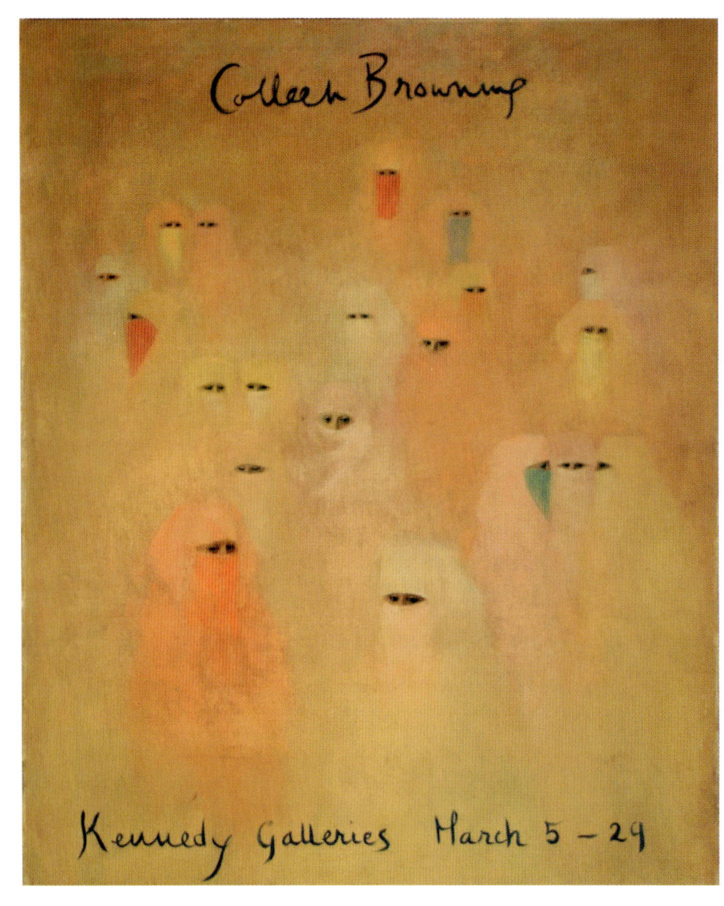

Colleen Browning, Browning Poster, *1968. Oil on canvas, 35½ x 28½ inches. Exhibition catalogue cover, Kennedy Galleries, March 5–29, 1969. Gift of the Estate of Geoffrey Wagner.*

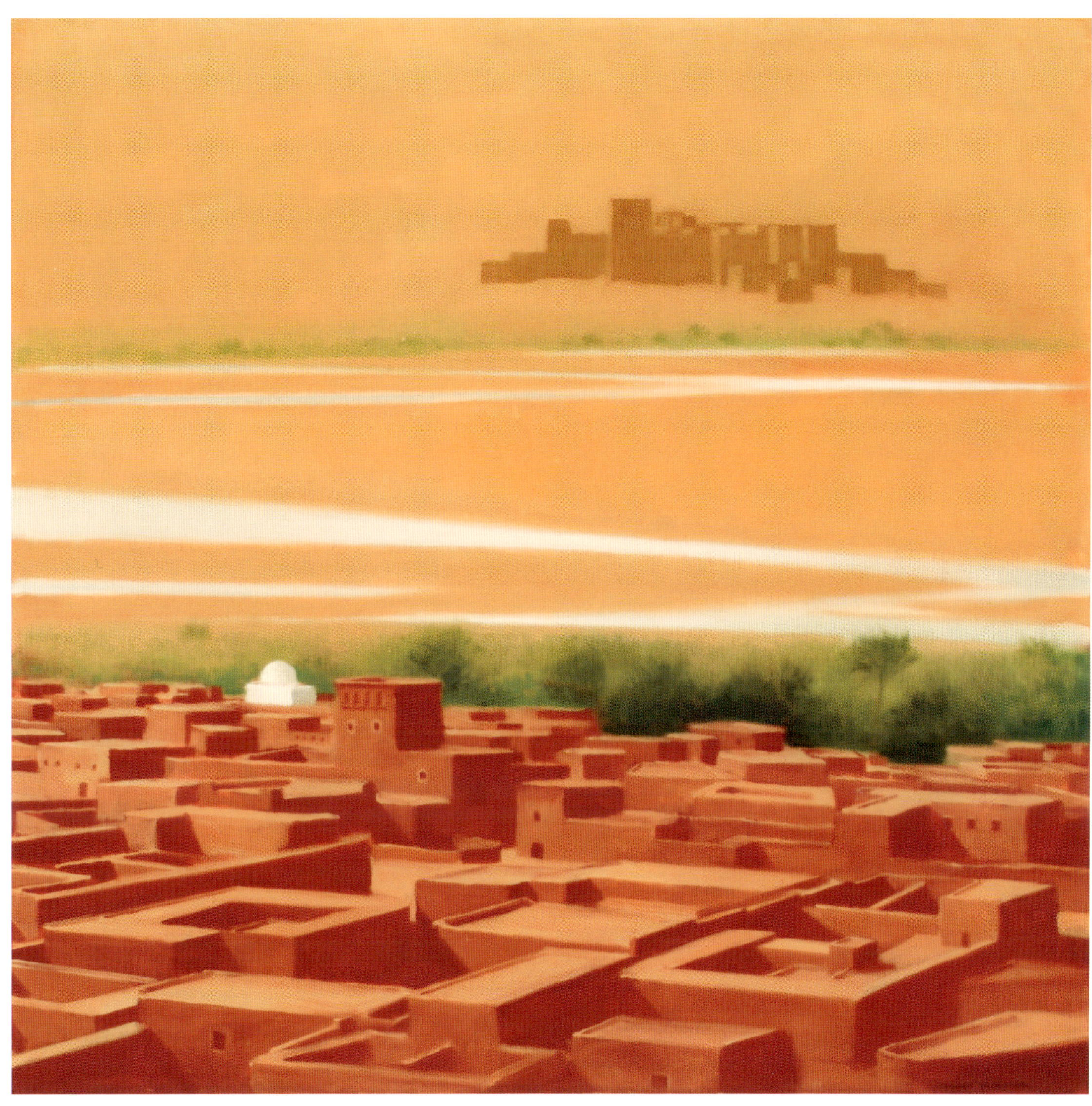

Another painting, with sunlight streaming through trees in a grove with gnarled branches and foliage, is described by Getlein: "almost allegorically, the forces of life and art that most concern the artist: the separating distance between ourselves and any reality, the solid resistance of that reality when encountered, and finally, the possibility of penetrating that reality to discern a deeper reality, an order, beyond it."[23]

Sensing Browning's affinity for the irrational, Getlein commented about the "ghostlike, mystical quality about the painting"[24] of veiled Moroccan women in *The*

Colleen Browning, Oued (River)*, 1968. Oil on canvas, 35 x 35 inches. Gift of the artist.*

Ghost Women of Essaouira, No. 1, 1983 (see p. 157). "The artist says that she came back from Morocco with 'references' in the form of sketches and photos to 'remind myself of the strangeness I had seen. That strangeness and the sense of seeing it and knowing it for the strange are palpable.'"[25] That "strangeness" became the essence of Browning's work. And the more she continued her quixotic search to find herself, the farther she went in holding up a reflecting mirror to nature's laws.

Speaking to future artists in her how-to-do textbook, she attempted to decode her own enigmatically developed methods. In *Working Out a Painting* (1988) she admitted: "I love painting…I feel it's an exciting challenge, like embarking on a voyage to an unknown exotic country."[26]

Even when understanding her tenacity to be true to herself while remaining artistically and commercially viable, Browning was forced to move toward more experimentalism. The proverbial handwriting was on the wall by the time John I.H. Baur, director of the Whitney Museum of American Art, indicated—in the past tense—the historically irreversible stampede toward abstraction in 1957: "American art has never experienced so sudden and so spontaneous a change as the general swing towards abstract painting that has taken place during the last fifteen years…. Whatever the causes, abstraction became the dominant trend in our creative painting soon after 1940."[27]

Adamantly loyal to her realist tendencies, she would not hesitate in experimenting with avant-gardist approaches as a way to remain *au courant*. Distinguished art critic Greta Berman for *Arts International* highlighted these chameleon-like abilities in 1984. Describing Browning as a "prolific, outspoken artist," Berman intuitively perceived Browning was painting "without sentimentalism…she is an untiring observer of beauty."[28] An important showcase for trendsetting galleries and artists of note, this glossy journal was published in Lugano, Switzerland, adding to its sophisticated following.

Berman focused on the tensions between Browning's early career and her success as an anachronism in the age of abstraction. "Colleen Browning's background and early success, together with her meticulous grasp of technique, were bound to militate against her acceptance in the New York Art Scene of the 1950s—dominated, as it was, by abstract expressionism."[29]

The experimental aspect of Browning's work was admired as "an abstract matrix underlies every realist painting she has ever made…. Paradoxically, she is a realist artist in love with abstraction…she herself stated: 'In translating these abstractions [color field, stripe paintings, and abstract expressionism] one is being a super-realist—which is a nice paradox!'"[30]

"Really my work is an accompaniment and a commentary on my life," Browning stated. And she adopted a variety of pictorial themes and guises to sustain this vacillating identity. Unraveling this riddle is requisite if we are to fully re-examine and validate her unquestionably noteworthy artistic achievements and properly bring Browning into the light of a new day.

Browning came of age between two world wars with an intensive game of loyalties—to king and country or to totalitarian party and fatherland—being played out. Rather than limit her possibilities, she donned appropriate cloaks but retained her autonomy. As a prerequisite of her survivalist instincts, she constructed an elusive artistic identity.

She also came of age at a time when those with guile and skillful intelligence could manipulate appearances. Embodying this strategy, the primary focus of her ever-evolving and marvelously inventive art was difficult to pin down. From afar, we come to realize that she was so wonderfully competent in her ability to create any type of visual reality that coming to terms with her artistic essence can be confounding, if not entirely impossible. The more we might think we understand her, the less we really can claim to know about her motives with absolute certainty. One just never quite comes to understand if she was looking out at the world with a sense of empathy or from detached emotional distance. By the late 1940s the abstract school was running away with a distinctively non-politicized pictorial field.

Another plausible argument for Browning's tactical evasiveness can be attributed to her understanding of the professional "glass ceiling" for female artists. Many women adopted circumventing choices and even outlandish forms of camouflaging their gender-limiting identities, biological age, or offspring. Forging a career within the particularly muscular New York art scene of the 1950s—with brawling action painters throwing boozed-up fists at each other—placed Browning in a defensive posture.

Decades after Browning decided to secretly alter her age and some elements of her identity, professor Linda Nochlin of Vassar College published a pioneering work answering the question: "Why Have There Been No Great Women Artists?" Nochlin's 1971 essay sparked a tectonic shift in art history's acknowledgement that "art is not a free autonomous activity of a super-endowed individual."[31]

In an updated interview published in *ARTnews* in 2007, Nochlin spoke of her own contributions in retrospect: "I don't think the work [of women artists] came out of the vagina or anything like that. I think it all came out of the thinking of very ambitious artists who happened to be women. These women wondered: How am I going to place myself in relation to the art language of today?"[32]

Furthering our understanding of social-cultural barriers, Germaine Greer took another giant step, authoring a best-selling book in 1979. In *The Obstacle Race: The Fortunes of Women Painters and Their Work*, now a classic in the field of feminist history, we can easily place Browning's vulnerabilities into Greer's assessment. She noted:

> *Women's painting reveals much that is of interest and concern both to the feminist and to the student of art, whether it shows the impoverishment of the oppressed personality, the sterile archetypes of self-censorship, the grimace of narcissistic introversion or the occasional flicker of rebellion in its latent content, or all of these.[33]*

Responding to this celebrated publication, which achieved international recognition, Browning felt compelled to enlist Greer as a prominent ally. A handwritten letter of 1987 was discovered in her correspondence file, with no evidence if it was a draft or even if the final document was ever posted to Greer. The letter's contents are a valuable insight into Browning's consciousness about her trials and tribulations. Characteristically, she reverted most of Greer's history of female artists—either by fame or obscurity—onto her own status. In identifying with these "obliterated women," Browning came very close to describing her own early "easy success" at a point later in time when her fame had waned.

"Anyone who has a continuous smile on his face conceals a toughness that is almost frightening," quipped Greta Garbo. Browning's alluring smile draws us closer by allowing us to appreciate the unsurpassed aspects of beauty, elegance, and artistic ripeness in her paintings. Many decades after she commenced her "Voyage to romance" we are still enthralled by the talismanic powers of her journey.

Browning's art envelops the viewer like the kiss from a visual sorcerer. Disarmed by our inability to imply literal descriptions or easy interpretations, we find ourselves released into its reservoir of its obfuscated meanings and poetically intoned mysteries. Her paintings gave contemporary emphasis to the core values of Renaissance pictorialism, fusing art and mystery by invoking the secrets of seeing versus representation.

In her remarkably productive career very little is obvious, expected, or taken for granted. Browning was an enchantress. Like a siren's call, her visual powers were deployed by purposefully acting as a beguiling manipulator of dreams, fantasies, and netherworlds. The thinnest possible cord binds these realms between the real and imagined.

NOTES

1. John Richard Craft, Foreword, *Colleen Browning: The Recent Paintings*, exhibition catalogue, Kennedy Galleries, NY, and Columbia Museum of Art, Columbia, SC, March 1972.

2. Georgina Ellen Challis, "Colleen Browning: A Rich Tapestry of Color," *American Artist*, September 1981, p. 40.

3. Ibid.

4. Michael M. Strueber, *Colleen Browning: A Retrospective*, Southern Alleghenies Museum of Art, Loretto, PA, 1997.

5. Howard DaLee Spencer, *Colleen Browning: Recent Paintings*, exhibition catalogue, Wichita Art Museum, December 6, 1986–January 11, 1987, p. 6.

6. Mark Stevens and Annalyn Swan, *De Kooning: An American Master* (New York: Alfred A. Knopf, 2004), p. xiv.

7. Mark Stevens and Annalyn Swan, *De Kooning: An American Master* (New York: Alfred A. Knopf, 2004), p. xiv.

8. Frances Trollope, *Domestic Manners of the Americans* (London: Whittaker, Treacher, & Co., 1832), p. 58.

9. Anthony Trollope, *North America*, vol. I (Leipzig edition, Bernhard Tauchnitz, 1862), p. 287.

10. Anthony Trollope, *North America*, vol. III (Leipzig edition, Bernhard Tauchnitz, 1862), p. 291.

11. Mary Ellen and Marvin Barrett, "Colleen Browning's Young Career," *Glamour*, June 1954, pp. 75–77.

12. Eric Burns, *Invasion of the Mind Snatchers: Television's Conquest of America in the Fifties* (Philadelphia: Temple University Press, 2010), p. 258.

13. Ibid., p. 258.

14. Mary Ellen and Marvin Barrett, "Colleen Browning's Young Career," *Glamour*, June 1954, p. 76.

15. Colleen Browning, *Working Out a Painting* (New York: Watson-Guptill Publications Inc., 1988), p. 72.

16. M. Therese Southgate, MD, "The Cover," *Journal of the American Medical Association*, April 26, 1995, vol. 273, no. 16, p. 1238.

17. Ibid., inside front cover.

18. Ibid.

19. Julian Weissman, "New York Reviews," *ARTnews*, vol. 75, no. 4, April 1976, p. 124.

20. Video recorded interview, Harmon-Meek Gallery, Naples, FL, March 1993.

21. Ibid.

22. Frank Getlein, *Colleen Browning*, exhibition catalogue, Kennedy Galleries, NY, March 1969, unpaginated.

23. Ibid.

24. Ibid.

25. Ibid.

26. Colleen Browning, *Working Out a Painting* (New York: Watson-Guptill Publications Inc., 1988), p. 9.

27. John I.H. Baur, ed., *New Art in America: Fifty Painters of the 20th Century* (Greenwich, CT: New York Graphic Society, 1957), p. 220.

28. Greta Berman, "Colleen Browning and the Texture of Life," *Arts International*, vol. XXVII/3, August 1984, pp. 18–25.

29. Ibid.

30. Ibid.

31. Linda Nochlin, "Why Have There Been No Great Women Artists?" *Women, Art and Power and Other Essays* (Boulder, CO: Westview Press, 1988), p. 147.

32. Barbara MacAdam, "Where the Great Women Artists Are Now," *ARTnews*, February 2007, vol. 106, no. 2., pp. 114–119.

33. Germaine Greer, *The Obstacle Race: The Fortunes of Women Painters and Their Work* (New York: St. Martin's Press, 1979), p. 7.

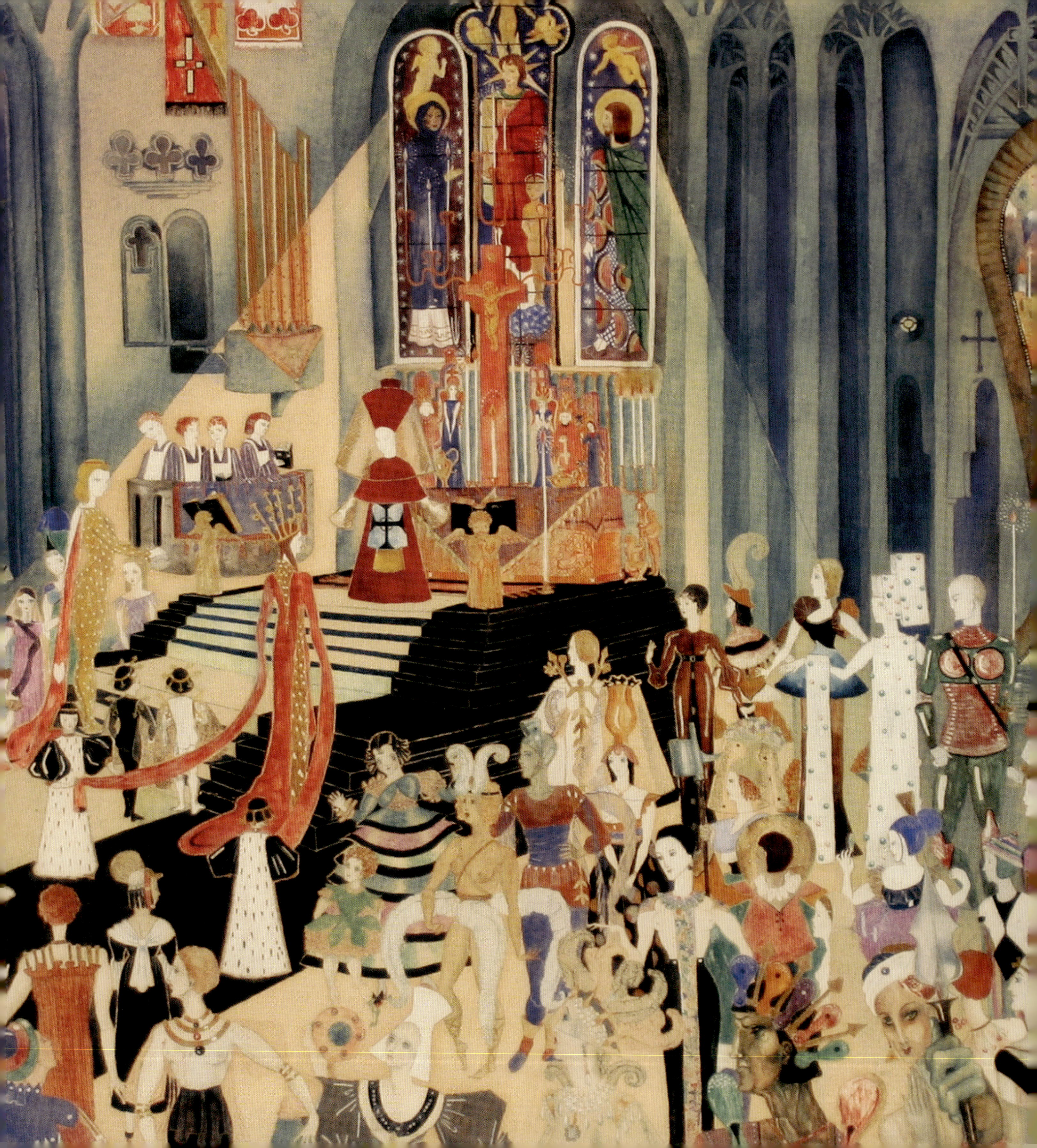

*"…five horses killed under me, and a German shell burnt off most of the hair
on my head…my right arm paralysed."*

—WW I memoirs of Captain Langley Browning

"…a brush with the famous Michael Collins…"

—Captain Langley Browning, 1920

COLLEEN BROWNING'S BIRTH ON ENGLISH SOIL in May 1918
took place toward the end of World War I in the military
town of Shoeburyness, an ancient fortified outpost on the southeastern tip of Essex at
the mouth of the Thames overlooking the English Channel.

With its strategic position as a coastal bastion, Shoeburyness was originally fortified by a Roman garrison in the first century AD. It served as a beachfront camp for the
invading Danes in their challenge to King Alfred in AD 894 and was eventually expanded
into a major strategic fortress defending England during the Napoleonic wars of 1797–
98. During the Great War it was a first perimeter coastal installation. Heavy six-inch
breech-loading artillery rimmed the seawall, searching for the Kaiser's lethal submarines
and battleships on the horizon.

Browning's birth at Shoeburyness was the result of her father's furlough from
battlefield injuries. With the armistice still six months away, Captain Langley Browning
(who would rise to the rank of Major General by World War II) was severely wounded
on a Belgian battlefield. He had the good fortune of reassignment for "light duty," leading an artillery training school at Shoeburyness, out of harm's way.

In "Irish Gunner," Major General Browning's autobiography, he presents us with
unimpeachable information, our most reliable testimony documenting his daughter's
early years. The unpublished manuscript, bound in a rugged leather binding, is a gold
mine. "I was pepping up our cadets or young officers to keep them up to date in the
constantly changing artillery technique. In May 1918 my first child, Colleen, was born.
I had been rather afraid about this because of the anxious and dangerous time my wife
[Violet Muriel Cairnes] had gone through but all was well and Colleen was perfectly
normal except for years afterwards she could not bear to hear people moving in a room

overhead. My friend, General Burrard (late editor of "Game and Gun") says he feels partly responsible for Colleen's arrival! He lent us a dog-cart and I took Violet out for a drive one morning. She was a bit shaken up by the drive and told me to get back quickly, which I did. We got back at noon and Colleen was born at 2 pm!"[1]

Colleen Browning's bracing, tough-minded worldview—both she and her father shared a characteristic tenacity, forbearance, and single-mindedness—was dramatically shaped by her father's service to the Crown. Major General Langley Browning's service included years away from family in the early 1930s when he was stationed in India to oversee the last chapters of the Imperial Raj.

A family history and subjective commentary on Major General Langley Browning's life and times, "Irish Gunner" is filled with pertinent information on his daughter's heritage. We can only sense a smidgen of the bloody carnage and emotional strains he must have experienced. With humanizing insights, Browning reported about life in the trenches on the battlefields of Loos, Ypres, Bernafay Wood, and the devastation of the Somme. In concluding one chapter, he wrote: "This ended for me the First World War— five horses killed under me, twice officially a casualty and three times unofficially, eight medals of various kinds and my health and strength unimpaired. I was lucky."[2]

With the Citation for America's Legion of Merit, signed by President Truman in August 1945, Major General Langley Browning's service reached its summit as one of the top Allied generals in Rome. He was charged with the supervision of the reconstruction of the defeated military in post–WWII Italy. He was an able servant of the king, devoting a lifetime to His Royal Majesty's army, the Royal Regiment of Artillery. Eventually, he would earn a chest full of decorations and honors. By the end of his storied career, he was ranked as Major General, C.B. (Companion of the Most Honourable Military Order of Bath, established by King George in 1725), O.B.E. (Officer of the Most Excellent Order of the British Empire, created by King George VI in 1917), and M.C. (Military Commander, given for gallantry in World War I).

The major general also took great pride in a special commendation, signed by the governor of Texas, making him an honorary Texas citizen. "Any Texan will tell you that as far as the U.S.A. is concerned TEXAS won the war with the assistance from the other States! Be that as it may, I found Texans the flower of American manhood—fine, big, upstanding, cheery fellows with an immense and justifiable pride in their state and themselves. I have a permanent invitation to visit "my" Lone Star State…to visit the very best chaps I ever met." Interestingly, although he would never visit America, his daughter would drive across Texas on her honeymoon trip in the summer of 1949, en route to meet the artist Diego Rivera in Mexico City.[3]

According to archives in *Burke's Peerage* (Burke's Irish family records), Langley Browning was born on July 28, 1891 and died on April 19, 1974. His father was, as noted previously, Lieutenant Colonel Winthrop Benjamin Browning, who was educated at the City of Dublin Hospital where he was trained to be a member of the Royal College of Surgeons. He married Annie Georgina Stevenson in 1887. His peerage was established in 1898 when he was invested as a Companion, Order of the Indian Empire (C.I.E.) and served successive governors in Madras. In 1910, he left the active medical service of the Indian Medical Service, retired into the hospital service as a professor at the medical college in Madras, and finally retired to his country estate, Cregg Castle House, Fermoy, County Cork.

Colleen Browning often spoke of Cregg Castle House as her Irish home, but how much time she actually spent at this wonderful ancestral estate is unknown. With its richly chronicled past, surely embellished with family lore, Cregg Castle always touched a vulnerable spot in her heart. A recently renovated national monument, Cregg is Irish for "a rock, rocky ground." In 1611, King James I gave a grant to David Lord Roche, Viscount Fermoy at the parish church of Cregg. "The walls of the old 13th century castle are still standing, but the rest is in ruin," according to a nineteenth-century description. Nearby to the Cregg Castle, at Kilcolman Castle, Edmund Spenser penned in 1590 his literary classic dedicated to Queen Elizabeth I, *The Faerie Queene.*

> *A mid-18th century structure, Cregg Castle House is a "rare example of a particularly fine Georgian country house set in an idyllic wooded setting on the banks of the River Blackwater. Behind wrought iron gates, a narrow winding avenue, flanked on one side by mature trees and woodland and the other side by views of the ancient castle.*[4]

Colleen Browning's grandfather, Dr. Winthrop Benjamin Browning, retired from the Indian Medical Service in 1910. Apparently he became world famous as a surgeon, having conducted the first successful surgery on elephantiasis disease. On retirement he returned to Tipperary where he permanently resided at Cregg Castle House. Waxing whimsically on his childhood recollections of this comfortable home, Langley Browning recalled those halcyon days:

> *Cregg epitomized the spacious days of Country Gentleman in the Victorian Era. An old estate, it had one of the best preserved castles covering a ford in all Ireland. The house was a fine old mansion…We owned 1 and ¼ miles of the River Blackwater at our door where the salmon and trout fishing was first class and there was good woodcock shooting on the property. Nearby there was over 100 miles of free fishing in the Funshion, the Bride and other rivers. Those were happy days. The world was at peace…the great exodus from Ireland of the English or rather of our class, had not been dreamed of. There was far greater happiness and pleasure in the simpler and more placid and natural amusements and pastimes of that era than there is in the nervous, hectic, synthetic non-stop roundabout which goes by 'life' today. It seems to me that there was then more honesty, more real friendliness, a greater sense of duty to one's job and one's neighbour.*[5]

The clouded lens of history framed Colleen's father's worldview: "Fundamentally I believe that the change in the last 30 years is a withdrawal from religion and Christian tenets…The dominance of the paterfamilias in the Victorian era may have been overdone, but it did produce a race which controlled with equity and justice a large part of the world, planning and working for others with a high degree of altruism. How different from today when so many people are 'on the make' for their own ends, irrespective of their duty to their neighbor and the world in general."[6]

The major general proved to be a man of great humility and humanity. "Judge a man by the company he keeps," Euripides proffered as a rigid test of character. Browning revealed profound admiration for a figure he met in 1923, when "I spent five weeks or so attached to my cousin, General Sir William of Malta,"[7] when Browning began teaching at the Staff College at Deepcut. This cousin was Lieutenant General William George Shedden Dobbie (1879–1964). "I enjoyed this very much and found Dobbie a sterling chap. As is well known he is very religious but I found him extremely human and pleasant…He was a firm believer that the Bible is full of hidden prophecy and quoted parts to support his ideas. He was also a British Israelite. I think he is one of the finest men I have ever met and with great moral courage."[8]

Langley Browning was deeply impressed with his cousin's sense of historical purpose and divine destiny. Dobbie had the Bible Society distribute New Testaments to his troops at the beginning of the 1929 conflict and had this printed notice inserted in each Bible: "You are stationed at the place where the central event in human history occurred—namely the Crucifixion of the Son of God. You may see the place where this happened and you may read the details in this book. As you do this, you cannot help being interested, but your interest will change into something far deeper when you realize the events concern you personally. It was for your sake the Son of God died on the cross here. The realization of this fact cannot but produce a radical change in one's life—and the study of this book will, under God's guidance, help you to such a realization." Late in his career in 1948, he authored *Active Service with Christ* and was named as a member of the Order of St. John of Jerusalem.

We can track Colleen Browning's first three years in southern Ireland, between 1919 and 1921, when her father wrote: "I returned to my home in Fermoy in the Spring of 1919."[9] We can imagine his relief in surviving the war and returning to his fishing in Fermoy. "It was a lovely easy free life and I hoped that I could serve in Ireland for most of the rest of my service, moving from one Field Brigade to another or promotion…. There were many lovely places all round where people lived on their ancestral acres, so there was jollity."[10]

But "the Troubles" were underfoot—the chasm splitting the Emerald Isle had come to their front door. As a senior ranking officer of the Crown, he was not in the least conflicted about apprehending those "Irish rebels…establishing a reign of terror and not stopping short of killing…. In 1920 the I.R.A. [Irish Republican Army] turned their attention to the British Army. Matters went from bad to worse."[11] He was responsible for his soldiers ensuring "law and order" for an area of more than 200 square miles of County Cork.

Captain Browning organized "flying columns" of 12 to 15 officers who wore "plain clothes and roamed about the country heavily armed putting the 'fear of God' into the populace and taking on any bad men they met…. They say that one has to be cruel to be kind and I entirely agree. Really strong action, even a few shootings, at the beginning of the rebellion may well nip it in the bud and thus save countless lives later on. This modern ideology of democracy just asks for trouble and only fits where people as a whole are highly educated. The majority of the world still only understands force—and it will take centuries to become otherwise."[12]

Events intensified. "Neither I nor my family were molested by the rebels in any way. Most of them were old friends of mine and that may have had something to do with it. We discovered after it was over that our excellent cook had been the C.O. [Commanding Officer] of the local I.R.A.'s women's battalion in Fermoy!"[13]

The local member of Parliament, David Kent—a man of "tremendous influence"—who was sentenced to be hung in 1916, was "on the run in 1920 [but after] six months was 'worn out.' We captured him sixteen miles from Fermoy and as he was an old man I put him on my horse and walked beside it all the way to Fermoy. This raised a terrific storm and I got word that evening I was to be shot for being so inhuman and making a parade of the old man. I felt, needless to say, somewhat disturbed, particularly as I had done a kindly act. So I went and saw David Kent in our Guardroom and told him what I thought. He was furious with the Fermoy people and sent word out that I was the "grand gentleman" and that neither I nor my family were to be harmed on any account…within half an hour of this getting out [by bush telegraph] I was completely safe and the most popular man in County Cork!"[14]

One historical point might be somewhat embellished as Langley wrote of his "brush with the famous Michael Collins [an Irish revolutionary leader]. A man came in one day and said he had slept the previous night in the same house as Collins. We doubted his veracity but laid out our trap. They said that Collins would be preceded over Fermoy Bridge by an old chap with both hands crossed behind him, so as to be able to draw two guns at once! Sure enough that man did cross over but we never caught Michael Collins, though he mentions in his book that one of his narrowest escapes was Fermoy."[15]

Military family life was disruptive. Browning's brigade was transferred to Yorkshire, England, in 1921. He was again reassigned and stationed in Cologne, Germany, between 1923–24. Colleen and her mother were allowed to stay nearby and they enjoyed their time with the "good burghers" of Cologne. It was in December 1924 that Browning was accepted into the Staff College at Camberley, "having passed the exams as one of the top cut of the 600 candidates." The entire family returned to England, and Colleen's residency there was continuous until her departure to New York, with the exception of summer vacations in the Mediterranean.

Camberley, about an hour by train west of London, became Colleen Browning's home at age 6. Soon a younger brother arrived as her father noted the "birth of my Shane on November 10th, 1925" was the "great event" of his two years at Camberley.

Colleen's father was extremely content to be teaching at the Staff College but then his superiors "stepped in and said that I had to go back to regimental duty—and thus to India because I had little foreign service. I therefore sadly left England in the Spring of 1927 en route for a Medium Brigade R.A. [Royal Artillery] at Ambala in the Punjab. I had to leave Violet and the children behind because Colleen was too old to be taken to India….They installed themselves in a house in Camberley and I left for India. I did not then know that I would not see my children for three years."[16]

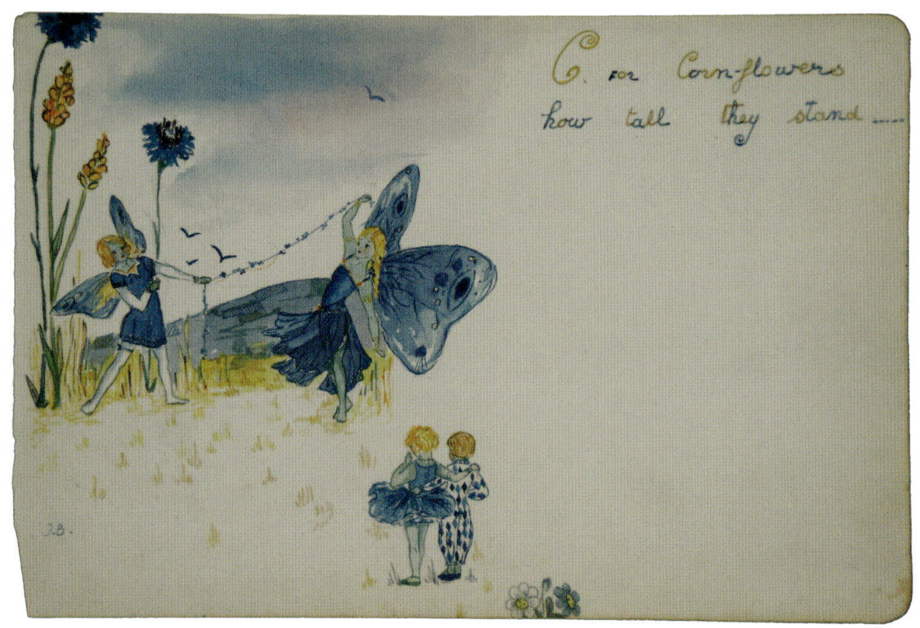

Song of the Apple Blossom
Fairy

I am dancing on the trees.
Up, up high
In the blue, blue sky
Where the lark will sing
And the birds are on the wing

THE WALL-FLOWER FAIRY

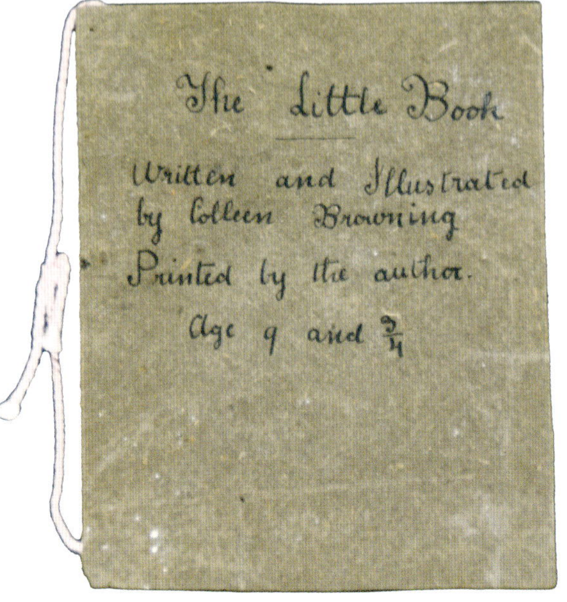

The Little Book

Written and Illustrated
by Colleen Browning
Printed by the author.

Age 9 and 3/4

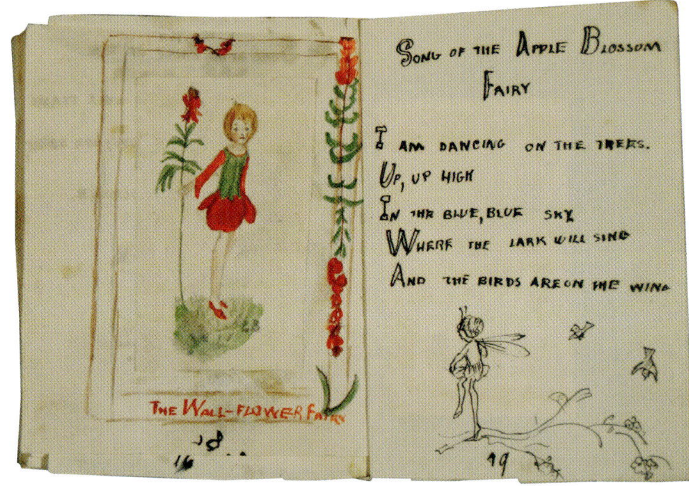

Song of the Celendine
Fairy

I grow
By a streamlets silver flow,
And I know
Where the rabbit lives.

THE PANSY FAIRY

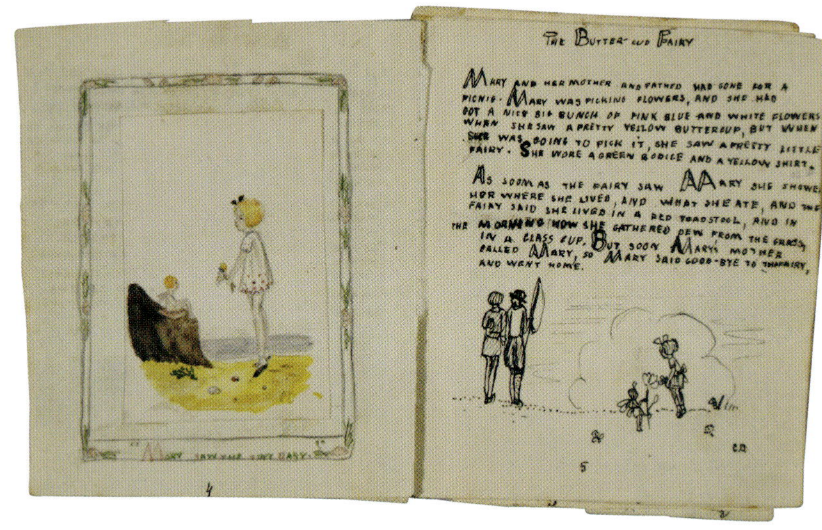

The Butter-cup Fairy

Mary and her mother and father had gone for a picnic. Mary was picking flowers, and she had got a nice big bunch of pink blue and white flowers when she saw a pretty yellow buttercup, but when she was going to pick it, she saw a pretty little fairy. She wore a green bodice and a yellow skirt.

As soon as the fairy saw Mary she showed her where she lived, and what she ate, and the fairy said she lived in a red toadstool, and in the morning how she gathered dew from the grass in a glass cup. But soon Mary's mother called Mary, so Mary said good-bye to the fairy, and went home.

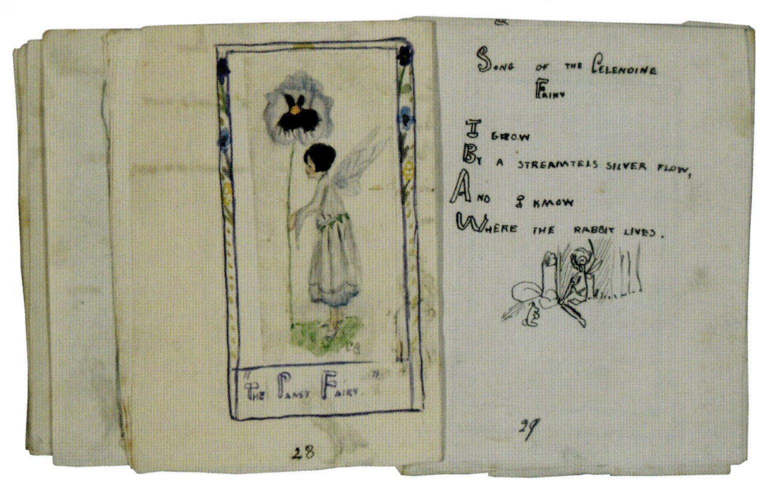

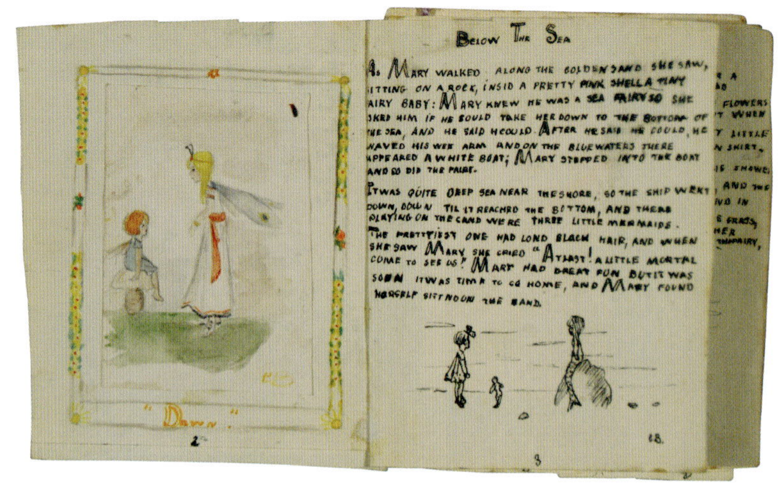

Below The Sea

1. Mary walked along the golden sand she saw, sitting on a rock, inside a pretty pink shell a tiny fairy baby. Mary knew he was a sea fairy so she asked him if he would take her down to the bottom of the sea, and he said he could. After he said he could, he waved his wee arm, and on the blue waters there appeared a white boat; Mary stepped into the boat and so did the fairy.

It was quite deep sea near the shore, so the ship went down, down, til it reached the bottom, and there playing on the sand were three little mermaids. The prettiest one had long black hair, and when she saw Mary she cried "At last! a little mortal come to see us?" Mary had great fun but it was soon it was time to go home, and Mary found herself sitting on the sand.

It was during her magical years growing from a child to a young woman that Colleen Browning's earliest extant drawings and sketches were created. *The Little Book* (fig. 3.1), written and illustrated by Colleen Browning and printed by the author, is the earliest evidence of her future vocation with its notation of "age 9 and ¾." From the start, her image of a faerie princess named Dawn is depicted with an utterly assured sense of confidence. The booklet, conceived, sketched, and sewn together by Browning, is more than a child's craft project: it reveals the hand of a prodigy. Next came her book *A Fairy Alphabet*, created at age 12 in July 1930. Dancing pixies stream across its pages as the young artist transformed period magazine photographs of ballet-diva Isadora Duncan into elfin spirits out of *A Midsummer Night's Dream*.

Displaying an advancing technique, her page with "C is for Corn-flowers" depicts four figures all turned at different angles from the picture plane. Remarkably, Browning had understood at 12 years old that figures standing in space occupy differing positions and spatial volumes.

A natural copyist, Browning used as source material a book she retained until her death, *A Floral Fantasy in an Old English Garden*, by Walter Crane (fig. 3.2), published in London in 1899 and inscribed as a gift to her from her mother. More evidence of her instinctive ability appeared with her decorously stylized image *Two Winsome Female Nymphs* (fig. 3.3), dated 1931. The entire mood—with its Aubrey Beardsley-inspired, serpentine figures—predicts her lifelong immersion in realms of fantasy, illusion, and fairytale magic.

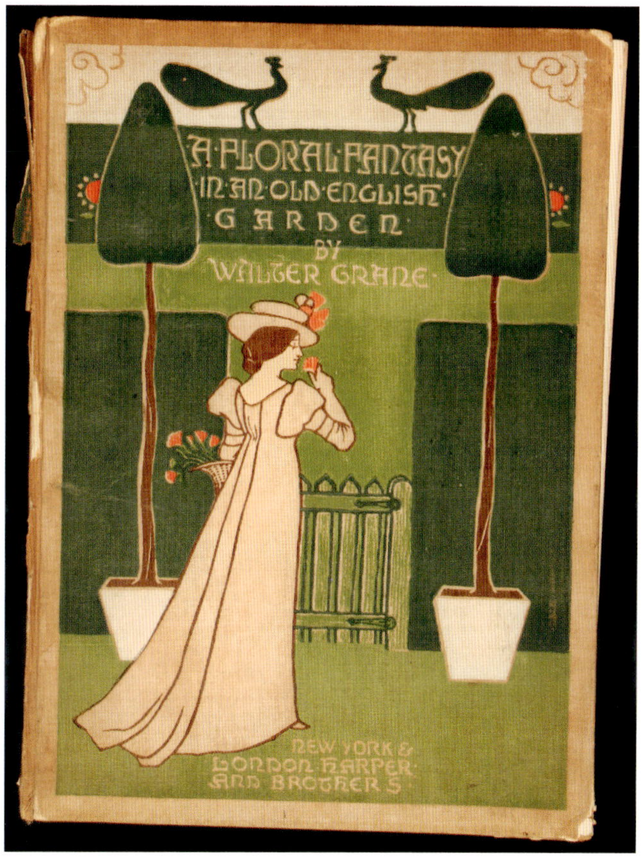

With the young Browning's obsessive daily activities focused on a steady torrent of imaginative watercolor sketches and pen-and-ink drawings, her parents wisely encouraged her development. Her father recalled: "Colleen had always shown great ability as an artist and she was starting to develop enormously in this line. Her imagination, sense of colour, and draftsmanship were quite extraordinary and a great future was prophesied for her."[17]

Noting that Langley Browning wrote this memoir in 1948, just at the moment when Colleen was having her first solo exhibition in London, it is particularly relevant to read of his sense of her future:

> This I am glad to say has been the case and the end is not yet I hope. This is
> a convenient moment perhaps to give a rough outline of her remarkable artistic career.

Fig. 3.2. Walter Crane, A Floral Fantasy in an English Garden, *1899. New York & London, Harper and Brothers.*

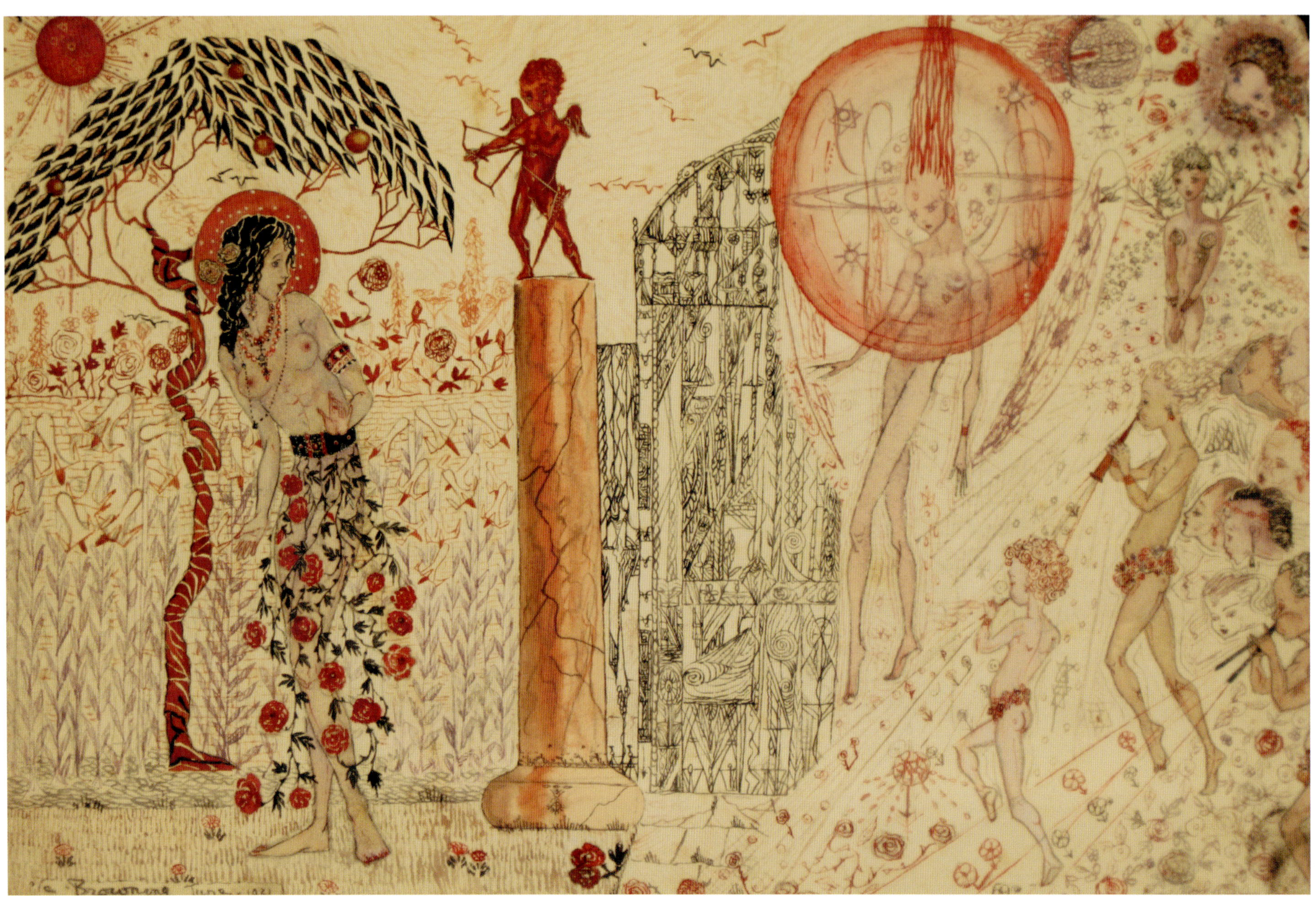

Fig. 3.3. Colleen Browning, Two Winsome Female Nymphs, 1931. Watercolor, graphite, and ink on paper, 7 x 10⅜ inches. Gift of the Estate of Geoffrey Wagner.

Violet and I felt in 1933 that it was no use sending her to a normal school to be crammed with algebra and suchlike subjects which are useless in after life. So we had a French governess for her and she went daily to the Farnham School of Art [established in 1866; James M. Barrie and his wife Mary resided at Farnham's Black Lake Cottage, where he wrote Peter Pan in 1904].

She started painting an imaginative picture called 'Cathedral Wedding' (fig. 3.4) which was exhibited at the Society of Women Artists in London. She was the youngest exhibitor ever, being only sixteen at the time [1934]. Then she competed for the 'Rome Scholarship' in 1935. She was not successful but she got great praise for her work. 'The Morning Post' stated that "the contributions of seventeen year old, rebel-

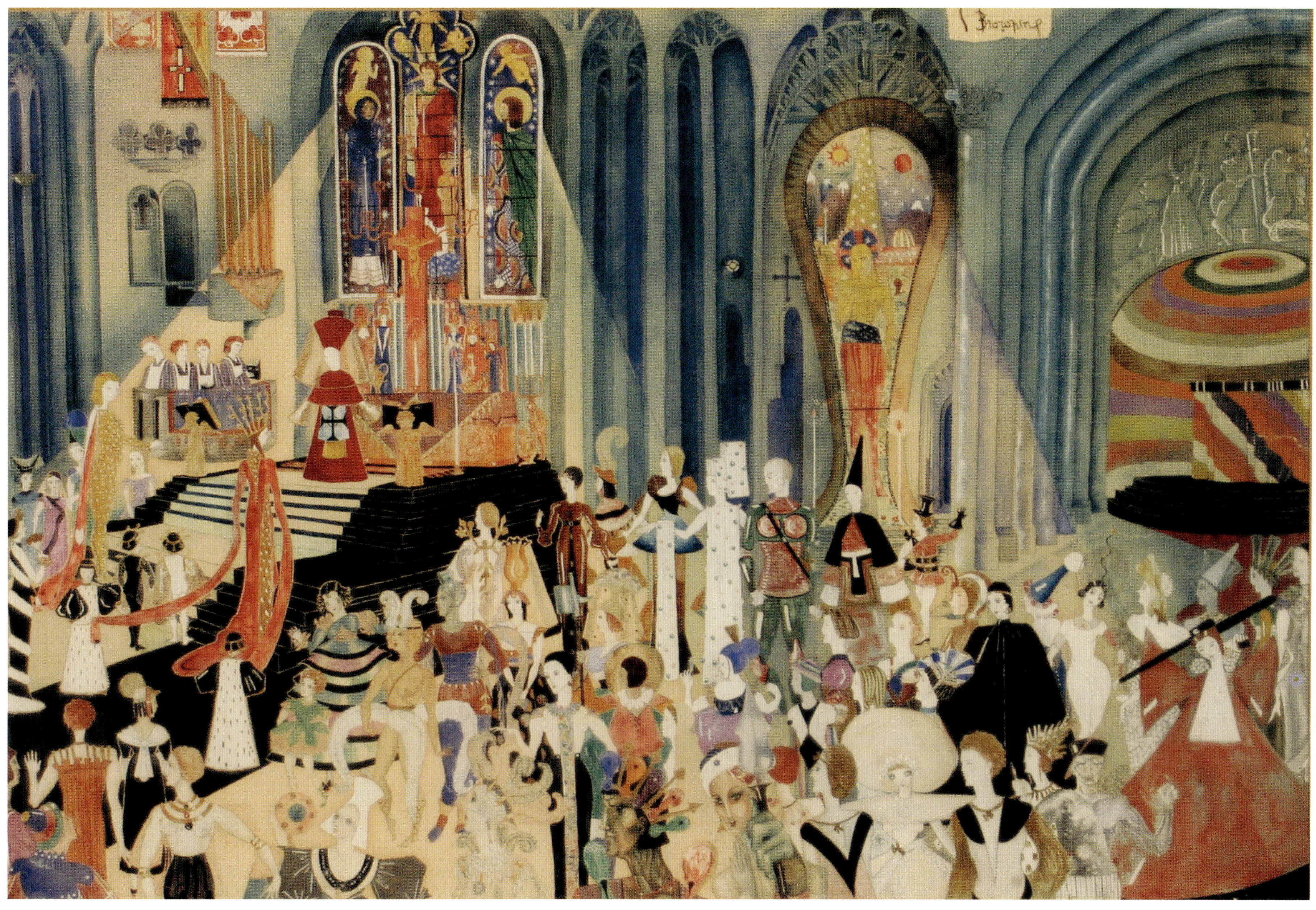

Fig. 3.4. Colleen Browning, Cathedral Wedding, *n.d. Watercolor on paper, 15 x 22 inches. Gift of the Estate of Geoffrey Wagner.*

With her father still in India, Browning, 16, and her mother moved to Amesbury, Wiltshire, to another country cottage. Just a short distance from home was the Salisbury School of Art and Crafts, which was something of a professional trade high school with a rigorous curriculum. Among the works from Browning's teenage portfolio is a highly

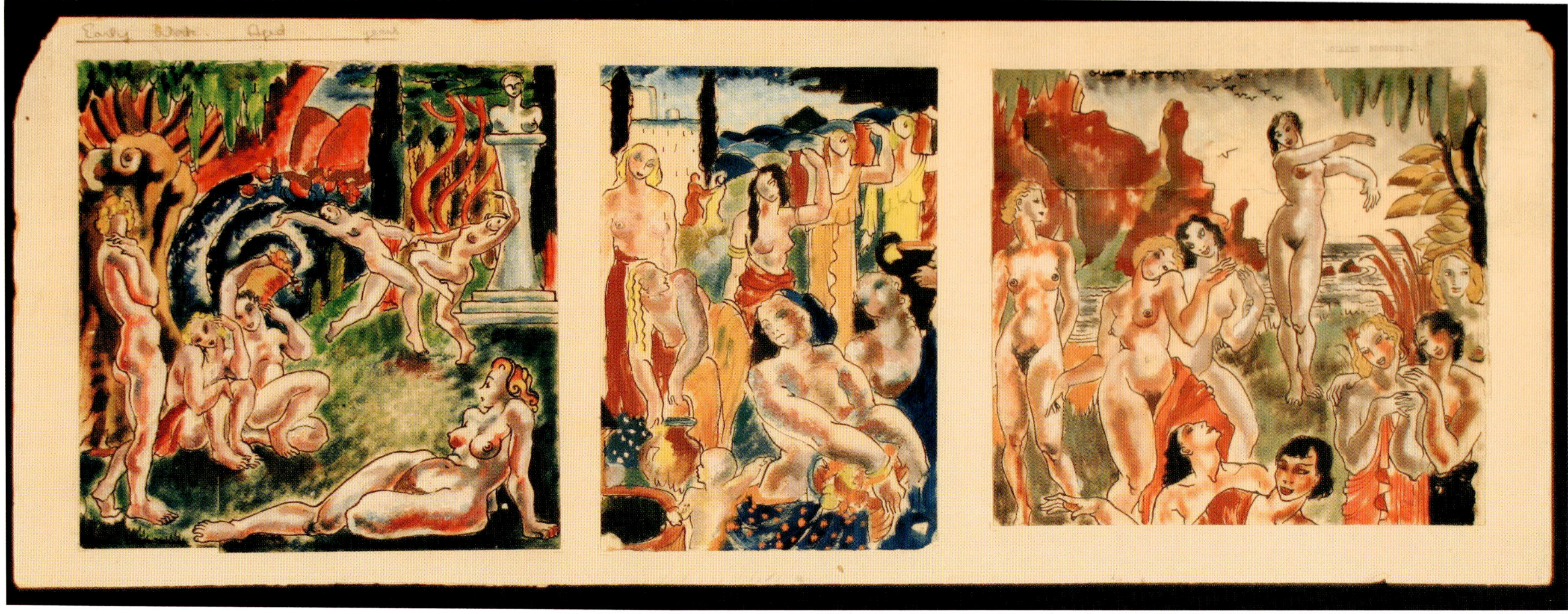

Fig. 3.5. Colleen Browning, studies:
The Dance, *10 x 9¾ inches;*
Gathering Water, *10 x 7 inches;*
and The Bathers, *9½ x 10 inches,*
1933–34. Oil and ink on paper.
Gift of the artist.

expressionistic triptych of nudes (fig. 3.5) with the inscription "age 16." Assimilating a variety of contemporary painting styles, she has freely designed intertwined female nudes into tropical landscapes. With a debt to Matisse in his Fauvist *joie de vivre* paintings and some formalized Art Deco inspired costumes and hair coiffeurs, Browning had begun to pick and choose her sources. The entire set of undulating figures vibrates with youthful vitality.

The Southern Daily Echo reported on February 17, 1937: "Pretty 18-years-old Colleen Browning of Amesbury, a student at the Salisbury School of Art and Crafts has secured one of the two Edwin Austin Abbey Memorial Scholarships for 1937…. Her work which secured the scholarship—including a copy of Botticelli's 'Madonna and Child'—at present on view at the Victoria and Albert Museum."

More details of the prize appeared in *The Irish Times* on February 22: "Miss Browning has just won the Edwin Austin Abbey Scholarship, which is open to the whole of the British Empire and United States…. Miss Browning must be an extremely able artist. The entrants…had to submit works which included a portrait, a number of life studies, perspective drawings and various other works needing a high degree of ability and training."

It is possible to assume that Browning's *Baptism: Homage to Piero della Francesca,* circa 1936–41 (fig. 3.6) painting, perhaps predated, is one of these copyist assignments mandated in the Abbey Scholarship competition of late 1936, which was awarded in 1937. Part of the scholarship's requirements was to visit London's National Gallery and to "copy, in oil, water-colour or tempera, a painting by an Italian master, such as: Michel

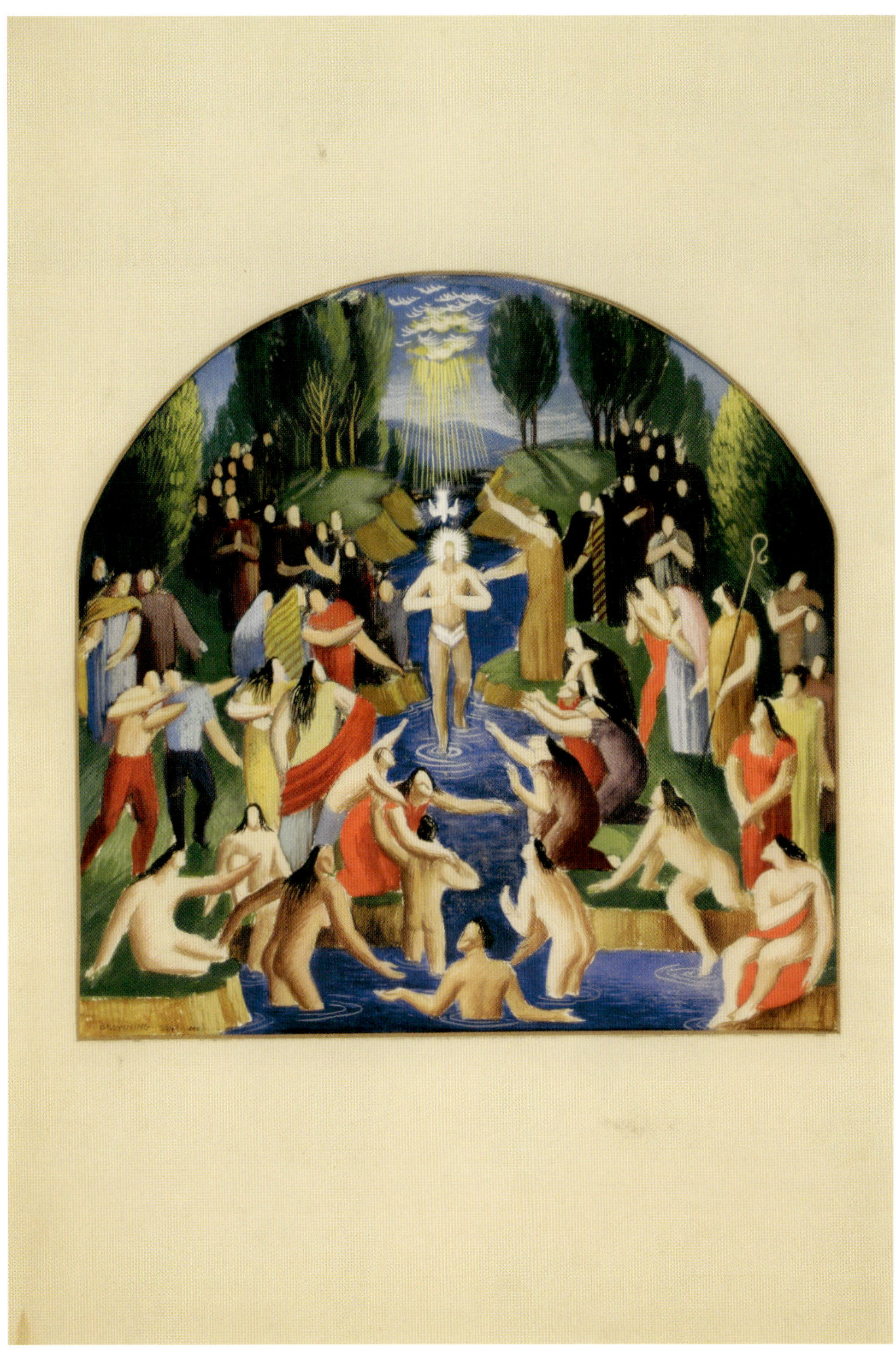

Fig. 3.6. Colleen Browning, Baptism: Homage to Piero della Francesca, *c. 1936–41. Watercolor and gouache on paper, 14⅛ x 12¾ inches. Gift of the Estate of Geoffrey Wagner.*

Angelo…Botticelli…or Piero della Francesca." In the lower left corner she indicated "1941 – Dec"—but there is good reason to believe this was part of the 1936 submission.

The winning entry must demonstrate "examples of application of perspective to pictorial composition showing the candidate's grasp of the scientific aspect of the subject." Elegantly contemporized into a sleek, *Art Decoratif* pattern, her *Baptism* trans-

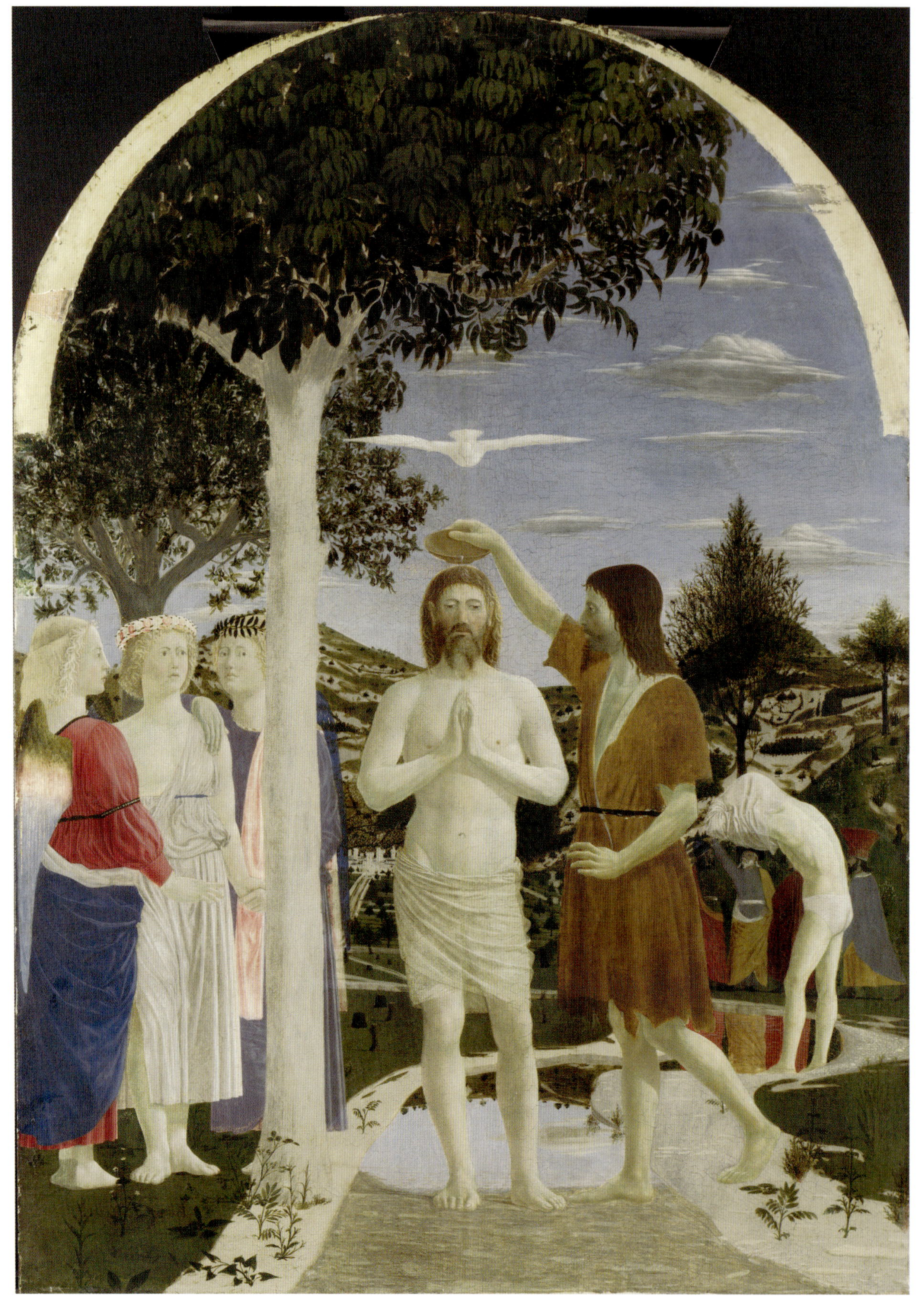

formed the Quattrocento image into a Parnassian scene. Iberian-styled nude bathers from Picasso's rose period join elasticized bacchants dancing in the spirit of Matisse in a Kermesse-like circle. Whatever inventive liberties she depicted with the surrounding figures, the three central elements: Christ, the Holy Spirit, and John the Baptist are directly quoted from Piero della Francesca's *Baptism of Christ*, 1450s (fig. 3.7).

A letter from Paris arrived dated 20 May 1937 to a "Madam"—the writer perhaps unaware that here was a girl who had just marked her 19th birthday—bearing this news: "We propose publishing a report on the Exhibition of the Royal Academy of Arts in London where our Editor desires devoting to you a biographical review." Browning was asked to supply background information concerning her "tastes, inclinations, and exhibitions in which you have taken part and those you contemplate."[19]

La Revue Moderne in Paris published her first international notice on September 15, 1937. Unfortunately, she failed to win the Prix de Rome prize, which would have been the ultimate feather in her cap. However, at this time, she was a finalist for the coveted Rome scholarship:

> *Mll. C. Browning. From an early age, Ms. Browning revealed her pronounced artistic temperament…. At the age of 18 she achieved the distinction of the Edwin Austin Abbey Memorial Scholarship for her mural painting. At the moment, Ms. Browning has made for herself an enviable reputation for her purely decorative art, theatre costumes and theatre scenes. Her portraits are a part of her essential work. In Rome where she will work in the midst of classical antiquity under the Italian sun, and in a school so rich in Italian masters, she will learn this artistic plentitude which justifies the very precociousness of her taste for form, color, and beautiful plastic design—which she treats with such eclecticism.*

Just two months before their star pupil would depart for London to attend Slade School of Fine Art with an annual scholarship valued at £125 pounds sterling, *The Salisbury and Winchester Journal* printed on July 16, 1937: "Even more attractive is Miss Browning's extensive display of mural painting design. This is quite the most attractive feature of the exhibition. The work shown begins with original compositions of Miss Browning when only fifteen years of age, and continues for about four years, so it is possible to see the gradual growth in power and composition…There is sound draughtsmanship behind her work, too, as may be seen in her life studies, some very cleverly rendered in pen and ink."

As if through a wrinkle in time, Browning's early years as a schoolgirl were re-connected to the children of the present. Sparkling with enthusiasm before a rambunctious group of sixth-grade students from Altoona's public schools, Browning relished being in the limelight as the video camera rolled. On the occasion of her 1997 retrospective organized by the Southern Alleghenies Museum of Art, the opportunity was not lost to capture the aging artist at a professional television studio in Altoona. Approaching her 80th birthday, she was a proud relic of her once former glory. Drenched in oversized jewelry and heavily applied makeup, she exuded the positive self-image of a dowager duchess.

Fig. 3.7. Piero della Francesca, Baptism of Christ, *1450s. Egg on poplar, 65½ x 45½ inches. Bought 1861 (NG665). National Gallery of London, Great Britain / Art Resource, NY. © National Gallery of London / Art Resource, NY.*

Indefatigably she spoke to the children with a marvelous ebullience, like a plume of champagne just uncorked but from an aged and rather dusty bottle. The slightly distracted local students, who could have been snatched right out of a Norman Rockwell sketchbook, were stretching, yawning, and responding in delightfully uninhibited ways. They listened politely and responded to the elderly woman's give-and-take in a scene that was staged with the limited budget of a local public television station. Browning performed flawlessly as though she were a vintage schoolmarm in this electronic classroom.

> *I grew up in England. My father was a general in the British Army. And although I'm Irish, I only went home for the holidays, which is why I have such an English accent. I was a complete misfit as a child. I had lots of girlfriends—but I liked being by myself and I liked painting. I hated social life.*
>
> *The only thing I can remember is drawing. My parents used to get catalogues, and I remember drawing elaborate necklaces and earrings on these ladies in their underclothes. I was a prodigy. I came from a completely uncreative background. My father was in the army and no one in my family has ever done anything in the artistic line at all. But my parents were very proud of it. And they encouraged me like anything by putting up my paintings and drawings. They even started framing some of my watercolors. They sent one of my watercolors into an ad-hoc exhibition—lady artists of England or something—and my God, I was taken. I was 11 or 12—I did a watercolor called* Cathedral Wedding.[20]

These young students had no conceptual ability to appreciate that the grandmother-aged lady before them was born at the end of World War I and had evaded the Luftwaffe during their murderously destructive bombings across England. For those innocent schoolchildren, this quirky lady with a funny Mary Poppins-like accent could have been from Katmandu, Zanzibar, or the moon. She spoke about the past as if she had been referring to distant Arthurian legends

NOTES

1. Major General Langley Browning, "Irish Gunner" (unpublished manuscript), pp. 60–61.

2. Ibid., p. 67.

3. Ibid., pp. 230–231.

4. Niamh Hurley, "18th century Blackwater Valley Grandeur," *The Sunday Business Post*, September 3, 2000.

5. Major General Langley Browning, "Irish Gunner" (unpublished manuscript), pp. 4–5.

6. Ibid., p. 5.

7. Ibid., pp. 79–80.

8. Ibid.

9. Ibid., pp. 68–70.

10. Ibid.

11. Ibid., p. 71.

12. Ibid., pp. 70–72.

13. Ibid., pp. 70–71.

14. Ibid., p. 73.

15. Ibid., p. 74.

16. Ibid., p. 93.

17. Ibid., p. 134.

18. Ibid.

19. Letter to Colleen Browning from the editor of *La Revue Moderne*, Paris, May 20, 1937.

20. Video recording, "A Visit with Colleen Browning," Southern Alleghenies Museum of Art, education program, Altoona, PA, April 1997.

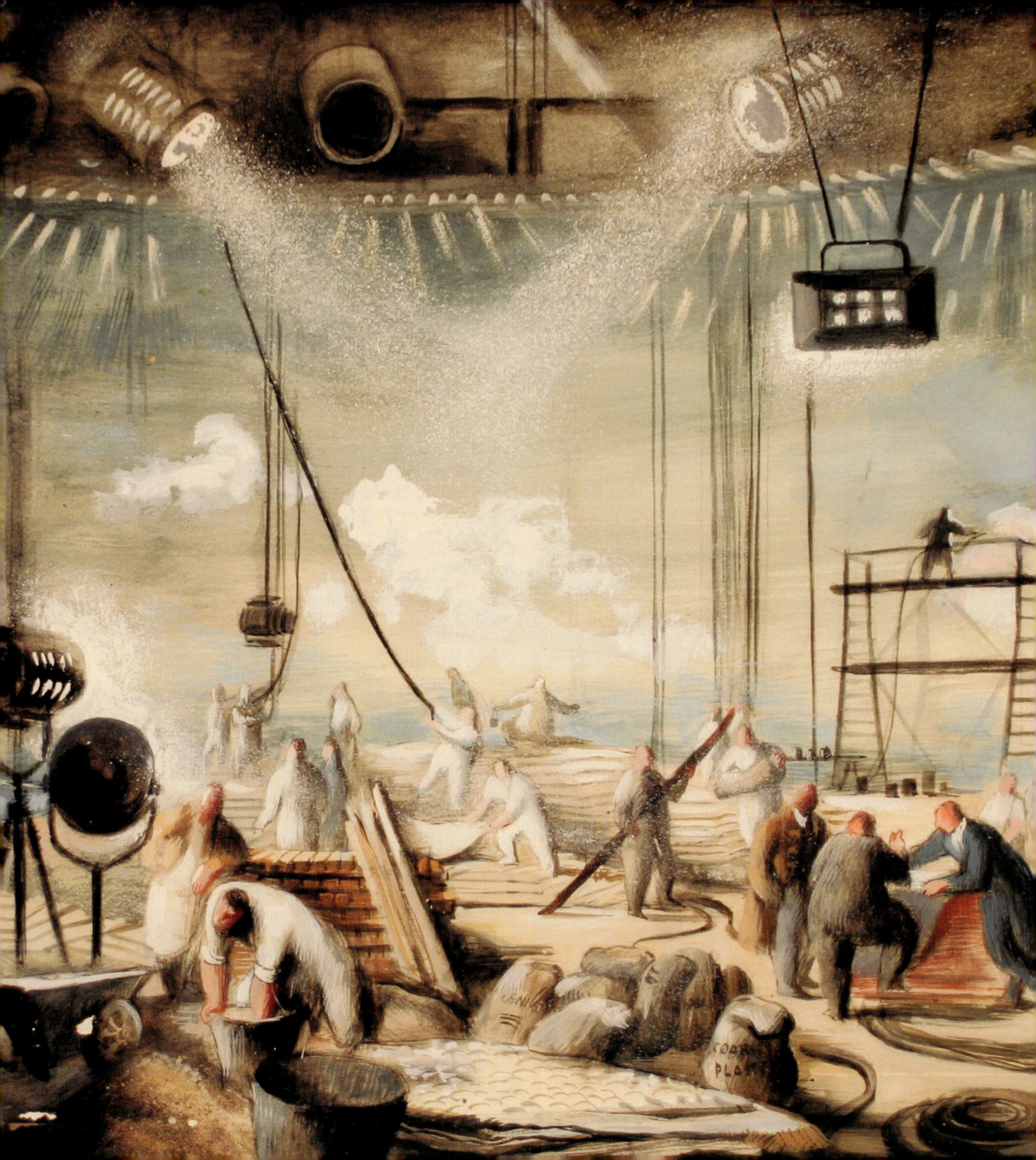
COARSE
PLASTER

IN THIS ATTEMPT TO RE-EVALUATE AND RE-POSITION Browning's career, we find her time in London before, during, and after the war represents the most challenging lacuna to reconstruct. Faced with a scarcity of reliable information, we are enabled in this search by a number of original paintings and sketches that can guide us through her artistic journey. Filling in the cracks, her father's family memoir continued to track her enormous forward leap after being granted the scholarship:

> *So we sent her for two years* [1937–39] *to the Slade School of Art, parking her out in London in a hostel for girls. In 1939 she was on her own in London starting a career as a portrait painter for which she has a flair. Soon she was getting thirty guineas for her portraits and her clients were passing her on to their friends.*
>
> *Unfortunately, the war supervened and she was called up to draw maps for the War Office. She was the first woman draughtswoman to be taken on by the War Office and she made a great success of it.*[1]

Attending Slade placed Browning at England's elite art academy with the equivalency of a college diploma. Established in 1868 when Felix Slade bequeathed funds to endow an art school at the University of London, it shared chairs in fine art with Oxford and Cambridge. Among its most illustrious faculty and alumni are Lucian Freud, Roger Fry, Augustus John, Alphonse Legros, and Wyndham Lewis. Organized as the applied fine arts program in affiliation with Oxford and Cambridge, the Slade is located near the British Museum in the Bloomsbury district.

CHAPTER 4

London Bridges: Renaissance Models to Avant-garde Cinema, 1937–1949

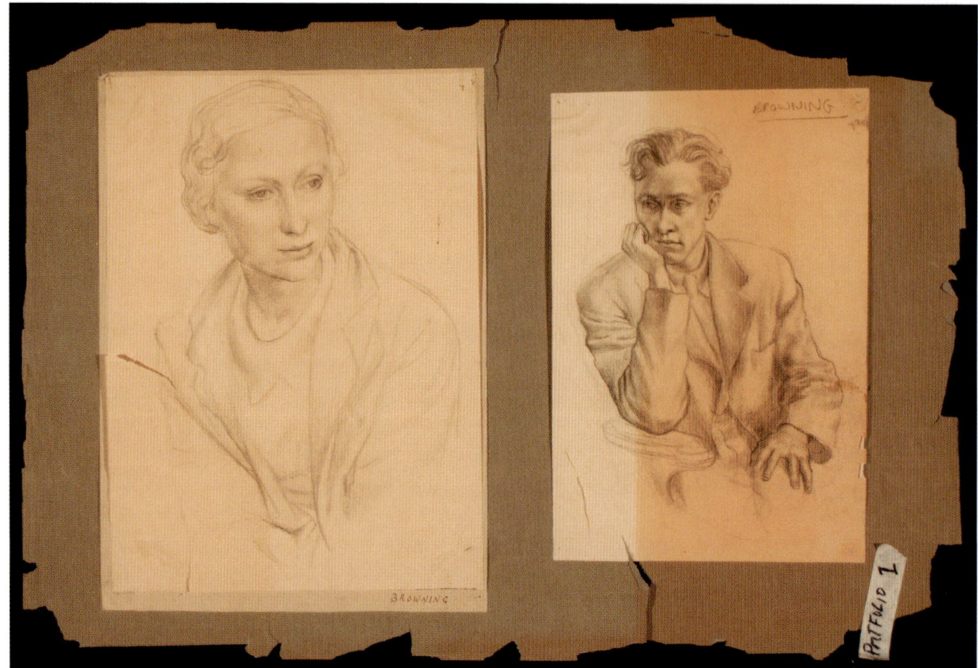

Colleen Browning, Seated Woman and Seated Male with Head Resting on Hand, *1939. Graphite on paper mounted on paper, 20½ x 30 inches. Gift of the Estate of Geoffrey Wagner.*

A sampling of academic sketches from the life class at the Slade demonstrated the quickening development of her rendering skills. The curriculum at Slade in those prewar years was fully consistent with the teaching of draughtsmanship, perspectival rendering, and composition from the pedagogic principles of the Rome Academy. Students progress from elementary classes where they learn to sketch and create inert still-life compositions. In the next term they toil before plaster casts of antique monuments to prove that they can convincingly render three-dimensional volumes and the recesses of form. Only upon passing those hurdles are they permitted into the restricted Life Class—the final frontier of any solid studio art degree.

Generations of artists from Poussin to Picasso had been trained in this academic method as it was adopted and implemented at institutions in Barcelona, Berlin, Dresden, London, Milan, and Stuttgart. The art academies of Paris were the epicenter of nineteenth- and early-twentieth-century classicism. But their pedagogical approach would soon be eclipsed by the individualism of modernist expressionism. It was, for purposes of artistic authority, a form of education intertwined with "official" standards of taste supporting rigid societal hierarchies of the French Republic.

To gain insights to Browning's formal education, we need to recognize how the discipline of drawing and the craft of creating formidable illusionistic pictures determine the very core of her art. As Mark Steven Walker points out, these fundamental elements were prerequisites to appreciate the almost angelic qualities of Bouguereau's major paintings. "One must submit to the mystery of illusion as one of painting's most characteristic and sublime powers." And it is logical to substitute "Browning" for "Bouguereau" as [her] "vast repertory of playful and poetic images cannot help but appeal to those who are fascinated with nature's appearances and with the celebration of human sentiment frankly and unabashedly expressed…"[2]

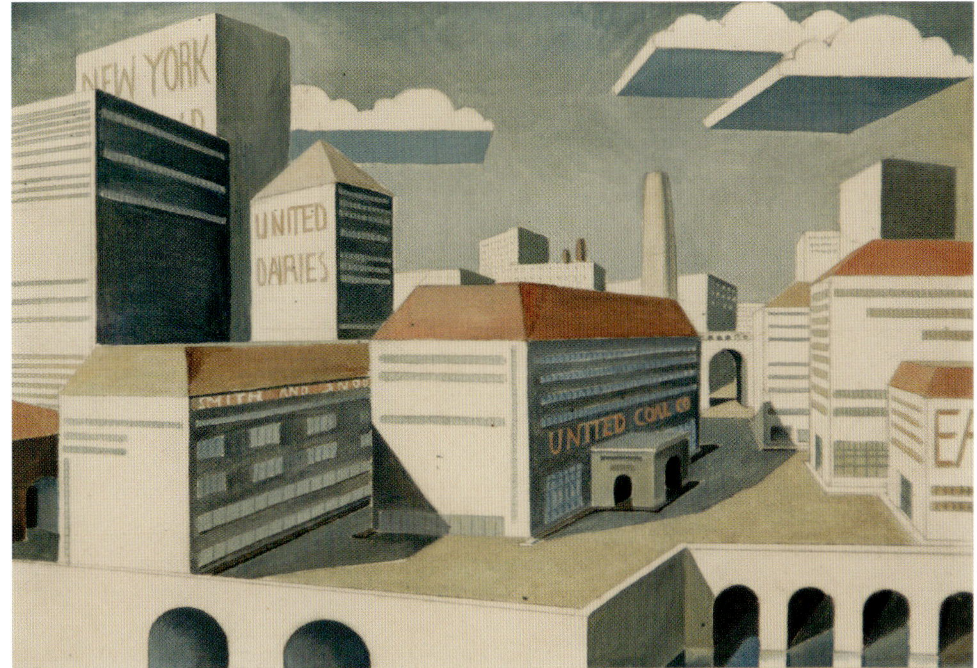

Colleen Browning, *Examples of the Application of Perspective to Pictorial Composition, image 1, c. 1938. Watercolor and graphite on paper, 9¼ x 10¼ inches. Gift of the artist.*

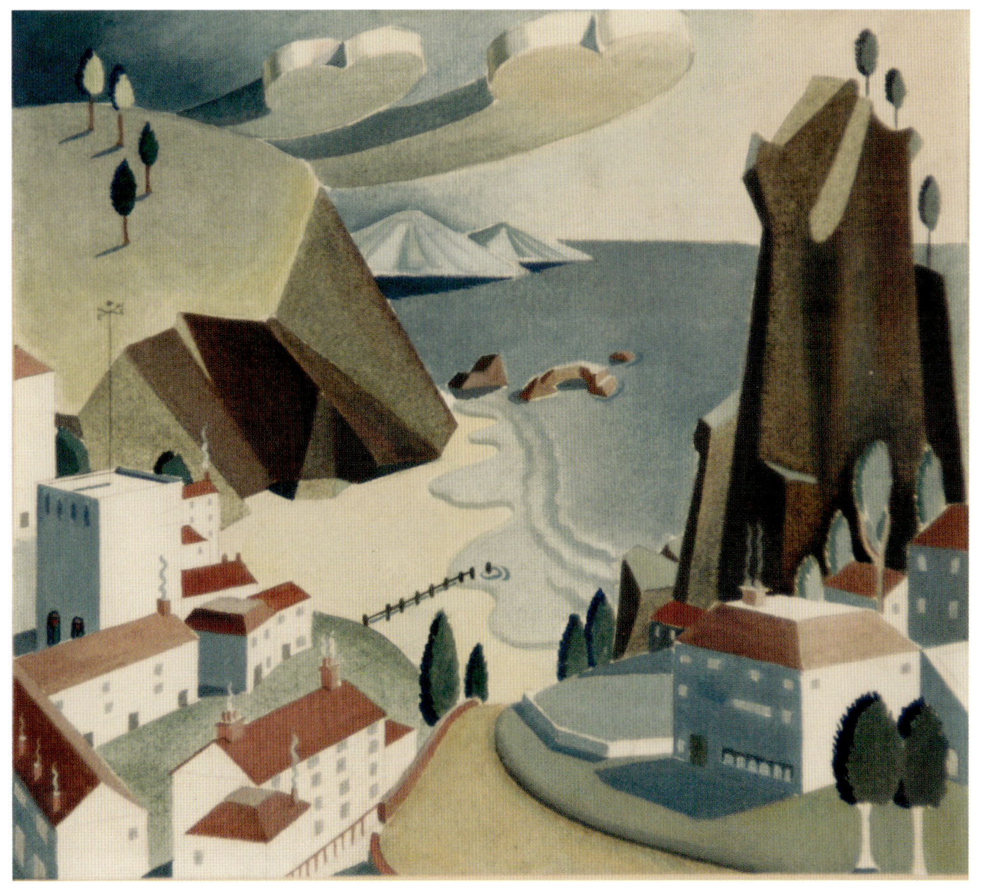

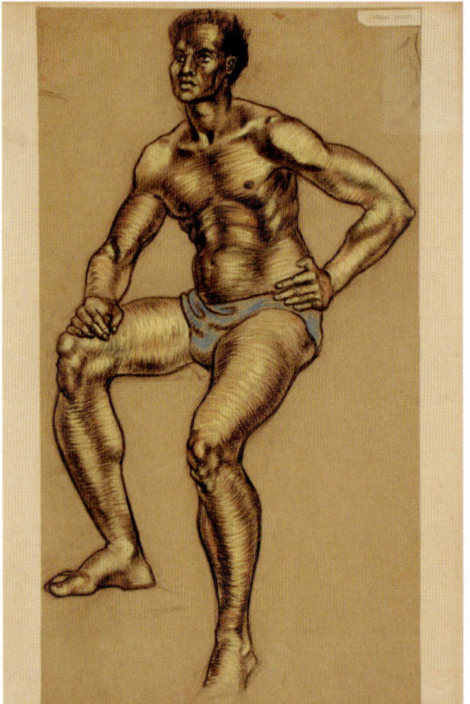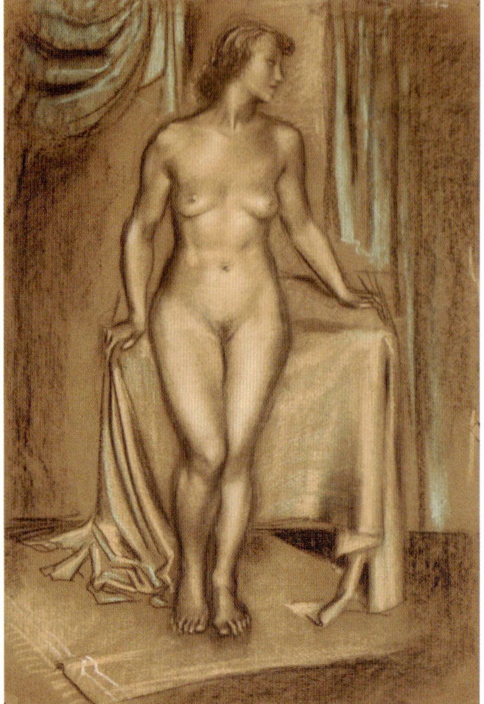

In spirit and applied technique every painting Browning created after graduation from Slade was precisely executed following this tradition: "Bourguereau and his fellow academicians practiced a method of painting that had been developed and refined over the centuries in order to bring to vivid life imagined scenes from history, literature and fantasy. The process of acquisition of the skills necessary to produce a first-rate academic painting was a long and laborious one.... The singular goal of traditional art instruction was to endow artists with the skills essential for the convincing pictorial actualization of their imagined visions. The figure drawings, compositional sketches, color studies and cartoons were all logical steps in a process that at the end magically congealed separately studied details into an impressive, illusionistic, and unified ensemble."[3]

Browning's earliest figure studies of this period, circa 1935, reflect some awkwardness in the transitional elements. The contour line around the limbs and torso set off the figure. In *Male Nude with Blue Loin Cloth* (fig. 4.1) we find a lingering heaviness in her hand as muscles, sinews, and cartilage are being forced onto the drawing sheet, giving the male model a rubbery, almost inflated appearance. This is understandable as student work in its misreading of Quattrocento *disegni* of Masaccio, Mantegna, or Signorelli. Crayon strokes—which replicated sculptural chisel marks on Michelangelo's drawings— are treated here as surfaces lines instead of modeling devices.

Her *Female Nude with Drapery* (fig. 4.2) eases up the rhythmical flow between sections of the body, while smoothing out the surface areas of the flesh and hair. A vigorously crosshatched pen-and-ink of a standing *Female Nude with Posing Block* (fig. 4.3) marks considerable accomplishment toward completion of her life class curriculum. Flesh and form move gracefully across the drawing with substantial achievement noted.

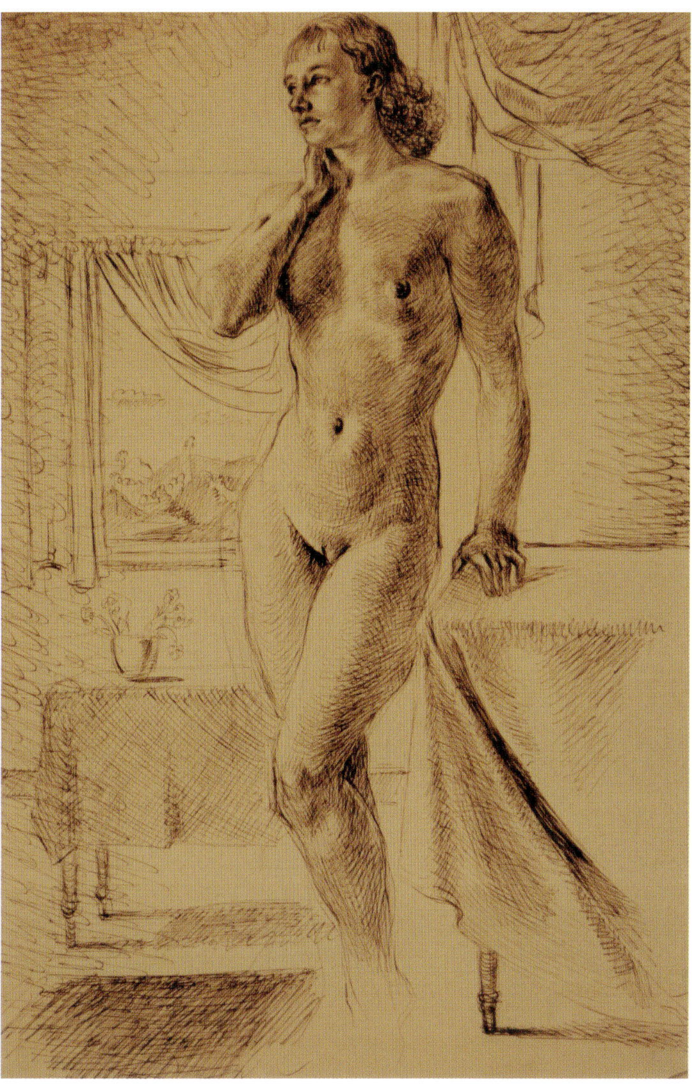

"Varnishing Day," April 26, 1937, at the Royal Academy was Browning's opportunity to complete the paintings she submitted for the juried show. She retained her "nontransferable" pass that allowed the exhibiting artists access to brighten up their paintings. Noteworthy at this exhibition is her decorously composed *Tennis Scene* (fig. 4.4), integrating its graceful figures into a rolling landscape. Flirting with a variety of modernist elements from Fauvism to Expressionism, Browning's personal idiom began to emerge in these academic thesis paintings. At the same time, she assessed contemporary British painting with a watchful eye.

The elongated plasticity of the figures set into the tennis court grid reminds us of Sir Stanley Spencer's (1891–1959) style of the same era in their eccentricities. Browning must have taken inspiration from Spencer's powerful *Resurrection at Cookham* (1924–27), one of England's most widely reproduced figurative murals. Just as she was completing Slade, Spencer produced another of his Christian-inspired masterpieces, *Christ in the Wilderness*, 1938.

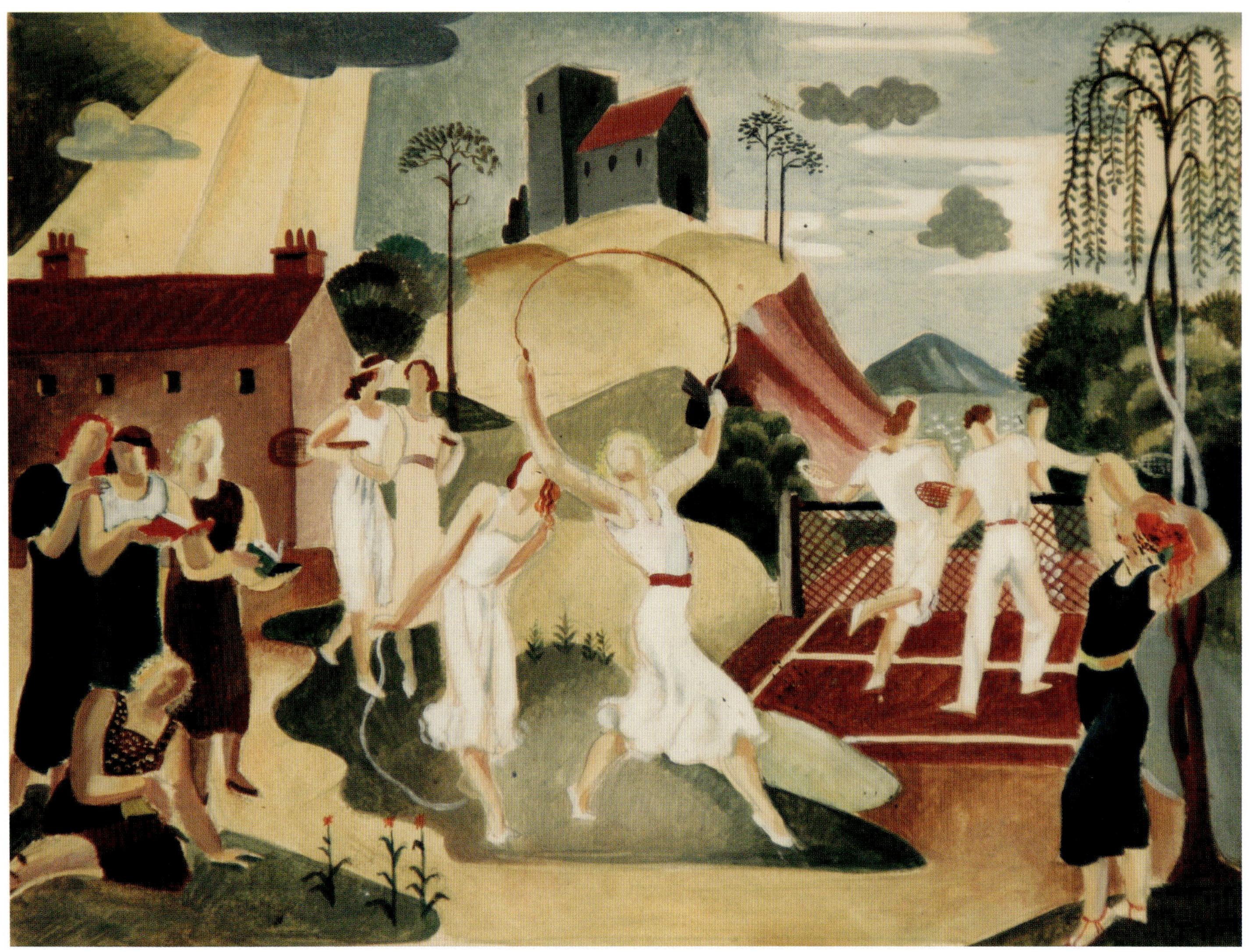

Spencer's visionary imagery must have had a profound impact on Browning's early painterly language. An example such as *The Builders, Bird Nesting, Human Effort*, 1935 (fig. 4.5), now at the Yale University Art Gallery, typifies his naturalist tendencies. "The interweaving of the natural and the human, the organic and the built, are typical and representative of Spencer's vision of the unity of all things."[4] Browning certainly revealed an abiding reverence for pantheistic reverie in her early paintings. Spencer created many paintings in an outdoor setting creating a "curious and moving sense of joyous solemnity."[5]

After receiving her diploma from Slade in June 1939 (awarded with distinction taking 2nd Prize in Decorative Painting at the end of the Spring 1939 term), Browning's first London period drew to a close. With her scholarship funds now consumed, it is possible that she returned to her family's country home out in Salisbury after graduation. Within three months the world was at war. Germany's blitzkrieg assault on Poland and virtually unchallenged invasion of France, and America's neutrality prior to Pearl

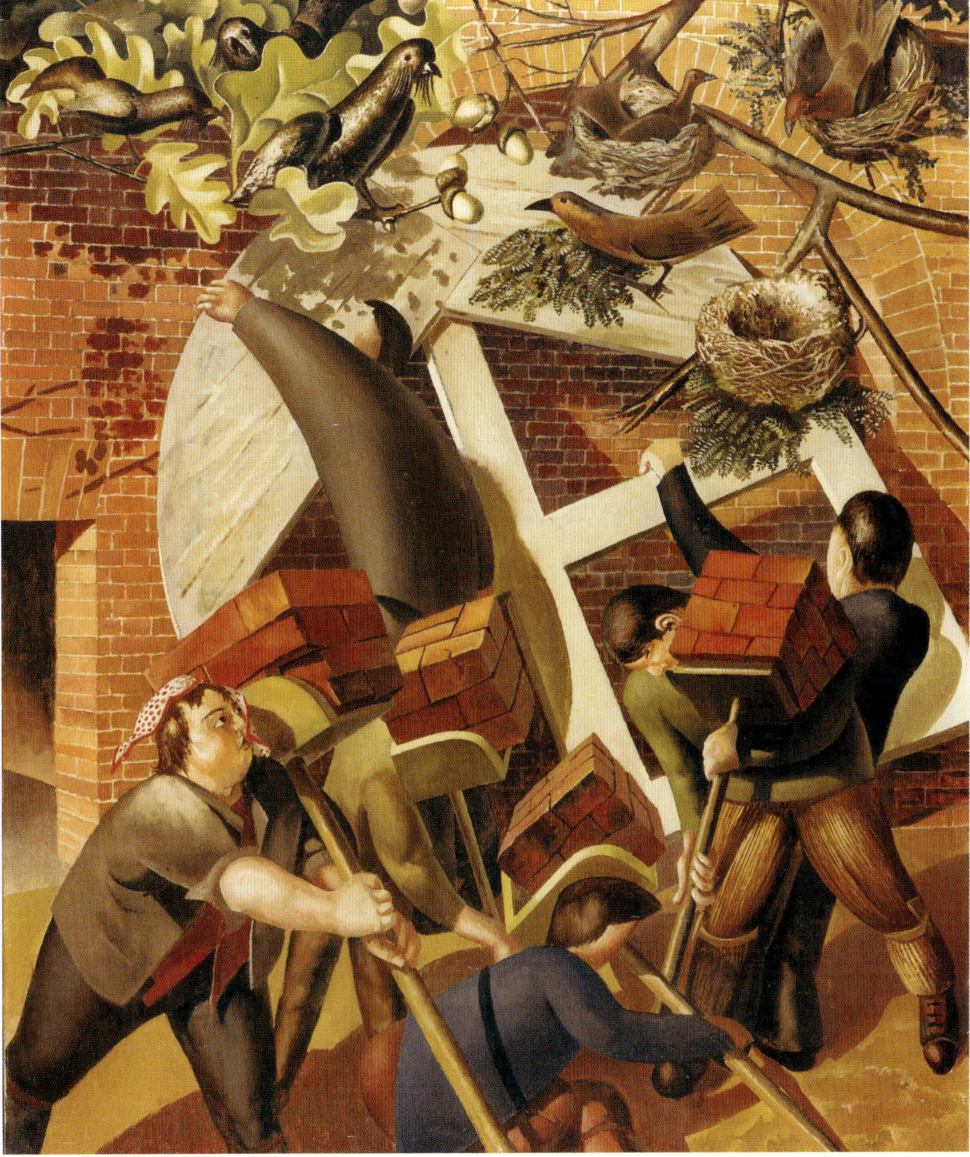

Harbor, left England at considerable peril. Having just earned her art degree seemed of little consequence against the foreboding winds of war.

England prepared for the worst as the Blitz began the following spring in 1940. We know that Browning traveled into London because a series of newspaper articles, dated May 28, photographed her with a painting in hand for submission to the Royal Academy's summer exhibition. "General's Daughter Is Academy Entrant" read the headline of the *Evening Standard* on May 28.

The photo shows a smiling Browning wearing a fashionable bird-decorated hat and a most-probably borrowed mink coat. "Miss Colleen Browning, artist daughter of Major General Browning arriving at Burlington House with her painting today—first day for the reception of works for the Royal Academy summer exhibition."[6] Within a few weeks any sense of calm was over as tens of thousands of Londoners began sleeping in Underground station shelters to avoid being burned alive in the firestorms created by the Luftwaffe's nightly raids.

The first bombs on the London Region fell on 8 June [1940] on open country at Addington. A fortnight later bombs fell in a field at Colney. A goat was killed… The authorities knew that these 'so-called air-raids' were only a foretaste of what the Germans were likely to direct at London…. If London be taken as [Richard Wagner's] Valhalla, then within a few days the Twilight of the Gods was to begin indeed.[7]

Where, when, and how Browning escaped harm during the Battle of Britain remains unknown. But we are certain of her complete involvement in the nation's defense during these terrifying days. Newly appointed as prime minister, Winston Churchill spoke in the House of Commons on June 4, 1940. Whether she might have listened to this memorable address on BBC radio or read its stirring message in the morning newspaper, Browning was surely aware of the dangers all Britons were to face. Nobody knew for certain, not even the daughter of an army general, the degree of commitment, sacrifice, and loss that England and the free world would endure.

Acknowledging England's isolation in the spring of 1940, Churchill spoke with inspirational confidence: "We shall prove ourselves once again to defend our island home, ride out the storms [to] outlive the menace of tyranny, if necessary, for years, if necessary, alone….A large tract of Europe and many old and famous States have fallen or may fall into the grip of the Gestapo and all the odious apparatus of Nazi rule…We shall not flag nor fail…We shall defend our island whatever the cost may be; we shall fight on beaches; landing grounds, in fields, in streets, and on the hills. We shall never surrender… until in God's good time the New World with all its power and might, sets forth to the liberation and rescue of the Old."

Expected to do her part, Browning also contributed to the war effort. An encouraging art review was published in *The Salisbury and Winchester Journal* in October 1940 about the young artist: "Girl Artist's Offer: A fine pastel portrait of a stately elderly lady caught my eye in the vestibule of the Gaumont Palace this week. So different was it from the portrait one usually encounters in a cinema theatre that I turned automatically to look at it. Some leaflets nearby told me that Miss Colleen Browning, who is the daughter of Brigadier Browning, of Winterbourne Dauntsey, was offering to do similar portraits for two guineas each and give the proceeds to the Red Cross fund…. I anticipate that Miss Browning will have many calls on her as the result of her offer because her prices usually range from 30 guineas."

The devastation of 1940 culminated on December 29 when "the most celebrated and notorious of all raids" ended the year. "The warning was sounded a little after six in the evening, and then the incendiaries came down like 'heavy rain.' The attack was concentrated upon the City of London. The Great Fire had come again…. One observer on the roof of the Bank of England recalled that 'the whole of London seemed alight! We were hemmed in by a wall of flame in every direction.' Nineteen churches, sixteen of them built by Christopher Wren after the Great Fire, were destroyed…St. Paul's was ringed with fire, but escaped. 'No one who saw will ever forget.'… One who walked through the ruins the day after the raid recalled that 'the air felt singed, I was breathing ashes.'… It was the invisible and intangible spirit of the presence of London that survived, and somehow flourished, in the period of devastation."[8]

Offering her talents as community service, Browning took on an ambitious mural project by decorating the newly built Women's Services Club at the Palace Hut, Salisbury. Similar to the U.S.O. clubs where American military servicemen were entertained, this "hut" was a Quonset structure described as a "bright and commodious structure with modern fittings and lighting."[9]

The Salisbury and Winchester Journal on July 24, 1942 remarked about the wonderful "mural painting by Miss Colleen Browning…22 feet across and over 5 feet high contains 60 figures representing such local worthies as the Bishop, the Dean…and figures from Salisbury history." Her Majesty, Queen Mary, attended the unveiling ceremony of the mural according to a note in Browning's records.

Although this was unremarkable in its static design, it revealed her capacity to compose and design large-scale pictorial projects. Her first professional mural project, it presaged her later stage sets for the British film industry.

Between the 1942 Salisbury mural project through V-E Day, May 8, 1945, Browning's activities as an exhibiting artist were curtailed by her service to the Royal Air Force (RAF) in their map-making workrooms. Her location is unspecified, but most certainly she was not in London and perhaps she worked in the outskirts of London around one of the airbases. Fortune smiled on her in the form of an indirect consequence of her father's position as a top Allied general in Italy. Serendipitously, he would eventually propel her—at a distinguished dinner party in London years later—into the next giant step, forwarding her art career.

In the aftermath of Operation Husky in the summer of 1943, Churchill's plan to attack Nazi-occupied Europe through its "soft underbelly" in the Mediterranean succeeded. Mussolini's Fascist government abandoned Rome on Sept 8, 1943, and Prime Minister Badaglio signed an Armistice Agreement with the Allies. The Allies gained a foothold in Sicily and then fought their way up through the Italian peninsula, arriving on the outskirts of Rome

Colleen Browning at Salisbury, 1942. Photograph from artist's scrapbook.

Colleen Browning, Salisbury AD 1942, *1942. Gouache and graphite on paper, 18¼ x 25¼ inches. Gift of the Estate of Geoffrey Wagner.*

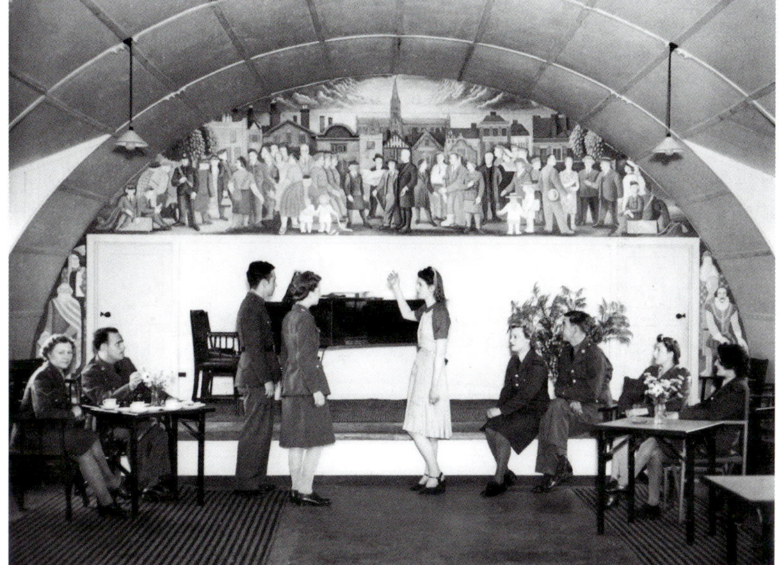

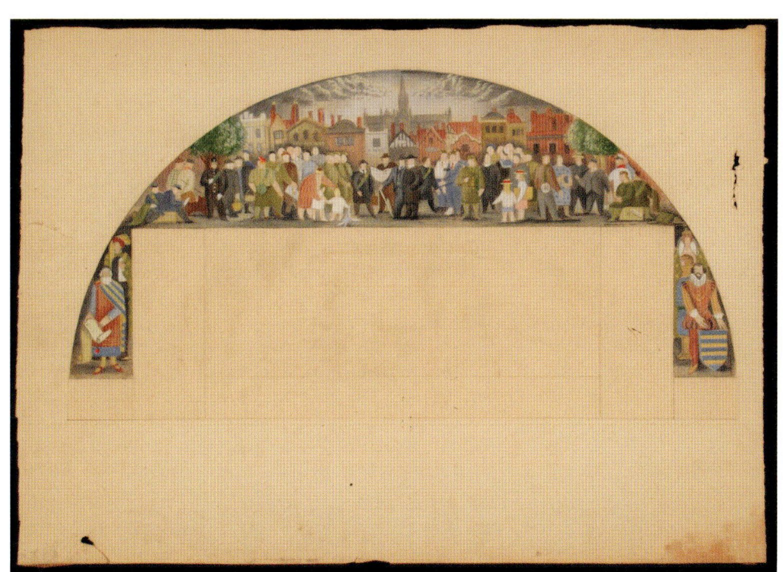

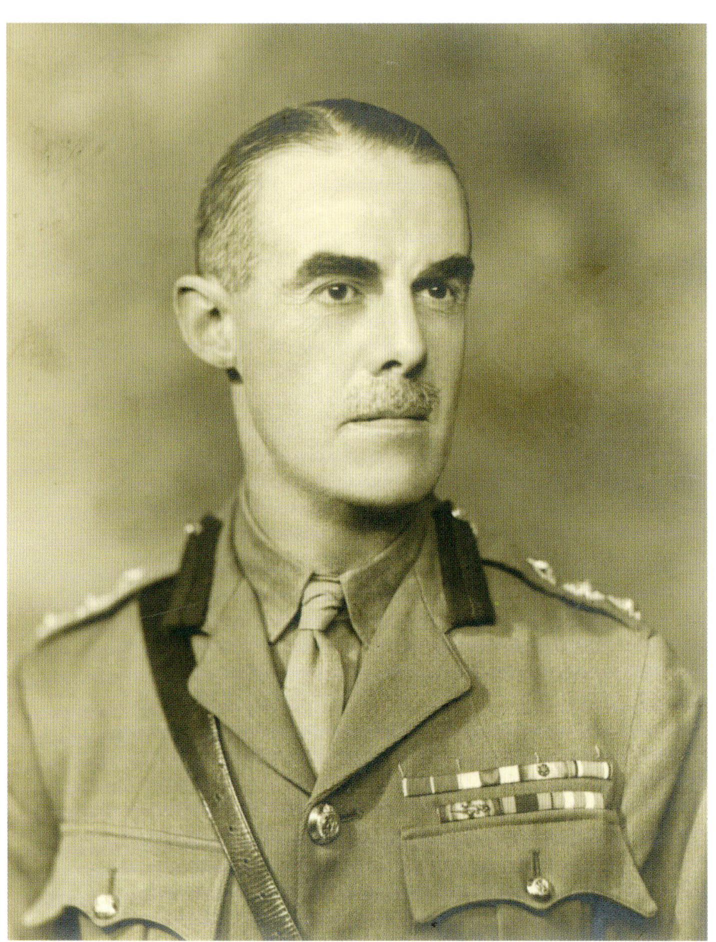

Fig. 4.6. Undated photograph of Major General Langley Browning.

in June 1944. Germany seized control over all of central and northern Italy while the scattered remnants of the Italian army disappeared overnight into the hills and back into civilian clothing. With reprisals, revenge, and the internecine conflicts of a completely chaotic situation in Italy, the Allies had to defeat the entrenched German army and rebuild Italy's infrastructure.

Major General Browning's Italian service began when in "April, 1944, I went down to an aerodrome in Cornwall with a view to flying to Italy…We flew a hundred miles out into the Atlantic [outside of radar range of Nazi-occupied France] and arrived in North Africa. The next morning we flew to Algiers where I had been told to report to Henry Maitland 'Jumbo' Wilson, the Supreme Allied Commander. Then on to Naples passing over Sicily and an excellent view of Mt. Aetna." (fig. 4.6)

I was to organize the Italian army. All orders to the Italian Army from S.A.C. [Supreme Allied Command] came through me and I passed them on or interpreted them to the Italian Minister of War direct. I was thus virtually the Minister of War and Commander-in-Chief of the Italian Army. I was responsible for organising what was then a complete rabble into units and formations, clothing them, equipping them, training and delivering them to the British or American formation that required their services.… All the Italian troops, of course, were terribly mixed up. Many commanders had taken their formations or units into the hills as the Germans retired and a large number of troops had just cleared off on their own.

It was a herculean task this reorganization of a complete Army from zero but a fascinating one. No soldier could have ever asked for a better job.… The Italians themselves were only too anxious to cooperate in every way. Many, if not most of them, had been against the Fascist Regime and wanted to rehabilitate themselves in the eyes of the world. As Mr. Churchill put it, they wished to 'earn their passage' so they would stand in a better light when peace came.

The [Italian] Minister of War was General Orlando…The line I took was this: 'It is no use living in the past'. It is the future that counts. I, perhaps more than most people, realise this because I am Southern Irishman and the fault of my country has been to look backwards instead of forwards…The bigger the fence the better the horse to jump it. I promise you that you will get a square deal.… The Italians are sentimental people, not unlike my own countrymen.[10]

Browning's father was elevated to a prominent position before and after V-E Day in Italy. Regardless of their leanings as former *fascisti* in league with Nazi Germany, the natural survivalist tendency for anyone of rank or title in Rome was to now switch allegiances with the arrival of their new British and American overlords. The major general was on the victorious side, which placed him in contact with many of Italy's nobility and governmental elite.

He wrote of his affection for Umberto II, prince of Piedmont and even king of Italy briefly in 1946. "I hope I shall not be accused of *lese majeste* if I say that I thought Prince Umberto a very fine man…. From the moment that he became the Head of State he applied himself to the salvation of Italy…and I admired his growth in stature, lofty outlook and practical common sense."[11] (fig. 4.7)

One can assume that Browning was frequently traveling between England and Italy in 1945–46, enjoying the spoils of war with her mother and father who were installed in a big villa in Rome. At one point the director of the Italian state railways put at their disposal a "diesel rail-car with sleeping compartments, dining-room, sitting-room, kitchen, etc."[12]

The Brownings were not the first, nor the last Anglo-Italophiles to taste the intoxication of this luscious *paessagio* and theatrical culture. With its sleepy medieval towns nestled among vineyards through Tuscany and northward to the Veneto, the major general was brought to tears on his "wonderful trip enjoying the scenic beauty of Italy."[13]

"Of Florence one could write a book—it breathes the spirit of the Italian Renaissance…. To my mind there are few countries in the world which have quite the same beauty and appeal as Italy. The Italians understand the art of living."[14] In contrast with fog-shrouded London and the stern military rigidity of English society he noted: "After all they [Italians] have the sun and the wine and the fruit and opera and beautiful women and scenes all around them. Who could not be happy under those conditions?"[15]

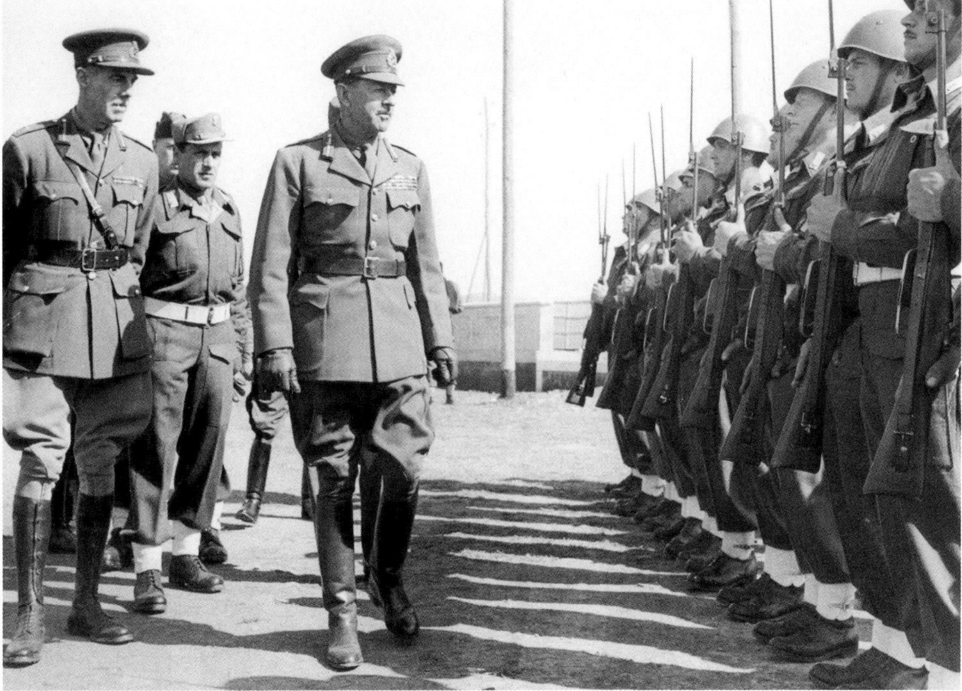

Fig. 4.7. General Browning inspecting troops with King Umberto II, c. June 1946.

Colleen Browning, Untitled: Theatrical Scene 1, *1947–49. Gouache, watercolor, ink, and graphite on paper, 19½ x 29¾ inches. Gift of the Estate of Geoffrey Wagner.*

Colleen Browning, Untitled: Theatrical Scene 2, *1947–49. Gouache, watercolor, ink, and graphite on paper, 17⅛ x 30½ inches. Gift of the Estate of Geoffrey Wagner.*

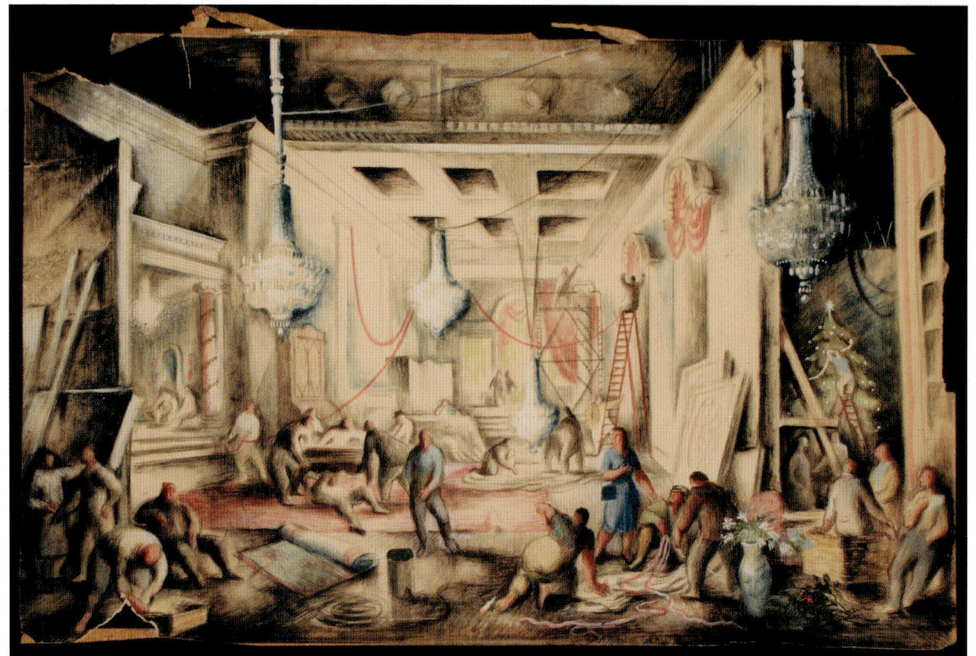

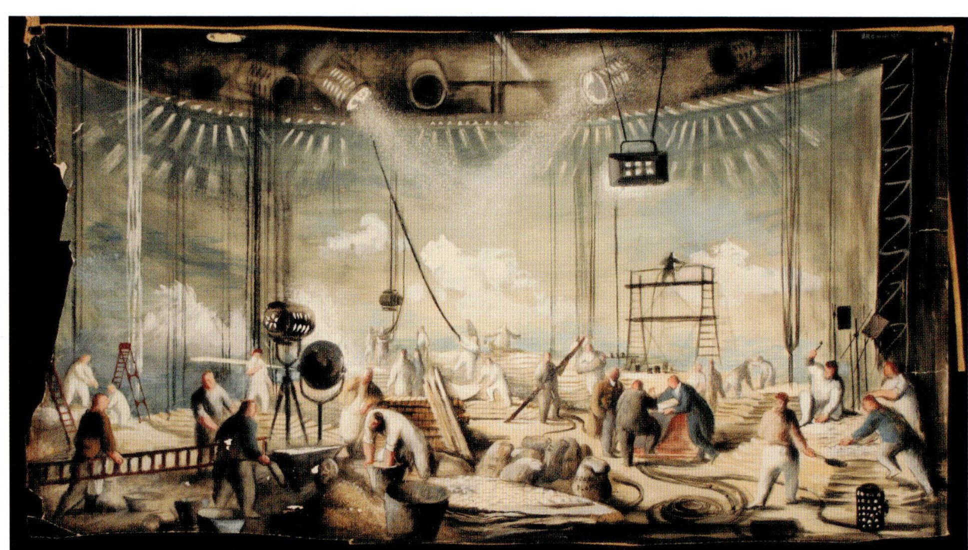

This was a time of living a charmed life, attending parties at the British Embassy, hobnobbing with the last of those who were hanging on to their princely titles. "Through the influence of a friend I was able to see many parts of the Vatican not normally open to visitors…I attended an audience by the Pope to service personnel…I was up on the dais within ten feet of him, so got a good view. His Holiness has a remarkable presence and the atmosphere of sanctity of the whole ceremony was most impressive."[16]

Toward the end of the war Browning reaped the rewards of these high-level contacts when her father was seated at a distinguished dinner party—of the type where "all the aristocracy and elite of Rome [or London] and their wives were present. The Diplomatic Force came resplendent with their stars and decorations and sashes."[17]

The setting was a dinner party hosted by Count Nicolo Caradini, the newly appointed ambassador to Great Britain at his London residence. "She happened to sit next to one [Filippo] Del Giudice…[Colleen] did not know who the famous 'Del' was but she talked art to him and he suddenly said, "I will give you a job at Two Cities Film Studios, Denham."[18]

Del Giudice (1892–1962), a lawyer who worked for the Vatican, had fled the Fascists in 1933 for England. Using his considerable negotiating talents, he founded the Two Cities film company in 1937. Two Cities granted exceptional artistic autonomy to its directors and actors. It was a highly regarded studio employing Sir Laurence Olivier, Peter Ustinov, and David Lean. His films are critically praised by cineasts for their avant-gardist techniques that appealed, with their innovative narrative, to sophisticated audiences.

Browning joined Two Cities in 1946, shortly after release from her work with the mapmaking services, just about the time that Two Cities was merged into the J. Arthur Rank Film Organisation. "Colleen had the luck to get in on the ground floor…but she could never had stayed there without exceptional ability and effort. I feel she is launched and I am very proud of her…Del Giudice is a most charming and able genius. He says and quite rightly that he has a flair for picking potential stars…. He 'spotted' Colleen and backed his judgment."[19]

Her chameleon-like ability to create any mural stage set, theatrical design, or even faux-paintings used for props was nowhere better demonstrated than in the 1947 Two Cities-Rank film *Odd Man Out*. Although not properly credited, Browning was among the four set designers for this suspenseful film noir. Starring James Mason as a doomed Irish Republican Army-type gang leader, it was filmed on the streets of Belfast. It is known as a masterpiece of postwar British cinema. "I still consider it one of the best movies I've ever seen," commented film director and producer Roman Polanski, "probably James Mason's best picture. No film ever made me happier."[20]

Film Studio, 1947 (fig. 4.8), is an ambitiously composed multi-figural composition. Its deep spatial recession removes the invisible "fourth wall" between the viewer and its sequential layers of ladders, scaffolds, and stage-flats. A rich spectrum of lighting effects dapples the areas of light and dark across the surface, concentrating on glowing areas of artificial stage lighting and gloomily recessed shadows.

Browning contributed to the film's wraithlike imagery of a nightmarish dream sequence. Dozens of quickly executed portraits in this hallucinatory scene are weirdly distorted, expressionistic faces in the manner of Edvard Munch or Oskar Kokoschka. If Browning had her hand in these, she showed an almost playful sense as an imaginative copyist of period styles and tastes.

Fortunately there are extant paintings of Browning's finest cinematic stage designs. They reveal a dramatic forward leap. For the first time she combined her instinctive use of the Alberti-Brunelleschi "framework" for figures within a proscenium arch-framed, recessed space. These movie designs show obvious expropriations from modern expressionism. To some degree, her career as a professional painter was truly launched during this period from 1947–49.

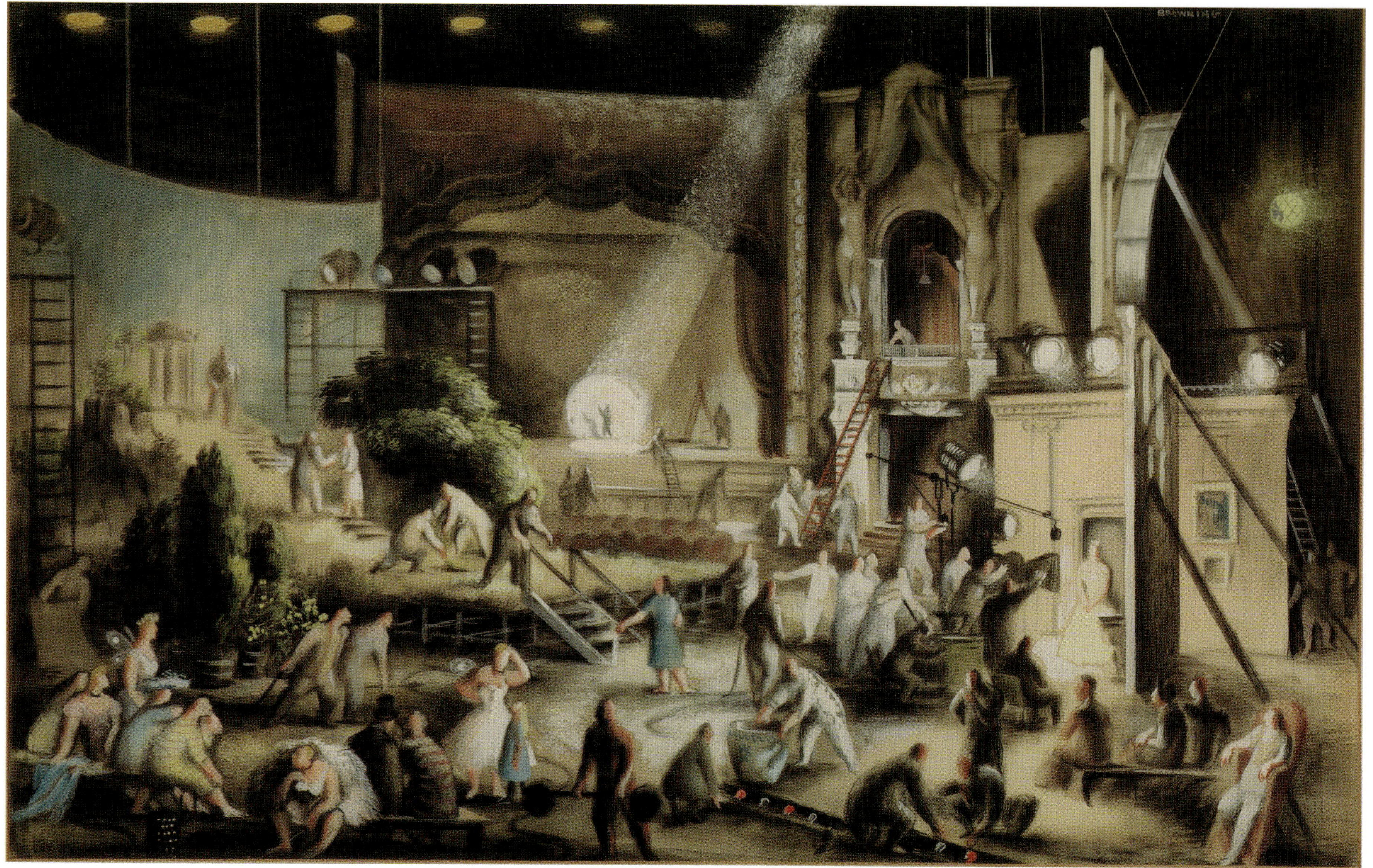

Fig. 4.8. Colleen Browning, Film Studio, *1947. Watercolor on paper, 18¼ x 28½ inches. The Butler Institute of American Art, Youngstown, OH. Museum purchase, 1989.*

At first she was only a sketch artist but rose swiftly to the position of a set decorator. One can appreciate how this new set of artistic assignments expanded her vision. At Slade School of Fine Art she was limited to Renaissance-inspired assignments with touches of modernist stylization. But the daily routine of designing sets for the modern cinema had the impact of broadening her reach into twentieth-century expression.

Browning's watercolor sketches and projects for murals of the late 1940s are consistently organized around central pictorial themes. *Crucifixion* (fig. 4.9) and *Resurrection* (fig. 4.10), circa 1948–49, are hemispherical designs placing intertwining figures into a receding landscape. Browning's figurative motif was to simplify the nude into bulbous, exaggerated shapes with minimal definition of facial or anatomical features.

Considering that Browning's exhibition record began as a 13-year-old, it was propitious that her exhibition, which opened on May 2, 1949, was her English swan song.

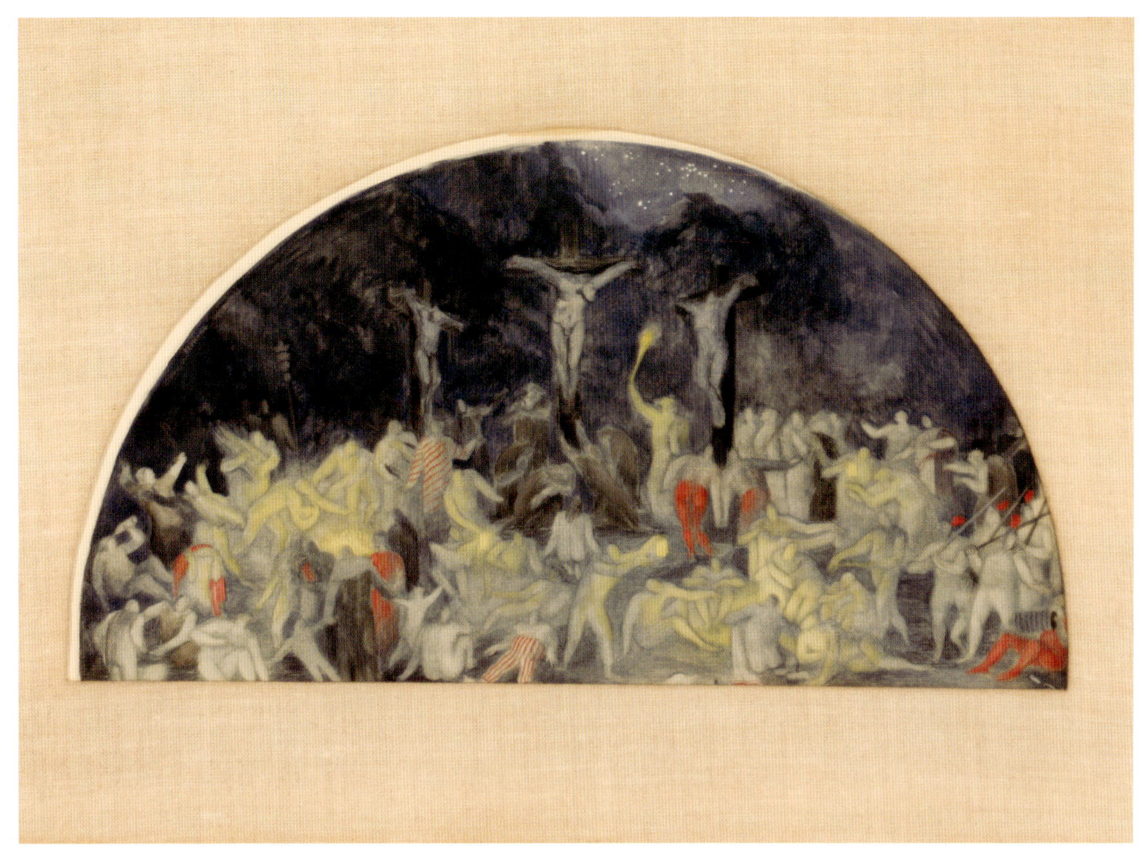

Fig. 4.9. Colleen Browning, Crucifixion, 1946–49. Watercolor on paper, 11½ x 20½ inches. Gift of the Estate of Geoffrey Wagner.

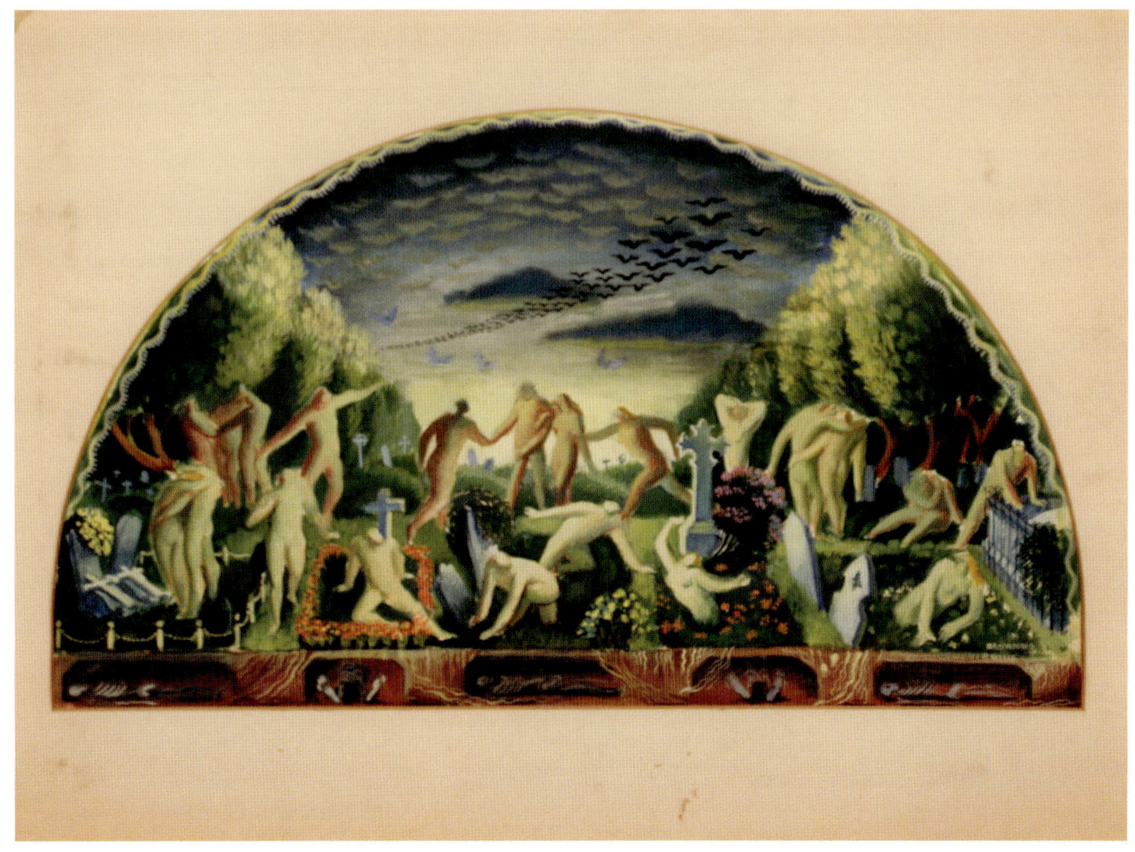

Fig. 4.10. Colleen Browning, Resurrection, 1946–49. Gouache on paper, 13¾ x 22¾ inches. Gift of the Estate of Geoffrey Wagner.

Variety, a London-based entertainment publication, reported about a "Quick Decision Woman." "Artist Colleen Browning…holds her first show at the Little Gallery, Piccadilly, today. At 26 [she was 30] Miss Browning is a young woman of dynamic energy—and quick decision." Referencing her instantaneous decision to marry "Geoffrey Wagner, Oxford scholar…I know very little about him, not even his age."[21]

"Energy? Every morning for the last two years she has left her flat in Highgate Village, taken a trolleybus to the Great North Road and there thumbed a lift to Denham film studios…. This pastime, she says, has kept her young and supple. She has ideal measurements, is a brunette full of high spirits."[22]

The Little Gallery was a boutique space ensconced within the Piccadilly Arcade. Opposite James Gibb's seventeenth-century landmark Burlington House, it was a sophisticated venue for a young artist's premiere one-woman exhibition. She presented twenty-three works in total, including eight studio scenes priced at 16 to 18 guineas.

These were fully conceptualized watercolors and gouaches that replicated what audiences would be enjoying on the screen. Smaller set sketches at an average cost of 5 to 6 guineas were executed in pastel and crayon as interior views for the movie set. The exhibition was rounded out with six mural studies for garden walls and interiors of great houses, covering ceilings and staircases. London's *Art News and Review* published a respectfully impressive review. A critic named Dorante opined:

> *The film industry today with its technicians…its eye fixed unremittingly on the box-office, might well seem an environment too cruel and deadly for artists. Yet for the seeing eye there is the richest material at hand in the fantastic scenes to be witnessed on the sets.*
>
> *For whereas it was regarded as a mere perversity of some artists, influenced by surrealism, to place objects not normally in juxtaposition, this is a commonplace of the film studios, and as in one of the pictures of this exhibition, we may see at one and the same time an interior scene at a theatre with a solitary lady in a box, or the delights of a picnic in the open air.*
>
> *Miss Colleen Browning…has the seeing eye, and has consciously appreciated the strange dream-world around her…She is a true designer, having the power to take raw, pictorial material, sometimes of a type which many people would ignore, and build it into something new and previously non-existent…. Like some of the Victorians also, Miss Browning is a most skilled and sensitive draughtsman…a delightful thing to find in a 20th century exhibition.*[23]

Almost at the same moment, when the British art community of collectors and critics was reading this generous critique announcing Browning's craftsmanship, she was packing her luggage, including her paintbox, drafting tools, and brushes. Culminating the first phase of her professional life in England, she boarded the *Queen Elizabeth*, and eighteen days after this complementary review appeared, she was sailing to the United States.

NOTES

1. Major General Langley Browning, "Irish Gunner" (unpublished manuscript), p. 135.

2. Mark Steven Walker, "Bouguereau at Work," exhibition catalogue essay, in *William Bouguereau: 1825–1905*, The Montreal Museum of Fine Arts, 1984, p. 71.

3. Ibid., p. 71.

4. Malcolm Warner and Robyn Asleson, *Great British Paintings from American Collections*, exhibition catalogue, Yale Center for British Art, September 27–December 20, 2001, pp. 232–233.

5. Ibid.

6. "General's Daughter Is Academy Entrant," *Evening Standard*, London, May 28, 1940 (unpaginated; artist scrapbook clipping).

7. Philip Ziegler, *London at War* (New York: Alfred A. Knopf, 1935), pp. 108–112.

8. Peter Ackroyd, *London: The Biography* (New York: Doubleday, 2001), pp. 723–30.

9. "Palace Hut for Service Women," *The Salisbury and Winchester Journal*, July 24, 1942 (unpaginated; artist scrapbook clipping).

10. This and the preceding three paragraphs are all from Major General Langley Browning, "Irish Gunner" (unpublished manuscript), pp. 192–195.

11. Major General Langley Browning, "Irish Gunner" (unpublished manuscript), p. 216.

12. Ibid., p. 198.

13. Ibid., p. 233.

14. Ibid.

15. Ibid.

16. Ibid., p. 220.

17. Ibid., p. 221.

18. Ibid., p. 135.

19. Ibid.

20. Michel Perez, "Interview with Roman Polanski," from *Le Nouvel Observateur*, 1988. Reprinted in *Roman Polanski Interviews*, ed., Paul Cronin (Jackson: University Press of Mississippi, 2005), p. 124.

21. "Quick Decision Woman," *Variety*, London, May 2, 1949 (unpaginated; artist scrapbook clipping).

22. Ibid.

23. Dorante, *Art News and Review*, vol. 1, no. 8, May 21, 1949 (unpaginated; artist scrapbook clipping).

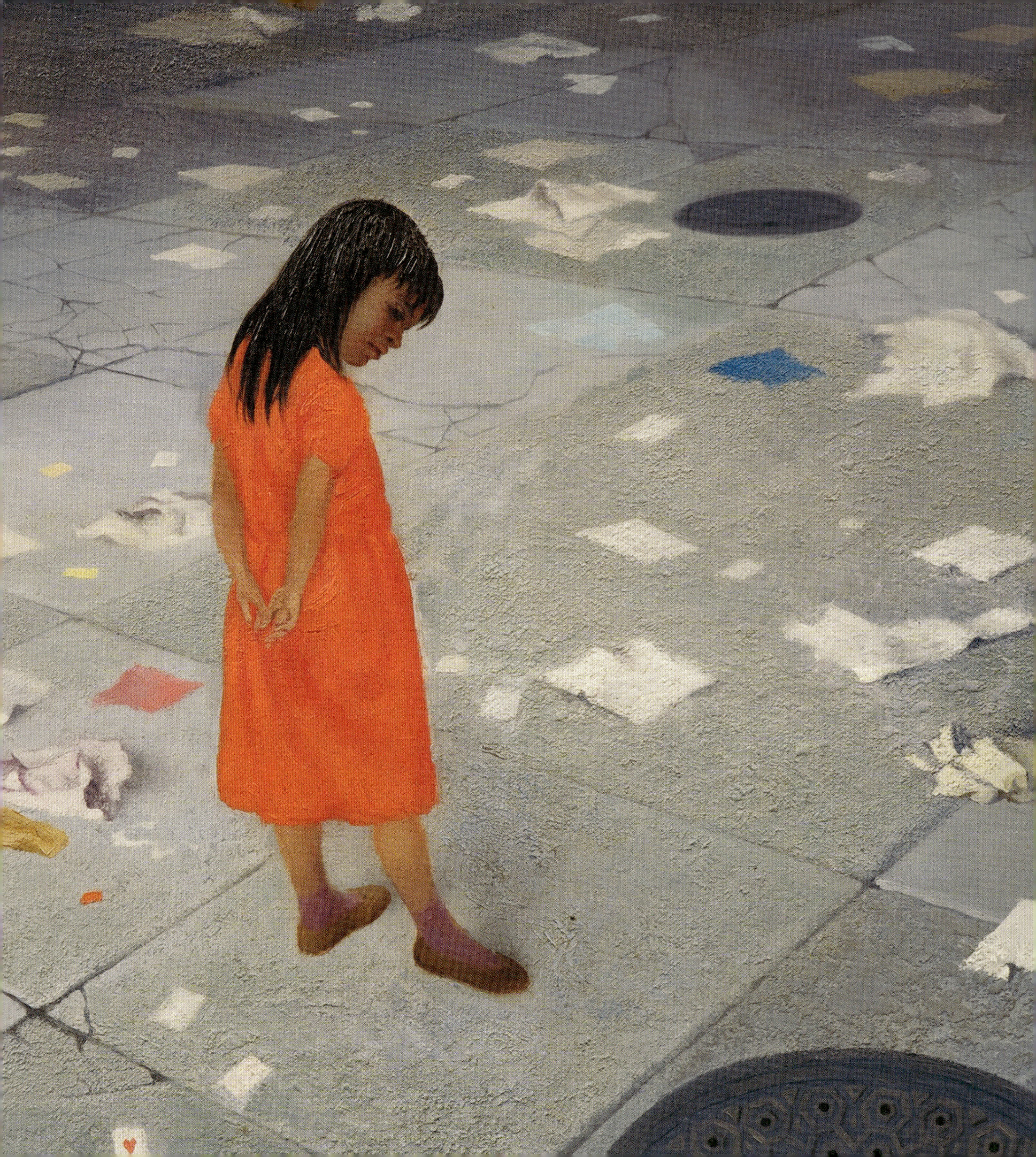

T
HE HALCYON SUMMER OF 1949 must have been an endless journey of discovery. Doubtlessly, it was thrilling, exhausting, and
overflowing with the new sights, tastes, and cultural customs of America. Fresh from her
transatlantic passage, a cross-country automobile honeymoon trip to Mexico City, and
then back to upstate New York, Browning's first moments of rest finally arrived by Labor
Day weekend as the newlyweds reached Wagner's apartment near his English department classrooms on the University of Rochester campus.

Her "Voyage to romance" would eventually toss her about on the high seas of
modernist art in transition. She arrived on the American art scene at the very moment
of its paradigmatic shift from realistic pictorialism to avant-garde abstraction. The carefree lass who posed so confidently on the deck of the *Queen Elizabeth* was unaware of
the brewing storm.

For an ambitious British immigrant, America was the newly crowned global power.
Browning had experienced the hardships and deprivations suffered in London and the
English countryside during the war. There were still severe shortages of consumer goods,
and the bitter taste of Europe's devastation lingered in the air. All was behind her now as
she bid England adieu that morning in 1949. Hope was in the air.

*'There never was a country more fabulous than America,' wrote the British his-
torian Robert Payne after visiting America in the winter of 1948–49. 'She sits bestride
the world like a Colossus; no other power at any time in the world's history possessed
so varied or so great an influence on other nations…Half the wealth of the world, more
than half of the productivity, nearly two-thirds of the world machines are concentrated
in American hands; the rest of the world lies in the shadow of American industry…"*[1]

CHAPTER 5

East Side, West Side, All
Around the Town: East
Harlem & Greenwich
Village, 1949–1952

Browning's dedication to Wagner was predestined—their life in the United States was yet another stroke of good fortune on their side. By chance, they had met on a volcanic beach on the fabled island of Ischia in the last two days of August 1948. With her father's high connections in Rome, she had ready knowledge of Italy's romantic resort islands. The *dolce vita* of a *Ferragosto* holiday required little hesitation for an English general's daughter, as this was the natural order of things.

Italian cities are deserted as the urbanites head for beaches and resorts for two weeks beginning every August 15. This ancient Latin festivity—*Fariae Augusti*—began with sexual excesses related to fertility and ripening in honor of the goddess Diana. By the Middle Ages it was transformed on the church calendar into the Feast of the Assumption of the Virgin.

Ischia, though less well known than the nearby isle of Capri, is a perfect stage-set of Mediterranean sun, sky, vineyards, deliciously inexpensive *trattorias*, and cozy *pensione* hotels. Lacking the swanky pretentiousness of Capri—with its exclusive clientele of movie stars and second-tier European royals—Ischia offered more of an authentically primitive experience.

Indicative of this casual chicness, Truman Capote spent time on Ischia in August 1948, and author Patricia Highsmith appreciated the island's artistic milieu, setting a portion of her 1955 novel *The Talented Mr. Ripley* on Ischia's beaches and in its cafes. It's a dreamy backdrop to enjoy a particularly *Italiana* style of *il dolce far niente*—the sweetness of doing nothing. Among the pleasures of idleness, like twirling *spaghetti alle vongole* and imbibing soft *vino bianco* from the volcanic slopes of Mt. Vesuvius, it also happens to be an ideal place to fall in love.

Characteristically curious and coquettish, Browning freely admitted she first approached Wagner while strolling along the picturesque Maronti beach on the island's southern tip. Deeply suntanned, with the physique of a perfectly proportioned acrobat, Wagner was a veritable Adonis—with an Oxford degree to boot! Their entwined destinies were stamped, minted, and cast in bronze at that moment.

Like two tropical birds exuding attracting pheromones, they flew into each other's arms. Swooning in their affections, they embraced for the next 72 hours until Wagner was forced to depart. He had to make his transatlantic voyage and show up in Rochester for his first American teaching position. Their brief interlude came to an end, and they faced nine months of separation that forged their passion into alloyed steel.

Wagner also engaged in professional subterfuge to mask his literary identity and age. He also falsified his age on many of his published biographical data entries. This deception included author information on the book jackets for his many novels and academic works, uniformly giving his birth date as 1927. From his school records we learn, in correspondence of August 19, 2010 from Catherine Reeve, development director at Lancing College, that Wagner was "one of our former distinguished pupils." She offered important data:

> *Geoffrey Wagner was born 27 December, 1920; his father was a barrister and practicing in Kuala Lumpur. Geoffrey came to Lancing in 1934 and left in July 1939. He was a keen sportsman at school and was captain of the cricket, football, and squash*

Dutifully writing to his fiancée to chronicle his two-week sea voyage, Wagner's stream of consciousness missives reflect his innate genius. Vacillating between his bibliophilism and a caustic sarcasm, he chronicles each moment like a Tolstoyesque narrative. The unnamed Italian steamship sailed from Naples on August 31 and arrived in New York on September 15, 1948. Quivering with a heart-stirring exhilaration, his log became a 15-page double-sided letter that he posted almost immediately upon arrival. Facing a brave new world together is episodically spelled out:

Naples was a lonely place without you my darling…I went to San Genaro [church] *and bid Him take care of you and of us* [31 August]. *I've been planning madly in my mind for next summer…I am sweating through a book on Milton's influence on Blake…*[mentions Jane Austen, C.S. Lewis, and Dryden]. *But poor Colleen's heart and love life are being turned into a receptacle for my literary loitering….The only hope is international socialism that it may be the only alternative—either a united non-national world or no world at all…. Oh dearest, dearest love…San Genaro's got the whole thing in hand, wait till next summer, Geoffrey* [1 September 1948].

The coast of Spain and gleaming porpoises oh my darling, oh I love you [2 September]. *I still love you* [3 September]. *I don't know if I can wait nine months. Five days on this ship have seemed like five centuries. Just finished Faulkner's 'Pylon.' This is a must if you like Steinbeck and the American school of romantic realism. Faulkner (also 'Sound & Fury') is to me the most controlled of the stream-of-consciousness school—even better. Thanks to Arlene* [earlier described as a 'very superficial American artist, social climber, but she possesses a glib mastery of technique…her work is quite hollow'] *I spend this voyage on the first class deck but I can't say the people are any more attractive there. The usual sprinkling of celebrities & cosmopolites seeking shelter from Europe & displaced Europeans—Where are you?* [6 September].

Arrival in New York—Sept. 15th—Oh dear, dear there is so much to tell you—the BEDLAM that is New York City—I cannot describe to you the sudden shock of being immersed in this dirty, sham, noisy, city. I am simply crazy to get to Rochester to hear from you. I sent you 3 pairs of nylons from here—tell me if you have to pay duty. CHRIST what wouldn't I do for a sight of you. This place is a mad-house, believe me…I haven't seen one building that doesn't revolt me…I can't speak, up here in my room on the top floor I can't breathe. Oh love, oh love…life is dead and empty here send me some cyanide or come yourself very soon—write, write WRITE—I must be reassured you exist, but love exists here. Geoffrey

On New Year's Day, 1949 (in Rochester)—"Our Year!"—in a lovesick, rambling, fourteen-page amorous declaration, Wagner gushes about "why we must get married

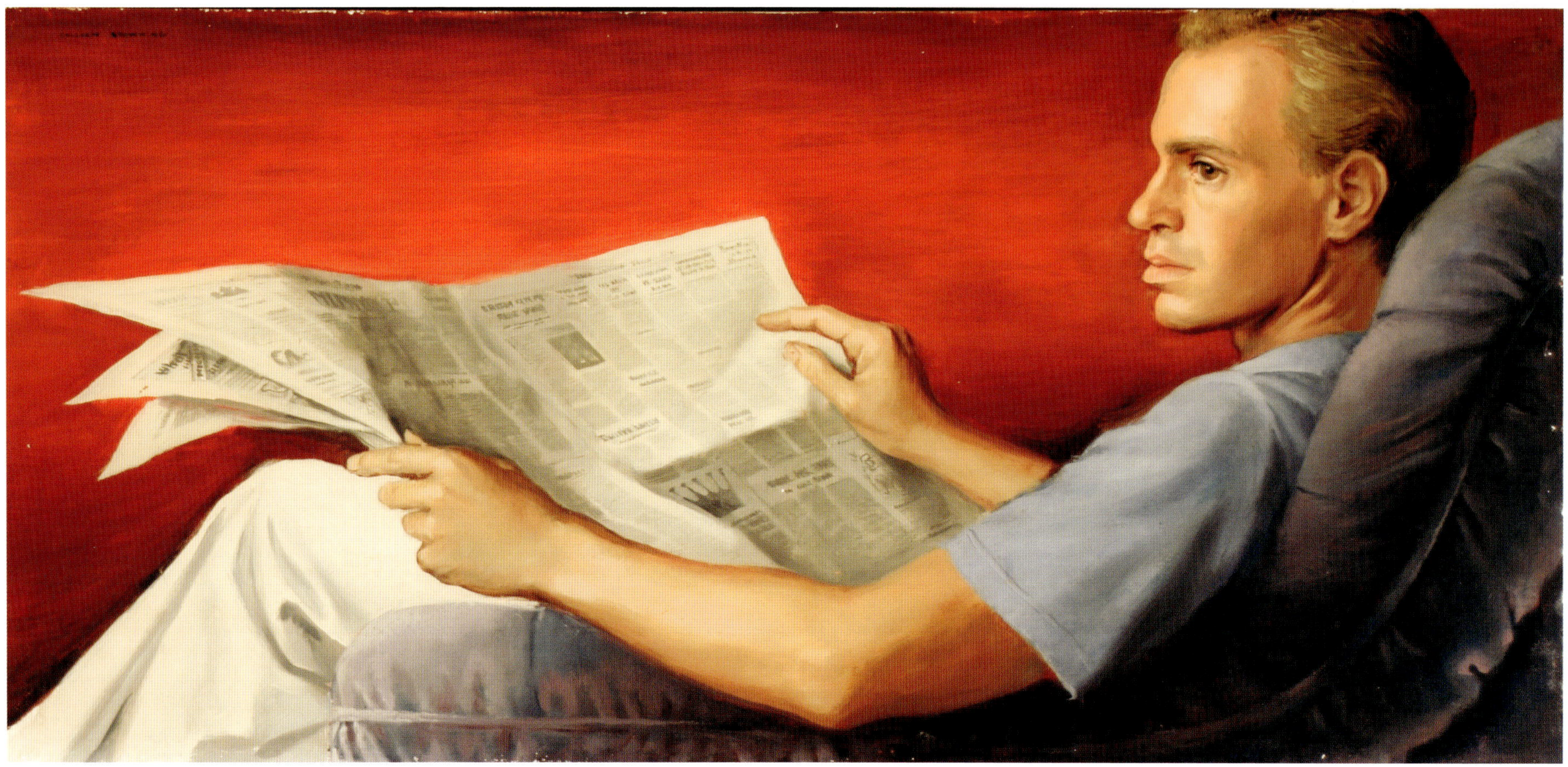

Colleen Browning, Geoffrey Wagner
Reading Newspaper, *c. 1955. Oil on
board, 15 x 29 inches. Collection of
Lancing College, West Sussex, England.
Gift of the Estate of Geoffrey Wagner,
LC/PUP/4313.*

at once as you know I'm awfully happy that we didn't live in 'sin' as they say (!), our
something for always—part of a whole fierce being not just sexual or tenderness—but
in marital love. I am so, so happy you want to marry me as I believe in the strong moral
representation of love as I feel you do."

He then confessed to Browning of an alienating desperation. His loneliness and
detachment from every familiar habit of hearth and home in England was exacerbated
during the holiday season. "Darling angel one: I've just come back from a very "European" talk at a house across the rivers—an Englishman, South African (!), Frenchman &
wife, Dutchman [this must have been a gathering of international faculty enjoying the
long winter break]." Distraught, Wagner condemned American values and wished he
could return to his British roots:

> *Oh my love I want to speak to you to pore* [sic] *out to you at once everything I
> feel. Oh love, we all agreed on all aspects of this ghastly, terrible country* [the United
> States]—*this selfish, panicky, amoral civilization with its hideous moronic culture, its
> jungle laws ('everyone' has a chance to get to the top—yes over everybody else's dead
> body) for morals, its vulgarity, & fantastic lack of breeding, its materialism (have you
> got a car? No? then you're a failure), its myth of its own virility (let's get stinking
> drunk, tell dirty jokes, have a whore, show ourselves what Men we are), its shallow-
> ness, its cheapness, its godlessness…*

Concluding with a vision of their future household, Wagner pointed out: "My only direction for next year is that New York is not America & that one can live in a reasonably civilized way there—let's keep European meal times—over here 'dinner' is 5:30–6:30, let's eat an enormous meal at 8pm…to hell with anything so American!"[2]

However torturous the wait, nine months later the attractive brunette, beaming and in high spirits, arrived in the United States with audacious ambition. And, a few hours after arriving, she married her great love and life companion for the next 53 years.

With a wedding ring in his pocket, Wagner whisked Browning off to a civil ceremony as soon as she arrived. Except for a few transatlantic phone calls and a stream of passionate love letters underscoring how he was unbearably at wit's end without her, the couple had only had 72 hours together on a beach in Italy. The torrent of letters that had crossed the Atlantic were filled with the languishing fervor of Jane Austen but eroticized with the raw sensuality of D.H. Lawrence.

Greatly worried about how they were to check into a midtown Manhattan hotel without a marriage certificate, Wagner chivalrously declared: "I am quite prepared, if you wish, to arrange for a single room till we are married—though I think this would be an unhappy arrangement and a dreadful defeat by bureaucracy! I'm prepared to swallow my Calvinism but I writhe at the red tape involved for two innocent and above-board single people getting hitched."

Back on May 16, 1949, Browning and Wagner were connected via a transatlantic phone call between Rochester and London. Her first solo exhibition at The Little Gallery in Piccadilly is referenced. In Wagner's excited letter, he writes of the exhibition's reception and then their imminent reunion in New York.

middle-class ideals of 'love' – 'marriage' – 'fiancing – 'engagement' & 'honeymoons saw the article before she received my letter [requesting that their marriage be kept quiet]. *I did wonder how much good it did your painting exhibition to know we are going to Mexico. Our hotel in N.Y. is The Winslow, 55th & Madison Avenue* [well located, this was an economical choice; a room at the Waldorf Astoria was $12 and the Pierre $10. The Winslow would cost approximately $2 for a double bed].

> *Also—I'm getting some tickets for 'The Madwoman' the night of June 14th – is it all right with you?* [on the day of her arrival, she is treated to the Tony Award-winning show, Jean Giradoux's *The Madwoman of Chaillot*, which ran for 350 performances at the Belasco Theatre]. *Incidentally, your father could not have been sweeter* [on the phone]. *I hope I conveyed to him just a little of how terribly lucky I know I am in this…I know darling because as the latest dance hit goes here 'I've seen a lot of places, I've been through quite a few'…I love you…P.S. after that* [phone] *call I feel more of a complete swine than ever dragging you away from home and hearth to America. – Yours, Geoffrey*[4]

Because they were so thoroughly fused into such a powerfully bonded couple, we need to take a deeper interest in Wagner's completion of Browning's persona. In some instances, his articulation in masterfully composed exposition leads us very closely into the ideas and thoughts that we see in her paintings. The rich trove of letters gives us valuable clues to her worldview—on the printed page.

In a formally typed letter dated May 22, 1949, on the collegiate letterhead of the English Department, University of Rochester, Wagner wrote to Browning's father seeking permission to marry her:

> *I am fully aware of what a wonderful person your daughter is. I have lived in all sorts of places all over the world and with all kinds and conditions of men, and I can assure you most sincerely that I know just how wonderful and exceptional she is. She has a gloriously happy and healthy personality, she has one hundred percent more guts and good sense than the majority of mankind (she has got where she is in her career solely through her own unaided and unremitting efforts), she has terrific tenacity, intelligence, loyalty, purpose, integrity, and enormous and perfectly terrifying (!) abundance of energy and what is more – I love her dearly.*

The fervently stricken *immorati* would be entwined in body, mind, and spirit as one of New York's most devoted couples for the next seven decades. Their life together as artist and author/scholar was a blissful partnership that was mutually self-limited in perfect devotion. They drew inspiration, encouragement, and an ongoing sense of fulfillment only from one another. Embedded within heaps of personal diaries, social calendars, or phone books, an analysis reveals only the most perfunctory connection to friends or like-minded couples.

Concerned about a snafu, uncertain about the U.S. residency requirements for marriage, Wagner proposed driving all the way to Mexico to circumvent a bureaucratic delay. An exasperated Wagner hatched another backup plan: "We can wed there [Mexico] by the British Consul…don't forget your birth certificate, time of birth, name of favorite colour, the weather in Dakar, grouse prospects next year and the predictions of your star. … WHAT A LIFE."[5]

On June 15, before two unrelated witnesses, Browning and Wagner were issued New York City marriage license #15870, and by paying $2, they were joined as life companions. He had driven down from upstate at the University of Rochester where he just completed the spring term as a teaching fellow specializing in nineteenth-century romantic poetry.

On December 8, 1949, in *The Rochester Democrat Chronicle*, a chatty newspaper column called "Seen and Heard" posted an article about the young professor and his "slim and vivacious" wife. It began with an unfortunate headline—"She Can Cook, Too"—reflecting gender-driven household norms in the pre-Betty Friedan era. Browning's art career was featured but in bold letters she answered Henry W. Clune's curiosity whether she had any cooking skills. "Yes, indeed," she answered promptly. "I'm quite proud of my accomplishments—ask my husband."

The Rochester society page provides us with tiny morsels about their honeymoon adventure. We learn that the Wagners' "real honeymoon was not in New York, but in Mexico, where they decided to spend the remaining weeks of Wagner's vacation…. Miss Browning, as Mrs. Wagner will continue to be known, professionally, is an artist of considerable distinction. In Mexico she wanted to study the murals of the celebrated Diego Rivera."[6]

There is much visual evidence in newly acquired peasant imagery that Browning had taken guidance under Rivera that summer, but we have no corroborating letters or photographs of her in the presence of the great master. The trail runs dry in attempting to find out more about the time that she would have been at the modernistic landmark house-studio of Diego Rivera and Frieda Kahlo in the San Angel district of Mexico City. Built in 1931 in the LeCorbusier manner by the architect Juan O'Gorman, it was the first modern movement residence built on the American continent.

As the elegantly dressed British subject first glimpsed the Statue of Liberty and Manhattan's skyline from the *Queen Elizabeth*'s deck on June 14, her heart must have been racing as she thought of her fiancé waiting at the base of the gangplank. It was unlikely that her thoughts would have focused on the larger critical issues under debate impacting New York's teeming art world. Looming in the distance, above those steel and glass skyscrapers, a pivotal stylistic shift was changing the very essence of modern painting.

That summer of 1949, Manhattan's cultural venues were brimming with nonstop events, Broadway hits, and gallery exhibitions. Rogers and Hammerstein's musical adaptation of James Michener's war memoirs, *South Pacific*, was the smash hit of Broadway. American G.I.s in Italy were dramatized in Roberto Rossellini's film *Paisan*. New best-sellers included Pearl Buck's *The Angry Wife*, John O'Hara's *A Rage to Live*, and Harold Robbins' steamy *The Dream Merchants*.

The uptown art galleries and museums were brimming with new exhibitions. George Bellows' "vulgar paintings" were being shown at the Allison Gallery, while The

Museum of Modern Art's director Alfred H. Barr and curator William S. Lieberman selected highlights of works by Cézanne, Degas, Picasso, and Renoir to show a succession of themes. Unexpectedly, the Whitney Museum's board announced plans to leave its home on West Eighth Street in the village and to lease a new proposed space adjacent to MoMA in its garden on 54th Street. This move uptown was reported as a form of "healthy competition" but the two museums would remain entirely independent.

As the great ocean liner was pulled by a fleet of tugboats from the Battery up the North River (the traditional term used by navigators for the Hudson), Browning probably had her first sighting of Greenwich Village and the shabby meatpacking district of the Lower West Side. Little did she realize that much was up for grabs in American art. More specifically, recently ballyhooed Abstract Expressionism was gaining traction as the ascendant artistic style.

Browning's arrival in New York City and her short time in Rochester could not have been more auspiciously timed. Virginia Mecklenburg, senior curator of American Art at the Smithsonian Institution, noted in her recent exhibition catalogue:

> *Indeed, the postwar period was a heady time for American art.* Life, Time, *and* Newsweek *brought images of contemporary abstraction throughout the country. With the blessing of the U.S. government, New York museums toured exhibitions to the capitals of Europe…. Aided in their efforts by a group of New York dealers, prominent critics, and the influential editor of* ARTnews *magazine, abstract artists gained credibility.*[7]

A dramatic debate and the vitality of New York in those days—the conversations in bars, saloons, and hangouts—were capturing attention in the highbrow literary magazines and avant-gardist art press. A raucous, sometimes cacophonous struggle had overtaken New York's art schools, clubs, studios, and downtown hangouts and bars. In these dimly lit caverns tough Irish dock workers from brownstones in outer borough Flatbush and Flushing in sweat-soaked overalls were strangely mixed with tweedy, Brooks Brothers-clad intellectuals from the Upper West Side or leafy Riverdale.

A salubriously hybrid mix of PhDs elbowed next to those just off the Interborough Rapid Transit (IRT). Tortoise shell rimmed eyeglass-wearing "eggheads," magazine editors, artists, and creative department types from Madison Avenue advertising agencies were cheek to cheek at the bar with their unlikely counterparts in this wonderful social mixed salad of races, ethnicities, and social castes. Downtown saloons equally welcomed subway transit workers, truckers, and ditch-diggers from ConEdison, who also converged on cheap Kentucky bourbon and pitchers of Schaefer, Piels, or Rheingold beer.

All of this privilege and striving upward mobility shaped America's incomparable dynamism in the era between Hiroshima and Kennedy's New Frontier. The ossified old guard and the rising working and middle classes of aspiring *arrivistes* were propelled into a new, unstoppable trajectory, making the United States the envy of global capitalism as the only economy surviving the war as a newly born superpower.

These conflicting issues of taste, style, and social class weighed heavily upon Browning and Wagner during their first years in the States. Did they view themselves as part of the unwashed proletariat or as newly arrived descendants of a patrician class?

Were their bloodlines in alignment with Mayflower connections in the New World? And how did they view the necessity of competing among New York's teeming masses for professional stature?

In terms of peerage, ancestry, and their British mannerisms, what was it like to be equalized with the people whose grandparents were shown in Alfred Stieglitz's memorable Ellis Island photograph of "those huddled masses yearning to be free" in *The Steerage*? This was an America no longer based on one's family standing in the social register but on the hard earned contributions individuals could autonomously register in the emerging fields of law, medicine, finance, and the new manufacturing technologies.

In one of his last missives to Browning, in May 1949, a few weeks before her departure for the States, Wagner wrote: "I feel I am the guilty European of this partnership and you are the Polyanna [*sic*] Anglo-Saxon…. There is nothing more depressing than failure in America; it is dreadfully demoralizing as I know. This is a country you have to come to with very sure values. All vulgarity—this country seethes with it. I believe in you desperately darling—somehow I think of you (artistically) as the postwar generation—uncynical, unglossy, essentially hopeful."

Giving his deeply cynical views was 1932 Yale graduate, cultural voyeur, and managing editor of *Harper's Magazine*, Russell Lynes. His 1949 essay, "Highbrow, Lowbrow, Middlebrow," set off shock waves in America's normally complacent plutocracy. Claiming he was genuinely "anti-intellectual" by attempting to expose effete pretentiousness, his caustic observations revealed an innate snobbishness. Perfectly symptomatic of this cultural chasm would be the appearance of Browning's painting *Holiday* at Pittsburgh's Carnegie International exhibition in 1952. It was her signature painting—somewhat akin to the sensation caused when MoMA purchased Andrew Wyeth's *Christina's World* in 1948 for $1,800, rocketing him into the stratosphere. Browning emerged into the national media and *Holiday* was her calling card image. We will come to see how Lynes' "anywhere but Manhattan" elitism was validated when the Browning painting won over popular audiences. It's difficult to justify the innermost values of a well-heeled, latter-day Flaubert who could write: "Any real New Yorker is a 'you-name-it-we-have-it' whose heart brims with sympathy for the millions of unfortunates who through…pure STUPIDITY live anywhere else in the world."[8]

Browbeating and offending almost every class, sector, and caste in America's increasingly diverse social strata, he launched a full frontal assault: "What we are headed for is a sort of social structure in which the highbrows are the elite, the middlebrows are the bourgeoisie, and the lowbrows are *hoi polloi* [common masses]. …An elite would like to see the middlebrow eliminated, for it regards him as the undesirable element in our, and anybody else's, culture….The highbrows would like to…devise a society that would approximate an intellectual feudal system in which the lowbrows do the work and create folk arts, and the highbrows do the thinking and create fine arts."[9] Lynes continued to wreak havoc on any vestige of democratic equalitarianism with later books, including *Snobs* (1950), *Guests* (1951), and *The Tastemakers* (1954).

The cultural leftists—despite their hypocritical airs of superiority belying their proletarian allegiances—enjoyed mixing with their ruffian working class opposites at these downtown saloons. Clinging to the leftist publications such as *Commentary*, *Partisan Review*, *The Nation*, or the *New Republic*, they argued art criticism with the same intensity as they argued international politics, while a good number of them were hiding their allegiances to the Communist Party of the U.S.A.

On the day after Browning boarded the *Queen Elizabeth*, the June 9 edition of *The New York Times* captured some sense of these internal tensions. Its disturbing headline: "Film 'Communists' Listed in FBI File in Coplon Spy Case – Denials Pour in from Those Accused: 'Absurd, Smear,' Un-American Tactics Seen." Actors Frederic March and Edward G. Robinson "were alleged in a secret report of the FBI to be members of the Communist party…Mr. March said the report was 'the most absurd thing I've heard of.'" Also named by the FBI's informants were the president of Boston University, a professor at Columbia University, and a reporter for the Columbia Broadcast System. Dorothy Parker, "reached at her Hollywood apartment, said: 'this makes me very sick. I'm damned glad to be an American."[10]

Beer- and gin-infused interactions could jump quickly from the weighty issues of the Red Scare to the subway competitions between Yankee Stadium, the Polo Grounds, and Ebbets Field. Fistfights could instantly ignite over mundane questions such as who would be the batting champ of 1949—Yankee Joe DiMaggio, Giant Bobby Thompson, or Brooklyn Dodger Duke Snider? Or a highbrow discussion would suddenly become rancorous with a question such as which Stalinist agent was responsible for having Trotsky hacked to death?

A seething cauldron awaited Browning's serene arrival into the New York arts and intelligentsia orbit as she descended from the *Queen Elizabeth*. Invectives were hurled about retrograde apologists for the retro-garde Stalinists versus the more internationalist Trotskyites, the darling of vanguardist camps. Art. Politics. Crime. Sports. All in a dizzying collage and in sight on newsstands, subway posters, and billboards. New Yorkers of all social and economic strata could read a bubbling broth of current events covering front-page hard news, sports, and gossip: the Bronx "Bomber" Joe Louis knocked out Jersey Joe Walcott in a punishing 11-round championship prize fight; Tammany Hall Democrats with ties to organized crime were backing William O'Dwyer as Mayor; and the tabloids were having a field day reporting on expanding racketeering and gangland violence among competing street enforcers.

Both Browning and Wagner had participated in the defeat of fascism in Europe, but the Soviet's "worker's paradise" was still being hotly defended by a substantial segment of New York's scholars. No artist, author, stage and screen actor, or theater director was spared from entanglement in this polarizing debate. Even those feigning being "nonpolitical" knew who was siding toward native "America First" conservatism or those "pink diaper babies" whose mother's milk was nourishing Marxist social theories. Everybody was suspect as the Red Scare was inevitably branching out like crushing tentacles of an international octopus from the Kremlin to Main Street U.S.A.

Just three months after Browning's British passport was stamped upon debarkation at the Port of New York, on August 16, 1949, Congressman George A. Dondero of Michigan rose to speak from the well of the United States House of Representatives. Alerting the nation to an insidious threat in the disguise of modernist art, the Congressman's speech was too closely paralleled in principle and example with the infamous tirades of Adolf Hitler when he assumed the role as Germany's chief art critic.

At the July 18, 1937 celebration for the opening of Munich's temple of Nazi iconography, the Haus der Kunst, eyewitnesses noted how the Fuhrer was "foaming at the mouth." But his rage was not targeted at Churchill or Roosevelt, but at Picasso and Modigliani. In his crosshairs were those deviants in the *Entartete Kunst* exhibition of "Degenerate Art." He promised that "those canvas smearers" [artists such as Brancusi, Matisse, Kandinsky or van Gogh] and "all of those cliques of chatterers, dilettantes, and art forgers will be picked up and liquidated." The hyperbolic language of *Kulturpolitik* had somehow jumped like a bullfrog from the homicidal artistic policies of the Third Reich to America's maniacal obsessions with artistic Bolshevism.

> *Mr. Speaker,* [A] *glib disavowal of any relationship between communism and so-called modern art is so pat and so spontaneous a reply by advocates of the 'isms' in art from deep, Red Stalinist to pale pink publicist,* [it will] *fool the public.… Art is a weapon of communism, and the Communist doctrinaire names the artist as a soldier of the revolution…I call the role of infamy: dadaism, futurism, expressionism, surrealism, cubism…and abstractionism.*
>
> *All of these 'isms' are of foreign origin, and truly should have no place in American art.… Abstractionism aims to destroy by the creation of brainstorms… We are now face to face with the intolerable situation, where public schools, colleges, universities, art and technical schools, invaded by a horde of foreign art manglers, are selling to our young men and women a subversive doctrine—Communist-inspired and Communist-connected.*[11]

"Browning recalls the art scene as eclectic when she started out in New York City in the '50s," Greta Berman and Jeffrey Wechsler reported in their 1981 interview with Browning. "She was aware of Pollock, and went to exhibitions of abstract expressionist, realist, and all kinds of art."[12] Refined in her etiquette, projecting an upper crust British elegance, she could not have found anything less appealing than the loutish, faux-machismo antics of the downtown world of *poete maudits*, grubby jazz musicians, and paint-stained abstract painters. Metaphorically, the aggressive brushstrokes of action painting were sometimes sublimated into boorish, juvenile behaviors. De Kooning's biographers Mark Stevens and Annalyn Swan described its milieu:

> *The Cedar smelled of spilled beer and tobacco smoke…the Americans were hard drinkers at a dive whose existential aura owed more to Brando on the docks than to Sartre at Deux Magots. The Cedar represented a perfect blend of high and low, of proletarian circumstance and intellectual aspiration. English hunting prints in elegant black frames hung, absurdly, on the dingy walls… With alcohol came a fashion for violence, usually not serious violence, but, instead, the kind of barroom swagger that Hemingway inspired in young writers. Pollock was celebrated for ripping the men's room door off its hinges at the Cedar…Drinking also made de Kooning pugnacious. He was quick to lose his temper, and he would sometimes take a drunken sock at people who offended him, including, on occasion, Pollock.*

Perhaps Wagner's most noteworthy literary achievement was the 1967 Alfred A. Knopf novel *The Sands of Valor*, which military buffs consider as the finest account of tank warfare in the desert of North Africa. Wagner retained shell-shocked recollections of his service in the British Brigade of Welsh Guards under General Montgomery. This fictionalized account was based on Wagner's experiential firsthand involvement in chasing General Rommel's (the Desert Fox) Afrika Korps across the Libyan and Tunisian desert.

The back-and-forth campaign pitted English Crusader tanks against Germany's heavier Tigers, which resulted in more than 50,000 killed or wounded English soldiers in the dunes. This compelling 434-page novel, filled with the grittiest of harrowing details, concludes: "And now gentlemen…let us exercise our calling. Let us go out and fight to the death."[14]

Four years after the end of WW II, in his proposal letter to Browning's father, Wagner was quick to admit: "I think you should know—I would not like to conceal it from you—that I am bitterly opposed to the army in all its many forms and manifestations. I shall continue ceaselessly and vehemently to oppose it and all it connotes in every aspect under which I encounter it. This has of course nothing personal in it…but it is a general sentiment I don't want to cloak from you in case you might meet it later on, for I make no compromises."[15]

Browning and Wagner passed a "year in exile"—1949–50—at the University of Rochester, often remarking about its provincialism. Nevertheless, it was surely rewarding. It gave her an opportunity to better understand Main Street USA before plunging into the Great White Way on Broadway. For the young scholar on a fellowship and his new bride, Rochester was a way station, an inconvenient stop on their life journey. But it was a valuable introduction for Browning as a typical midsize American city with a population in 1950 of a little less than half a million, the third largest city in New York State. It gave her a strong insight into how "real Americans" lived in an urban setting. With its intense seasonal changes—an average of 100 inches of snow in winter—and lovely springtime that she enjoyed at the area's waterfalls and gorges, she experienced the "real America." Later, when she moved to Harlem—an exotic, almost foreign country—it was unlike anything else in the USA.

Wagner's modest rented flat in Rochester became home as they pulled up in front of their love nest. They lived at 292 Alexander Avenue, just a few blocks from the university and only a short distance behind its Memorial Art Gallery. Established in 1913 when Rochester's gilded age merchants and manufacturers generously endowed its collection, the Gallery has impressively expanded into an encyclopedic institution with more than 11,000 works of art today.

After their grueling summer road trip of hot dog stands, uncomfortable rooming houses, and a crossing at the Texas-Mexico border in the pre-air-conditioning era, the Memorial Art Gallery must have seemed a small oasis of European history. Among its collection's highlights are good Renaissance altarpieces, a fine Titian, an original Ghiberti sculpture, and Dutch old masters, including a Rembrandt portrait of a young man and a handsome Frans Hals.

"Miss Browning is a slim vivacious young woman with dark brown eyes who is eagerly interested in every phase of her new life in America. As yet she has made few friends in Rochester," a local society writer noted.[16] Considering her brief residency in Rochester, from September 1949 to June 1950, Browning cut a small but well-notched niche across the art landscape in upstate New York. The local newspaper reported her industriousness: "Since her arrival in this country she has been far from idle. She has done several paintings of American scenes, one of which showing the rowdy goings-on of an American Halloween celebration. Also, she has just finished the mural decorations for a new and novel Alexander Street restaurant, the Rio Bamba."[17]

A determined collector recently discovered the *Rio Bamba Restaurant Mural* (fig. 5.1), which reveals Browning's extraordinary artistic inspiration. Following her work with London film sets, this painting is reminiscent of the incredibly imaginative set decorations created by Salvador Dali for Hitchcock's 1945 classic *Spellbound*, which features Rochester prominently.

Offering dining patrons an eyeful, adding to the avant-garde décor of this upscale Rochester establishment, Browning employed her scenic design talents and created a clever homage to Salvador Dali. Its phantasmal apparitions include several quotations from a Dali painting such as *William Tell*, 1930 (fig. 5.2). Direct visual quotes from *Spellbound*'s dream sequence—a landmark in cinematic history—are the menacing eyeballs. Browning inserted floating umbrellas that morph into winking eyeballs.

The Rochester mural includes a red-haired femme fatale in fishnet stockings lurking behind an eyeball mask; a seductive female nude sprouting a flowery head with a snap whip in her right hand; a zebra wearing a monocle; and detached, sensual lips filling the sky while an eighteenth-century balloon basket rises and is eclipsed by a crescent moon. More so the charming product of an instinctual copyist, the restaurant mural was imitative of the past. Now Browning had to discover genuinely American themes to

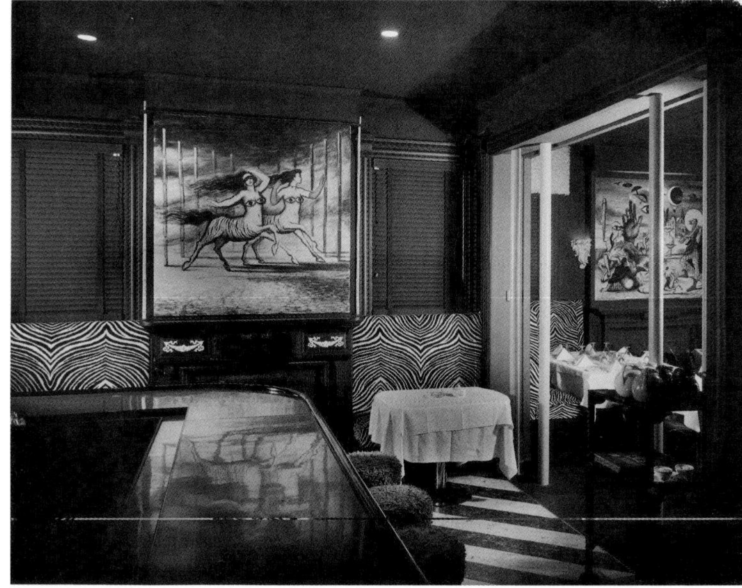

Interior of Rio Bamba restaurant, c. 1950. Rochester, NY. Photograph from artist's scrapbook.

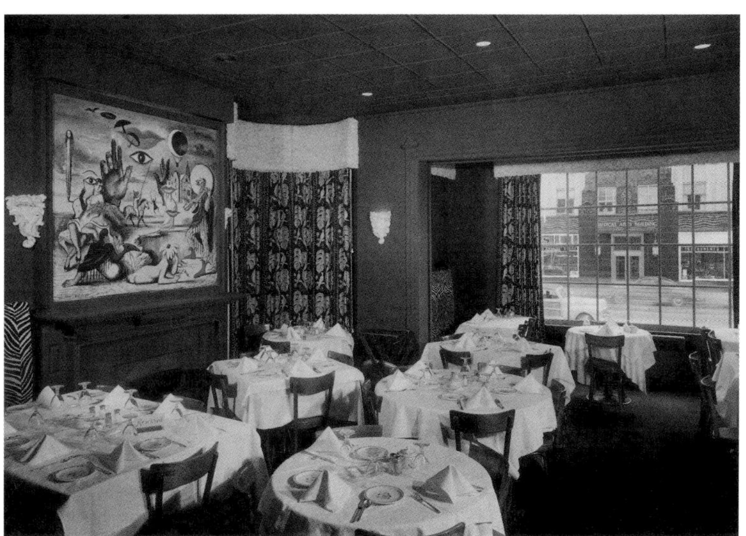

Interior of Rio Bamba restaurant, c. 1950. Rochester, NY. Photograph from artist's scrapbook.

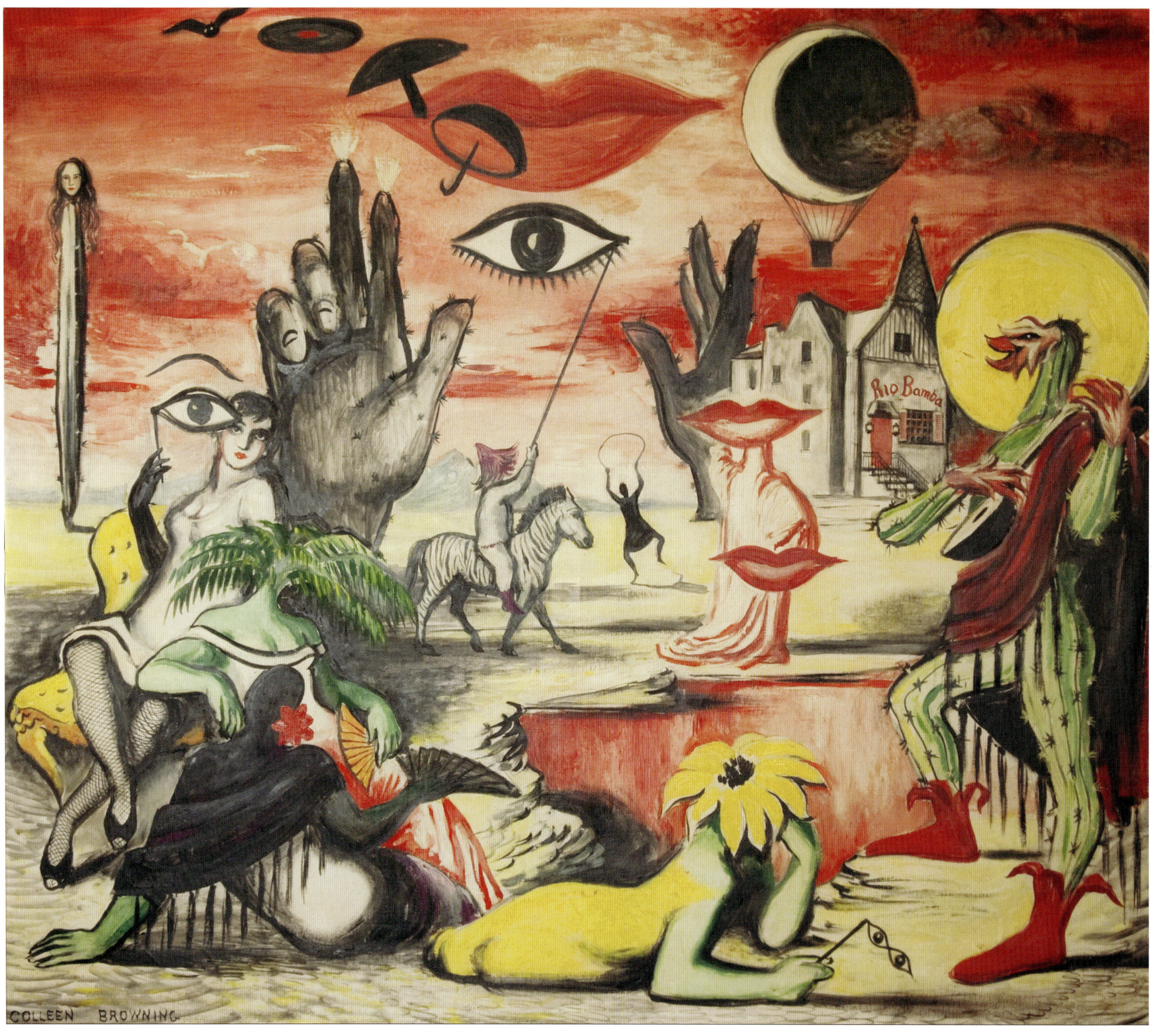
Rio Bamba
COLLEEN BROWNING

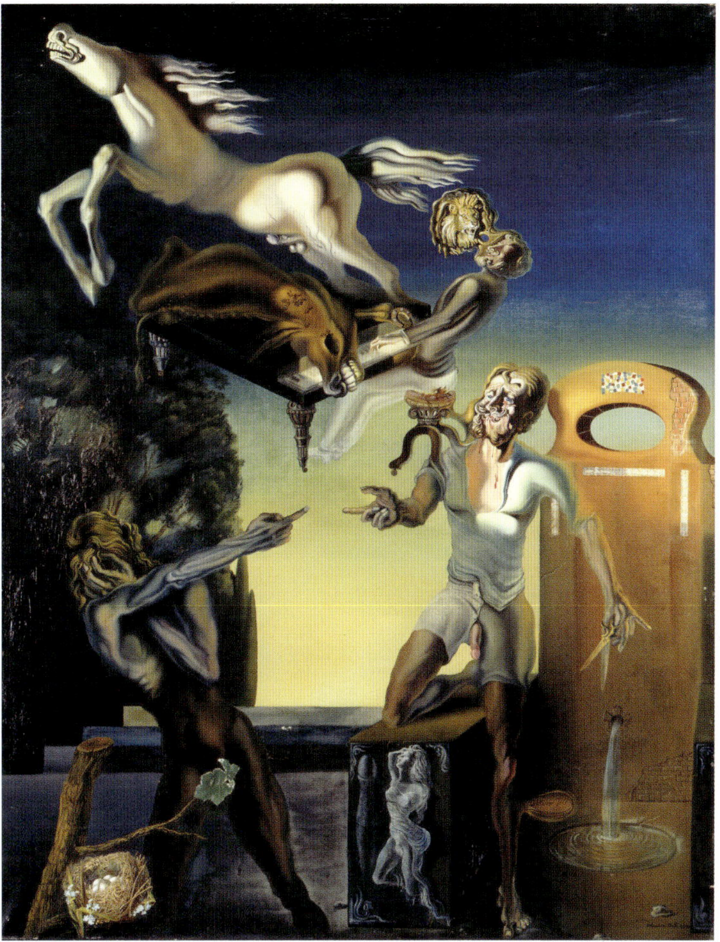

Fig. 5.2. Salvador Dali, William Tell, 1930. Collage of diverse materials, textile, paint, 44½ x 34¼ inches. Musee National d'Art Moderne, Centre Georges Pompidou, Paris / Art Resource. CNAC / MNAM / Dist. Réunion des Musees Nationaux / Art Resource, NY. © 2010 Salvador Dali, Gala-Salvador Dali Foundation / Artists Rights Society (ARS), New York.

Fig. 5.1. Colleen Browning, Rio Bamba Restaurant Mural, 1950. Oil on canvas, 59 x 65 inches. Private collection.

successfully assimilate into her new environment, like a chameleon changes its colors as part of its survivalist instincts.

Browning's reconnaissance of realist imagery by the leading painters of that day showed an attachment to the American scene. As a newly landed immigrant, she wanted to incorporate herself within the artistic milieu of her new home. Browning had indicated that an early influence for her own developing style was found in the style and localized settings of Ben Shahn. His social realist–based *Ohio Magic*, 1945 (fig. 5.3), served as a strong model to emulate.

This is evidenced in her painting, *Churchgoers*, 1950 (fig. 5.4), which takes a similar view of a typical American main street with its rows of brick buildings and church façade. Browning's painting won the Juried Art Patrons Award at the 1950 Finger Lakes Exhibition. It is now in the permanent collection of the Memorial Art Gallery. This earliest known American painting, created soon after her arrival in upstate New York, convincingly demonstrated Browning's aptitude as a quick study.

Searching around for other leading models, she snatched the look and feel of Charles Burchfield's Buffalo street scenes right out of the winter atmosphere. As aliens often need to learn English as their introduction to American culture, Browning manip-

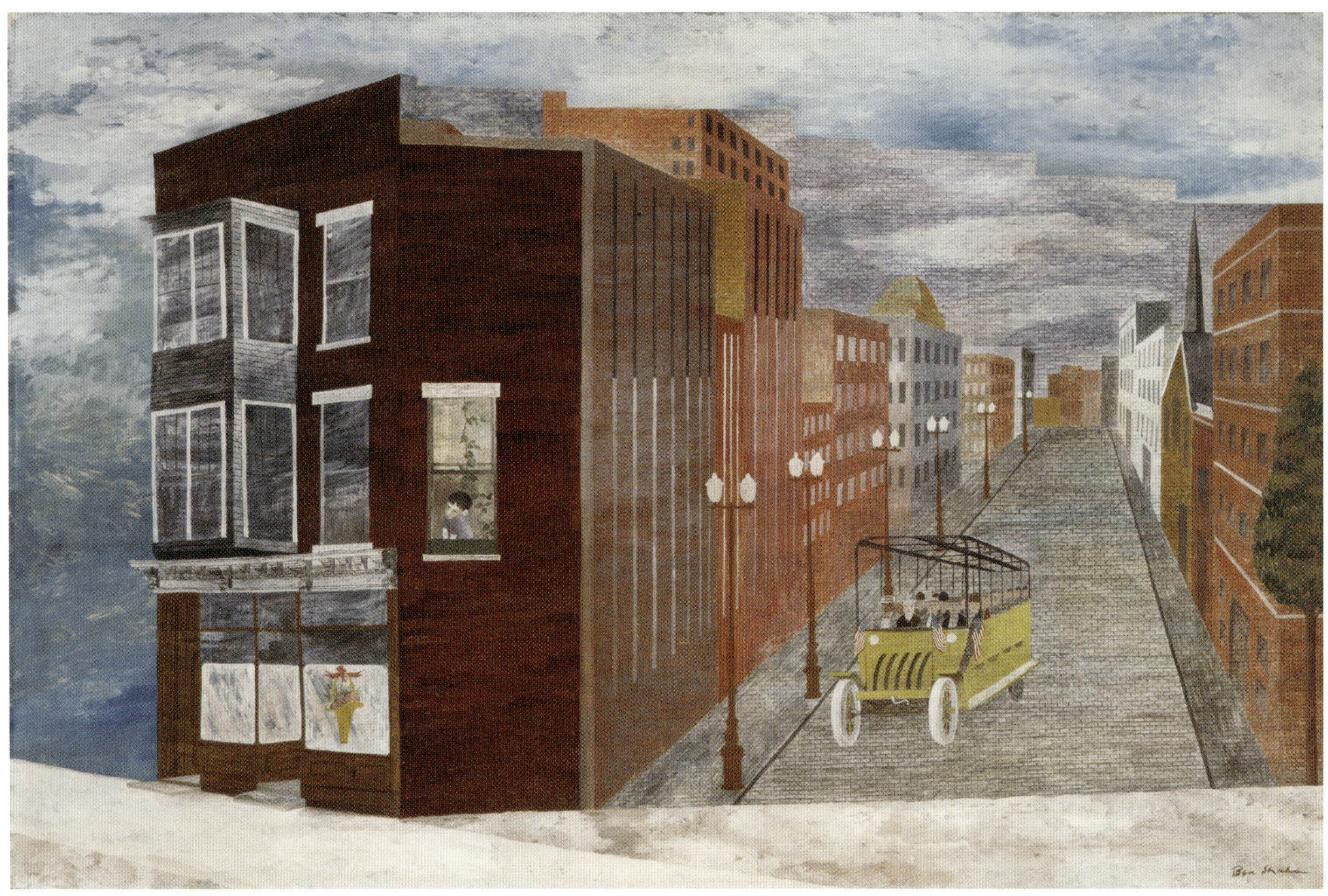

Fig. 5.3. Ben Shahn, Ohio Magic, *1945. Tempera on paperboard mounted on hardboard panel, 26 x 39 inches. Fine Arts Museums of San Francisco. Museum purchase, Mildred Anna Williams Collection. 1948.14.*

ulated her artistic language into an upstate, regional vernacular. *Churchgoers* is a perfectly unglamorous snapshot of a bustling street anywhere in small-town America as evening vespers concludes. The parish church on the corner, gossiping doyennes in their furs and stoles, and neighborhood children are depicted. They all seem to work their way into this entry-pass painting composed by a British woman observing the streets of Rochester.

On February 23, 1950, at the Rochester Historical Society's landmark building, Woodside, an exhibition formally entitled *Paintings by Miss Colleen Browning (Mrs. Geoffrey Wagner)* was presented. We have ample evidence of her swift progress in adapting and translating her new experiences into paintings. "Originality and liveliness are two marked qualities in the paintings in gouache and tempera…Miss Browning, at 28 [*sic* 32] has an exhibition record of 15 years behind her," wrote art reviewer Amy H. Croughton, in the *Rochester Times-Union.* Browning presented "four studies for murals, five sketches for 'American Scenes,' and 10 film scenes." The film sets had been in her steamer trunk aboard the *Queen Elizabeth.* The "American Scene" sketches were premonitions of her future.

Wagner recognized that his Oxford undergraduate degree required a capstone PhD from an American Ivy League institution in order for him to continue on his

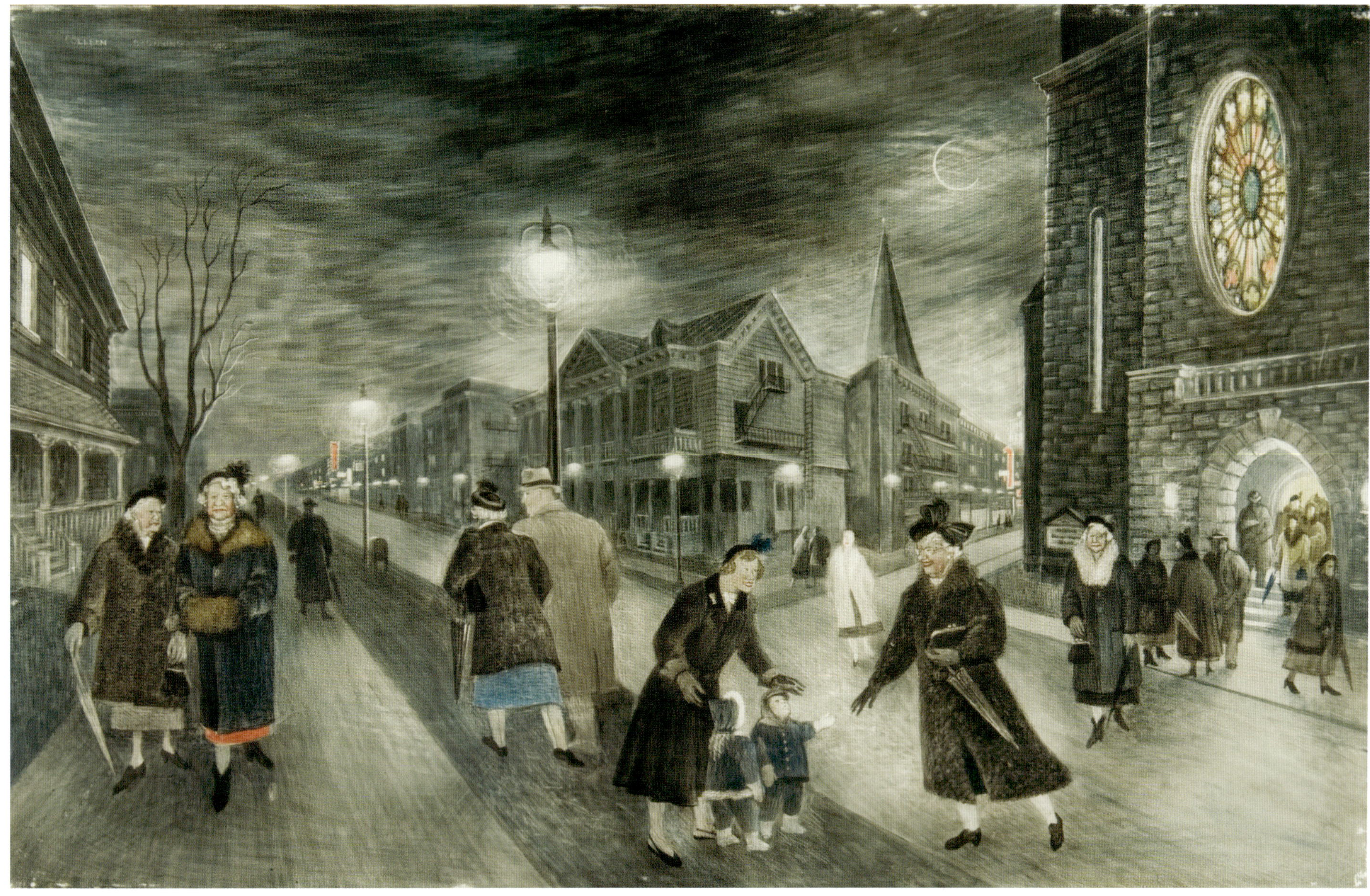

trajectory of laboring in the groves of academe. Wagner began his doctoral studies at Columbia in September 1950. One cannot calculate the enormity of this decision upon Browning's career. Had he chosen the doctoral program at Harvard or the University of Pennsylvania, his wife's art career would have been anchored in Boston or Philadelphia.

Unpredictably, moving into a tenement block, fourth floor walkup in East Harlem had the same effect on Browning as van Gogh moving from Paris to Arles, or Edward Hopper decamping to Cape Cod. Her change in location was like Dorothy finding her way from Kansas onto the wonders of the Yellow Brick Road.

By the late summer of 1950, Browning and Wagner set up household in what was then "Italian" East Harlem at 2310 Second Avenue and 116th Street. This broad intersection, a perfect crossing of uptown and cross-town streets, served her perfectly as the scenic stage for her earliest New York paintings. Even for the visitor of today, this

Fig. 5.4. Colleen Browning, The Churchgoers, *1950. Oil on board, 19⅝ x 30 1/16 inches. Memorial Art Gallery of the University of Rochester. Purchased through the Art Patrons Fund. 50.22.*

"anywhere uptown" streetscape retains its vibrantly pulsating sensation of urban energies. One can still clearly see Browning's perch at her fourth-floor window in a newly gentrified and restored area of Harlem today.

By the time Browning and Wagner arrived, East Harlem's Italian population was moving out to the newly created postwar suburbs on Long Island and in New Jersey. She painted black children in the neighborhood just at the time when the seesaw balance was shifting from a lingering Italian population to an increasingly African American community. This fact amplified the social history she documented—almost unintentionally—from her fourth-floor window.

During her initial New York City years in the early 1950s, Browning achieved unimaginable fame and critical recognition for these "American scenes." A memorable series of paintings, perhaps her most significant contributions to American art, captured East Harlem's newly arrived black and Puerto Rican children at play.

Even as this was a transitional period for Browning and Wagner, it was also a time when East Harlem was undergoing a sociological transformation. Their neighborhood had been a predominately Italian section of Manhattan with a deeply entrenched religious and cultural heritage. As Manhattan's first Italian parish and home congressional district of Fiorello La Guardia, East Harlem was a truly polyglot, ethnically diverse neighborhood for the newly transplanted artist and professor.

At the core of the southern Italian immigrants' worship was the Our Lady of Mount Carmel shrine at 447 East 115th Street, just around the block from the Wagners' apartment. Housing one of only three images of the Blessed Virgin crowned by pontifical authority in the Americas, the shrine is generously decorated in gold and adorned with precious stones. Not accidentally, Browning began creating a number of paintings where mystical adoration of religious icons, sometimes illuminated by a flickering candlelight, entered into her repertoire.

"The Wagners: Harlem Without Tears" was the outcome of another inquiring house visit to this irresistible couple's life by a curious journalist for New York's *Daily Mirror* newspaper, on March 27, 1953. Columnist Sidney Fields began: "The reasons why Colleen Browning, the artist, and her husband Geoffrey Wagner, the writer, live in a fourth floor walkup flat in Harlem, are simple: It's cheaper… 'This is Italian Harlem,' Colleen adds, 'within a few blocks are Puerto Ricans and Negroes. Whenever I do my household shopping I take a three-hour tour of a living gallery.' Colleen, born in Ireland [*sic*], is the daughter of a British general…. 'Imagine fiestas in a city like New York,' says Colleen with a child's wonder. 'Long processions of people carrying pennants. Women with bare feet carrying candles. All the faces full of light.'"

Debunking negative stereotypes, the article continues: "they heard their neighborhood described as a 'verminous, crime-ridden slum,' which shakes their British reserve to anger. 'The real estate ads stop at 90th Street…and anything above it is not the city. The impression is everyone walks around with a gun, even the children. The most spectacular things we've ever seen was a car crash at the corner,' says Colleen.

"They knew they belonged and were grateful and happy for it, when, one day Colleen went to the big Puerto Rican market on Park Ave., and the vegetable man asked her: 'Where were you yesterday? We missed you.'"[18]

No wonder Browning was so enchanted by the realism of everyday observations in East Harlem's limitless pageant of life. We sense some of what she experienced from the vivid recollections that Robert A. Orsi documented in *The Madonna of 115th Street: Faith and Community in Italian Harlem, 1880–1950*. He described the street festival on the Virgin's feast day of July 16. Orsi explained how parishioners were "walking barefoot behind the Madonna, kissing the statue in church and penciling petitions for love and health on them…. Religious idioms like those associated with the Madonna's cult (the technical term for Catholic devotional practices) have been designated as 'magical,' 'superstitious' …ambiguous amalgams of the sacred and profane."[19]

By 1950, a swelling population was bringing waves of southern blacks to the north as part of the second Great Migration to Harlem. Isabel Wilkerson, a Pulitzer Prize winner, journalist, and professor at Boston University, spent 15 years documenting her own family's history in the great migration. In a National Public Radio interview she explained, "At the beginning of the twentieth century, before the migration began, 90 percent of all African Americans were living in the South. By the end of the Great Migration, nearly half of them were living outside the South in the great cities of the North and West."[20] By mid-century, a massive exodus—sparked by Jim Crow laws and the threat of physical violence—had left the rural South and had completely transformed the neighborhoods of America's industrial cities.

Earlier in the twentieth century, the first Great Migration had established Harlem as the "Black Mecca" and as the "Capital of Black America." The greatest voice of that period was the anonymous *Invisible Man* of Ralph Ellison's 1952 novel. Living in the closed-off basement of an all-white building outside Harlem, Ellison's character states: "….a hell of a lot of free current is disappearing into the jungle of Harlem. The joke, of course, is that I don't live in Harlem but in a border area."[21]

A major early work of 1951–52, painted soon after her arrival in Harlem, is her iconic *Holiday* (fig. 5.5). In keeping with her stated interest of exploring the "world around me," this early masterpiece is cohesively connected to American artists who were acknowledged models. She effortlessly fell in step with her recognized heroes of that time. She often cited her visual debt at this time to older American masters, Ben Shahn and Henry Koerner. We also know that both Wagner and Browning felt very honored in their personal relationship with social realist painter Joseph Hirsch. He freely offered avuncular advice to her about breaking into the New York gallery scene.

Holiday establishes an overlooking view of a diffident child who is lost in her thoughts. Crumpled newspapers are strewn about across a Renaissance-inspired checkerboard of trapezoidal pavement sections. A grayish pallor denotes a moody somberness. The discarded papers might be a clue, representing society's apparent ease in abandoning the fragile inner lives of its most precious resource: children.

Almost at the same moment, Robert Vickrey (1926–2011) was also depicting street waifs whose graffiti drawings and wonderfully free markings on New York pavements were equally sympathetic to the struggles of adolescents. Vickrey's *Lines, Lines*, 1971 (fig. 5.6), is a later version of a Manhattan sidewalk scene that Browning might have known.[22]

In a handwritten script, "Picture of a Painting" (probably from the late 1980s) intended for an undated radio or video broadcast at some future point, she begins:

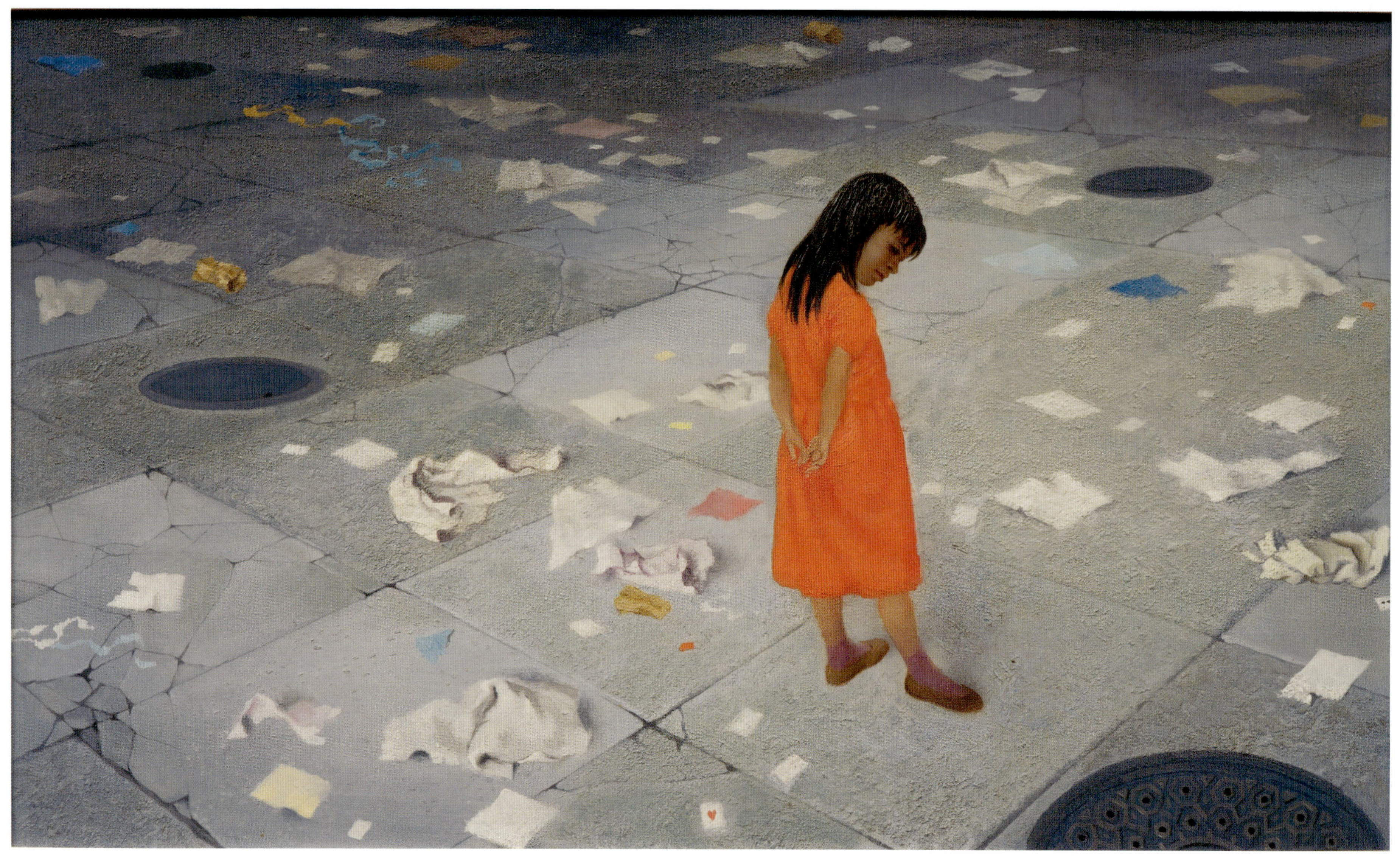

Fig. 5.5. Colleen Browning, Holiday,
*1951–52. Oil on canvas, 21¾ x 30½
inches. Collection of the Coleman
Barkin Family.*

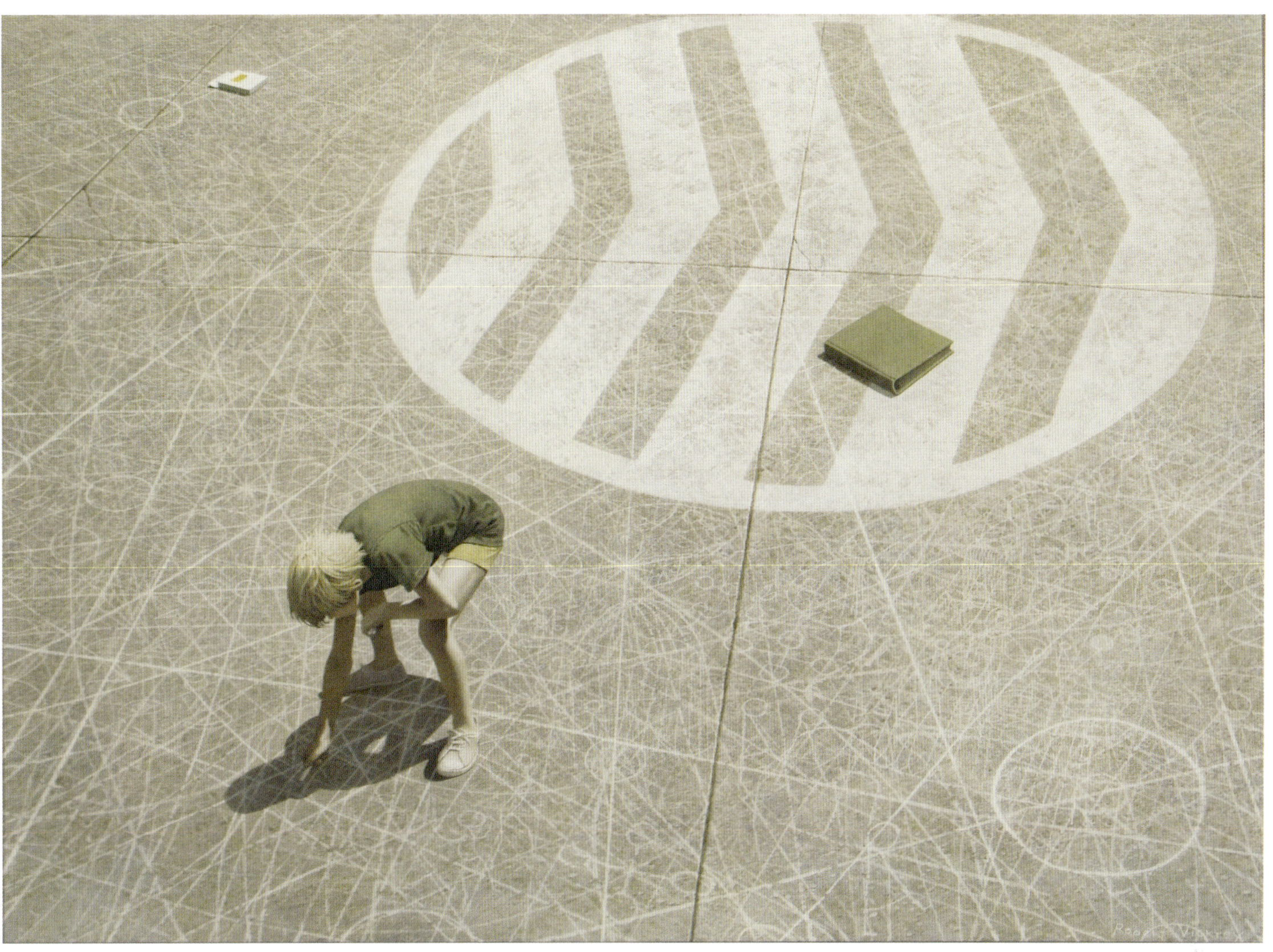

This is Colleen Browning speaking. I want to give you an insight into some of my paintings, their circumstances, and why I painted them. Holiday is an early work done in my second year in America. We had no money, so a cheap apartment was essential. We found one in East Harlem—a fourth floor walkup with no phone, the front windows overlooking the avenue. We paid $85 a month which the landlord reduced to $75 after being impressed with my painting the bedroom walls red with white tasseled drapes.

We didn't realize it was supposed to be the worst area in New York. In about a year, and by that time, I was a neighborhood character and didn't worry about it and nobody worried about me. The windows overlooking the avenue gave a marvelous view of activities below and after a holiday the sidewalk was showered with litter making another pattern on top of the pattern of manholes and the sidewalk rectangles. In preparing for the painting I went out and collected samples of the litter as I couldn't get the really squashed look from jumping on my own paper bags!

Fig. 5.6. Robert Vickrey, Lines, Lines, *1971. Egg tempera on gesso panel, 30 x 40 inches. Canton Museum of Art. Gift of the Hoover Foundation, Canton Museum of Art, Canton, OH.*

Fortunately, a younger generation of art historians, Greta Berman and Jeffrey Wechsler, had the opportunity to interview Browning about these early Harlem paintings. *Holiday* was prominently discussed as they were preparing for their landmark exhibition, *Realism and Realities: The Other Side of American Painting 1940–1960* (Rutgers University Art Gallery, January–March 1982). We have fragmentary quotes from their artist interview session at Browning's studio-apartment in Morningside Heights, on May 9, 1981.

In hindsight, we should recognize that the full circle from realism (1930s) to abstraction (late 1940s, dominant through the 1950s) to Pop (1960s), photorealism (1970s), and New Image painting (1980s) had sparked a renewed interest in the agenda of figurative painting. After many years of inattention, Browning must have savored this visit, realizing her work would be re-evaluated in the forthcoming Rutgers show with its revisionist sweep.

In this extremely important interview with two leading scholars late in her career, Browning said she had felt like an anachronism during her lonely years in London (again misrepresenting her attendance at Slade by nine years, claiming in the interview she graduated in 1948, instead of 1939).

Supporting the so-called Realist Revival of this era were massive new studies on academic painting by a young generation of unbiased art scholars. It began with major new studies on the careers of French academic artists such as Adolphe William Bouguereau, Rosa Bonheur, Alexandre Cabanel, and Jean-Léon Gérôme. The academy was considered the common "enemy" to the insurgent Impressionists of the 1870s, and this carried over to the American scene as social realists (Reginald Marsh, Isabel Bishop, and Philip Evergood) and regionalists (Thomas Hart Benton, Grant Wood, and John Steuart Curry) were all dismissed as anti-modernists.

In Berman-Wechsler's preciously documented catalogue, future generations of scholars are rewarded with amazingly detailed insights into the working methods of the normally reclusive or by-now embittered social realists, and nearly forgotten Magic Realists. No single publication has been of greater sustained value to this author than this informatively organized exhibition catalogue with the Berman-Wechsler interviews.

Presciently, they recorded remarkably authoritative interviews with key "lost generation" artists including Edward Laning, Balcomb Greene, Jack Levine, Henry Koerner, Bernard Perlin, George Tooker, Alton Pickens, Priscilla Roberts, Elmer Bischoff, and Hyman Bloom. These artists had been swept aside by the hurricane winds of Abstraction and modernist Expressionism that left them like flotsam and jetsam at low tide on the deserted beach of American art by the 1960s.

The Carnegie International Exhibition of Contemporary Paintings was at the top of the A-list as a competitively open arena. Visibly noted were the newly eclipsed realists versus the up-surging modernists, who were all equitably exhibited. One could easily discern the overt tensions as opposing artistic approaches were battling for primacy. This created a dramatic schism between more effete critical tastes and popular appeal. The official jury gave top honors to British abstractionist Ben Nicholson. But the intriguing vox populi placed Browning very near to the top of the pack. The outstanding reception to *Holiday*, reproduced as the "third best canvas in the exhibit" was noted in *The Pittsburgh Post-Gazette*'s coverage of the International Exhibition of Contemporary Paintings held at the Carnegie Institute. The December 9, 1952 morning edition ran a bold headline: "Public Ignores Abstract Art in Picking Winners at Show: Conservative Paintings Cop Top Prizes as Pittsburghers Disagree with Experts." The *sturm und drang* of the realist versus abstractionist debate was fueled by the popular choices in stark opposition to the highbrow art critics. Pirates fans gave thumbs down to pretentious painters as a result of the poll.

> *Pittsburghers don't just vote for abstract art. At least, not the current collection at the* [International] *exhibit. Disagreeing strongly with the expert art critics who awarded most of the cash prizes to abstracts, the public gave conservative works the nod for the top prizes. The abstract 'what's it' didn't stand a chance…. Third place in the popular vote went to* Holiday *by Colleen Browning of Harlem, N. Y.* Holiday *shows a young girl gazing at a Harlem street littered with paper.*[23]

Less sensationalized was the extensive write-up for "The Popular Prize" in the museum's January 1953 more staid bulletin. *Carnegie Magazine*'s coverage listed the top 13 choices from the public as "each visitor was given a ballot and was asked to nominate, according to his own taste and standards the best in the show."

Holiday was ranked third after the second place *Farewell* by Bernard Perlin. Perlin, who designed memorable propaganda posters for the Office of War Information in WWII, was also an intimate of the Kirstein-Cadmus circle and another blossoming Magic Realist. Rather astonishingly, Andrew Wyeth's painting, *The Toll Rope* (now in the Delaware Art Museum), was number 8 on the list, five notches lower than Browning's entry!

Reporting that "Miss Browning, born in Ireland in 1923 [*sic*] received the third largest number of votes, has this to say about her painting: 'Holidays always seemed an anticlimax to me as a child, so looked forward to, and yet often so flat and empty when they came. I am reminded of this when I see the lonely streets, littered with paper, after public holidays in…Harlem. It was this feeling that I tried to express in my picture."[24]

A bit of populist indignation versus highbrow disdain from the Pittsburgh hoopla reached the art pages of *The San Francisco Chronicle*. Eminent art expert Alfred Frankenstein, who championed American trompe l'oeil masters William Harnett and John Frederick Peto in his 1953 groundbreaking study, was then serving as the newspaper's music and art critic. Reporting on some ill will between the elitists and the attending public, Frankenstein's column bore an ominous headline: "A Word of Warning – Take the Pittsburgh Art Show Slowly."

> *Some of the artists and collectors of Pittsburgh were a little rueful about the way in which their local press treated the Carnegie Institute's international exhibition of modern painting, which moved last week to the California Palace of the Legion of Honor. The Pittsburgh reviewers, I was told on a recent Eastern visit, stated their likes and dislikes with little elaboration or development, and a show full of color, vivacity,*

and the clash of ideas was therefore rather palely reflected.[25]

Frankenstein writes indecisively of those paintings in the American section, which he felt merited discussion "at a later time." His transparently anti-abstractionist stand was easily known: "It seems scarcely worthwhile in a piece like this to list the things one doesn't like, nor the things like Robert Motherwell's *Castille* and Franz Kline's *Leda*, which one does not understand."[26]

What did one of America's most respected authorities point to as the highlight of the show? "But I seem to have omitted mention of one of the most striking romantic-surrealist-anecdotes which the American section contains—*Holiday*, by Colleen Browning, a recent arrival from Ireland."[27]

NOTES

1. David Halberstam, *The Fifties* (New York: Fawcett Columbine, 1993), p. 116.

2. This and the preceding four quotations are all from Geoffrey Wagner, letter to Colleen Browning, January 1–2, 1949.

3. Geoffrey Wagner, letter to Colleen Browning, mid-April 1949.

4. Geoffrey Wagner, letter to Colleen Browning, May 16, 1949.

5. Geoffrey Wagner, letter to Colleen Browning, May 16, 1949.

6. Henry W. Clune, "She Can Cook, Too" ("Seen and Heard" society column), *The Rochester Democrat Chronicle*, December 8, 1949, p. 25.

7. Virginia Mecklenburg, *American Abstraction at Mid-Century*, exhibition catalogue. Smithsonian, Washington, DC, 2008, p. 17.

8. Russell Lynes, "Highbrow, Lowbrow, Middlebrow," *Harper's Magazine*, February 1949, pp. 19–28.

9. Ibid.

10. "Film 'Communists' Listed in FBI File in Coplon Spy Case – Denials Pour in from Those Accused: 'Absurd, Smear,' Un-American Tactics Seen," *The New York Times*, June 9, 1949, p. 1.

11. Congressman George A. Dondero, "Modern Art Shackled to Communism," speech, U.S. House of Representatives, August 16, 1949, published in the Congressional Record, First Session, 81st Congress; reproduced in Herschel B. Chipp, *Theories of Modern Art* (Berkeley: University of California Press, 1968), pp. 496–97.

12. Greta Berman and Jeffrey Wechsler, *Realism and Realities: The Other Side of American Painting 1940–1960*, New Brunswick, NJ, Rutgers University Art Gallery, 1981, p. 31.

13. Mark Stevens and Annalyn Swan, *De Kooning: An American Master* (New York: Alfred A. Knopf, 2004), pp. 361–365.

14. Geoffrey Wagner, *The Sands of Valor* (New York: Alfred. A. Knopf, 1967), p. 434.

15. Geoffrey Wagner, letter to Langley Browning, May 22, 1949.

16. Henry W. Clune, "She Can Cook, Too" ("Seen and Heard" society column), *The Rochester Democrat Chronicle*, December 8, 1949, p. 25.

17. Ibid.

18. Sidney Fields, "The Wagners: Harlem Without Tears" ("Only Human" column), *Daily Mirror*, March 27, 1953, p. 30.

19. Robert A. Orsi, *The Madonna of 115th Street: Faith and Community in Italian Harlem, 1880–1950* (New Haven: Yale University Press, 1985), p. xv.

20. "Great Migration: The African-American Exodus North," "Fresh Air," NPR radio interview, September 13, 2010. Isabel Wilkerson, a Pulitzer Prize-winning journalist, was discussing her book *The Warmth of Other Suns: The Epic Story of America's Great Migration* (New York: Random House, 2010).

21. Ralph Ellison, *Invisible Man* (New York: Random House, 1952), p. 5.

22. It is difficult to determine between these competing artists who first invented the "pavement graffiti"-type painting—only to say they each developed it into a productive series in their own voices. Browning might have seen Vickrey's paintings using the distinctive theme of a rueful youth lost within a field on a plunging plane of concrete pavement. Vickrey's *Hopscotch* and *The Edge of the Shadow*—with a child immersed in a sea of graffiti scribbles—were exhibited in December 1951 and discussed in *ARTnews* the same month. With remarkable clarity, 84-year-old Vickrey once recalled: "The first time I saw a painting with black children on the street by Colleen Browning was a painting called *Lenox and Mondrian*—which I thought was a very strong composition [reproduced in *TIME* magazine, January 28, 1952]." Robert Vickrey, phone interview with author, January 24, 2011.

23. "Public Ignores Abstract Art in Picking Winners at Show: Conservative Paintings Cop Top Prizes as Pittsburghers Disagree with Experts," *The Pittsburgh Post-Gazette*, December 9, 1952 (unpaginated; artist scrapbook clipping).

24. Paul A. Chew, "The Popular Prize," *Carnegie Magazine*, bulletin of the Carnegie Institute, Pittsburgh, PA, January 1953.

25. Alfred Frankenstein, "A Word of Warning – Take the Pittsburgh Art Show Slowly," *San Francisco Chronicle*, February 1, 1953 (unpaginated; artist scrapbook clipping).

26. Ibid.

27. Ibid.

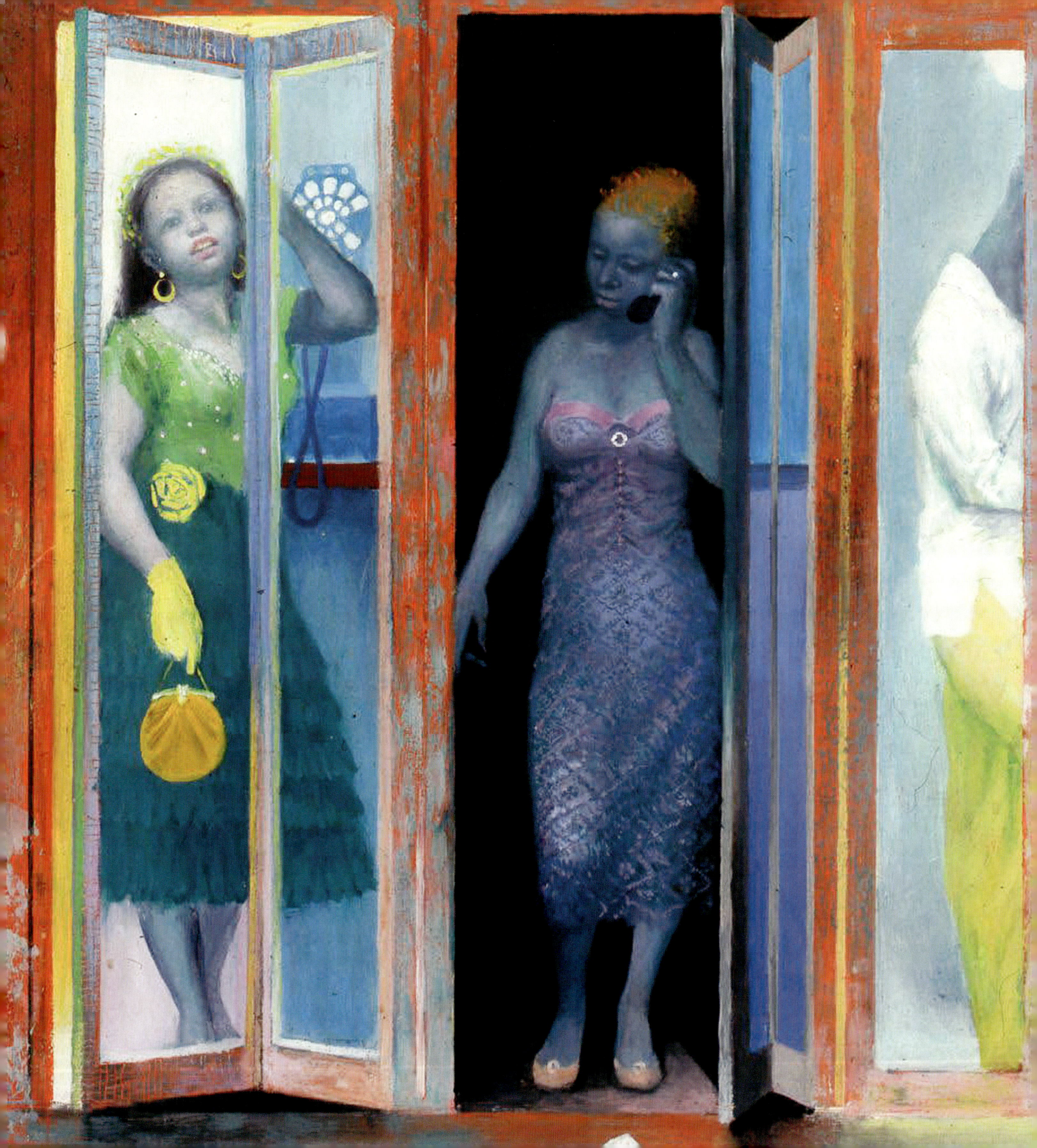

"…a painter with sharp eyes and a facile brush…"
—Unsigned review, *Newsweek*, January 28, 1952

"I am a recluse…"
—Colleen Browning, in "The Campus," *City College* newspaper,
March 26, 1965

Browning opened her premier New York exhibition at the Edwin Hewitt Gallery on East 69th Street in late January 1952. It was an ambitiously presented affair for a painter who had quickly surveyed and visually documented New York in the manner of a nineteenth-century artist-explorer documenting the Swiss Alps or volcanoes of South America. With an acute sense of perception and uncanny ability to translate her observations onto the canvas, Browning quickly earned attention.

Harlem was a uniquely American reality—a state of mind and picturesque subject that demanded visual investigation. Browning's painting *Jungle Gym* (current location unknown), a complicated labyrinth of steel bars imprisoning a daisy chain of street waifs, was purchased from that exhibition by the formidable tastemaker and ballet impresario, Lincoln Kirstein (1907–96).

Similar early Harlem paintings shown at her 1954 exhibition observed children entwined in back alleyways or playground mazes. *Between the Walls*, 1953 (fig. 6.1) and *See-Saw*, 1953 (fig. 6.2) developed this theme, always contrasting the innocence of youth against decaying surroundings. The characteristic motif in each painting is the placement of urban children in a restricted, usually narrowed vertical space.

Edwin Hewitt was a wealthy, well-connected gallerist ensconced in a coterie of homosexually oriented esthetes including W.H. Auden, Truman Capote, Tennessee Williams, George Platt Lynes, Pavel Tchelitchew, and Philip Johnson. This was a cosmopolitan, erudite charmed circle that exerted considerable cultural and literary influence and shared literary or artistic connections to the powerful Kirstein.

Browning found a sympathetic refuge for her figurative art that esteemed the human figure as an idealized form and the subject of carnal desire. An adoration for the

CHAPTER 6

The Enchantment of Magic Realism: Fame & Seclusion from "The Family of Man," 1953–1960

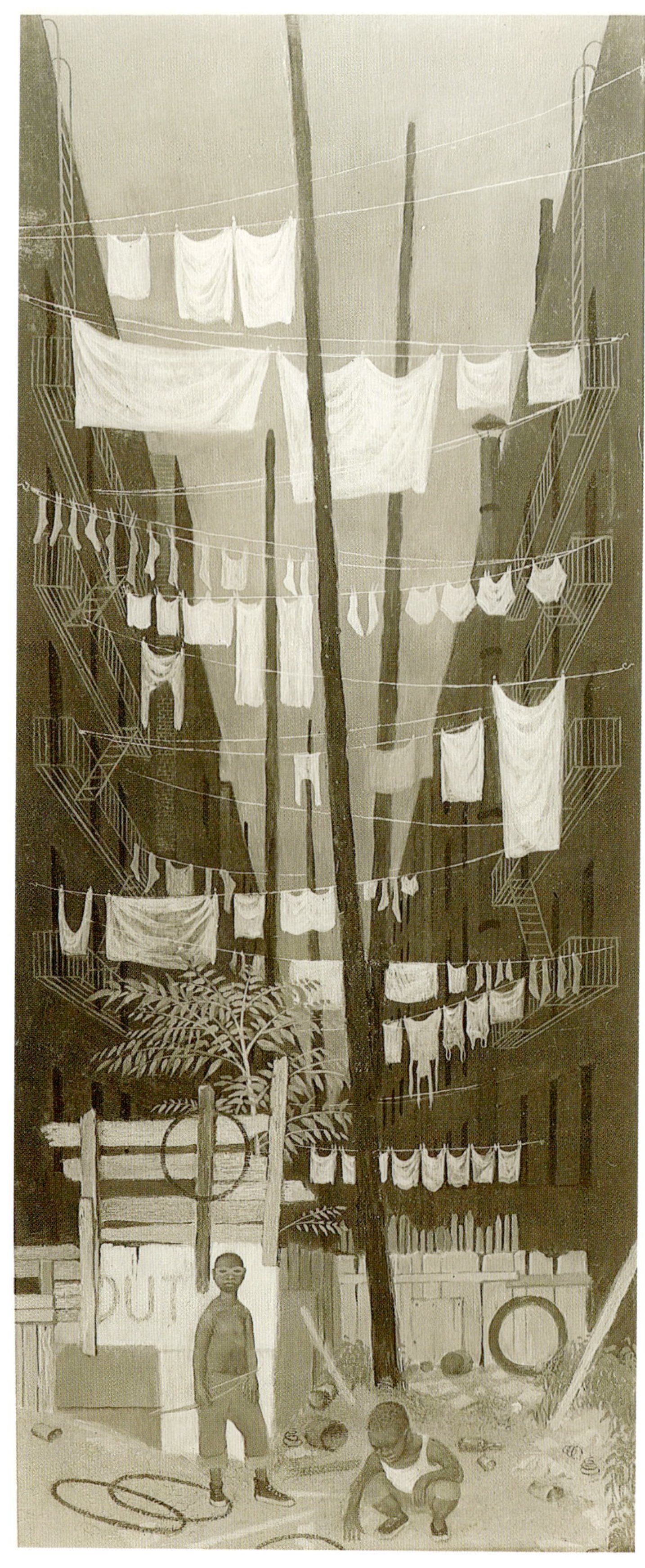

Fig. 6.1. Colleen Browning, Between the Walls, *1953. Photograph from artist's scrapbook.*

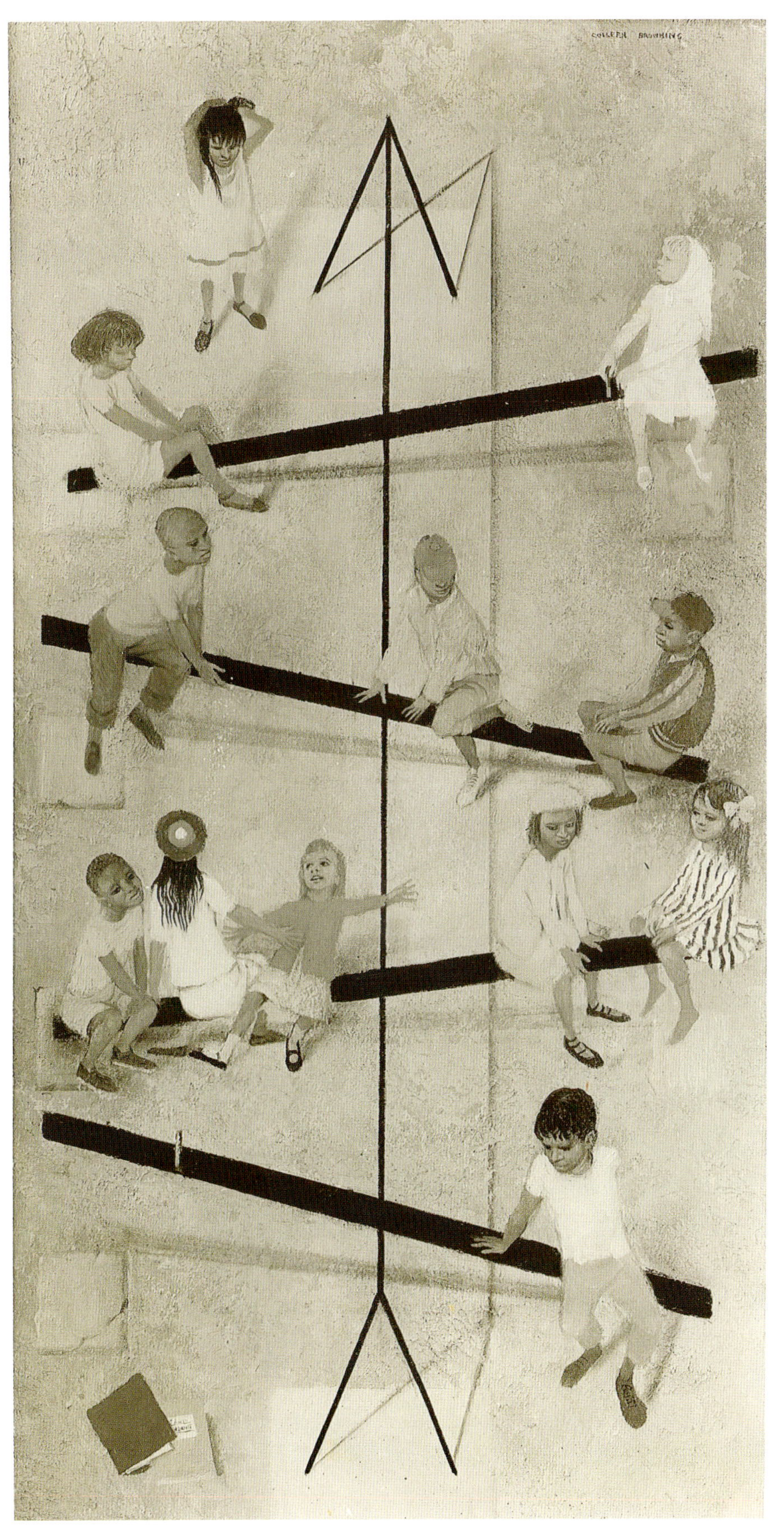

Fig. 6.2. Colleen Browning, See-Saw, 1953. Photograph from artist's scrapbook.

Apollonian model of the male nude and the living example of the Ballet Russes was transformed into Kirstein's New York City Ballet Company. Within this micro-universe of artists, authors, choreographers, and dancers, a tightly knit community of "underground" homosexuals made monumental contributions to the New York art world.

Of the multitudes of galleries in New York City, she slipped easily into the libertine, freethinking milieu of the Kirstein-Hewitt circle. Paul Cadmus, Jared French, and George Tooker—whose shows often followed Browning's on the exhibition calendar—frequented this venue. Robert Cozzolino, curator at the Pennsylvania Academy of the Fine Arts and co-author of a recent comprehensive book about Tooker, provides noteworthy insight into the undercurrents among Hewitt's artists.

> *Just as scholars have discussed the gendered, explicitly masculine discourse that accompanied abstract expressionism, it is possible to identify a sexualized undercurrent in the Kirstein and magic realist literature. Because many of the artists supported by the Hewitt Gallery were gay or bisexual, in-jokes and assumptions about the 'effete' implications of 1950s realist painting spread through the art world.*[1]

Unquestionably and instinctively, Browning's artistic training and theatrical background formed an intuitive sympathy for a Hellenic model and Platonic appreciation of homosexuality. Trained entirely in the manner and methods of Florentine art of the Quattrocento, her attention was focused upon the most noble traditions of Renaissance art in the *alla antica* style.

Browning certainly appreciated the coveted prestige of having one of her early Harlem paintings included in Kirstein's highly celebrated art collection. His legacy for cultural patronage placed him among the most eminent tastemakers of the twentieth century. An alacritous passion for the Russian ballet motivated his missionary role as the impresario for classical dance in America. Along with Harvard classmate Edward M.M. Warburg, he recruited George Balanchine in 1933 and established the School of American Ballet, which eventually evolved into the world-class New York City Ballet's creation in 1948.

Casting his refined tastes in support of the Magic Realists, Kirstein became this tiny movement's philosophical mentor, staunch advocate, and verbally pugilistic defender. After meeting Paul Cadmus at a Greenwich Village party in 1938 and being rejected as a potential lover, he eventually married the artist's sister, Fidelma Cadmus, in 1940. Kirstein's bisexuality was an openly known secret in circles of the art and ballet world.

His genius was found in the rather peripheral artists he promoted such as George Tooker and Jared French (who were both romantically linked to Paul Cadmus) plus Bernard Perlin, Edward Laning, Priscilla Warren Roberts, Robert Vickrey, and Andrew Wyeth. Each offered peculiarly hyper-realist imagery at the very moment when new avant-gardist painting was achieving a dominating position.

The underground nature of this restrained movement was noted by Jeffrey Wechsler in a 1985 cornerstone article, "Magic Realism: Defining the Indefinite." Noting that "Magic Realism has always been an elusive term," he pointed out that major scholarly resources such as the *Art Index* "never used magic realism as a subject heading."[2] Even more frustrating was the ambivalence or outright rejection of the term by a few of the artists counted among the group—including Colleen Browning—as no consensus of language could be negotiated. Considering their obsessive concern for van Eykian microscopic detail, some artists were not prepared to settle for the vagaries of language.

The Kirstein-Hewitt axis became the de facto launching pad for the marginalized Magic Realist movement. Only an esthete of his stature could confidently go mano a mano with the leading proponents for abstraction and action painting. By definition, Magic Realism, sometimes called the "Quiet Movement," was never to become a mainstream style. Its rarefied ideology was an almost Calvinist reaction to the art press's embrace for the novelties of abstractionism.

From this nascent exhibition, Kirstein organized his own special event at Hewitt's gallery in April 1950. "Symbolic Realism" became the avatar of Magic Realist theory, with Kirstein plunging headfirst into his dismissal of the current vogue of abstract painting: "This modest demonstration of American symbolic realism takes painting from an intellectual, more than an emotional or manual, profession and responsibility. It assumes the durable products of this art are expressions of ideas rather than of craft or the demonstrations of self-love or self-pity. It accepts painting as the triumph of the orderly, the intelligent and the achieved rather than as a victim of the decorative, the fragmentary of the improvised."[3]

Fire Escape II (fig. 6.3) was painted in 1953 and first exhibited at the Hewitt Gallery's solo show for Browning in January 1954. Its boxed and checkerboard patterning within a grid of horizontal and vertical lines responds to two organizational devices: theater design and the reality of tenement apartment blocks. Browning had transferred her London stage work into this slice of everyday life of a Harlem scene.

Instead of stage flats being lowered from the rafters, they outline delicate trellis-like forms of the wrought-iron fire escapes. Seizing upon the ubiquity of New York's grid design, the picture's theme hangs on the multi-tiered levels of the humble public housing structure. Browning's presciently sharp eye and theatrical sensibility focused on four juveniles who appear trapped within the cage. A similar scene was employed a few years later when the Broadway hit *West Side Story* opened in 1957. A fire-escape meeting of Tony and Maria is evocative of Shakespeare's balcony scene in *Romeo and Juliet*.

Browning had landed herself in one of New York's most prestigious galleries. *New York Times* art critic Stuart Preston offered a whiff of its significance: "The Edwin Hewitt Gallery presents a group show of paintings whose clear color and narrative emphasis pro-

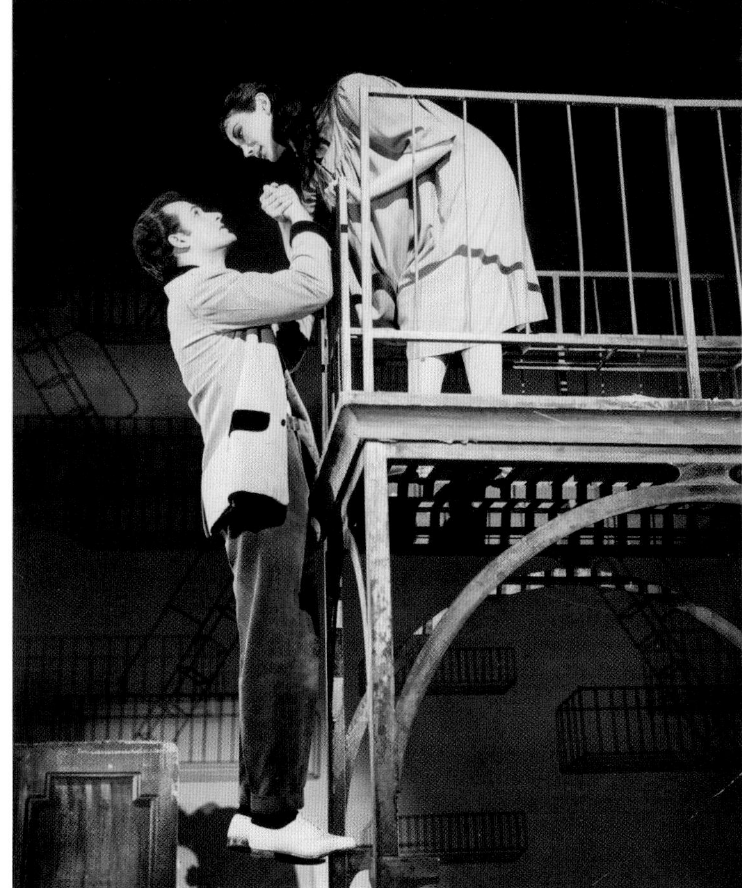

"Balcony Scene" from original Broadway production of West Side Story, *Museum of the City of New York.*

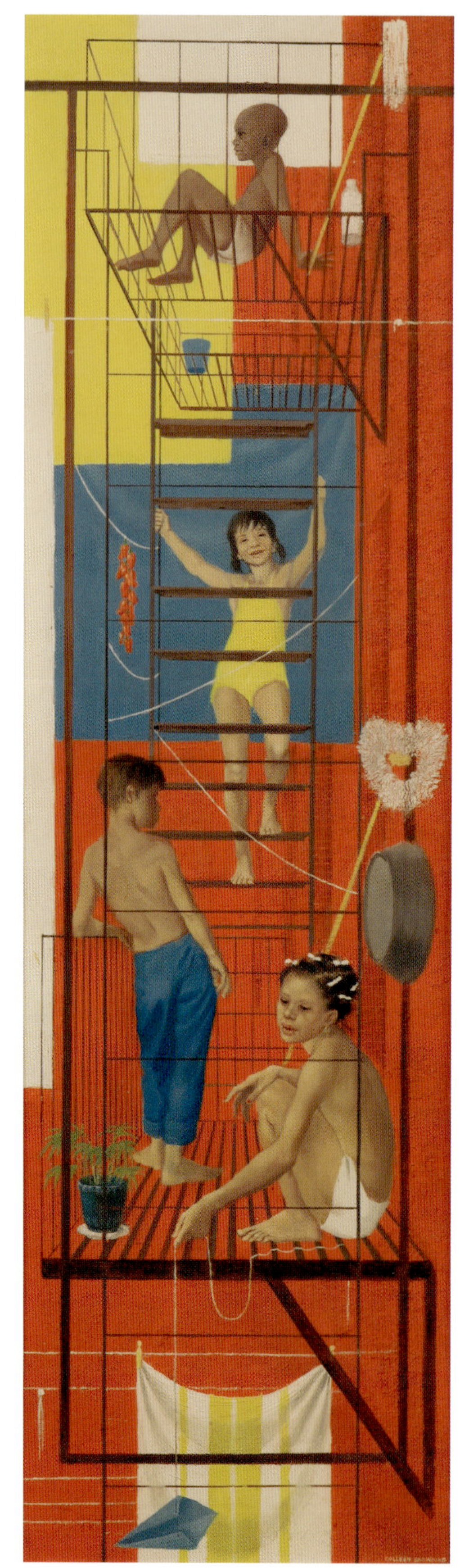

Fig. 6.3. Colleen Browning, Fire Escape II, *1953. Oil on linen canvas, 38¼ x 16½ inches. Collection of the Coleman Barkin Family.*

claim their allegiance to Magic Realism…Here is a delicate portrait of Lincoln Kirstein by Fidelma Cadmus; two paintings by George Tooker…and other work here, pleasantly in Colleen Browning's "Siesta I" and far from pleasantly in Jared French's "The Rope.""[4]

TIME magazine highlighted the recently arrived artist in her first triumphant review of her Hewitt exhibition: "Harlem has been painted more expertly, but seldom with more sympathy or with a quicker eye for vivid detail."[5] Especially noted was her unique ability to observe "children teeter-tottering dizzily up a perpendicular canvas. Another Browning trick: painting her Harlemites from above, so that the figures can be seen against a background of pavement and litter and sidewalk doodles."[6]

Newsweek resonated with equally admiring praise: "A painter with sharp eyes and a facile brush, Miss Browning might well have portrayed nothing but the bitter, poor and melancholy of the streets about her present home. In failing to be obsessed by these things she has painted with respect and responsibility towards mankind."[7]

Berman–Wechsler offers us insights from the artist about her all too overwhelming critical success. "Her first exhibition at the Hewitt Gallery generated an 'indecent' [Browning's words] amount of publicity. She had just begun to feel her strength as a painter when in 1952 full-page articles appeared about her in *Newsweek, Time* and other periodicals. She remembers this as 'too much, too soon'; she doubted and mistrusted the critics, ironically unable to paint for the next six months."[8]

> *Browning and her husband lived in Harlem during the '50s because it was cheap; they knew nothing about New York City's ghettoes. Like so many painters before her (Miller, Marsh, Laning, and Bishop come immediately to mind) she painted the people and the neighborhood around her. In this instance, that happened to be poor and black, usually subject matter indicative of a socially committed artist.*
>
> *To Browning however, it simply was visually appealing in form and spirit; had she lived in another neighborhood, she would have painted that. She particularly enjoyed painting children as 'fresh young things,' counterparts to urban decay. This has elicited much praise, but also some accusations of sentimentality—most of it unwarranted. She remembers that she 'did not particularly like children' and today sees them as possible self-portraits. Basically a loner, she knew few artists, and has never socialized much.*[9]

One might assume that Browning's rapport with these rope-skipping, chalk-drawing Harlem children extended to her interactions with their lives. But there is sparse evidence of her taking any personal interest in these street waifs or their impoverished families. From her bird's-eye view—a fourth-floor apartment looking down on the pavement—she observed these carefree ghetto kids at play. But we have no corroboration that she consciously felt an inner desire to actually engage these children by joining them at play or entertaining them with imaginary games.

"Humanitarian" themes dominated post–WW II figurative painting as an immediate response to the previous decade's apocalyptic events. In a "statement" published in 1953, a reactionary group of entrenched painters published *Reality: A Journal of Artists' Opinions*. A manifesto authored by Milton Avery, Philip Evergood, Joseph Hirsch, Edward Hopper, Jack Levine, Reginald Marsh, and others called for art that would express their "kinship and love for the human qualities in painting….All art is an expression of human expression."

Resisting abstraction as a form of "textural novelty," they aspired to "restore to art its freedom and dignity as a living language." This humanist current was widely viewed in Edward Steichen's *Family of Man* international photographic survey, first presented at The Museum of Modern Art in 1955. Paul Tillich, a giant of modern philosophy, penned the preface for MoMA's 1959 exhibition *New Images of Man*, apologizing for the newly demoted role of classical figuration. "The image of man became transformed, distorted, disrupted and it finally disappeared in recent art…[The artists shown] want to regain the image of man in their paintings and sculptures, but they are too honest to turn back to earlier naturalistic or idealistic forms…"[10]

Summing up her career in her preface for the Southern Alleghenies Museum of Art's retrospective catalogue (1997), Browning stated: "My interest has always been the human condition and the world around me, and the magic that can occasionally inform it; I hope that these images can sometimes touch on universal archetypes, so that there is a direct understanding between viewer and artist."[11]

Paradoxically, her engagement with the "human condition" was usually at arm's length. She was of the time and place when figurative art drew its raison d'etre from its sympathetic concern for the "family of man." Innocent children, indigenous mothers nursing babes in arms, or entrapped passengers peering out from subway windows are too often reduced to situational props in a visual field. Constantly exploring exotic locations, she often painted natives in Corsica, Morocco, Ecuador, or Mexico. Each place offered a visual opportunity to examine these "universal archetypes" while she elected to remain at a safe distance from the human condition surrounding each situation.

At a comfortable distance, she converted their plight into arresting compositions. An unresolved tension questions the emotional engagement between the artist's eremitical personality and the interior lives of her human subjects. Browning's annoyance, intolerance, and sometimes openly expressed disengagement with individuals who comprised the human condition are unavoidably the Achilles heel of her art. She was a figurative master who reduced some of her models to studio props.

To some degree, Browning's art is intellectually accessible, but one wonders about its ability to mirror her own soul. For instance: how much of herself was made visible on the canvas? "Portrait of the Young Artist Depicts a Prodigy and a Hermit" headlined a flattering story in the City College newspaper, *The Campus*, on March 26, 1965. The story announces Browning's forthcoming exhibition at 57th Street's Jacques Seligmann Galleries. "Mrs. Colleen Wagner (Art) paints under her maiden name of Browning. She is a 'born hermit' who does not want any part of the limelight her artistic achievements have won her. 'I'm a recluse who hates parties and nightclubs,' she says adding, 'I don't have a telephone, television or car.' Despite all the fame, Mrs. Wagner thinks of herself as a person who tries to avoid other people. She only likes deserted beaches and becomes 'intensely annoyed with 300 other people around swimming and waterskiing.'"

In an endearing personal letter to Ben and Shirley Barkin, among her most avid collectors, she wrote about an extended trip in 1986 to South America, visiting Chile, Argentina, Brazil, and the breathtaking Iguassu Falls. Now at their home in Grenada, she admitted her pleasure in "living the life of a total recluse. I never go out socially at all, just swim three times a day, paint, garden and cook." For an artist of such unimpeachable skills, boundless energy, and undistracted devotion to her work, one questions what limitations impeded her rise to the highest plateau of American art. That emotional distance between observer and subject might have been a thread too overstretched.

This prompts us to ponder: where is the true Colleen Browning? United with the camouflaged patterns in her landscapes, posed figures, or still-life arrangements, her own presence is artfully disguised. Once penetrated, one can surmise there is a deeply self-engaged narcissism that left very little concern, save for an endearing, self-gratifying obsession for her husband. Her brother Shane, seven years younger, and his son Rory (born in 1957) were entirely overlooked.

This characteristic ambiguity, painting a rather idealized portrait of her biological age or genealogical origins, reveals her cloaked representation of self-hood with peek-a-boo opacity. As a creative image-maker, Browning was a watchful observer—ever conscious of when, where, and how she would disclose or obscure her own presence.

Perhaps focused on a need for professional validation, she lost track of the human family—her own and the mass of humanity in the abstract—which was the central theme of her field of vision. The real was artfully dismissed as she chose to slip conveniently into states of romantic fantasy, and the dreamy realms of fables beyond. Invention, fabrication, and things imaginary were far more appealing than the dreadfully banal details of human existence.

Enchantment was sparked by her incantation of things seen and imagined. Sorcery often morphed into art. And she developed into the enchantress that transformed the invisible into the visible, but always behind the veil. As stylistic labeling and naming is an imperfect craft, we come to appreciate and understand Browning as a gifted magician. Eventually she would be loosely associated with the tail end of narrative artists who adopted mundane contexts for surrealistic fantasies. That ambiguous boundary between the known and the invented was a stylistic territory called New Objectivity, or Symbolic or Magic Realism.

Taking bearings of the longitude and latitude of Browning's artistic navigation, one comes to appreciate that she rarely drifted off course. She was steady at the helm as a realist practitioner who fully commanded her assets as a deftly equipped inventor of deceptive images. Interestingly, her work began in the 1940s with direct academic realism and then briefly flirted with Freudian-inspired Surrealism.

Arriving in the States, she surveyed the leading American realists, joining the Magic Realist mode in the 1950s. By the 1970s and toward the later stages of her career, Browning continually adapted to shifting attitudes in subject and themes. Overall, it was a highly diversified portfolio; each decade witnessed her expansion into the demands of each decade's successive styles as realism continuously unfolded. Her life achievement is nothing less than a prolific conglomeration of artistic production. In this densely seeded forest with many varieties of constantly growing plants, Browning's self was intertwined within each twig, branch, and leaf.

Enlisting this indiscernible air, Browning was perfectly in step with the painterly advances of her time. An increasingly mystery-laden content comes to dominate postwar-era painting as hallucinatory Surrealism moved toward mundane, magically inspired quotidian reality. Marlene Dietrich once said, "I envy Greta Garbo because mystery is a woman's greatest charm. I wish I could be mysterious like her." And Browning's strength was in maintaining an inscrutable veil of evasiveness.

Optically, her compositions playfully exposed the deceptive nature of invented imagery. In doing so, she relied upon her lifelong ability to conjure up magical apparitions. Her natural instincts as a chimerical personality flowed through her beguiling artworks, joining the recognizable with the invented.

Like many of the other twentieth-century European artists, Browning crossed the Atlantic into unknown places and uncertain new modes of expression. Leaving everything behind—a loving family and supportive art school friends—she had set out, starry eyed, to begin an unpredictable new life amidst totally unfamiliar environs.

And it was here in New York City—the great capital city of finance, commerce, and art—that a new form of artistic expression was about to explode. Doing her best to firmly establish her artistic reputation, Browning could not have predicted her American passage would be so tenuously timed. She possessed a strong character with unfailing determination on that bright morning when London's newspapers auspiciously witnessed her departure as she sailed forward. Unbeknownst to her, Browning's maiden voyage to the U.S. occurred simultaneously with a transitional moment in the twentieth-century art world. Competing with tangled skeins of paint from Pollock's sticks and hardware store paint brushes, the slashing calligraphic splashes found in Motherwell's monumental canvases, and Rothko's pulsating clouds of indescribable hues, Browning found herself in the eye of the hurricane.

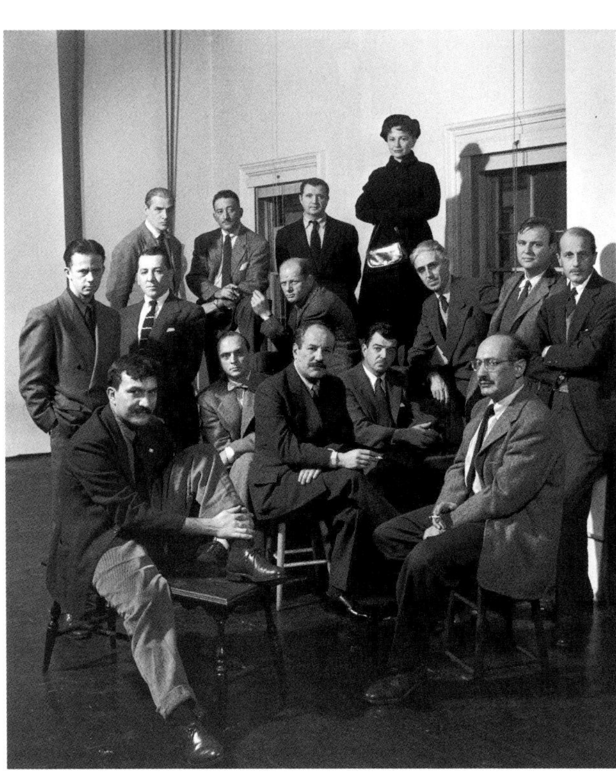

Fig. 6.4. "The Irascibles," 1950. Nina Leen, Time & Life Pictures / Getty Images.

The heavily male-dominated, machismo downtown world of the Abstract Expressionists was photographed by Nina Leen. *Life* published "The Irascibles" (fig. 6.4) on January 15, 1951 (the first winter Browning lived in New York) as part of an article about the group of prominent abstract artists who bitterly protested conservative policies at The Metropolitan Museum of Art. Among the 18 leading-edge modernists of the day captured in the image—including Jackson Pollock, Willem de Kooning, Mark Rothko, Barnett Newman, Clyfford Still, and Adolph Gottlieb—only one female, Romanian born Hedda Sterne, was included.

At a downtown New Year's party attended by a motley swarm of artists, intellectuals, and critics, the end of the decade that saw unimaginable global destruction, genocide, and the unleashing of atomic weapons was cause for raucous celebration. Philip Pavia, an avant-gardist sculptor who worked in France in the 1930s, raised his glass on the night of December 31, 1949 to exclaim: "The first half of the century had belonged to Paris, but the second will be claimed by New York!"

For Colleen Browning, the next half of the century would confirm an artistic rise and fall—and certain resurrection. In retrospect, we can now see some awkward, even embarrassing, moments when she was overtaken with ambition—and Wagner was an accomplice in their overreaching.

The publication of Wagner's spring 1954 article, a snappy, whip-lashing critique about the currents of American art in *The Antioch Review,* might very possibly have been forgotten. The journal was established in 1941 by a collegial group of faculty members at Ohio's Antioch College and became an open forum for social commentary, literary criticism, and philosophy. In the 1950s, contributors included Daniel Bell, James T. Farrell, and Sylvia Plath. *The Review* identified Professor Wagner as the translator of a new edition of the poetry of Baudelaire and an infrequent essayist for *The Manchester Guardian*, *The New Statesman and Nation*, and *The Spectator.*

As British subjects, years before declaring their American citizenship, Browning and Wagner must have felt some degree of alienation from the mainstream. Perhaps it was this safe sense of distance that created a false sense of security. What possible quixotic motive could have compelled Wagner to raise his lance to a towering windmill in his attempt to de-throne America's reigning art guru, Harold Rosenberg? Along with the more philosophically bent Clement Greenberg (1909–1994), the Rosenberg-Greenberg axis was an unassailable fortress of highbrow culture.

Rosenberg (1906–1978) was Abstract Expressionism's most avid proponent, hailing the postwar breakout as "the most vigorous and original movement in art in the history of this nation."[12] It was his seminal 1952 article in *ARTnews* that gave birth to the term "action painting." This essay was adapted as a virtual manifesto for the transcendence of abstract faith. Generations of readers savored every word of his uncommon sagacity in his closely read critiques published in *The New Yorker* as well as his essential books.

Presuming he was shielded, Wagner ensnared himself in a critical minefield with the publication of his article in *The Antioch Review* titled "The New American Painting." If a wantonly cocky Wagner was looking to pick a fight, he chose the biggest target imaginable. He would escape somewhat bruised from this intellectual kerfuffle. Whether out of heedless arrogance or virtuous, outspoken courage, Wagner pulled the emergency cord to instigate an academic train wreck. Without considering the ramifications of such a rash and ill-considered verbal attack, the outcome must have severely damaged his reputation among New York's insular community of academic highbrows.

He might have simply admitted that the article was cast under Cupid's spell and said his motive was an irrational act of love. Shakespeare's admonition from *A Midsummer Night's Dream* is apropos: "Lord, what fools these mortals be!" Only a brilliantly gifted, silver tongued, outrageously assertive, and recently minted doctoral fellow could have exhibited such self-inflicting harm.

In his preamble to the spring volume, editor Freeman Champney proudly proclaimed the historic mission of *The Review* as "one of its basic purposes, the building of bridges of understanding between layman and specialist…it is vital for a democratic society to maintain a broadly-based interchange of learning, opinion, and interpretation. In Mr. Wagner's article on modern art…cut through the tight little enclosures which tend to make private property of what should be the open range. This comes close to being the moral core of democratic society."[13] Regrettably, that mission was undermined in Wagner's subversive use of *The Review*'s pages.

Beginning in a jocular mood, Wagner describes a recent cartoon of a studio art class in *The New Yorker*. Choosing that perfectly highbrow publication assured his readers that he too was fluent in intellectual banter, and they would not have to endure oafish comments about so-called modernist art from a philistine.

The cartoon shows a classical life model posing; "all but one" student deviated from the cubistic "distortions," according to Wagner. The joke concludes when the studio instructor leans over to the only competent figurative realist among the group and laments: "I'm afraid you have a long way to go." With that segue, Wagner began his 88-howitzer denunciation of the "drip, splash, gouge, spray or rub-a-dub school" comprising American art of the day: the "action" painters. Tongue-lashing Harold Rosenberg, the inventor of the term "action painting," Wagner decried it as a "religious movement."

Revealing his own distrust of popular American tastes, he wrote with considerable condescension: "The general public in America, of course, often sees this painting as advanced, being as it is so far removed from recognizable reality…These humorless [art] articles, that appear with such doctrinaire regularity in the pages of Art news, [ironically, where Browning's exhibitions would be praised in future issues] would not be worth worrying about, even for their obvious efforts to hustle museums into acquisition of 'action' painting…I mean they are diagnostic of an uncivilized condition. It is odd, is it not, that there is so little 'action' art in Europe today?"[14]

Meandering toward his concluding remarks, Wagner then went beyond a mere questionable error in judgment. He veered off his assignment into defamatory references to Browning's closest competitors actively showing in competing galleries in New York.

"It is indeed significant that it is the emptiest and most banal realists (like Vickrey, Steumpfig, or Sharrer, their figures more limply cavorting each season) who are taken seriously by the Art news dogmatists."[15] Assuming the identity of a truly objective, independent arts reviewer, he then spread his calumnious remarks with slanted recommendations of worthwhile galleries: "The Durlacher Gallery knows something about painting, as does the Edwin Hewitt Gallery, and here alone we may find the formal and the assured, rather than the fragmentary and unfinished, the pseudo-spontaneous. We may even find in such galleries as these that compromising emotion, joy and authentic emotion after all."[16]

There is an unsettling realization that Professor Wagner used his typewriter so questionably to promote his wife's career in the unsuspecting pages of *The Antioch Review*. Against the entire panoply of American art, and considering the countless deserving artists he might have submitted to bolster his argument, he then asserts: "For have we not reached some fantastic critical conceit when a good realist like Colleen Browning has to apologize for presenting beauty? 'I have enjoyed the last years very much,' she is quoted by *Newsweek*…as saying, 'and I'm afraid it shows through.'"[17] Two pages later he lands yet another punch, this time pleading about Browning's unjust rejection from a recent grant competition. "The Tiffany Foundation has recently rejected Honore Sharrer, George Tooker, and Colleen Browning, three young realists under thirty with a considerable record of national and international exhibition, in favor of doctrinaire abstractionists."[18]

Harold Rosenberg, an intellectual titan of his age, did not take kindly to the junior professor's acerbic comments. In the next issue of this respectable journal, Rosenberg replied: "Dr. Wagner's main point about The New American Painting is that there isn't any. It's all a big hoax put on by Art news, Henry Luce, Look, Sam Kootz, Clem Greenberg, and me…. Roughneckism aside, balance, new or restored, demands that he honor, if not his self-selected opponents, at least his readers with an honest account of his subjects."[19]

Rosenberg enumerates three areas of "distortions and falsifications Dr. Wagner uses to support his arguments" and wonders if the "Humanism he wields as a brickbat has to do with humanity or human values….[his article] seem to me in the present atmosphere much more malevolent."[20]

But, "all's fair in love and war"[21] and after all, art criticism is never more than subjective, well-informed opinion. Occasionally, when erring in its mission, it may become biased by personal affections for the artist under discussion. But when the author inserted personal favoritism by proselytizing into the text of his critique, the curtain was lifted and the veil of objective scholarly discourse was shredded. More than half a century later, this could have been forgotten, had it not been discovered in one of America's most distinguished academic journals.

Surely the editorial committee at *The Antioch Review* was hoodwinked in this escapade. Exploiting an academic journal's neutral pages for the advancement of a family member was egregious. We shall never fully understand what act of undying love or misguided compulsion overtook Wagner. This desultory exchange is an enigmatic episode that tarnishes an otherwise sterling academic reputation.

But the sardonic tone and dismissive attitudes toward abstract painting continued a few years later in the British publication *Truth*. Wagner blew another full thrust of steam through his nostrils in this Tory publication's October 4, 1957 issue. Its editorial described the Labour Party's liberal policies as "disgraceful" and a "blaze of irresponsibility."[22] Feeling even greater encouragement to satirize American art, he wrote to his conservative sympathizers a caustic putdown. Without naming Browning, he tips his hat to her: "And the fact is that some very fine painting is being done in America today… the American genius is a fairly realistic affair, applying itself to the natural world rather than theorizing it."[23]

Titled "Slashing and Sloshing," he demonizes the "late Jack the Dripper Pollock" by pointing out that "non-figurative abstraction is the vogue, the academy, in America today and commands most space in the national salons and slick magazines alike…What Pollock & Co. Inc. did was to develop the art of the flat surface…Pollock groped his way, slashing and sloshing, towards a very small metaphysical radius of recession in the picture…. This, then, has been a hit-or-miss school and it has undoubtedly produced some of the worst painting ever seen in the history of the world."[24]

Such a lame defense or unwarranted attack was actually unnecessary. Browning began to hit her stride in the late 1950s. The sweet fruits of success began arriving in a cornucopia of delicious prizes, awards, and professional distinctions. She was now a formidable force. Respected by her peers, adored by her students at City College—where she had taken on an adjunct teaching position—and always desired by an expanding circle of discerning collectors, she had attained all the hallmarks of a well-honed reputation.

Browning was now a known entity within the entrenched Realist camp of the New York art scene by the 1970s. Well represented by the "blue-chip" Kennedy Galleries, her unpredictable and always evolving subjects were selected for exhibitions at prominent institutions. Although never quite arriving at the level of a household name to the degree that other female artists trained in her era came to enjoy, such as Isabel Bishop, Louise Bourgeois, Helen Frankenthaler, Lee Krasner, Georgia O'Keeffe, or Alice Neel, Browning had etched out an enviable niche. She was exhibited throughout the nation in some of the most prestigious events at the Carnegie Institute in Pittsburgh; The Butler Institute of American Art in Youngstown, Ohio; Stanford University; Pennsylvania Academy of the Fine Arts; Detroit Institute of Arts; the University of Illinois at Urbana; and the Walker Art Center, Milwaukee.

Appearing in competitive shows around the country, Browning earned best-in-show awards and purchase prizes, thus gaining entry into leading museums. Curators were now selecting her works as acquisitions for the permanent collections at many of the nation's most respected regional art museums. Although she could never be fully satisfied, Browning kept striving for greater visibility. She was relentlessly self-promoting, believing firmly in her artistic vision.

She participated in a group show organized by the American Federation of Arts staged at New York's Museum of Modern Art (1968); *Twelve American Realists* at The Cleveland Museum of Art (1975); *Painting Today* at the Indianapolis Museum of Art (1976); and *Contemporary Landscape Painting* at the Philbrook Museum of Art, Tulsa (1977).

Compelling evidence of her prominence was John Canaday's selection of *Telephones* (1954) (fig. 6.5) for a big pictorial splash on April 19, 1964, titled "The People of Our Town" for the Sunday *New York Times Magazine*, a special supplementary guide to the 1964 World's Fair. An elite group of artists were selected as representative for this global invitation, and *Telephones* was prominently featured. Canaday wrote:

> *Part confessional and part coffin, the communication chamber of the telephone booth is New York's closest approach to a common denominator uniting Harlem with Park Avenue, the Battery with Bronx, in a network of wire that has become as basic to existence as the food New Yorkers eat or the air, such as it is, that they breathe.*[25]

With its combination of glass-enclosed phone-booth stalls and insouciantly posed Harlem residents, *Telephones* signaled the feel and look of a now bygone era. Seven figures flow in a frieze-like pattern across the rectilinear picture plane. The gentle curves of each figure play against the geometrical frame.

The rather extended rectangular proportions—14" x 32"—were intentionally scaled. They became a key hallmark of Browning's pictorial design. She explained, "Meanwhile, a purely formal problem I enjoy working out is that of balance and imbalance—dividing a picturing in half down the middle and relating the two sides so that it reads as one—or again, weighting a picture down at one end, and so on."[26]

The elasticized, undulating black characters in *Telephones* are among the finest mannered figures of American art in the 1950s. These random figures are imprisoned momentarily for the duration of their three-minute phone calls—or before they need

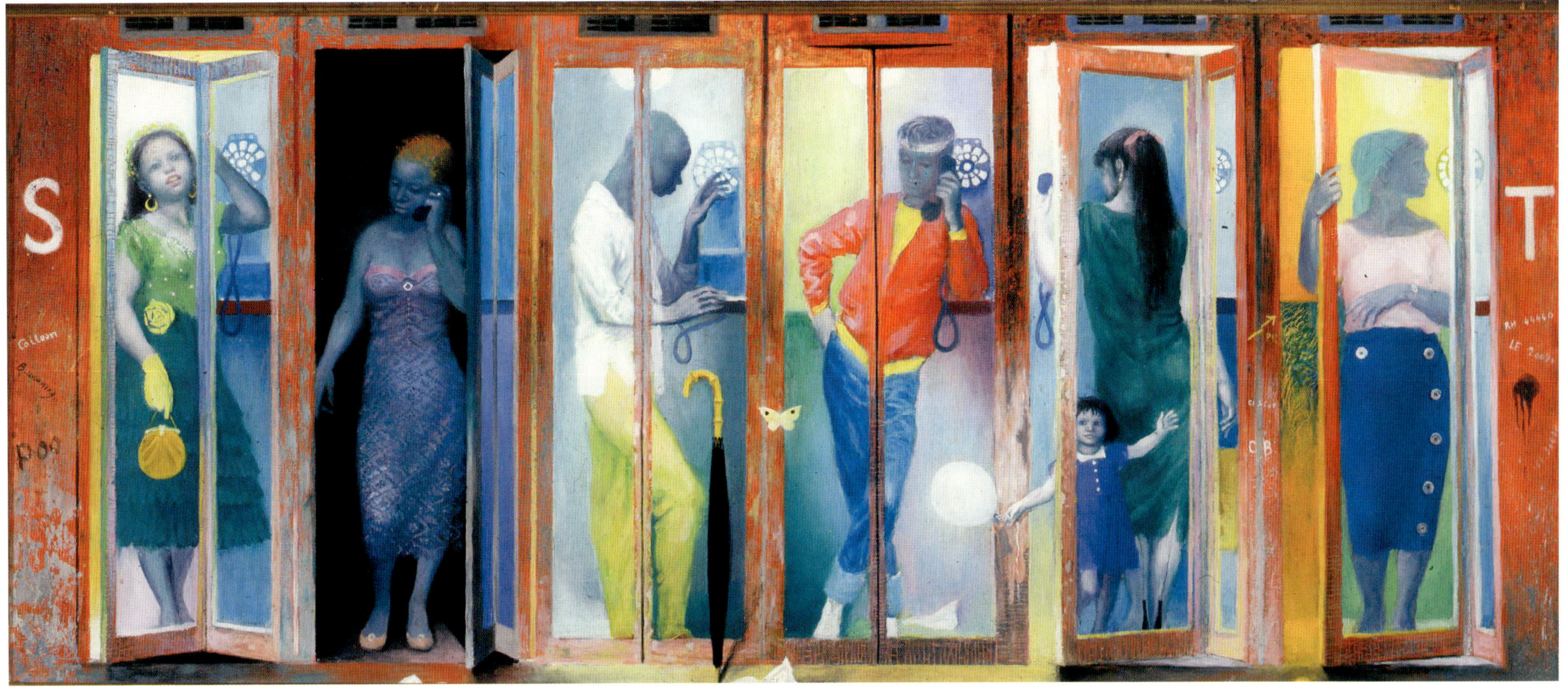

another coin to continue their conversations! Browning confined each form into its almost perfectly realized rhythmical cadence. The jazzy pulse in this painting sways to its internalized syncopation. It is arguably a mid-century masterpiece that fuses time, place, and local observation.

Drawing a direct comparison to George Tooker's parallel approach at this time, one astute critic, Meyer Levin, writing for the *National Weekly*'s pictorial of March 25, 1973, suggested the common pose of a female against the grid of a windowpane. "Tooker's girl shared with Colleen Browning's girl something of that mysterious musing suggested by all girls at windows. Both paintings have the evocative quality of magic realism, an evocation abetted by our general psychological response to the 'mystery of life' behind a glimpsed situation."

We can validate these assertions by enumerating a small selection of national exhibitions and awards. Included five times in the premiere event for all living American painters—the Whitney Museum of American Art's closely watched Annuals (1951, '56, '57, and '63)—Browning had achieved a visible presence. Making the Whitney's cut was akin to being placed on the Olympic team in that era. Just being admitted into the show was enough evidence of her artistic habitation in this most demanding field of competing talents with New York's most rarefied curatorial judges.

"The show began in 1918 as the Annual designed to provide attention and encouragement to neglected American artists when European art was all that mattered…. In the fifties…American art finally lost its peripheral status. Instead of a shining light in a

Fig. 6.5. Colleen Browning, Telephones, *1954. Oil on plywood, 13¾ x 32 inches. The Butler Institute of American Art, Youngstown, OH. Museum purchase, 1955.*

forgotten corner, the exhibit became a beacon. What fresh look was America giving the world?" commented *New York* magazine's Mark Stevens of its now hallowed history.[27]

Indicative of her increasing presence was a full-tilt feature in the February 1957 issue of *American Artist*. "Happily, in the present instance, we found Colleen Browning as clear in her expression as the pictures she paints. In fact the character of the work, its fundamental design and its creative order, is patently consistent with the personality of the artist. To reveal exactly how ordered her mind is and to show that an artist can be objective about her work without recourse to esoterics…"[28]

Increasingly recognized throughout the 1950s, Browning had gained a solid foothold on the American scene and established her own distinctive painterly voice. An identifiable style emerged within the framework of a tightly organized space, usually rectangular in design, with figures strategically inserted into compositions, such as a peasant cottage on Ibiza, Spain, or along a series of storefronts in East Harlem.

Mother and Child, 1952 (fig. 6.6), originally purchased by the San Francisco Palace of the Legion of Honor for its permanent collection, is an exquisitely rendered composition. This deftly arranged picture marks an increased maturity. It was executed on location during the Wagners' summer holiday in 1952 on Ibiza. The arrangement moves away from her cinematic space toward an intensified vision of painterly precision.

Fig. 6.6. Colleen Browning, Mother and Child, *1952. Oil on canvas mounted on panel, 11⅞ x 24¼ inches. Private collection.*

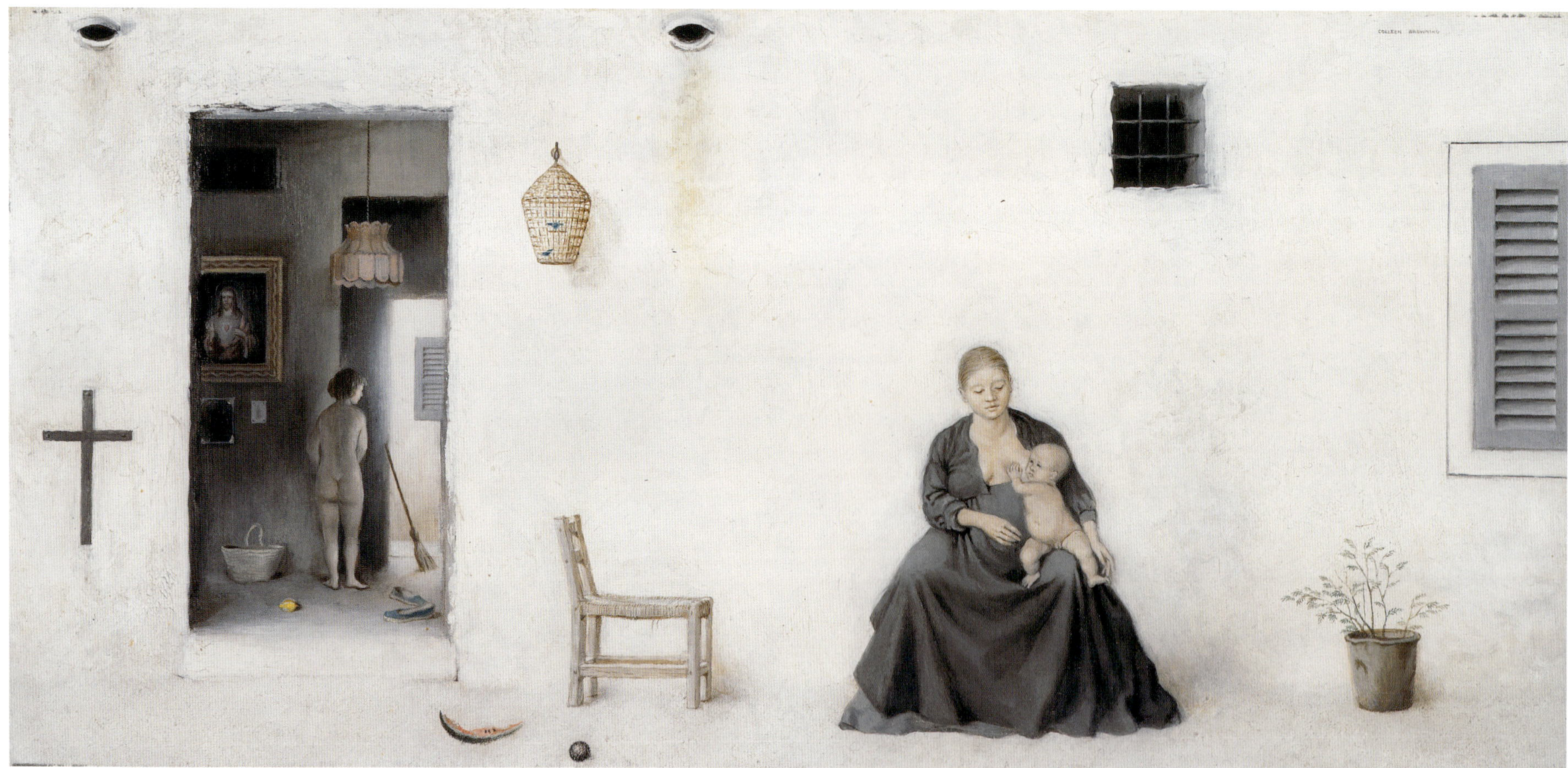

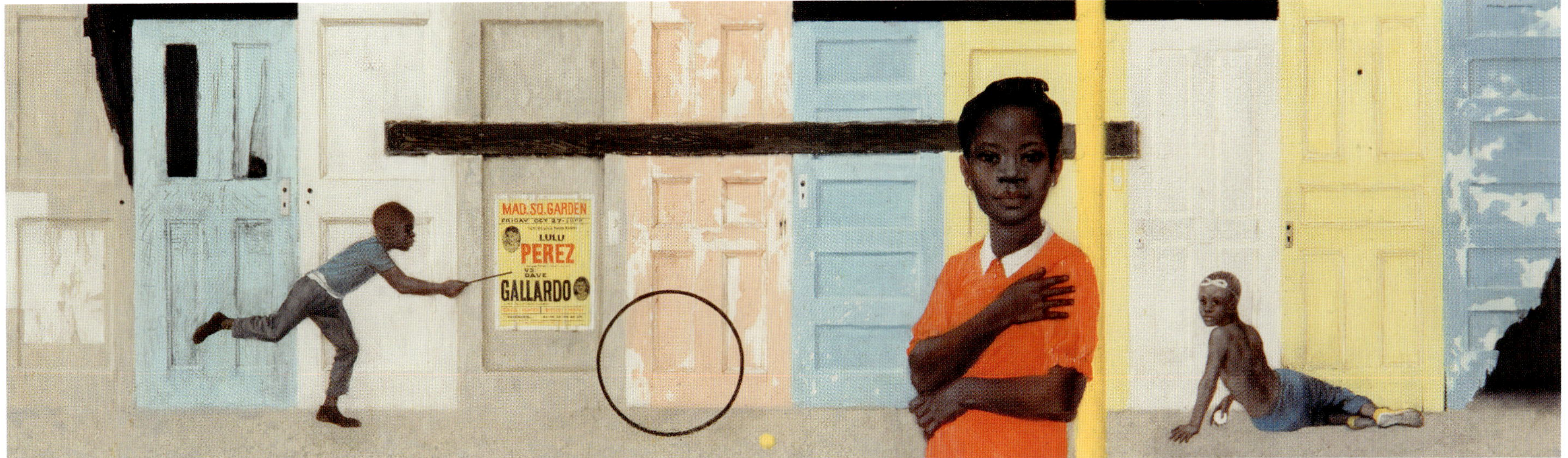

Spartan organizational geometry positions a mother and child in the foreground with allegorical elements of a cross, fruit of the vine, and an iconic portrait of Jesus Christ in the background. Enigmatically, a female nude is depicted within the cool interior, creating a soft contrast from the white stucco exterior. Only a scenographic painter could possess such a wonderful ability to paint a trompe l'oeil of the flaking stucco wall's surface.

Closer examination reveals microscopically detailed porous cracks and crevices in the wall, executed with a Vermeer-like degree of realism. Her signature in the upper right is painted in a brushstroke no thicker than one strand of sable hair, a conceit learned from early Dutch painting. Even the rainspout is meticulously depicted with a textured quality, imitating its worn surface abrasions. Beyond painting local color, Browning transcended time and space, extending subtle symbolism of the Virgin and Child into a hot, lazy summer afternoon on a Mediterranean island.

Other key paintings of her Harlem period are *Door Street* (fig. 6.7), circa 1953, in the collection of the Milwaukee Art Museum and *East Harlem Street Scene* (fig. 6.8), 1953, recently purchased and restored by a private collector. Both images respond to the successive frames of windows, doors, and right-angled spatial geometry of Harlem's sidewalks and streets (fig. 6.9 photo). The former is a closer view of three black youths cast in a frieze-like relief across a set of wooden doors. Pieces of the doorframes are torn, broken, or splintered off— indicating the fragmentation of these ghetto youths on the margins of American society. In its internalized patterns and flowing multigenerational depiction of Harlem residents, the *East Harlem Street Scene* casts her roving eye across a stage-like intersection carved out of a deeply recessed crossing of two city streets. Her fully embraced American palette is now gauged toward the strong primary colors of red, yellow, and blue; she has taken her clues from street signage and cheaply painted exteriors.

A stream of semiotic messages is spelled out with word fragments: "beauty – Soda – Lunch – dentist – fish – Universal – Canaan." The barbershop's traditional red-white-blue is contrasted with the circular and horizontal typography of Coca-Cola. Fabric dyes

Fig. 6.7. Colleen Browning, Door Street, *c. 1953. Oil on canvas, 11½ x 36½ inches. Milwaukee Art Museum. Gift of Mrs. Harry Lynde Bradley. M1966.150.*

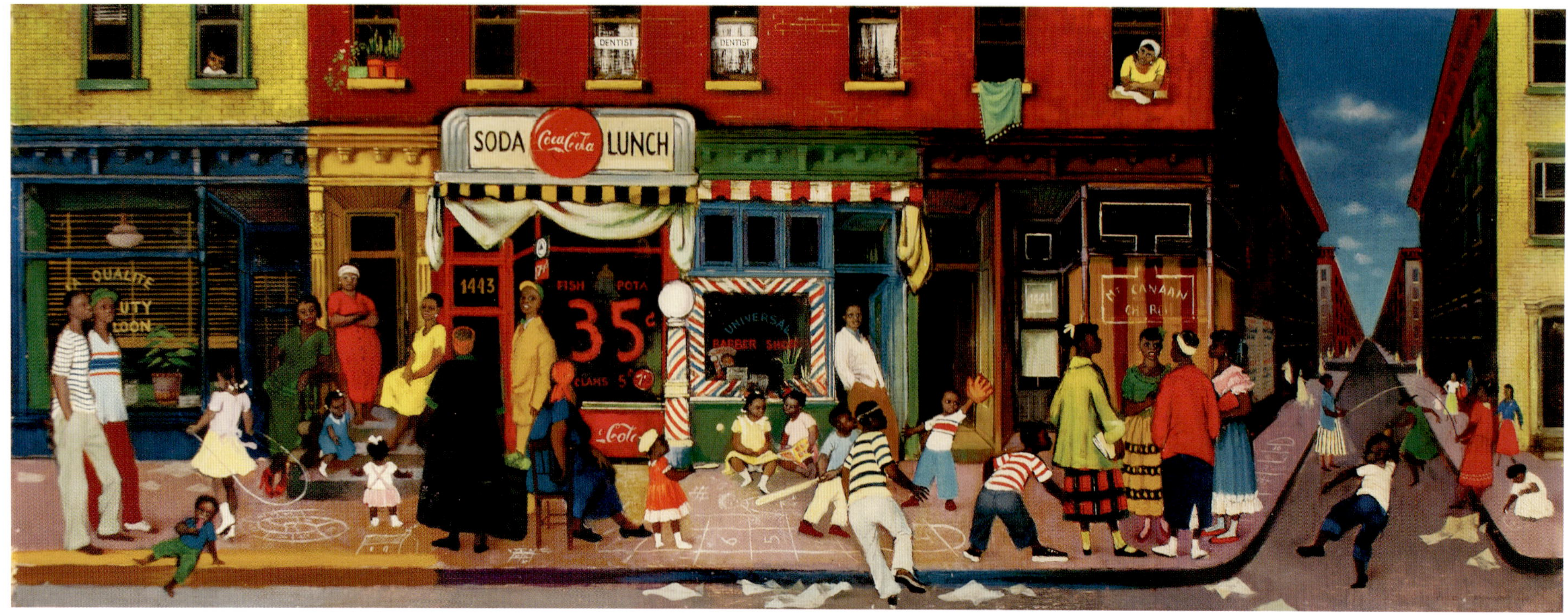

Fig. 6.8. Colleen Browning, East Harlem Street Scene, 1953. Oil unvarnished on board, 15½ x 40 inches. Private collection.

Fig. 6.9. "Children Playing in Fire Hydrant Water," c. 1938. © Photo collection Alexander Alland, Sr. / Corbis.

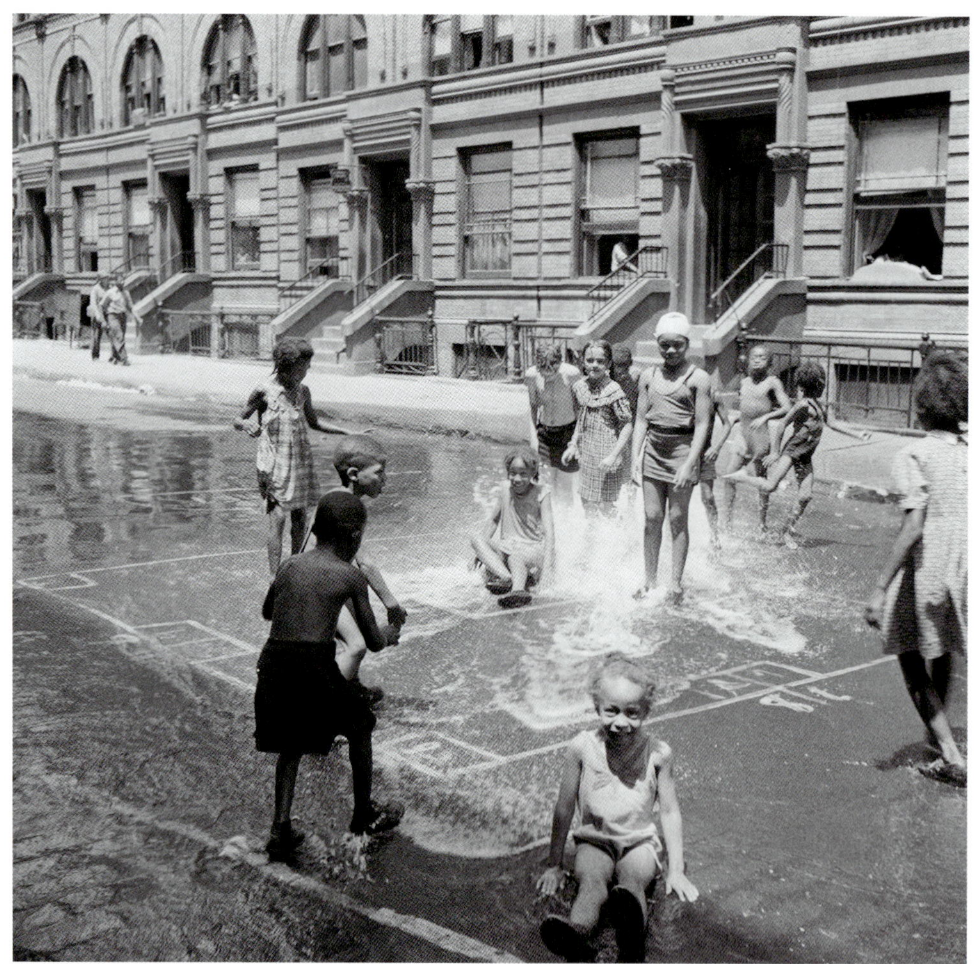

and textile patterns in horizontals and verticals from pale greens, orange-tinted reds, and turquoise create visual accents. Browning captured the rhythmical harmonies of the street. Harlem Renaissance poet laureate Langston Hughes felt this undercurrent in his 1923 poem, "The Weary Blues":

> *Droning a drowsy syncopated tune,*
> *Rocking back and forth to a mellow croon,*
> *Down on Lenox Avenue the other night,*
> *By the pale dull pallor of an old gas light*
> *He did a lazy sway…He did a lazy sway,*
> *To the tune o' those Weary Blues.*

An instructive comparison is made with *East Harlem Street Scene* of the early 1950s and another urban view—*Storefront* (fig. 6.10) of 1965. Instead of the rollicking, saturated street brimming with humanity, the latter is an isolated, abandoned, ghost-town image. Whether consciously or not, Browning has captured the fate of New York's neighborhoods from the optimistic postwar energies of the '50s to the blighted, urban decay of the mid-1960s. *Storefront* exudes an air of despair, neglect, and societal abandonment. As the Vietnam War was percolating in 1965, America's attention was not directed toward investment in its urban, largely black neighborhoods. Within a few years, the Watts riots and the burning in Newark and Detroit after the assassination of Dr. Martin Luther

Fig. 6.10. Colleen Browning, Storefront, *1965. Oil on canvas, 21 x 47 inches. Gift of the artist.*

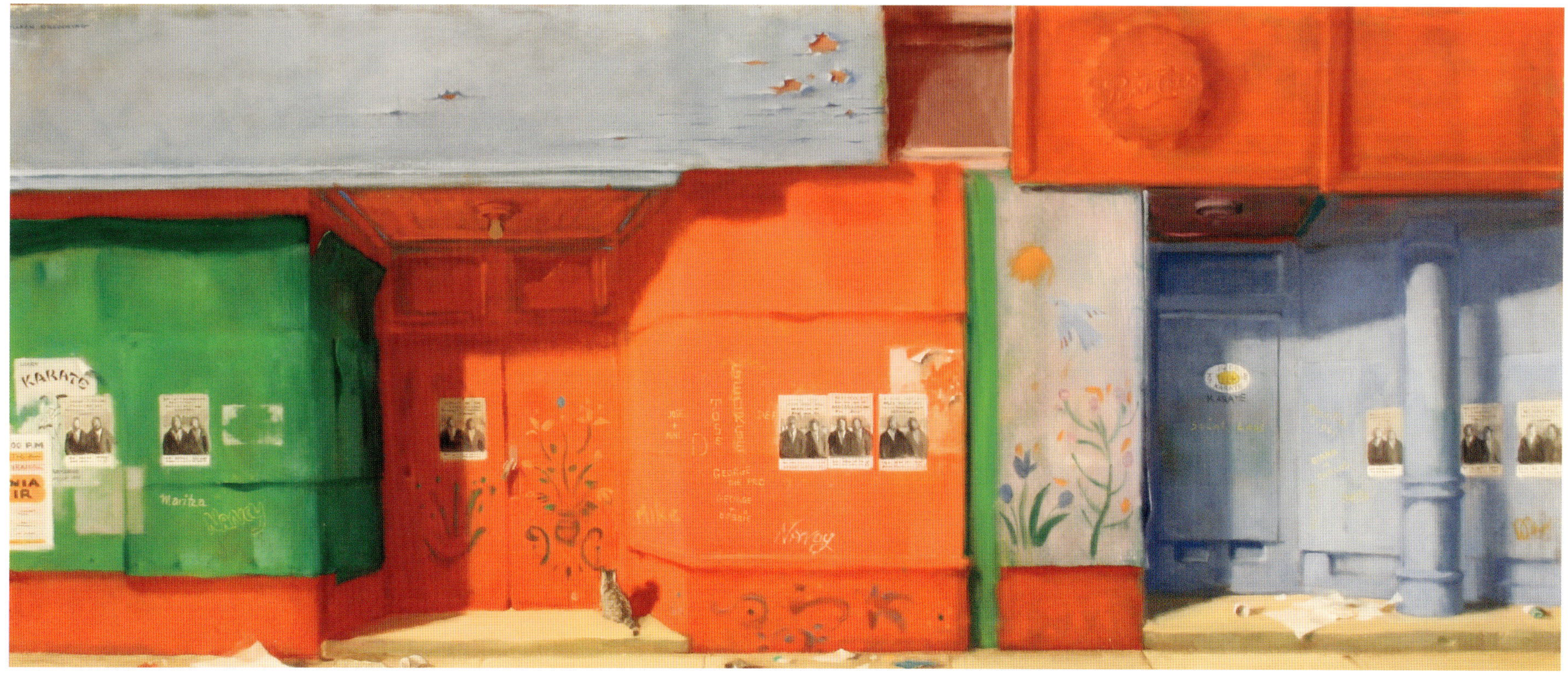

King, Jr. in April 1968 would bring black ghettos to their very nadir. Browning continued to observe America's underclass in her "subway" series. She was always watchful of, yet detached from, the individuals in the context of a decaying environment.

Browning's reputation surged in the mid-1950s while the overall demand for realist painting was losing ground. Virginia M. Mecklenburg charted this unfortunate demise: "The increasing attention to abstraction alarmed leading New York realists. Edward Hopper, one of the country's most successful realists, had sold $30,000 worth of paintings in 1954, but he and…forty other figurative artists were distressed at the increasing amount of press devoted to abstract art. They formed a group called Reality to affirm the validity of figurative art and to protest the widespread endorsement of abstract expressionism."[29]

Intuitively alert to this seismic shift, Browning enlarged her frame of reference, even as the coming decade was marked by intensive social change. As tastes and styles fluctuated so dramatically in the 1950s toward abstraction, the '60s and '70s posed an even wider agenda, for the very nature of art itself was to be challenged in the coming cultural upheavals.

NOTES

1. Robert Cozzolino, *With Friends: Six Magic Realists*, exhibition catalogue, Elvehjem Museum of Art, University of Wisconsin-Madison, 2005, p. 13.

2. Jeffrey Wechsler, "Magic Realism: Defining the Indefinite," *Art Journal*, College Art Association, New York, vol. 45, no. 4, winter 1985, pp. 293–298.

3. Lincoln Kirstein, "Symbolic Realism," foreword, exhibition catalogue, Edwin Hewitt Gallery, April 3–22, 1950.

4. Stuart Preston, "About Art and Artists: The Edwin Hewitt Gallery Reopens," *The New York Times*, October 9, 1954, p. 15.

5. Unsigned, "Colleen in Harlem," *TIME*, January 28, 1952, vol. 59, no. 4, p. 72.

6. Ibid.

7. Unsigned, "Realism Without Tears," *Newsweek*, January 28, 1952, vol. 39, no. 4, p. 63.

8. Greta Berman and Jeffrey Wechsler, *Realism and Realities: The Other Side of American Painting 1940–1960*, New Brunswick, NJ, Rutgers University Art Gallery, 1981, pp. 29–31.

9. Ibid., p. 31.

10. Paul Tillich, *New Image of Man* (New York: The Museum of Modern Art, 1959), p. 9.

11. Michael M. Strueber, *Colleen Browning: A Retrospective*, Southern Alleghenies Museum of Art, Loretto, PA, 1997.

12. Leonhard Emmerling, *Pollock* (Köln, Germany: Taschen, 2003), p. 46.

13. *The Antioch Review*, vol. 14, no. 1, spring 1954, inside front cover.

14. Ibid., p. 9.

15. Ibid., p. 10.

16. Ibid.

17. Ibid.

18. Ibid., p. 12.

19. Harold Rosenberg, "Old Song and Dance," reply to Dr. Wagner, *The Antioch Review*, vol. 14, no. 2, summer 1954, pp. 251–255.

20. Ibid.

21. Francis Edward Smedley, in *Frank Fairlegh*, 1850.

22. Geoffrey Wagner, "Slashing and Sloshing," *Truth*, October 4, 1957, vol. 157, no. 4228, p. 1134.

23. Ibid.

24. Ibid., p. 1134.

25. John Canaday, "The People of Our Town," Sunday *New York Times Magazine*, April 19, 1964, pp. 32–33.

26. Norman Kent, "Colleen Browning," *American Artist*, February 1957, pp. 20–25; 62–65.

27. Mark Stevens, "The Biennial Question," *New York* magazine, February 19, 2006, page unknown.

28. Norman Kent, "Colleen Browning," *American Artist*, February 1957, pp. 20–25; 62–65.

29. Virginia M. Mecklenburg, *American Abstraction at Mid-Century* (Washington DC: Smithsonian Institution, 2008), p. 47.

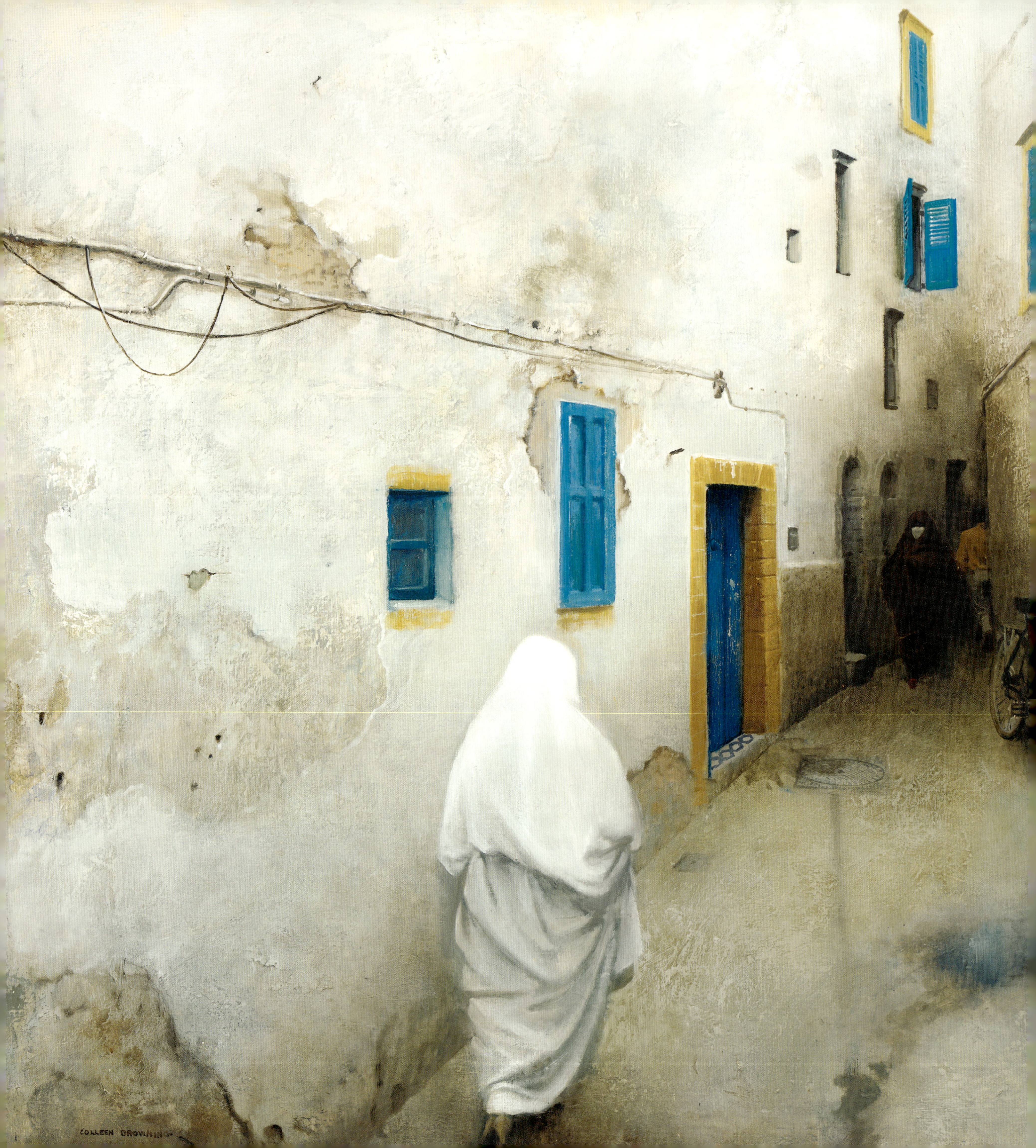
COLLEEN BROWNING

KEEPING IN STEP WITH MANY ARTISTS well into the second half of their lives, Browning came upon a new subject or thematic concept. She abandoned all restraints by digging deeply into its essence, spun off some variations, and ultimately found resolution in an extended series of paintings. At this point we can re-group to reflect on thirteen distinctive groupings or periods. Spanning five decades, this list roughly traces her major paintings as both an autobiographical and chronological thread from the late 1940s through her death in 2003: 1) London film and stage designs; 2) Harlem and the human condition; 3) travels, exotic locations near and far; 4) umbrella and "shielded" woman series; 5) Edenic gardens and lush jungles; 6) portraits—the self and others at close range; 7) still life—studio equipment and fruit displays; 8) nudes and bathers—beaches, pools, and public spaces; 9) semi-abstractions—mindscapes and scrambled television images; 10) subway series; 11) mythologies and romantic fairytales; 12) fireworks; and 13) the hidden psyche—mystics, clairvoyants, and dreamers.

By the 1960s and well through the 1970s, Browning rode a wave of continuing commercial success. As a self-driven individual, by all indications she was blissfully content. She was by now well ensconced in the New York art world with enviable gallery representation. In 1965, she was elected into membership at the National Academy of Design, the nation's oldest and most prestigious organization founded and directed by a constellation of celebrated artists.

Traditionalist collectors who remained unfazed by modernist trends continuously appreciated her. These diversified themes gave her a license to move toward more creative, and even contemporary, directions while never really abandoning her realist outlook. In a revealing letter to the chief curator at the Wichita Art Museum, Browning wrote from her studio in Grenada about her forthcoming exhibition:

CHAPTER 7

The Academician and
the Professor: Barbarians
at the Gates—Exotic
Travels & Underground
Graffiti, 1960–1980

The surging tide of abstraction, followed by Pop, Photorealism, and then Mini-
malism, presented Browning—a diehard easel painter—with some particularly tough
artistic decisions. The "barbarians at the gates" incensed both Browning and Wagner as
their classically defined standards were being assaulted in the galleries, the classroom, and
society at large.

Browning was vigilantly aware of the necessity to stay on top of her game as
"Countless artists, working in their studios and talking about everything they were
doing and looking at everything that everybody else was doing, had pushed New York
to the point where this was at last a city where painters and sculptors could take the
metaphysics of art history for granted and pour all their energies into the specifics. New
York, having found its place in the history of art, had left the artists with the glorious
paradox of their individuality."[3]

Being of the moment meant a great deal to her. But easel painting was being
transformed into a series of nihilistic stunts, anti-art productions, and site-specific instal-
lations. Well beyond Action Painting's re-imaging of pictorial space, avant-gardism was
pushing into new territories, reflecting the upheavals in the culture at large.

As the velocity of change—societal, academic, and artistic—increased with intensity, both Browning and Wagner began taking on a number of defensive postures. In
some instances, they were unfortunately on the wrong side of social progress in the
trajectory of American history.

In 1961, they moved into a light-filled, two-bedroom apartment on the nineteenth
floor at 100 LaSalle Street. Ironically named Morningside Gardens, this colossal urban
renewal facility was the first owner-occupied development project that replaced a slum
area of the Upper West Side. It is composed of six towers of twenty-one stories, each
with a total of 980 apartments, all within a nicely landscaped eight-acre campus between
Broadway and Amsterdam Avenue.

With a sweeping view of the Hudson River, the apartment's panoramic vista
included views to the north of the George Washington Bridge and the upper reaches of
the Palisades almost directly out from generous windows, a small terrace, and the West
Side piers to the south. The apartment was conveniently close to Wagner's classrooms

at the City University of New York, where he had been a senior professor and tenured member of the English department since the 1950s. When the Wagners passed through their metal front door, virtually the same as hundreds of thousands of such protective barriers in New York City public buildings and rent-controlled corridors, they entered into their private paradise.

When the complex opened in 1957, many of its residents were affiliated with neighborhood institutions such as the National Council of Churches, Columbia University, the Jewish Theological Seminary, and the Manhattan School of Music. Justice Thurgood Marshall was an early resident of this urban cluster. High-quality amenities and social services were offered at affordable rates for a racial, ethnic, and economically diverse community.

Because of the Gardens' dehumanizing scale, neighborly relationships were difficult. Each apartment was merely a cubic box in the sky. But a mimeographed newsletter, "The Morningside Gardens News," reported on January 22, 1977 that Browning "conducts the Bldg. I Sunday sketch group for tenants wanting to keep their drawing hands in shape."

Always able to catch the attention of a curious journalist who could not resist the combination of British class and earthy candor, Browning allowed another "at home with the artist and author" feature story that was published in the *New York Daily News* on January 5, 1972. Again taken by her "beautiful" appearance, gossip writer Sidney Fields ran a photo of the couple with the caption: "Color amid the decay." The couple are "living in a big co-op near Columbia with a fine view of the Hudson, Grant's Tomb, Riverside Church and seedy rooftops sown with TV antennas. 'It's so impersonal

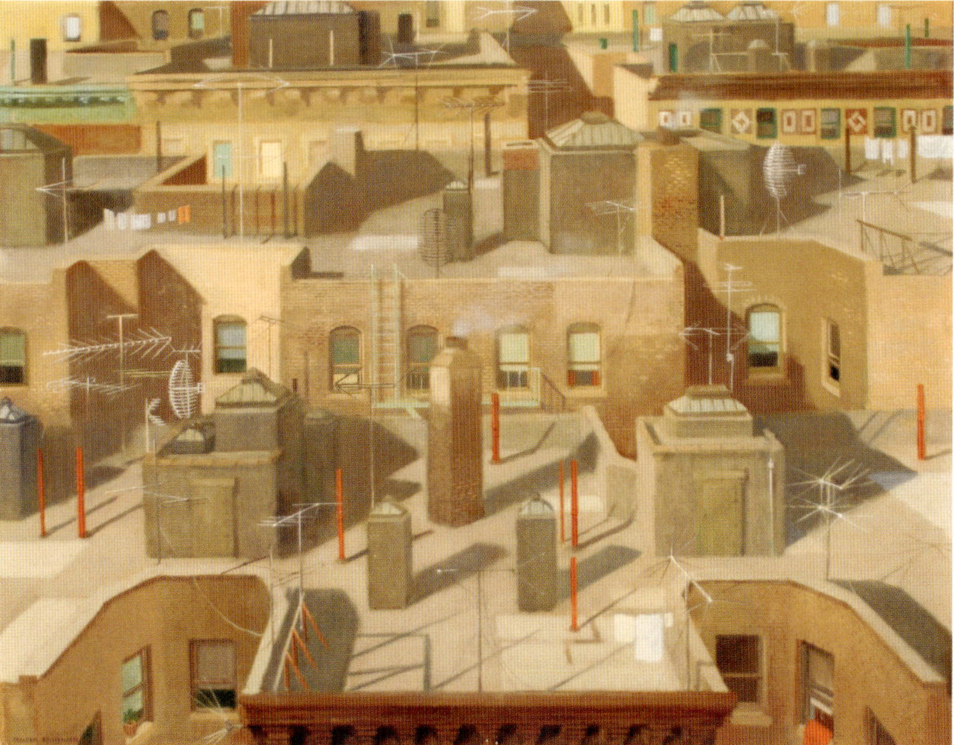

Colleen Browning, Roof View, *1965. Oil on canvas, 28¾ x 36¼ inches. Gift of the artist.*

here,' said Geoffrey… 'and it's less safe than East Harlem was. We're stiff with guards here.' 'I was never afraid to walk down Second Avenue,' Colleen said. 'Our neighbors knew us. It was a street of individuals.' From time to time they go back to East Harlem to buy squid and cheese. But mostly they go back to East Harlem to look for the teeming life from which the stuff of art comes. They lived in Italian Harlem, but a few blocks away were Puerto Ricans and blacks. Whenever Colleen went shopping it was like a three-hour tour of a living gallery…[Her] works are in the permanent collections of 10 museums from here to San Francisco and are treasured by private collectors around the country including George C. Scott, Henry Fonda, and Nelson Rockefeller."

By this time they had settled into a comfortable rhythm as artist and author. Browning took on adjunct teaching status at City College and was invited to teach life drawing at the National Academy. No greater affirmation for her contribution to the official narrative of her adopted land could surpass Browning's election to the National Academy of Design.

Proof of her elevated professional status was Browning's acceptance as a peer at this national institution. Founded in 1825 by Thomas Cole, Asher B. Durand, and Samuel F.B. Morse to "promote the fine arts in America through instruction and exhibition," it was a bastion of artistic standards exhibiting, every year since 1826, works of the highest caliber. The constantly changing nature of styles and approaches are reflected by the works of more than 2,000 artists who have been elected.

Browning felt greatly honored when she was named an Associate of the National Academy (ANA) in 1965, and then by a two-thirds majority of the membership named a Comprehensive Academician in 1966. This placed her in an exclusive club of America's most notable artists of the past: Albert Bierstadt, Frederic E. Church, Thomas Eakins, Winslow Homer, and John Singer Sargent and contemporaries Will Barnet, Paul Cadmus, Chuck Close, Robert Cottingham, Richard Estes, Robert Rauschenberg, George Tooker, and Andrew Wyeth.

An announcement was made in June 2010 by the National Academy Museum & School of Fine Arts to "renovate its exhibition galleries" funded by bequests from a former student, Eleanor D. Popper, and "author Geoffrey Wagner in memory of his wife, Colleen Browning Wagner, an American realist painter and National Academician (NA)." This is the first renovation in more than 100 years for the galleries at the National Academy's historic beaux-arts home on Fifth Avenue, allowing for the "informative, thought-provoking, and revelatory exhibitions of its collections." Carmine Branagan, director, expressed deep gratitude to "Geoffrey Wagner for [his] farsighted generosity and contribution to our reinvestment in and re-imagining of the institution's relationship with its remarkable collection of American art."[4]

Becoming an intrepid Manhattanite—enjoying and enduring the grueling daily pace and pulse of the great city—prompted Browning to produce a major series. Highly imaginative, her Subway series translated her daily subterranean adventures into eye-popping, high-voltage paintings. In 1976, she applied for an official New York Transit Authority press pass that gave her free access to photograph and sketch the entire subway system. Some subway riders pulled coats and scarves over their heads to hide their identities, believing she was from a law enforcement agency doing surveillance!

New York has 468 stations, where 5 million people daily ride 26 train lines covering more than 800 miles of track. Operating 24 hours a day, the system connects all the boroughs (except Staten Island) by the Interborough Rapid Transit (IRT) and the Brooklyn-Manhattan Transit (BMT) companies. Too often the city's subway system is maligned for its infernal heat and grimy, soot-encrusted iron and steel bowels. The atmosphere ranges from an eerie silence to a deafness-inducing screeching, usually ignored as part of the experience.

And yet, Wall Street managers, executives from Fortune 500 corporations, and Broadway stage and screen stars pass through the subway turnstiles daily. Being a true New Yorker means sliding onto the "local" as naturally as eating a pastrami sandwich or a boiled hot dog from a corner stand. Begun in 1900, the IRT's first day of operation was October 27, 1904, with 28 stations from City Hall north to 145th Street and Broadway. This was Browning's line where she jumped off at the 125th and Broadway station.

I.R.T. Eye, 1977 (fig. 7.1), jolts us into the Stygian darkness below New York's streets, as we stand on the platform waiting for the mechanical doors to fling open. "This is almost a direct quotation of the faceless eye on a Lexington Avenue local," she noted. "The light from the green-walled, dimly lit car made the people seem as if they were in an aquarium."

The marvelously unpredictable subway would become a major breeding ground for the artist. It combined her "human condition" imagery of the 1950s with the social consciousness of the America of the '60s, defined by its March on Poverty, and the new image painting-graffiti and allover patterning styles of the '70s. Browning hit her mark here—perhaps her last great burst of innovative originality.

Browning's series premiered at Kennedy Galleries in January 1979. Lawrence A. Fleishman, chairman and chief executive officer, introduced his featured gallery artist in the catalogue statement. "Browning! This interesting painter is showing us an urban art with a totally American flavor…. In our service to the lovers, users, and collectors of art, we are once again delighted to offer Colleen Browning's work."

Fleishman, one of America's greatest collectors and art patrons, is remembered for his countless gifts, including the endowment of a chair at The Metropolitan Museum of Art's department of American art. He was also the founder of the *American Art Journal* and a tireless sustainer of the Archives of American Art, which are all today supervised by the Smithsonian Institution.

The unusual exhibition catalogue cover included Browning's self-portrait peering out from a circular window on a subway car door. If ever there was an indication of her deliberate attempt to define herself as a newly rehabilitated painter—open to current trends—this show was that turning point. Notching up her imagery toward a hot zone, she competed fearlessly with the youthful street language of aerosol spray-bombers and barrio "tagging."

A refined, middle-aged woman, she earnestly tried to turn back the clock to drink from the fountain of art made by ghetto youth. Just as she had once learned the almost

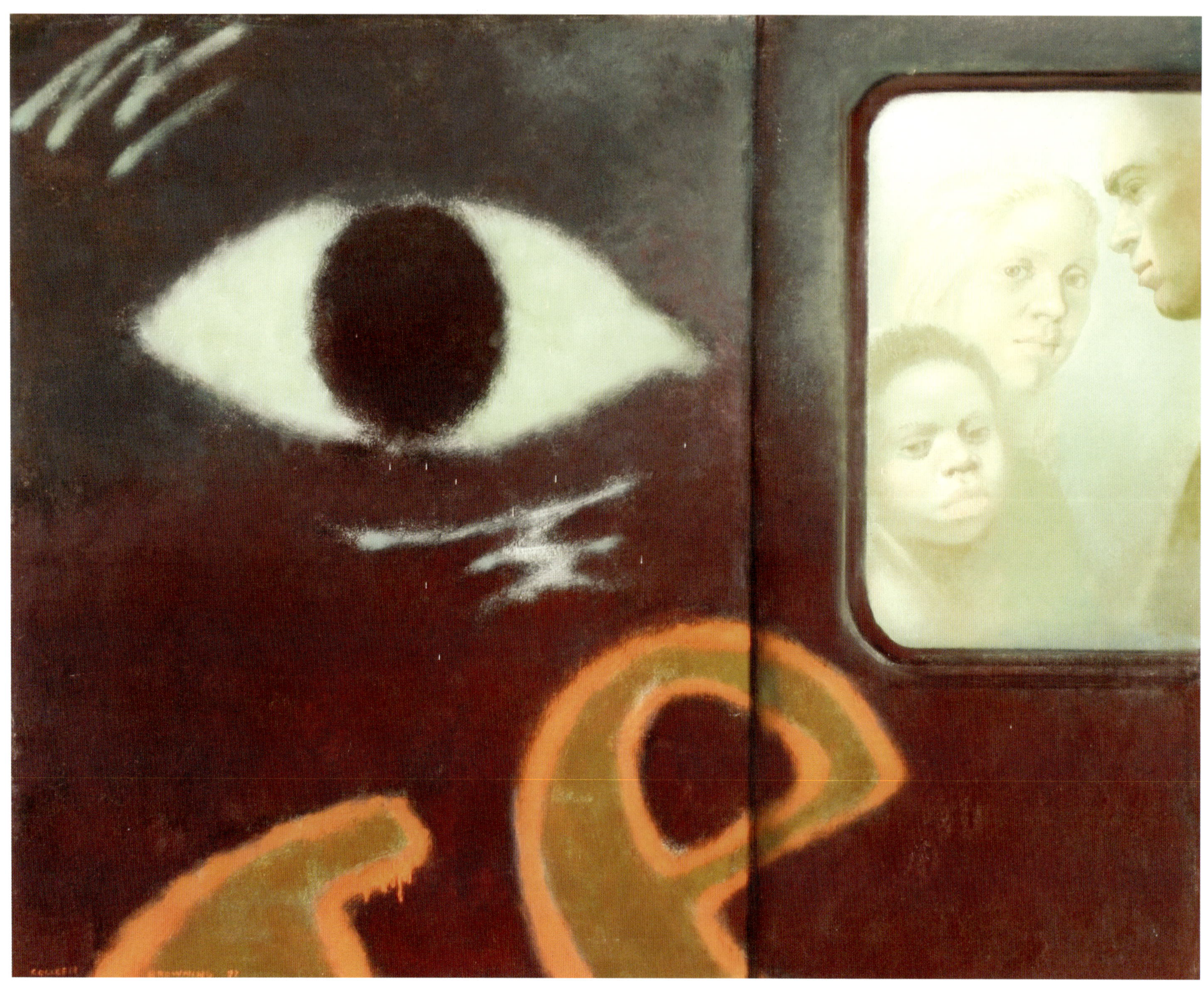

*Fig. 7.1. Colleen Browning, I. R. T. Eye,
1977. Oil on canvas, 33 x 40½ inches. Gift
of the artist.*

imperceptible stylistic differences between Florentine and Venetian painting "hands" of the Cinquecento, she said: "I have to admit I miss the excitement of coming on a new major whole-car creation by one of the masters or the pleasure of comparing borough styles on different lines!"[5]

This artist—eight years older than Queen Elizabeth II, trained in Renaissance methods at Slade, and the epitome of British civility and high-bred elitism—was bravely down in the gritty subways rubbing shoulders with Latino hip-hoppers from Sedgwick Avenue in the Bronx.

Giving a background about the series, Browning wrote in the show catalogue: "I've found the subway graffiti phenomenon an endlessly fascinating subject. This genuine urban folk art—done under dangerous conditions—some of the artists were electrocuted—has a rough magic in its archetypal images—circles, stars, spirals…" And showing her hand—as well as her intention to incorporate a mini-history of modernism into her latest series of paintings—she hints at her respect for "the vocabulary of modern high art, such as color field, stripe painting, abstract expressionism…but in translating these abstractions one is being a super-realist—which is a nice painterly paradox!"

That "painterly paradox" defined the unavoidable dilemma of this series, played out with her "faux-abstractions." Nowhere was this issue more directly exposed than in her *WOW Car*, 1977 (fig. 7.2). This amazingly well-executed work continues down this track with its exuberantly recreated slashes, arrows, and zig-zagging galaxies of aerosol paint. The counterfeited graffiti alone was a virtuoso performance of imitative art, harkening back to Browning's stage set methods.

Taking a simple idea—capturing a subway car's explosively decorated patterns—she exploited this experience to its maximum intensity. In this exclamatory image, the painting bombards any remnant of a cohesive picture plane. In an almost atomic burst of superimposed patterns and sub-patterns, *WOW Car* is a multidimensional field of energy of colors and designs imploding and exploding. Mural size in scale and polyphonic in its hallucinatory hues of glaring hot neon and death-star blacks, this was her great "baroque" moment, unleashing the full fury of her swirling, dizzying dynamism.

Browning's incognito preparations—lurking around subway stations, observing its denizens with a watchful eye—were documented in a January 1979 newspaper interview with Jerry Talmer of *The New York Post*: "Nobody with red hair like that and dark brown eyes like that should be hanging around subway stations all the time. Doesn't she get a lot of propositions? 'No, I don't actually,' she said.'" The point being that Browning didn't really belong deep within the bowels of the subway, but it was a fascinating place for her to gather "local color" for painterly exercises.

She noted about *WOW Car*: "This painting kept growing. I started out on a small canvas with just two windows, then began a larger one, abandoned it halfway, and started on the final version. The man in the moon and all the faces are portraits."[6] True to herself by not just recreating the colorful aerosol gestures of street youth, she made the ghostly portraits of the strap-holding riders bring these subway paintings into sharp focus.

Chevron, 1978 (fig. 7.3), reduced and enlarged the ghostly portraits in the subway car's portal window. Executing a series of preliminary thumbnail sketches for this painting, Browning had minimized the composition into two subordinate units: the circle and

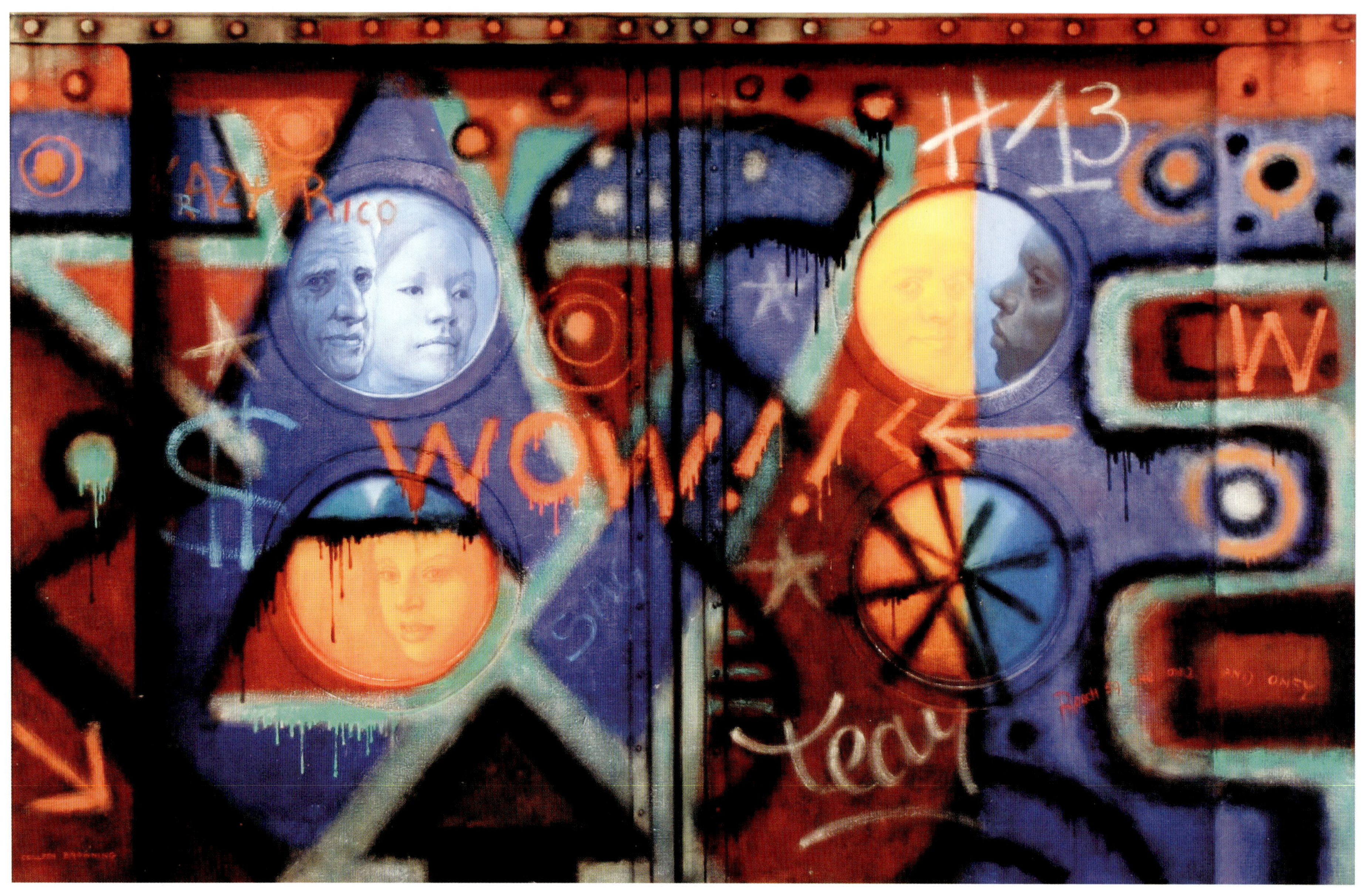

Fig. 7.2. Colleen Browning, WOW Car, *1977. Oil on canvas, 36 x 54 inches. Gift of the artist.*

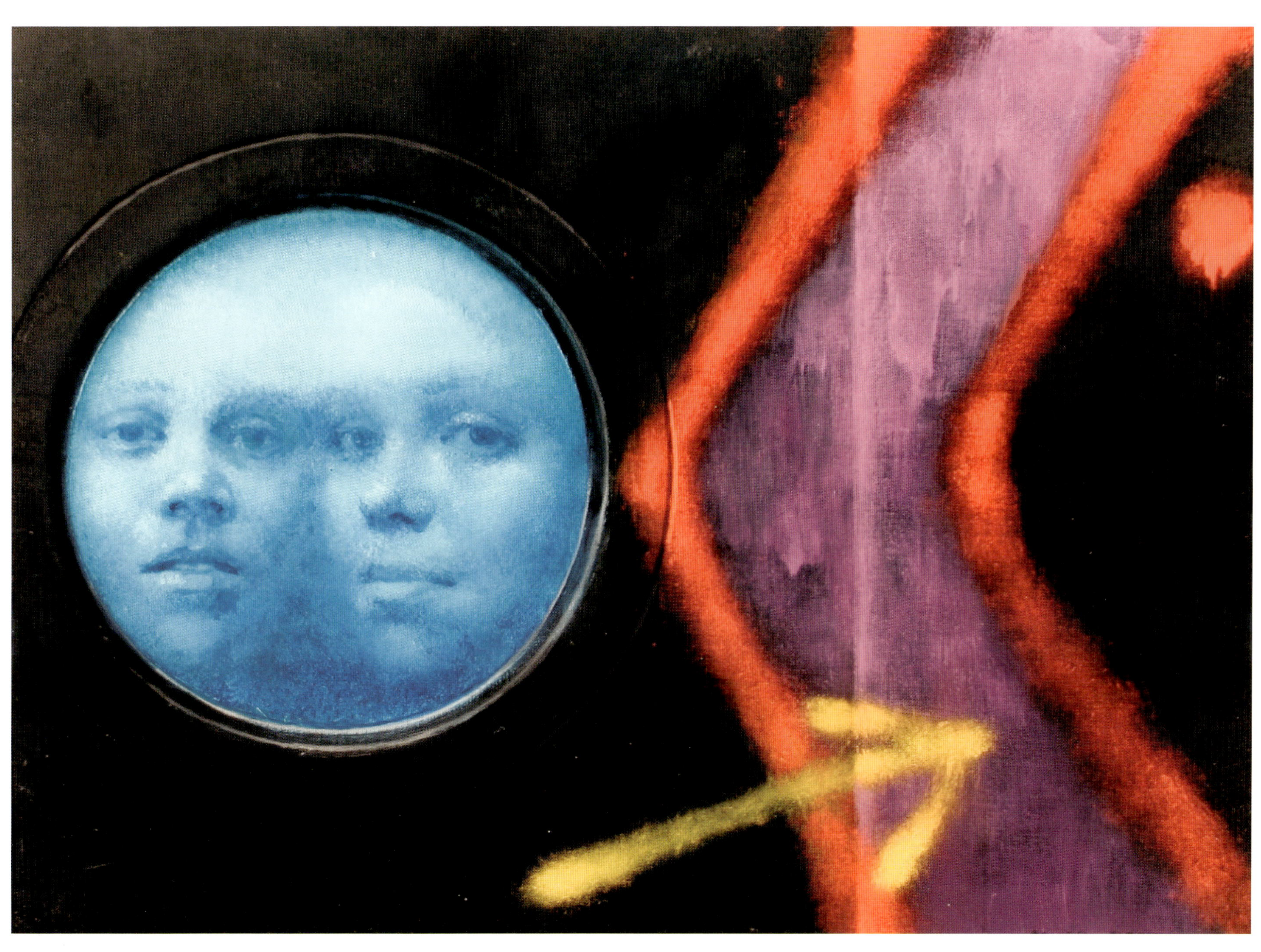

Fig. 7.3. Colleen Browning, Chevron, *1978. Oil on canvas, 17 x 23½ inches. Gift of the artist.*

chevron. Its genesis worked out of a highly gestural form of abstraction in these early light/ground sketches—more in the calligraphic mode of Adolph Gottlieb or Robert Motherwell. The play on invented patterns is an underlying abstractionist approach.

> *I wanted the most effective and dramatic relationship between the two bold, simple shapes within the circle. The faces are blue, from the spray paint on the window glass, which ties them into the design and removes them somewhat from naturalism.*[7]

A consistent element of the Subway series, unifying her concept and image, are facial details—eyes, ears, partial mouths—in a successive number of exquisitely rendered portraits. Trapped behind an oculus or a horizontal window in the car, each baleful face expresses the wanderings of Gogol's lost souls. In this, Browning gave a nod to her contemporary George Tooker, whose iconic subway painting of twenty years earlier depicted alienated souls symbolically repressed behind steel barriers and turnstiles.

The Subway series yielded respectable critical success. At this point in her career, getting a full-page review in *ARTS* magazine was something of a coup. Critic Leonard Kriegel elaborated on the subway paintings with a number of generous observations:

> *The canvases in this show are large and imposing…. We see the car from the outside, but while it is the eye that first asks for our attention, the surface expands until we take in everything that is there…. The boldness of the color—the depth-ridden blues which sink away from the orange sun of the pupil, the heavy drifting green of the subway car interior—manipulates one's attention so that the effect of the painting is ultimately judgmental…. It is our world, vibrant, tearing itself apart, perhaps even on the verge of destroying itself—yet decisively ours. In the window of one door, a face floats out from the collective refugees of our century…. It is a splendid picture, balancing the depth of color and form with the everyday resignation of its subject matter.*[8]

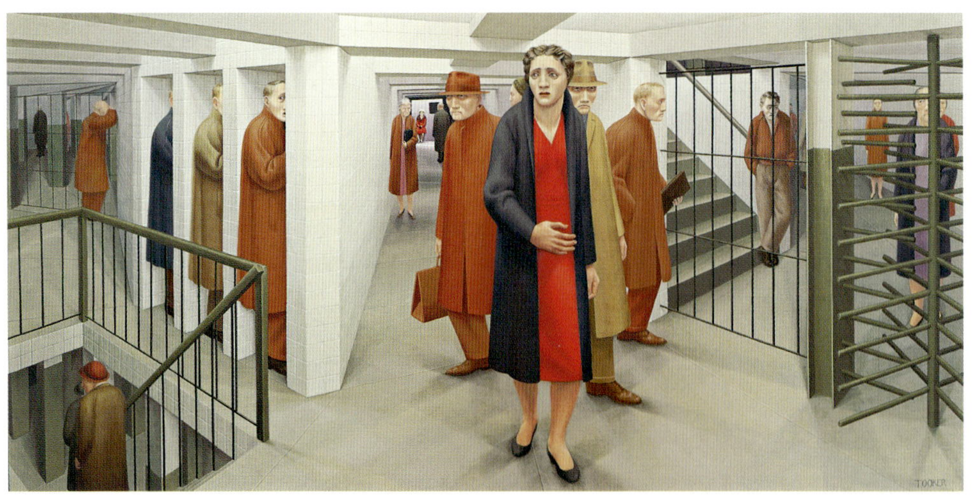

George Tooker, The Subway, *1950. Egg tempera on composition board, 18⅛ x 36⅛ inches. Whitney Museum of American Art, New York. Purchase, with funds from the Juliana Force Purchase Award. 50.23.*

Capturing the zeitgeist of its age, when New York was devastated with utter economic, infrastructure, and social decay, Browning's subway paintings were a valid litmus test of the squalor that permeated the 1970s. Translated into Hollywood films, the subway played a significant role in Hollywood productions of that era, including *The French Connection* (1971); *The Taking of Pelham One, Two, Three* (1974); and *Death Wish* (1974). Kriegel knew that Browning sensed this anarchical moment:

> *The power of the show lies in the decisive relationship between the swirling violence of the surface that moves—the graffiti stained doors and sides of the subway cars—and the artist's interest in the world, her insistence that art can be the recreation of the created form. Browning has given us a superb show, filled with forms that impose themselves on a viewer's consciousness, a sense of siege out of which a grudging beauty is born.*[9]

In essence, we are being asked to swallow some of the tough, new street imagery that eventually became the signature of Jean-Michel Basquiat, Keith Haring, and David Wojnarowicz. Browning was standing at arm's length, recycling these energies in a copyist format. She could imitate the "cool" new graffiti art, making sensational art world headlines in the morning, and, if she wished, could have stenciled Roman wall painting motifs of gargoyles or cherubs in the afternoon.

Benefiting from their frequent semester breaks from their teaching duties and free of the restrictions of having school-age children, Browning and Wagner were truly like *wandervogel*—traveling freely like migratory birds. Their holidays were frequent and lengthy. With Browning using each trip as field research in exotic locales, Wagner employed his powerful writing talents as a freelance writer for descriptive travelogues.

The liberty of Wagner's full-year sabbatical leave in 1967 afforded Browning an enormously diversified series of geographical locations for her paintings. She increased her rate of production and exhibited an unprecedented number of new works for her premier exhibition at Kennedy Galleries in March 1969. Inspired by locations from Morocco, Corsica, and France, her work evolved into an expanded "Browning look." Expanding her range of subjects and locations, these travel pictures seem to enlarge the compass of her global vision. They also show a broader range of painterly effects.

In *Adieu I*, 1968 (fig. 7.4), she painted a cemetery she had discovered in Corsica. She made "endless sketches and photos" of the flowers and wreaths, determined to capture the unique characteristics of this Mediterranean burial site. "I find Corsican cemeteries touching and friendly places….The graveyard is very much a social gathering." The reality of an entire family being shown—in vintage photographs—on the headstones created an intersection of the living and the spirit world. Eventually she dabbled in the theme of conjuring up the spirits of ancestors in her clairvoyant paintings.

Her paintings' dimensions were also getting larger—some up to 50 inches—and more colorful. Glazing and scumbling with her oils, surface textures for landscapes became looser, and blurrier. Her brushwork style departed from the extremely fine

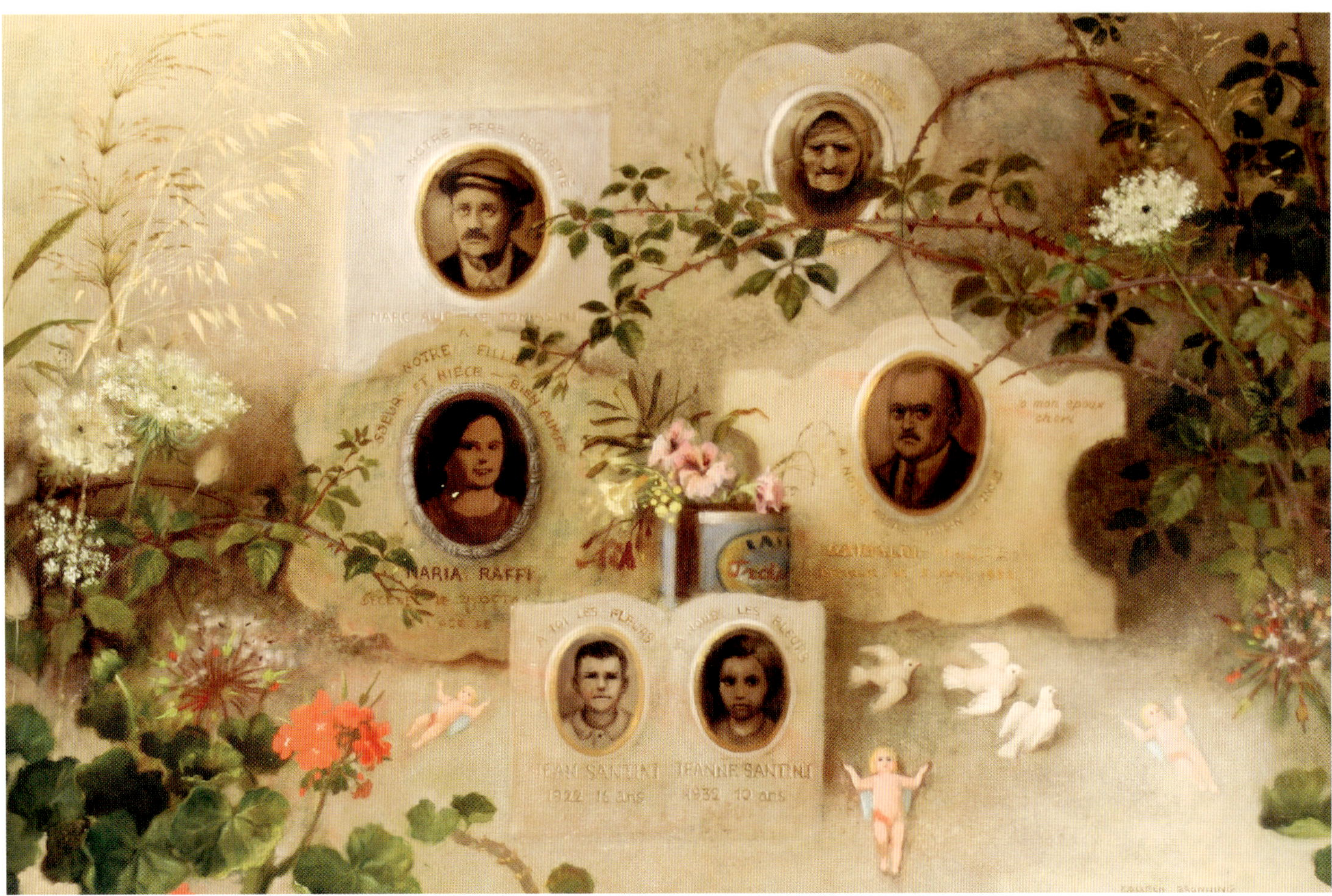

Fig. 7.4. Colleen Browning, Adieu I, *1968. Oil on canvas, 21 x 31 inches. Gift of the artist.*

linearity of the past into an intensive muscularity. Granularity seeped into the paintings as she used thicker, heavy brushes to create atmospheric effects, as in *The Grove*, 1966 (fig. 7.5).

Exploring the casbahs, souks, and ancient villages of Morocco brought Browning a newly charged sense of color and subject matter. The timeless imagery at Fez and Marrakech drifted into her paintings. Instead of the hard right angles of Harlem's tenement blocks, a painting such as *Village*, 1968 (fig. 7.6), depicts a desert landscape of mud-brick shapes in an abstract arrangement.

Browning's unyielding technical strength for rendering three-dimensional forms in space—a skill she mastered while slavishly imitating Renaissance perspectives at Slade School of Fine Art—now came to its full force. An entire enclave of stuccoed buildings was painted with each surface meticulously bathed in the fading afternoon sunlight.

Glowing in the late afternoon heat, a zig-zagging pattern of reddish forms with recessed courtyards and planar surfaces was created. "It was a wonderful experience," Browning said, taking notice of the "medieval ways in people, in commerce, in dress and in architecture."[11] The powerful sense of unity between landscape, indigenous tribal costumes, fabrics, and textiles found in the workshops of dyers and weavers were an incredibly rich source of imagery.

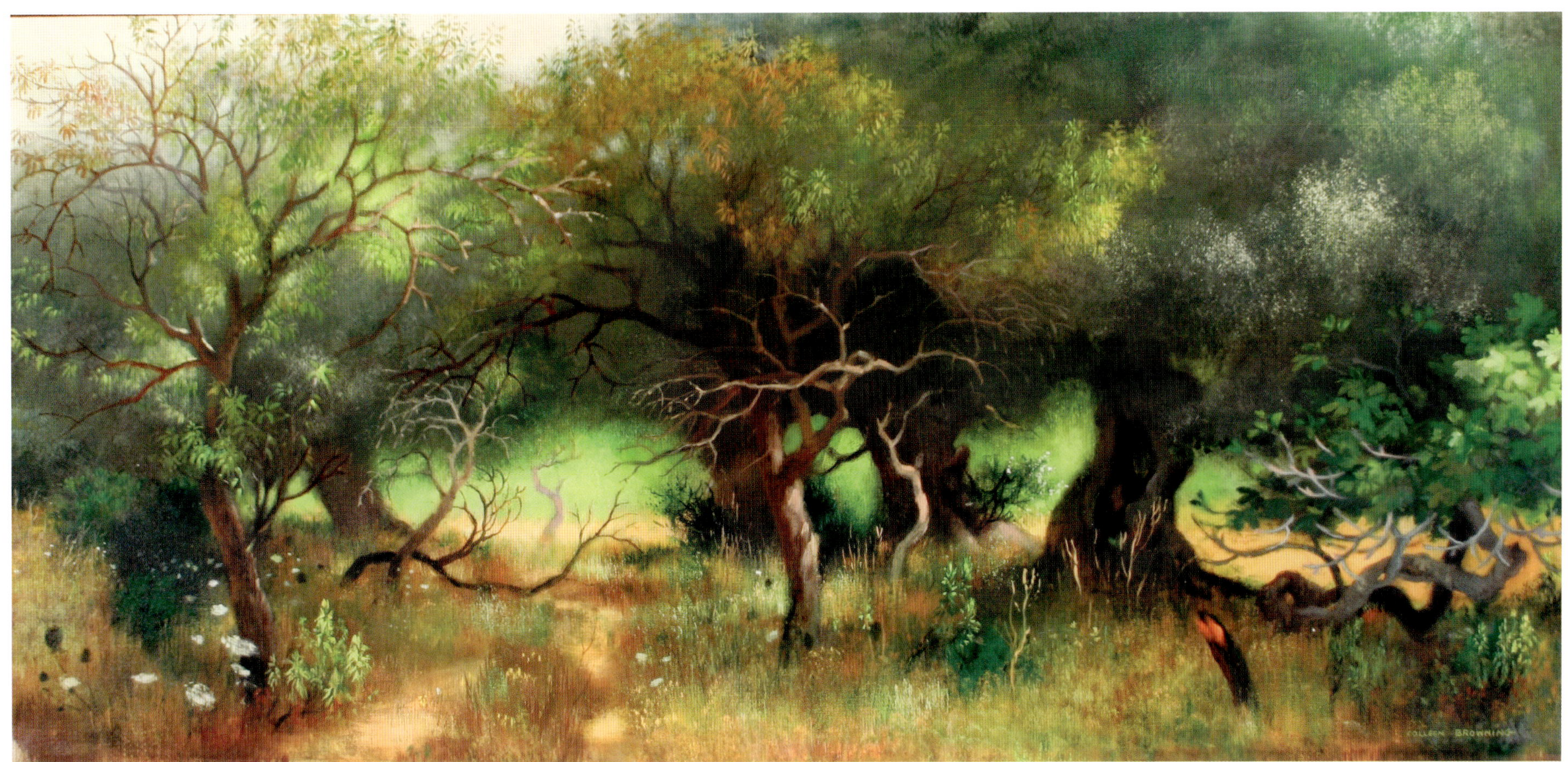

Although completed years later, *The Ghost Women of Essaouira, No. 1*, 1983 (fig. 7.7) is among Browning's finest paintings. The ancient fishing village of Essaouira, on Morocco's Atlantic coast, is the setting for this remarkable painting. Originally known as Mogador, the city's richly indigenous Arab heritage was layered into stuccoed ramparts and labyrinthine alleys. It offered an irresistible natural backdrop for one of Browning's exotic travel paintings.

Portuguese traders built fortifications here in the fifteenth century because its geographic location was on the caravan route to Timbuktu, thus opening access to the resources of the African continent. After Morocco gained independence from France in 1956, the town was re-named Essaouira, meaning, "well designed." Orson Welles appreciated its picturesque setting and filmed his *Othello* within Essaouira's walls in 1952. In the 1960s it became a popular hippie destination with Jimi Hendrix dedicating his "Castles Made of Sand" lyric to its magical aura. With all its historical and cultural layers, one can grasp why Browning was drawn there. Returning from Morocco, she mapped out her schematic plan for the painting in an unpublished notebook:

> It is a fascinating place, with its narrow, twisting alleys and women swathed
> from head to toe in white so that they seem like phantoms—yet they wear high-heeled

Fig. 7.5. Colleen Browning, The Grove, *1966. Oil on canvas, 23 x 47 inches. Gift of the artist.*

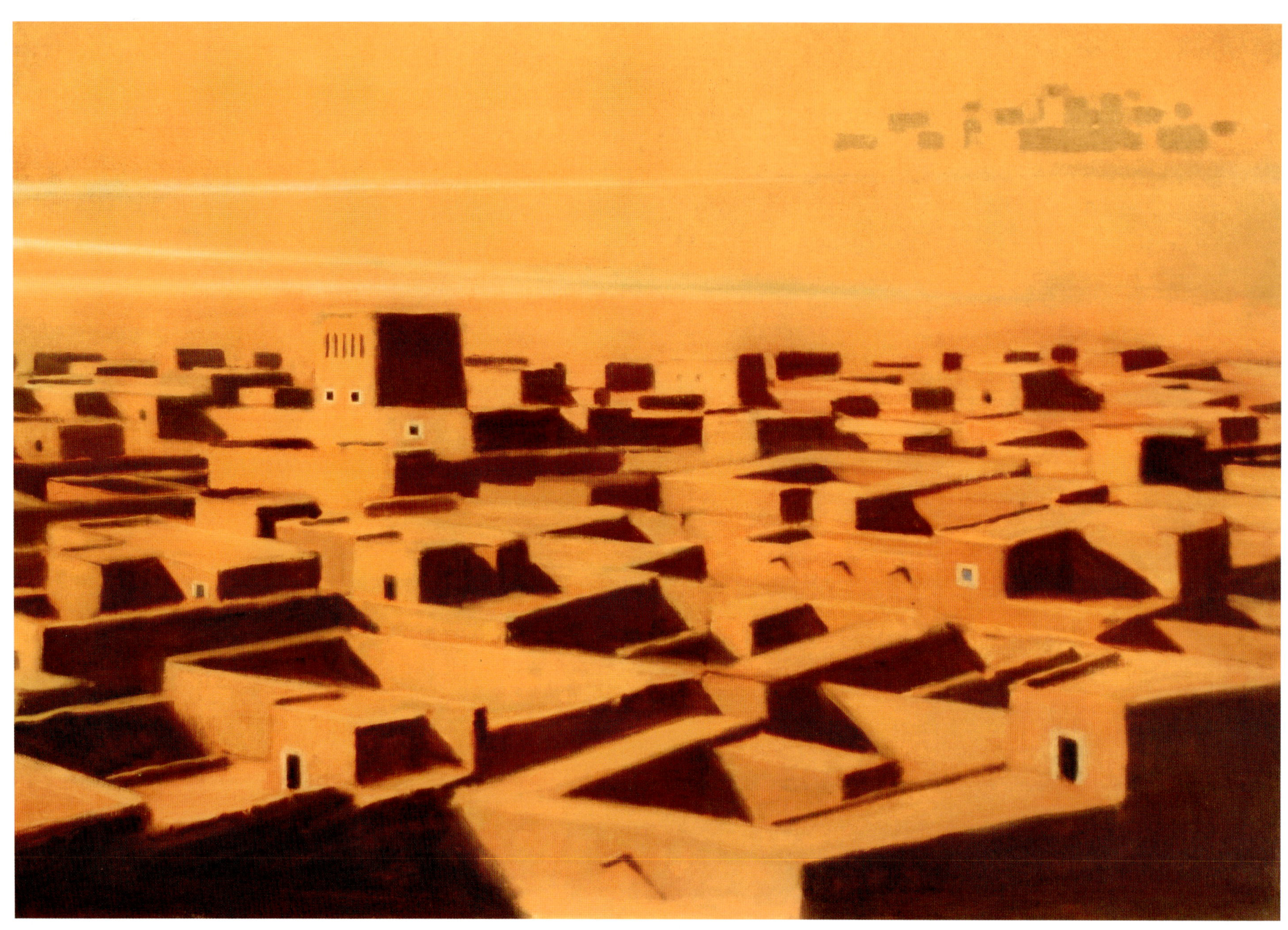

Fig. 7.6. Colleen Browning, Village, 1968.
Oil on canvas, 18 x 25 inches. Gift of the
artist.

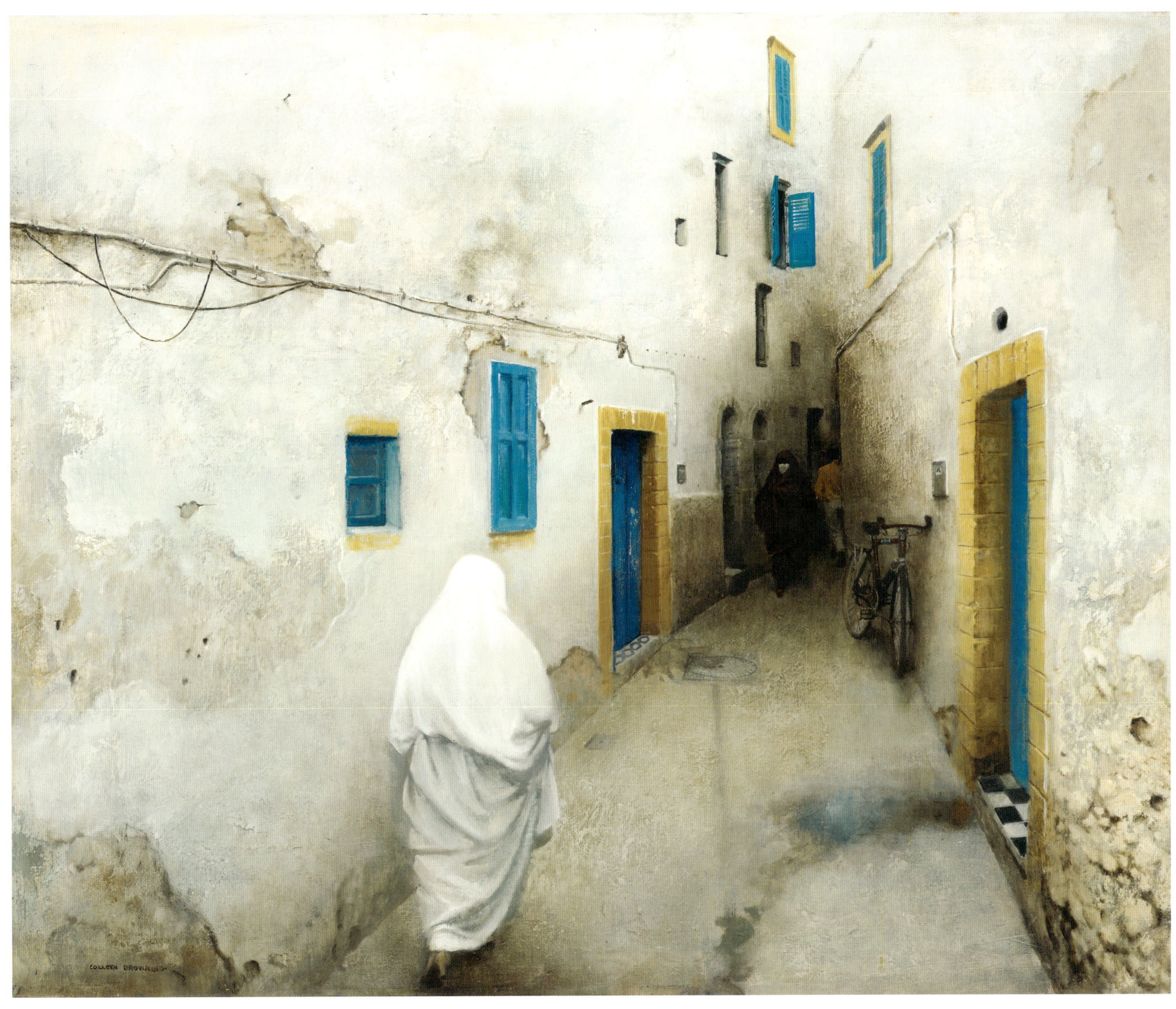

Fig. 7.7. Colleen Browning, The Ghost Women of Essaouira, No. 1, *1983. Oil on canvas, 40½ x 48⅜ inches. Museum purchase, the Lulu and Kenneth Brasted, Sr. Memorial Fund, Wichita Art Museum, Wichita, KS. 1986.83.*

Because she has not been treated to much-deserved museum research, nor has she
enjoyed more recent critical analysis, an anomaly is the Wichita Art Museum's archi-
val text. This is a curatorial highlight insofar as Browning is rarely observed with such
exceptional sensitivity. Enormously welcomed are the keen insights and tactile sensibili-
ties revealed in Wichita's reading of *The Ghost Women of Essaouira, No. 1:*

> *Two women heavily cloaked in traditional Eastern dress and one male in west-
> ern garb seen in the far distance—who are walking along a narrow, alley-like street in
> Morocco. But the primary interest of the painting stems not from the theme but from
> the powerful formal dynamics of the composition itself. Indeed, the arrangement of
> line, shapes and colors is geometrically planned to draw the eye to a central focal point.*
>
> *For the vast stretches of wall surface that border the narrow street are punctuated
> by the bright blue and yellow windows and doors that cluster near the center of the
> composition and hold the viewer's attention. At the same time, the eye travels along
> the narrow street into the composition's depths where it halts as the street bends to the
> right in the murky atmosphere of ominous shadows. It is there that visibility ends and
> imagination takes over.*
>
> *Another aspect of enormous interest relates to the sensorial responses vicariously
> experienced as the result of the artist's treatment of the scene. For the attentive viewer
> readily becomes aware of the stench of the stale air trapped in the narrow street, the
> reverberating clack of the footsteps in an otherwise silent setting, and the unsightly
> stains both on the walls and on the street…. [She varies] the thickness of pigment
> applied…[giving the] impression of crumbling stucco and patched wall surfaces so
> commonly found on actual house walls in the Mediterranean region.*[12]

On other occasions, we follow their travels, encountering a sensory overload as
Browning and Wagner explored a resort's innate charms. Reporting from Martinique
in 1967, Wagner paints an image with words for beloved Colleen to fill in the patches
of tropical tangerines and lemons: "With this perpetually shifting kaleidoscope of color,
one notices the charming and provocatively tied doudou headdress, wherein the madras
scarf is twisted in various shapes…. Perched on hills are old farmhouses with the scal-
loped russet tiles peculiar to the island…Everywhere in Martinique there is a feeling of
color. *Jou ouve*—it's daylight, as the Creole saying goes…There is a fine sophistication
apparent, and the food, notably the spicy Creole curries and fish dishes, is delectable. Too,
the remoter hotels return one to the faded light of another world."[13]

Finding their place in the sun, Browning and Wagner negotiated the purchase of
a tropical hideaway on a luxuriously verdant hillside overlooking the waterfront capital

of the "spice island" of Grenada. Deep in the Windward Islands group off the coast of South America, it became their home away from home when construction was completed in 1972. But we learn that they had begun exploring Grenada back in 1964 when Wagner filed this travelogue with *The New York Times*.

Browning's luscious palette is vividly recalled in every breath: "For those visiting the Windward Islands of St. Vincent or Grenada, a voyage between the two can be relaxing, inexpensive and beautiful…Grenada has developed fast of late, and its Grand Anse beach hotels are most comfortable. None destroys the quality of this famous two-mile stretch of platinum sand, with its frieze of leggy palms and its mauvish shadows cast by sea-grape trees…. Tropical gardens lead to the volcanic peaks at the island's northern end. In the rain forests, the vegetation is exotic enough to seem artificial to the city eye. Everything is excessive, especially the wild orchids…Torn-shirted youths fish each evening off the wooden jetties. The washed-out atmosphere is intact, and there is a sort of ragamuffin divinity in the air. Riviera girls parade barefoot out of affectation; on Grenada, it is more a matter of comfort."[14]

The adobe dwellings and a colorfully wrapped peasant woman walking in solitude form the sharply painted foreground of another vivid sightseeing image, *The Andes*, 1983 (fig. 7.8). The contrasting textures of man-made and natural forms that are smoothly depicted are expertly treated: the cobbled street, terra-cotta roof tiles, and the high-pitched colors of the woman's native clothing from organic vegetable dyes all add to the composition's flawless rendering of a specific time and place in this Ecuadorian village at the base of the Andes mountains. In the manner of Frederic E. Church, who explored the interiors of South America a century earlier, Browning opened her painterly lens to a gigantically scaled vista. Anchoring our perspective with finely brushed details in the foreground gently allows the viewer to discover the majestic depths of the snow-capped peaks in the distance.

Even as a senior professor, surviving in Manhattan on a modest academic salary was always an economic challenge for Wagner. To support their adventuresome lifestyle—travel to sun-drenched Mediterranean and Caribbean islands, tennis in the Hamptons, squash tournaments and galas at the exclusive University Club on Fifth Avenue, and the construction of a house on a scenic hillside in Grenada—he adopted a slew of epigraphic pseudonyms with an income-producing, moonlighting alternative career.

In an undated letter to Browning, who must have been working alone at their Grenada home, Wagner bubbled over with his psychoanalysis of the notorious Patti Hearst kidnapping from her Berkeley apartment by Donald DeFreeze ("General Field Marshal Cinque") of the Symbionese Liberation Army. This scenario dates the letter to the spring of 1974 when Wagner noted: "DeFreeze bought some kind of drug, he then put Patti in a dark cupboard, blindfolded, for a few days, on this drug and when she came out she thought she was 'Tania'—and still does!" He then proclaimed, "Did a quick article last night (pseudonymously) and sending it to *Playboy*. I've given up covering up."

Exploiting his exquisite prose style and fertile imagination in the spirit of the Marquis de Sade, he authored dozens of "bodice-ripping" erotic novellas under a diverse

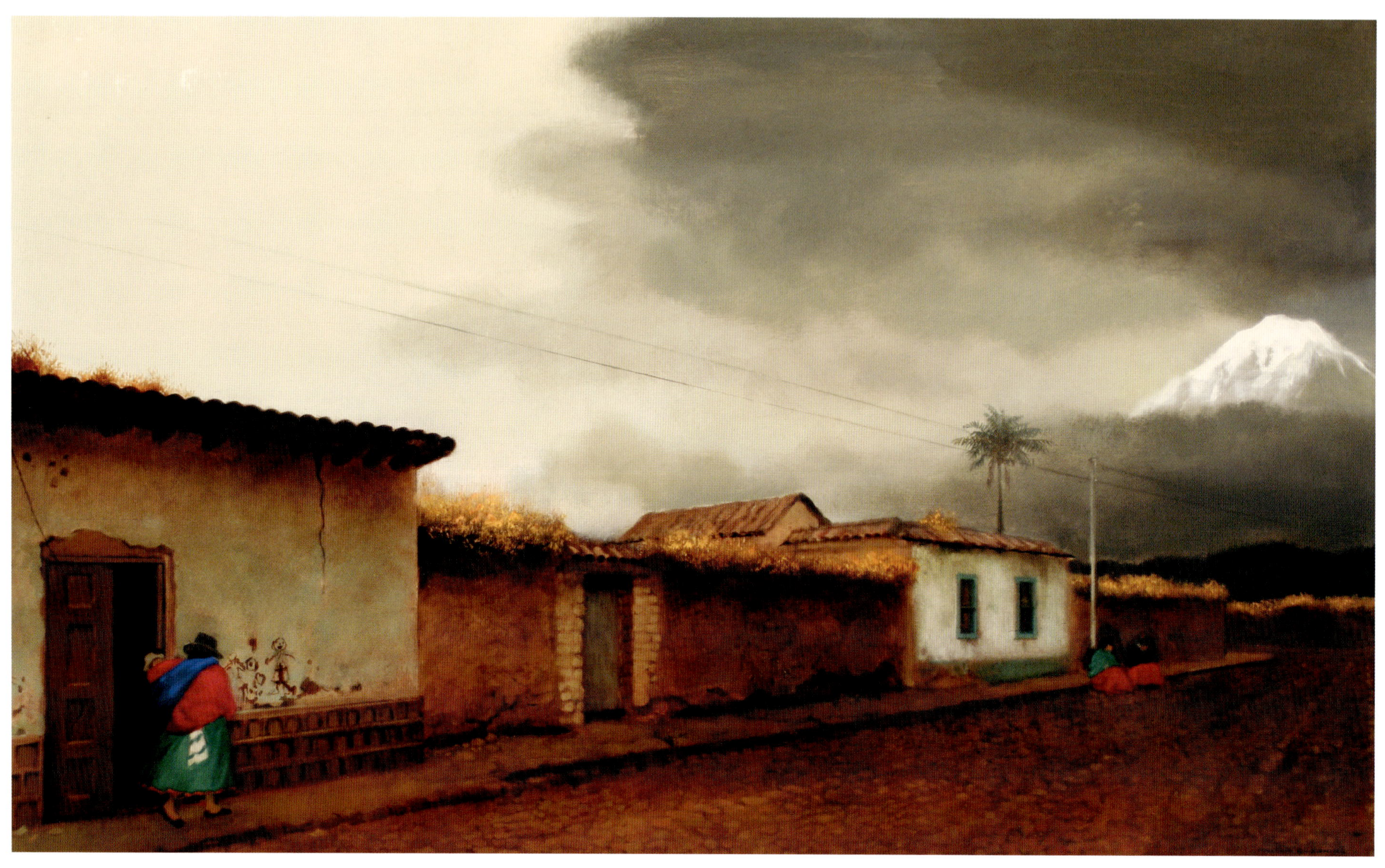

Fig. 7.8. Colleen Browning, The Andes,
*1983. Oil on canvas, 29 x 46 inches. Gift
of the artist.*

160

list of noms de plume. Readers relished Wagner's promiscuous imagery expressed in the most erudite Oxford vocabulary. He described their pot-boiler production in several letters as an almost mindlessly pursued hobby that brought sustaining royalty checks in the mail. He frequently wrote about a stream of scholarly articles being "sent off to Grove Press"—the *sina qua non* of underground publications during the time the sexual revolution of the 1960s and '70s was heating up.

Based on Grove Street in Greenwich Village, the press was a cornerstone of the literary avant-garde, publishing major works of Jack Kerouac, William Burroughs, and Allen Ginsberg. Most famously, Grove published the unexpurgated version of D.H. Lawrence's *Lady Chatterley's Lover* in 1959, which was confiscated by the U.S. Post Office. Wagner was repeatedly published by Evergreen, which was Grove's erotica publishing arm next to sister imprints, Black Cat and Venus. It was all a perfectly disguised beard for the literary scholar, offering a steady stream of side income.

The Wagner-Browning marriage appears to have been entirely monogamous save for one moment of medical crisis, infidelity, and forgiveness. Apparently in late spring 1973, Browning was in Lenox Hill as an early stage of uterine cancer had been diagnosed, and she immediately underwent a total hysterectomy. Wagner, now at the end of the school term and beginning summer vacation, must have been required on Grenada to maintain their property and to take care of business on the island. In a humble voice, Wagner wrote to her on June 25 from their home in Grenada.

He alluded to his "tennis match" at the club "watched by the Premier who talked briefly to me afterwards" and other small talk. Little details crop up, like "Mr. James has done the table top…it was certainly a right idea of yours, darling, because I find it so convenient for sitting at and reading and even working at, outside. Just the right height. Lawrence and Cephas poured some cement for retaining walls."

But the real issue comes up quickly: "I shall be thinking of you every single minute, believe me; oh my darling Poo, I do hope I am not deserting you in your misery by being here…. I calculate that if you're to be in Lenox Hill ten days this ought to be the last I'll address you there…. And so terribly hope all went well and that all your misery is now over, my love, and they are looking after you well. Believe me, a belly scar is not disfiguring so far as I'm concerned. Actually, rather interesting, in fact!"

A crisis of fidelity reared its head in his correspondence at this very delicate time. In his next letter of that week, Wagner wrote in a confessional manner. Perhaps regretful of this abandonment, he wrote to her in a voice of complete emotional enslavement, beseeching her for renewed trust:

> *My precious, I think of you all the time. Do get well and hurry down; I can't settle down to any writing at all at the minute….*
>
> *I promise you I never wrote to Ellen Kessler from that day to this—and I beg you to prove it by opening her letter… After all that happened at that time I'd have been crazy to have written to her in Brooklyn, let alone not having the slightest desire to, after releasing myself to you…. My love, my love, I long to see and hold and kiss you again. XXX Poo XXX*[15]

The totality of their physical-emotional bond is thus explained: "I do agree you have a total force of concentration unlike anyone I've ever met before. It's almost a spiritual force and comes through the walls when you're painting hard in one room and I'm in another."[16] With the one documented exception of the Kessler affair, the Wagner-Browning marriage was nothing less than a fanatically self-contained unit. Their interlocking of mind, body, and spirit gave each of them the courage to pursue their art with the unequivocal knowledge that "only if one person in the world recognizes your genius"—it was the marital partner who believed totally.[17]

Sought after by rare book dealers as a collectible item and recently auctioned is Wagner's 1954 exposé *Parade of Pleasure*. With academic insights he delves into an underworld of "girlie" and male "physique" magazines, pin-ups, and newsstand erotica. The newly formed Comic Authority Code, ensuring prohibitions for "racy" content of any illicit sexuality, profanity, or vulgarity, imposed strict regulations in 1954. Wagner was an expert and invisible presence in this secret world of pulp fiction and was a truly respected authority in fringe areas far beyond his Oxford and Columbia degrees.

Wagner's reputation within a tiny circle of erotica authors was probably the reason for his selection as the English translator of Joseph Kessel's 1928 French classic, *Belle de Jour*. Its unflinching eroticism, delving into a tormented female psyche, was published in 1967 in conjunction with the release of Luis Bunuel's film. Winner of the Venice Film Festival's Golden Lion award, the film starred Catherine Deneuve as Madame Severine, the conflicted female protagonist who was living a double life.

This willingness to artistically craft a unique identity—first as individuals, then as artist and author, and finally as an inseparable marital unit—was agreed upon at an early point in the Browning-Wagner courtship. Just a few weeks after their brief interlude and initial meeting, Wagner wrote to Browning in London from upstate New York of his wish to be liberated from any class encroaching on his freedom:

> *Incidentally on the marriage question, we seem to be happily suited since we are both (evidently) part of a new generation in England which cares little for the mores of the past (on which our elders are living). I for one am a class traitor. I have no class and no nation. It makes life so much simpler, you don't have to live up to anything— except yourself. To be true to oneself is all that matters in life, Vide Polonius* [wise father of Ophelia who is murdered].[18]

Liberal democracy was to be defended versus state-imposed socialism as the political map of Europe was being re-configured. A strain of detached indecisiveness enabled Browning and Wagner to stand back with an emotional coolness. One never knew what they were thinking while in the company of others. Wagner once expressed his pleasure in this masquerade with his colleagues at the University of Rochester. He had reported to Browning decades earlier:

> *The English boy here is as delightfully vague as ever. I am tickled to death seeing how he impinges on the great Yanks.... Arguing with him on Soviet Russia is a good practice in chasing your tail but that's about all. We differ fundamentally*

As art was Browning's all-consuming passion, we have scarce evidence of her political leanings. Within her artistic persona, she left virtually no expression of her political
ideologies, and remained behind the veil of her paintings. Since they appeared to agree
about virtually everything—from food to fashion to literature—one might comfortably
assume she approved of Wagner's outspoken views. There is significant documentation
of Wagner's political transformation from that of an Oxford new-world romantic to a
defensively armored, academic curmudgeon espousing reactionary policies. He became
a regular contributor to William F. Buckley's *National Review* and developed a reputation
in the faculty senate and lounge at City College at the peak of the era's cultural revolution as an archconservative.

An Oxford-bred humanist who warmly embraced anti-capitalist utopianism in
his youth, Wagner declared to Browning in 1948 that "international socialism is the only
hope." Inexorably, Wagner migrated toward the Anglo-American traditionalist conservative movement in his later years. Shifting dramatically on his political compass, he
became associated with High Tories of England's conservative establishment. It was poet
Robert Frost who marked a very different coming-of-age trajectory when he commented in 1936: "I never dared to be radical when young for fear it would make me
conservative when old."[20]

Another curiosity in the Browning–Wagner narrative offers additional insight into
their private versus public facades. We pick up the first rumor of the Open Admissions
policy controversy in a letter to Browning in May 1974 as Wagner confided to her:
"Latest rumor swanning around, for what it's worth is that the BHE [Board of Higher
Education] are gradually going to phase out the CCNY liberal arts college, which will
simply be replaced with remediation for the neighborhood! If this happened I still think
there'd be enough English majors going through to last me four more years; which is all
I need [his pension would kick in at age 58] but the red light is up."[21]

He goes so far as to identify the "missionaries" of the New Left who are determined to educate the "noble savage" with or without his acceptance. His indignation
is not disguised: "I am paid for a certain competence in English language and literature,
not for understanding the inner compulsions of Joe Blow yawning his head off in the
back row."[22] An academic goad, he staked out a socially intolerant, if not openly hostile,
position toward the inclusivity of the Open Admissions process offering advantages to
minority and economically distressed students.

As a live studio guest on William F. Buckley's widely watched forum, PBS's *Firing Line*, Wagner appeared on national television on April 25, 1977 in a verbal duel with
a pro-Open Admissions colleague from C.U.N.Y. With Buckley moderating, a debate
was engaged, asking, "Is the Experience of Open Enrollment a Threat to Higher Education?" Introducing his guests, Buckley announced to the world: "Geoffrey Wagner is
perhaps the most prominent and certainly the most acerbic critic of open enrollment."[23]

Five days later, on April 30, an opinion-editorial by Wagner was published by *The New York Times*, which opened a full salvo: "Dismay about the Way Things Are Going at CUNY." Noting who was previously "excluded, who came from ghetto schools where preparation was inadequate," Wagner charged that the change in Board of Higher Education mandates was directed by "six revolutionary individuals who negotiated mainly by obscenity, with an erstwhile City College president…" He continued to rail against the unfairness in the idea that rigid pedagogy is "elitism," the loss of "penmanship" due to the typewriter, the inability to do basic arithmetic operations caused by the "miniature electronic calculator," and the "reduction of English course and the liberal arts." "Soon, like the Cheshire cat, there will be little left of our liberal arts professor but his smile."[24]

Relentlessly, Browning and Wagner thought as one, as a perfectly tuned operational unit. One can only raise questions about the sincerity of her plea to the chairman of the art department in a formal letter dated December 5, 1973. Apparently, Wagner was granted a full-year sabbatical leave for 1974–75, she explains to her supervisor. Browning was attempting to protect her non-tenured teaching appointment, realizing she was departing for travels and leaving her part-time position at risk. It is somewhat amusing at best and calls into serious question her self-defense. A case could be made for playing both sides of the coin in the context of the heated environment surrounding racial relations during that time. "I feel that I am particularly appropriately placed in a college of the composition of CCNY since the body of my work has been concerned with Black subject-matter; I helped pioneer the Doubleday Zenith children's book series aimed at reevaluating America's Black heritage…my latest book jacket is the imaginative portrait of Sojourner Truth, 'an ardent fighter for the rights of Blacks and women.'"[25]

Art critic Frank Getlein visited Browning at her studio-apartment to interview her in advance of writing a thoughtful essay as a preface for her March 1969 Kennedy Galleries exhibition. His immediate observations were perceptive. "Still on the edge of Harlem, in a high rise with a view of the Hudson, the Wagners live a hermit existence, each immersed in his own work and admiring the other's."[26] And her chameleon-like appearance—not so much painting what she felt, but what she conveniently sought to exploit for its visual richness—was also sensed:

> *The beauty of Colleen Browning—aside from the cascade of auburn hair and the Irish eyes—the beauty of Colleen Browning as a painter is that no one, herself least of all, knows exactly where she'll turn up next. The Harlem paintings were good for her and for those who saw them.*[27]

Browning's jet-setting adventurism was fed by Wagner's abilities in gaining assignments from the travel editors at *The New York Times*. For a couple, these travels were the basis of numerous key artworks about places near and far. Wagner became an infrequent correspondent for the Sunday travel pages of *The Times* during the 1960s and '70s, which surely subsidized these frequent getaway jaunts. During their peripatetic wanderings to sun-drenched resorts in the Mediterranean and Caribbean—giving both Browning and Wagner leathery, perpetual suntans—he shared his expert methods of scrimping and how to be frugal.

At their Upper West Side sanctuary-apartment-studio, bookshelves were perfectly aligned and triumphantly displayed Wagner's published works. His entire literary oeuvre was bequeathed by the terms of his will to the permanent care of his public school, Lancing College in West Sussex. Lancing, founded in 1848, was a place of High Anglican Church values where young men matured into formidable intellectuals guided by spiritual values. Lancing was the type of cold-shower English public education that Americans imagine as an erudite military boot camp with Latin, rugby, and evening song.

Prolific but never fully recognized beyond a small cadre of academic specialists in his field, Wagner authored nineteen novels, eight scholarly works of literary criticism—including studies on Charles Baudelaire, Wyndham Lewis, and Gerard de Nerval—a series of travel guides focusing on Corsica, and editions of anguished poetry. One wonders if in his classroom presence and pedagogical methods he was a friend or foe to English students squirming in their seats at City College.

Meanwhile, Browning remained deeply immersed in her surveillance of contemporary artistic trends. While visually arresting, the stylistic appropriation of an external source impacted *Nine Times One (Self Portrait)*, 1970 (fig. 7.9). Taking a cue from Andy Warhol's playbook, Browning projected her own image into Warhol's easily identified iconography. Without the celebrity status to warrant the multiple-grid portrait Warhol used in the mid-1960s featuring Marilyn Monroe, Jacqueline Kennedy, or Liz Taylor, never-bashful Browning still created a double-whammy.

In an overt visual quotation, she was both imitating Warhol's *Six Self-Portraits* of 1967 and inserting herself into the demi-monde of Warhol's downtown factory scene. More on the outside looking in than invited visitor, she was a trans-generational voyeur of sorts. In practice, she looked around the art scene to constantly drink an elixir of youth from its fountain.

In a videotaped interview in 1972, Browning commented about her multiple-grid self-portrait. But she made no mention of its source—Warhol's multiples, which had become ubiquitous by this time. "I just wanted to do an experiment of all the ways one could treat a face, or if you'd like it, mess up a face; turning it red, brown, or gray with very bright lips so it becomes almost a mosaic pattern, as well as, just lines between portraits. And like most artists, I don't like painting myself, but I'm the only model there full time and free."[28]

A copyist by training, and intensively ambitious by nature, Browning seemed to have adopted a perceptible strategy in her later years of production. She sought out newly popularized elements in the contemporary art world, reflected on their most appealing aspects—color, form, and subjects—and regenerated her own versions within her formal compositions. It worked with limited success to keep her in the game, but did not advance her standing as a late-career innovator.

Breakfast Garden, 1977 (fig. 7.10), brought Browning back into her formalist training. It focuses on what she called the "essentials of painting" in her manifesto, *Working Out a Painting*. As avant-gardist trends were overtaking her position, *Breakfast Garden* is anchored in its no-frills approach to the "principles of value, color, and composition."[29]

The journeyman artist throughout history has learned that a still life is merely a platform for representational theories and solutions. Browning was so fully aware of this

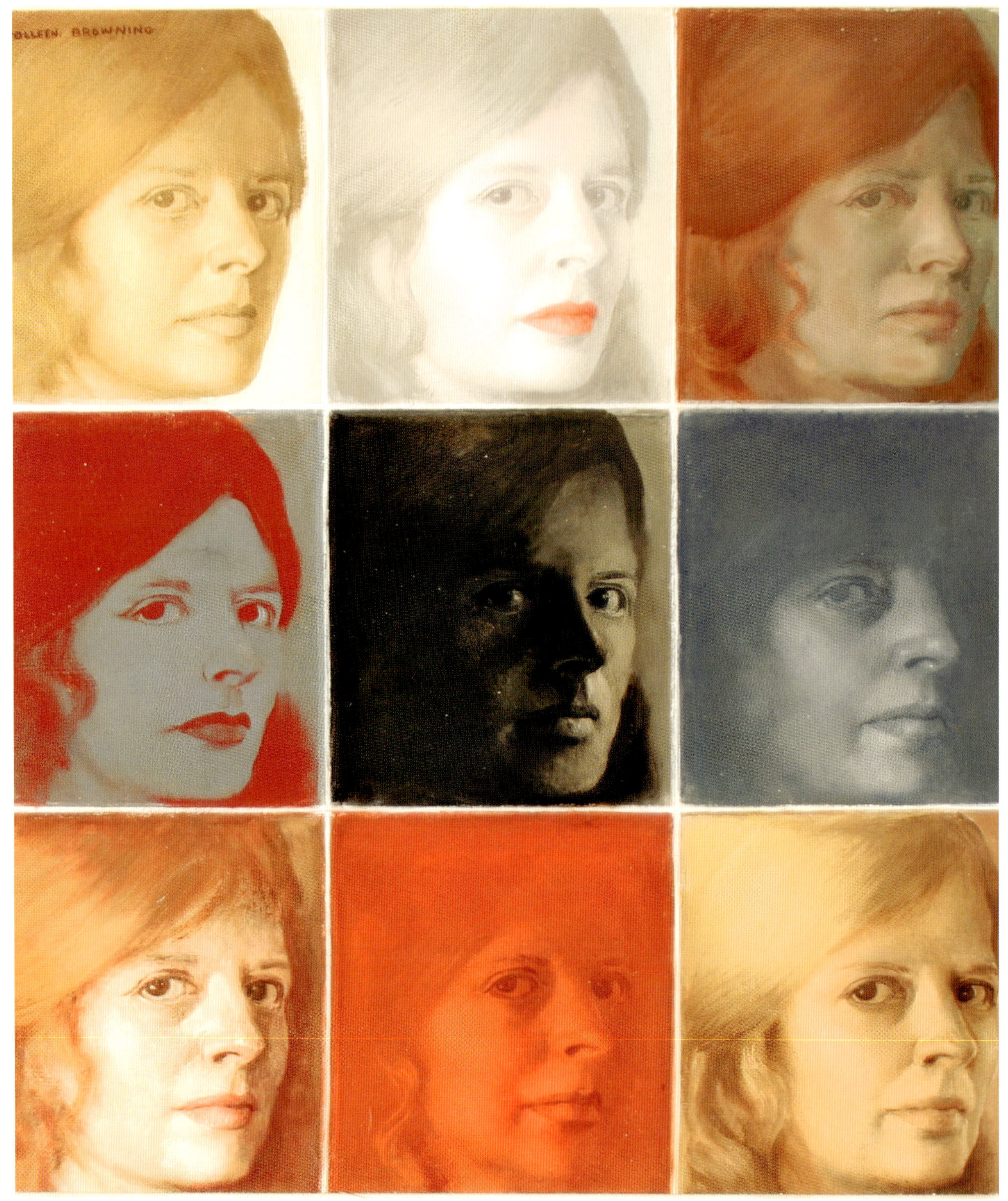

Fig. 7.9. Colleen Browning, Nine Times One (Self Portrait), *1970. Oil on canvas, 25 x 19 inches. Gift of the artist.*

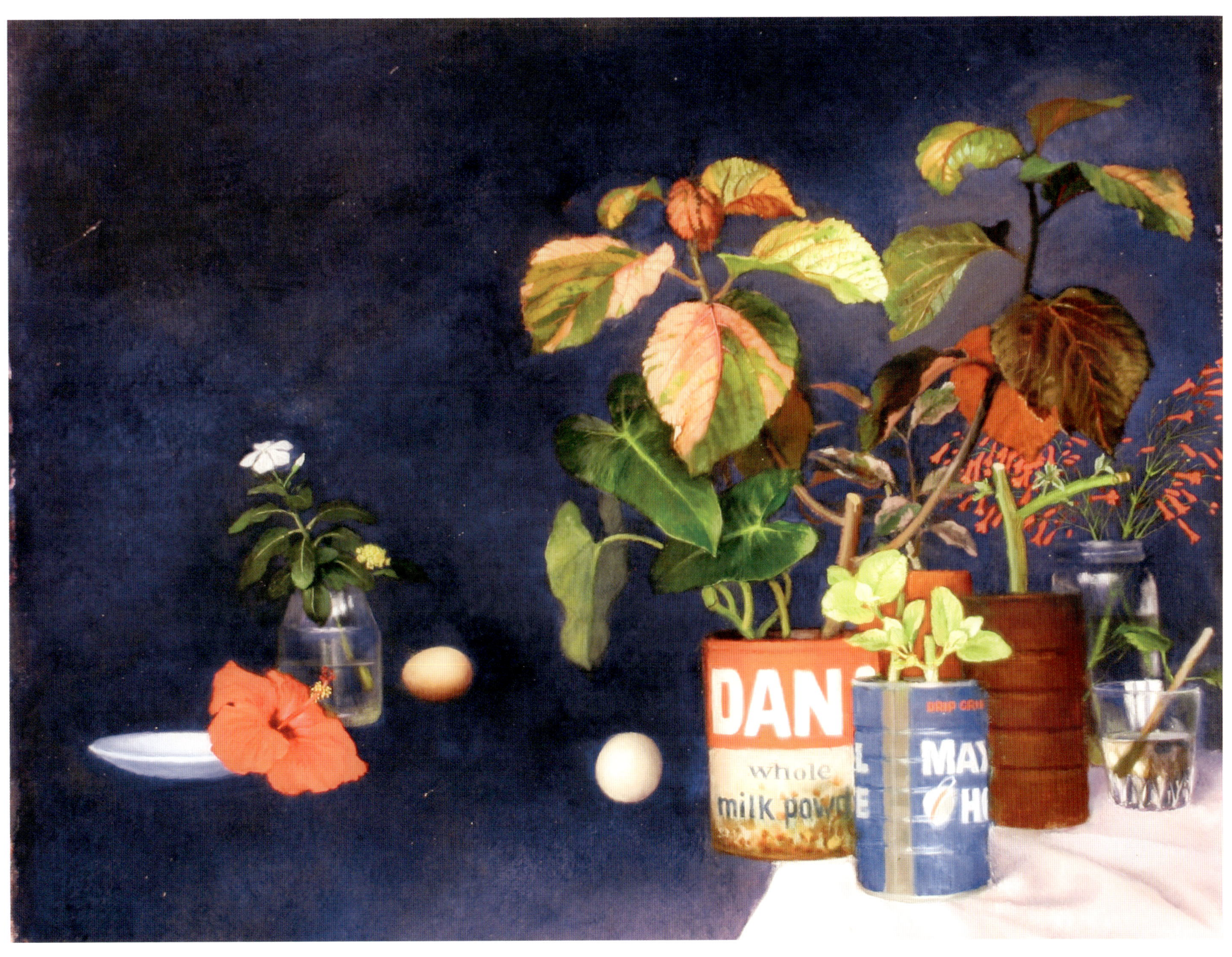

Fig. 7.10. Colleen Browning, Breakfast Garden, *1977. Oil on canvas, 28 x 36½ inches. Gift of the artist.*

visual lexicon that her trompe l'oeil compositions pushed to the next level and disclosed how nature bears the true fruits of art. She is easily allied with other twentieth-century masters who stood on the precipice of Western painting by separating artifice from art. In her heightened awareness, she responded to that very small group of modern artists who could implement William Dobell's definition for the still life: "A sincere artist is not one who makes a faithful attempt to put on a canvas what is in front of him, but one who tries to create something which is, in itself, a living thing."[30]

From such a simple studio setup—an arrangement of houseplants growing out of humble coffee tins—she created unassailable evidence of her mastery. Objects placed on the right side of the composition carry physical weight. The left is a counterbalance as a vacuum where two eggs, a glass carafe with wilting flowers, and a simple white saucer are magically floating within the composition's space. Inevitably, the more we look the less we realize is arbitrarily arranged. This utter simplicity is the most reliable indicator of a master's touch.

Fruit and Friends, 1978 (fig. 7.11), scatters organic materials across a rainbowed background with incredibly perfect details. Within every piece of the puzzle—lemons, apples, berries, eggs, and oranges—the ripeness of each object is magnified into a hyper-visual reality. Browning carefully arranged the shapes into an orchestrated symphony of curves and arcs; the direction of the pattern across the surface moves the viewer's eye into absolute seduction. The focus is not on any one particular squeezed orange or split grapefruit, as each form is defined in relationship to its counterparts on the table. It's as if Browning took the high-fidelity precision of Willem Kalf and deconstructed the formality of the composition with a debt to Cézanne's playful relationships.

Browning's ambitiously painted *Mindscape* (fig. 7.12) and *Face to Face* (fig. 7.13)—both painted in 1973—prefigured her nascent attraction to phantasmagorical allegory. They originated as "results of a technical accident," Browning wrote. "This time it was blotting off a painty smear on a white canvas. The creases in the rag left intriguing lighter marks in the darker film of paint. By changing the material of the rag, from softer to firmer, or even using bunched newspaper, I could vary both the size and character of my blots…As the forms were semi-automatic, like Rorschach blots, it seemed logical to put this flux inside a head! I tried to avoid any too specific images with the profiles, though there is an arrow for a penetrating eye!"[31]

Unabashedly taking cues from the barrage of hip countercultural ideas in the post-Woodstock zeitgeist of the early 1970s, Browning began a journey into mysticism, occultism, and psychic phenomena. In her unpublished studio guide, she cited key elements of her working method. "Q = quandary: how to ask yourself questions when in difficulty; X = The Unknown Element that informs and inspires a painting; Z = Disappearance of Time and almost mystical state when you are in a Zone and absorbed utterly in your work."[32]

These strangely composed images convey variants of psychedelic surrealism that permeated the popular realms of rock album covers and concert posters of that time. A superficial reading would merely dismiss these two paintings as Browning's response to the

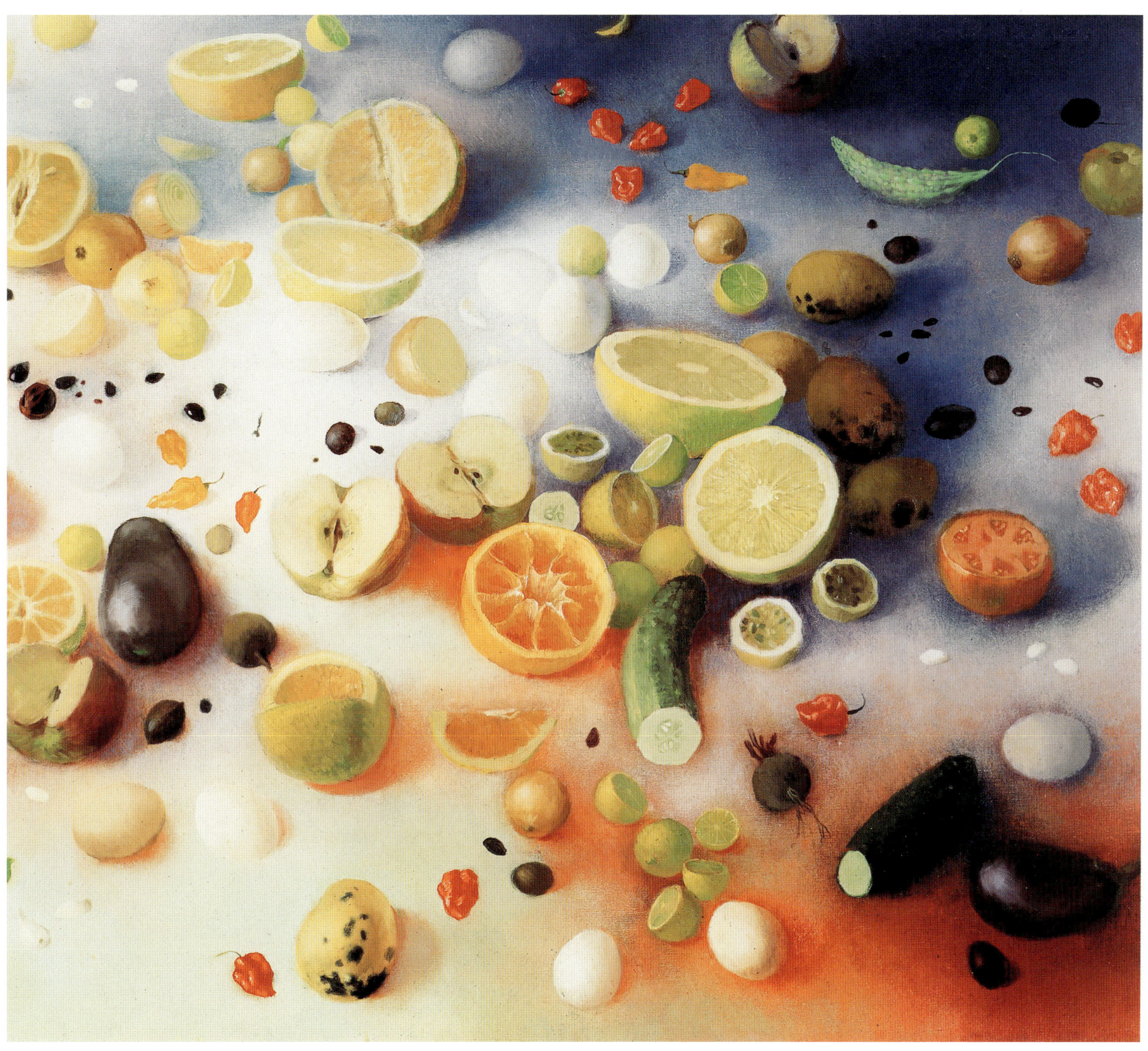

Fig. 7.11. Colleen Browning, Fruit and Friends, *1978. Oil on canvas, 31 x 48 inches. Private collection.*

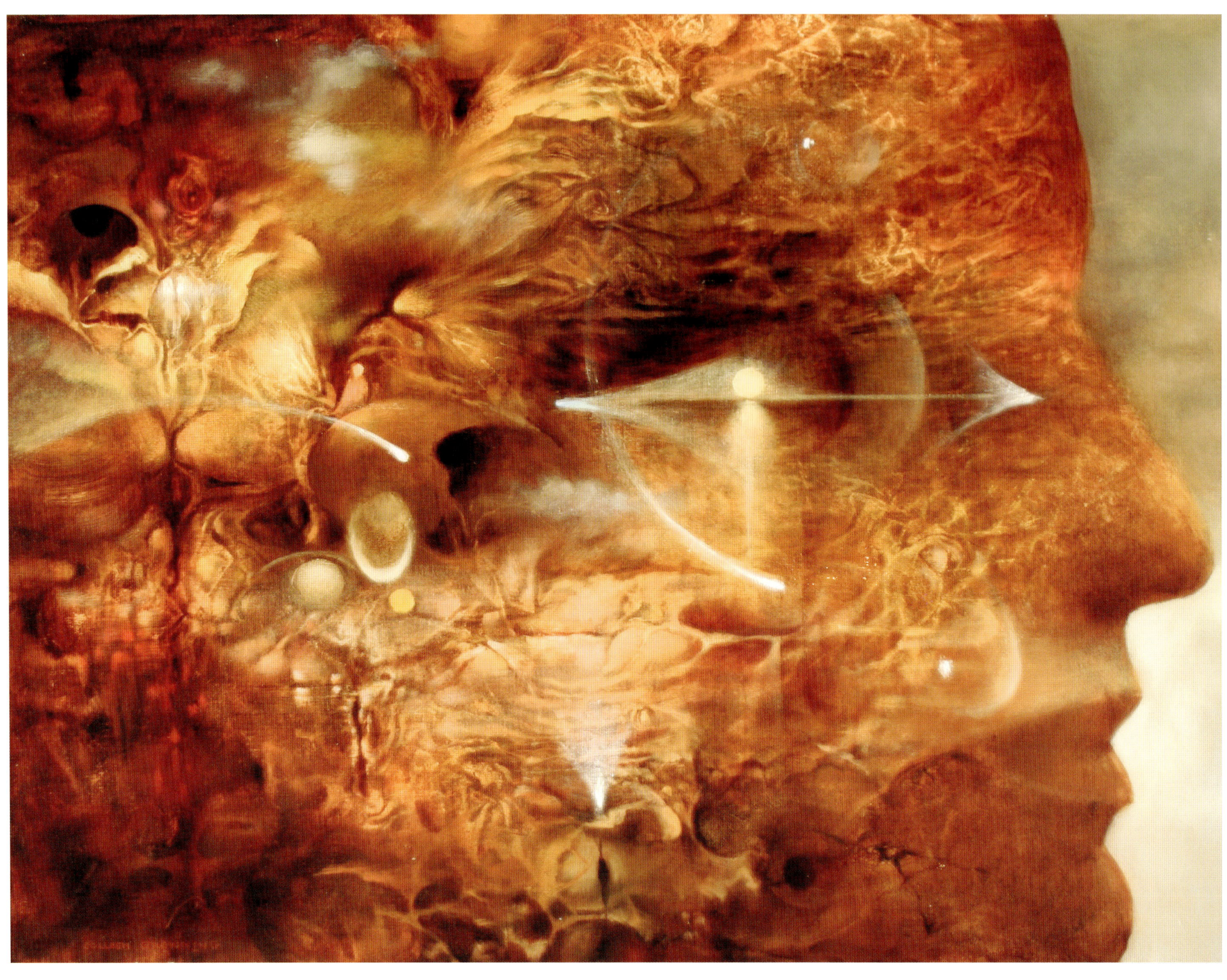

Fig. 7.12. Colleen Browning, Mindscape,
1973. Oil on canvas, 28½ x 36¼ inches.
Gift of the artist.

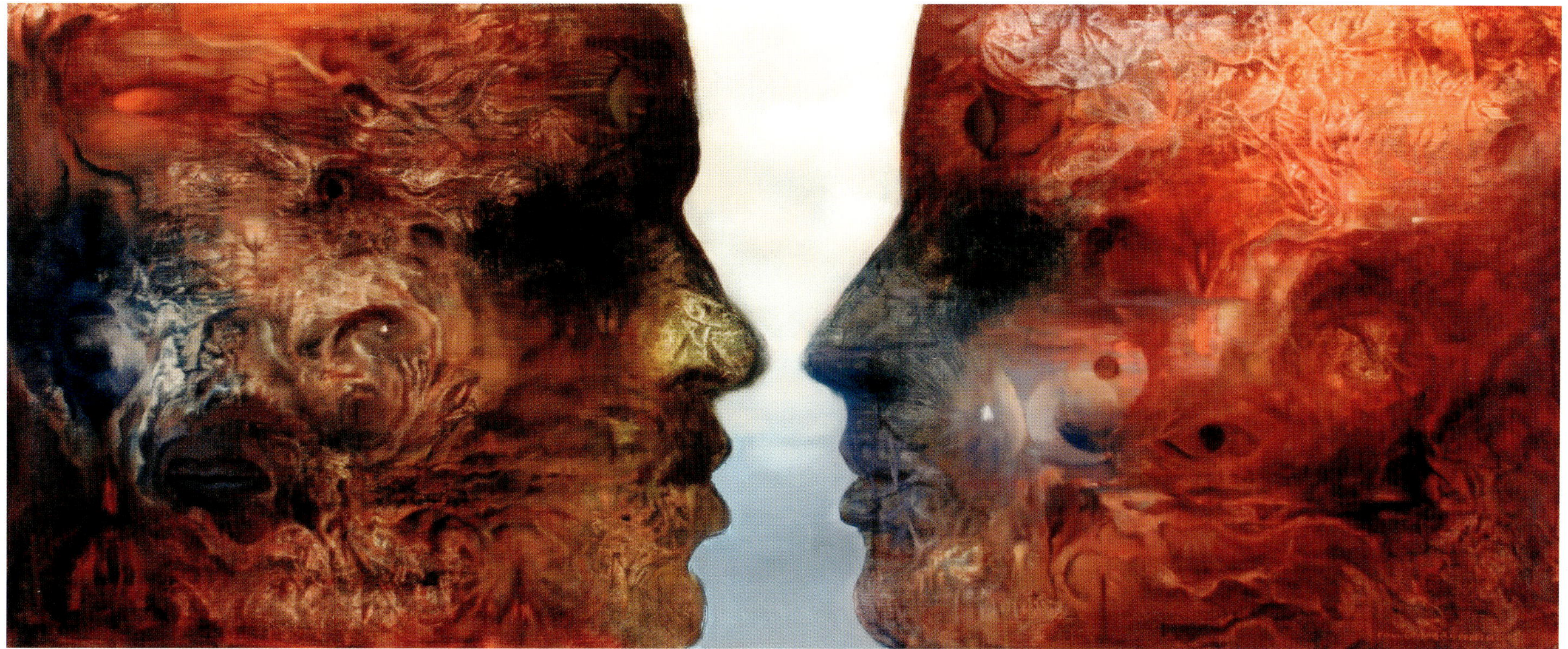

realm of hippie-induced swirling fantasies. "Browning has always been 'fascinated by and nervous about the occult,' but she never shied away from the curious or controversial."[33]

These canvases are both time capsules, revealing her immersion into psychic phenomena, reflecting and bouncing off a cultural trend at the time. The most probable sources of these unusual paintings are album covers of 1973 with occultist images, such as Pink Floyd's *Dark Side of the Moon*, Led Zeppelin's *Houses of the Holy*, or Todd Rundgren's *A Wizard*. She recreated the amoeba-like, "blink-twice" images on the screen of the sound and light show at Bill Graham's legendary Fillmore East or the uptown Broadway rock palace, the Beacon Theatre.

It would be unthinkable—because of her very conservative tastes—that she would ever have attended any of these now-famous rock shows. But instinctively, she worked to siphon off the vibe, attempting to rejuvenate her subject matter. "In my Face to Face I have used bands of color.…They sort of connect to a certain extent that their interior understanding is always running on different wave lengths," she noted.[34]

The counterculture's energized frenzy was unavoidable. New York's newspapers, handbills, and street poles exploded with commercial posters announcing these events. The visual impact of these posters was documented in 2010 when the staid New-York Historical Society presented an unexpected survey of posters and miscellanea resurrecting ubiquitous memorabilia from the vaults of the Grateful Dead. The survey included medieval grim-reaper iconography for their 1973 album, *Wake of the Flood*. Known for its conservatism, the Society was sold out during the unprecedented run of the exhibition, causing the show's extension for an additional two months.

Fig. 7.13. Colleen Browning, Face to Face*, 1973. Oil on canvas, 20 x 47½ inches. Gift of the artist.*

A better interpretation of these paintings comes from knowing of her dabbling in that era's rediscovery of the Swiss psychiatrist Dr. Carl Jung and German symbolic fantasist author Hermann Hesse. Browning recharged her batteries by synthesizing intellectual themes and popular trends of the day. We know she and Wagner were avid subscribers to *The Village Voice*, the quintessential potpourri of weekly countercultural news. Unlike the more restrained *Times*, the *Voice* was enjoyed by professors and their students who kept abreast of hip and novel arts, culture, and social trends. This was not casual dilettantism for Browning, but more of an attempt to expand the sources and influences for her next set of projects and constantly morphing ideas.

Jung's archetypal imagery, related to ideas about the collective unconscious, was being widely embraced by the "alternative culture" at the close of the psychedelic 1960s and into the early 1970s. It offered a rejection and response to the mainstream culture as the United States experienced the Watergate break-in and the fall of Saigon. With the background rock anthem of The Doors—"People are Strange"—*Mindscape* and *Face to Face* were Browning's surrealistic reactions to larger societal events shaping American culture.

NOTES

1. Colleen Browning, letter to Howard DaLee Spencer, St. George's, Grenada, 3 August 1986, archives at Wichita Art Museum.

2. Jed Perl, *New Art City: Manhattan at Mid-Century* (New York: Random House, 2005), p. 556.

3. Ibid., p. 557.

4. This and the preceding three quotations are all from National Academy Museum & School of Fine Arts, New York, press release, June 23, 2010.

5. Colleen Browning, "By the Artist," catalogue statement, *Colleen Browning: Recent Paintings*, Kennedy Galleries, January 31–February 17, 1979, unpaginated.

6. Jerry Talmer, *The New York Post*, January 1979.

7. Colleen Browning, *Working Out a Painting* (New York: Watson-Guptill Publications Inc., 1988), pp. 124–125.

8. Leonard Kriegel, "Colleen Browning," *ARTS Magazine*, February 1979, vol. 53, no. 6, p. 6.

9. Ibid.

10. Kennedy Galleries, exhibition catalogue, March 5–29, 1969, unpaginated.

11. Frank Getlein, *Colleen Browning*, exhibition catalogue, Kennedy Galleries, March 5–29, 1969, unpaginated.

12. Wichita Art Museum website, "Permanent Collection" http://wichitaartmuseum.org.

13. Geoffrey Wagner, "The Enduring Old-World Charm of Martinique," *New York Times*, July 16, 1967, p. 322.

14. Geoffrey Wagner, "Lazy Cruising in the Windwards" *New York Times*, April 5, 1964, p. 30.

15. Geoffrey Wagner, letter to Colleen Browning, Grenada, June 27, 1973.

16. Ibid

17. Ibid.

18. Geoffrey Wagner, letter to Colleen Browning, October 1948.

19. Ibid.

20. Nancy Lewis Tuten and John Zubizarreta, *The Robert Frost Encyclopedia* (Westport, CT: Greenwood Publishing Group, 2001), p. 284.

21. Geoffrey Wagner, letter to Colleen Browning, May 1974.

22. Anatole Broyard, "I'm Majoring in Me," book review, *New York Times*, December 2, 1976, p. 41.

23. Transcript, "Firing Line," taped in NYC on April 25, 1977, telecast on PBS, April 29, 1977. A production of Southern Educational Communications Association (SECA), Columbia, SC, Leland Stanford Jr. University.

24. This and the preceding six quotations are all from Geoffrey Wagner, "Dismay about the Way Things Are Going at CUNY," *New York Times,* April 30, 1977, p. 20.

25. Colleen Browning, letter to Professor Mervyn Jules, chairman, art department, CCNY, December 5, 1973.

26. Frank Getlein, exhibition catalogue, Kennedy Galleries, March 5–29, 1969, unpaginated.

27. Ibid.

28. Colleen Browning, script for a videotape (never produced), circa 1972.

29. Colleen Browning, *Working Out a Painting* (New York: Watson-Guptill Publications Inc., 1988), p. 42.

30. Judith White, "William Dobell: Yours Sincerely," *Australian Art Collector*, no. 12, April–June 2000, page unknown.

31. Colleen Browning, "A Studio ABC – A Talk with an Imaginary Studio Visitor," unpublished manuscript, c. January 1990, pp. 78–82.

32. Ibid.

33. Howard DaLee Spencer, "Colleen Browning: Recent Paintings," exhibition catalogue, Wichita Art Museum, December 6, 1986–January 11, 1987, p. 12.

34. Colleen Browning, "A Studio ABC – A Talk with an Imaginary Studio Visitor," unpublished manuscript, c. January 1990, p. 78.

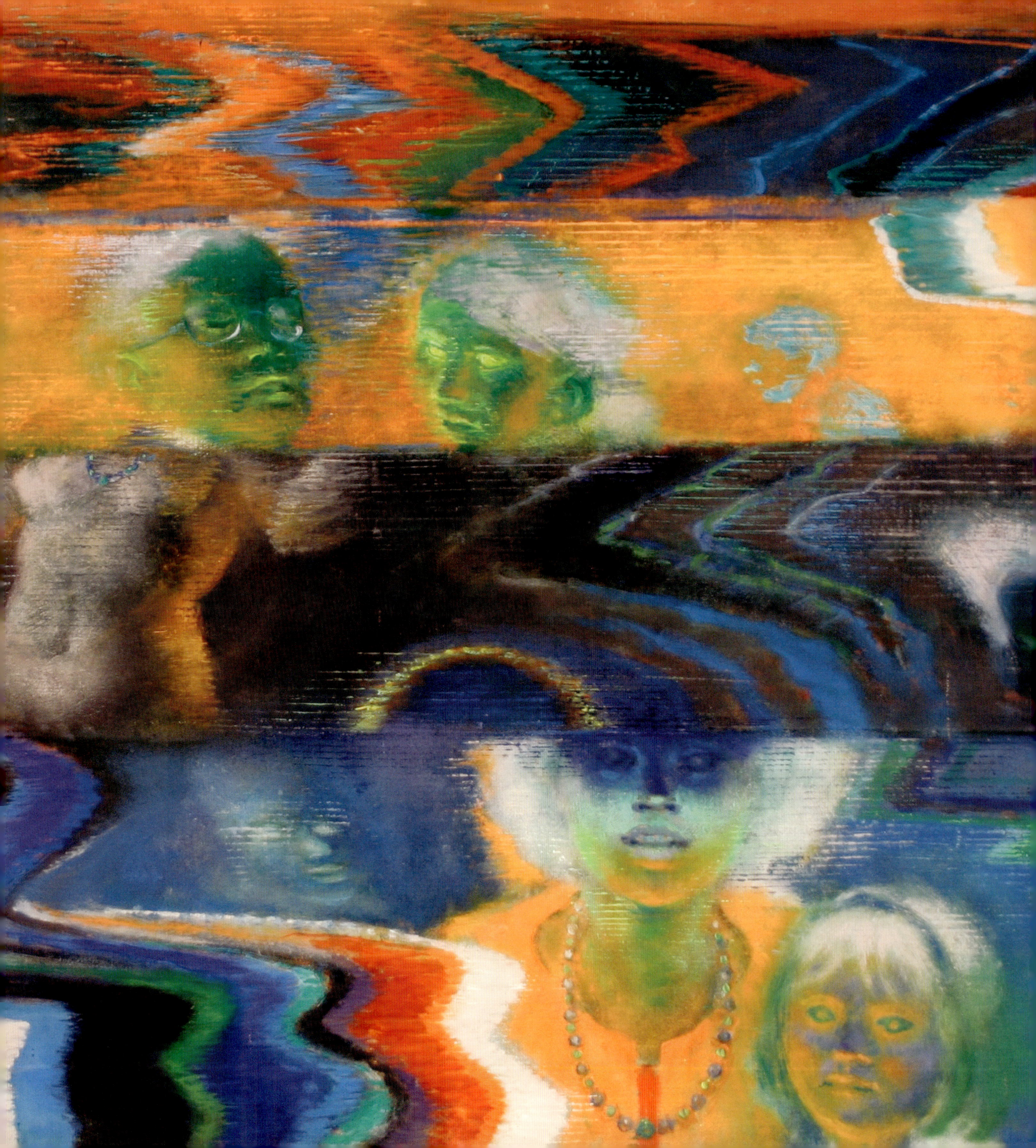

COLLEEN BROWNING'S *alter stil*—old-age style—was a regenerative series of images expanding into new worlds. On canvas and in paint, she seemed preoccupied with how things seen are merely emanations revealed by cosmic consciousness. Seeking to paint the comprehensible versus the unknown, her last decades questioned all the rest she had yet to discover. "The most beautiful thing we can experience," according to Albert Einstein, "is the mysterious."

Browning's spiritual re-awakening came gushing forth in a series of New Age paintings. Pantheism, gnosticism, and spiritualism were the alternative platforms of her advancing art and age. Her late paintings are filled with inexpressible wonder and a final burst of psychic energy to enshrine and ensure her lasting fame. These include female goddesses finally achieving their long overdue acclaim (*Target*, 1991) (fig. 8.1); fireworks bursting in the night sky (*Jubilee*, 1988); (fig. 8.2); television screen patterns scrambling into confounding puzzles (*Rising Tide*, 1994) (fig. 8.3); and in the tarot card theme of *The Adept*, 1984 (fig. 8.4), a proclivity for deeper self-knowledge.

Browning dabbled and explored but was never fully a certified believer in anything but herself. The sacred aura of her 1987 painting, *Ave Maria* (fig. 8.5) is a fine example of her versatility. In its Caravaggesque lighting effects—a magical tenebrism backlit with glowing candlelight—*Ave Maria* simulates a tactile spirituality within its devotional figures at a shrine.

Cautiously remaining on the periphery—just as she observed street waifs in Harlem 30 years earlier while never entering into their interior realities—she plucked pictorial information from her various tarot card readers and oracles without being sucked into the web of their spells. She maintained self-control but wanted to imagine she understood the ineffability of magic.

CHAPTER 8

The Dream: Myths &
Seances Late into Her
"New Age," 1980s–2003

In *Target*, one of three paintings (along with *Noon*, 1981, and *Studio*, 1998) accepted into The National Museum of Women in the Arts, Browning added yet another self-validating layer to her portfolio. Among the spectrum of New Age movements she observed—although from a distance—was the momentous shift toward a new feminist art history. Browning would have sympathized with the Victorian artist Anna Lea Merritt. In a letter written in 1900 to her sisters-in-arms (women who struggled for parity in the "man's world" of art history), Merritt wrote: "The chief obstacle to a woman's success is that she can never have a wife. Just reflect what a wife does for an artist."[1]

Target is a dynamic synthesis of various New Age themes reflecting Browning's ongoing desires to be current, recognized, remembered, and enshrined. There's little doubt the red-haired female is a self-portrait. We can assume she was admiring the work of photo-realist artist and feminist celebrity Audrey Flack in this period. Always capable of achieving top billing in the art press, Flack was being heralded for a series of goddess consciousness sculptures and public monuments in the 1980s. Developing a repertoire of New Age figures, Flack's woman warriors were redefining millennia of patriarchal imagery.

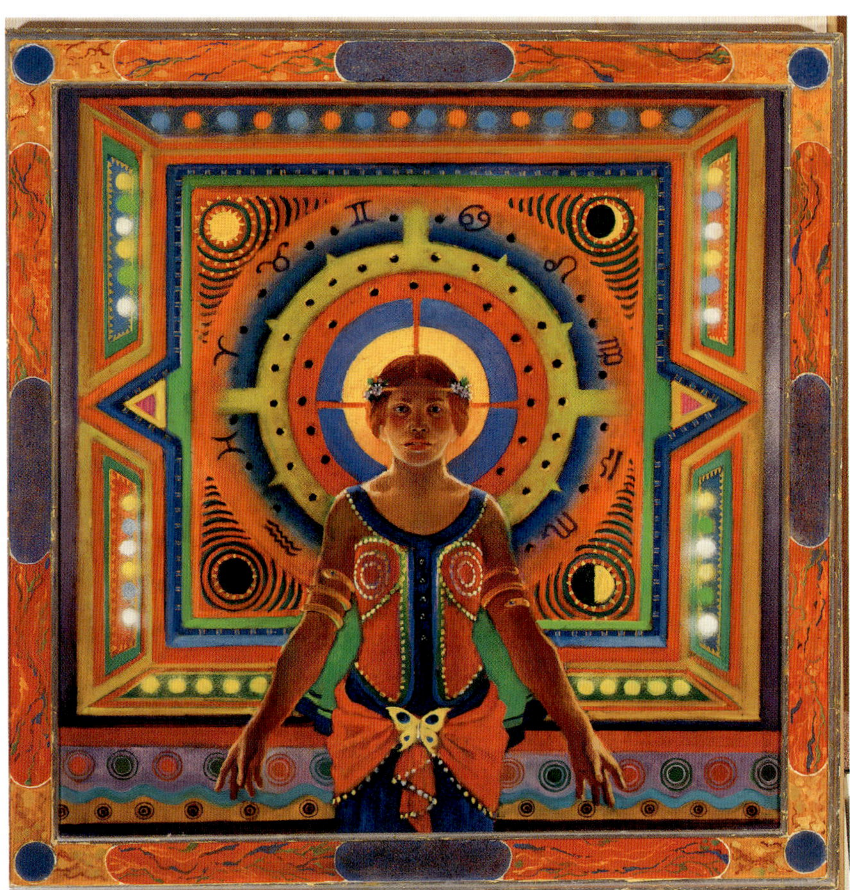

Fig. 8.1. Colleen Browning, Target, *1991. Oil on canvas, 51½ x 50½ inches. Collection of The National Museum of Women in the Arts, Washington, DC. Gift of the artist and the Harmon-Meek Gallery.*

Browning saw herself de facto as part of that unwritten narrative, and cultivated writers and critics to champion her role as an underappreciated female artist. Receiving major coverage in the national art press, The National Museum of Women in the Arts opened its doors in 1987 in the refurbished Masonic Temple, a massive beaux-arts monument on New York Avenue in the nation's capital, Washington, DC. Witnessing a new surge of historical and curatorial projects that identified undervalued female masters such as Sofonisba Anguissola, Mary Cassatt, Frieda Kahlo, Georgia O'Keeffe, and Louise Bourgeois, Browning felt driven to take her rightful place in the ranks as yet another unsung feminist artist. She orchestrated her acceptance into the collection with gallerist Bill Meek's always-skillful and supportive intervention.

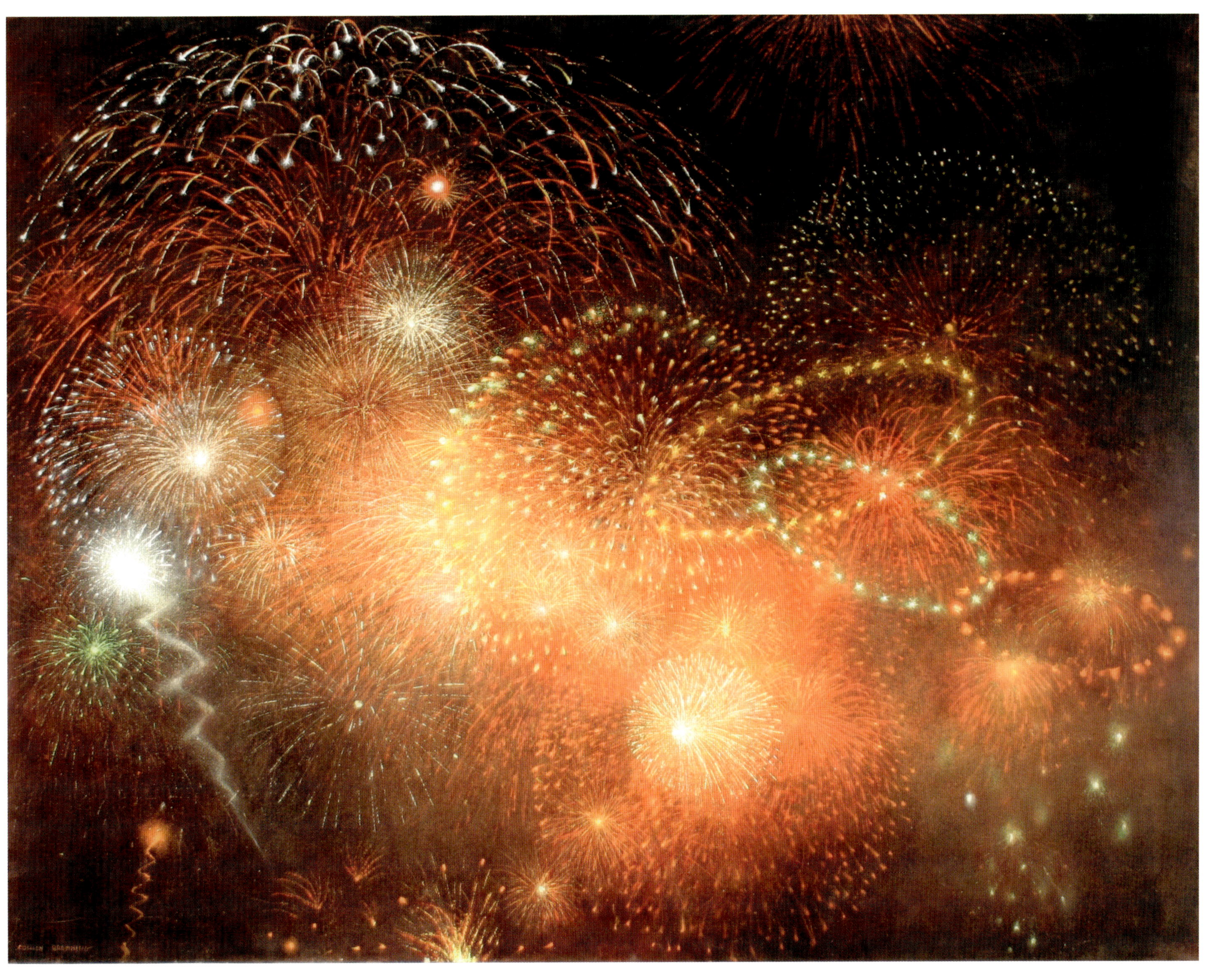

Fig. 8.2. Colleen Browning, Jubilee, *1988. Oil on canvas, 49 x 62¼ inches. Gift of the artist.*

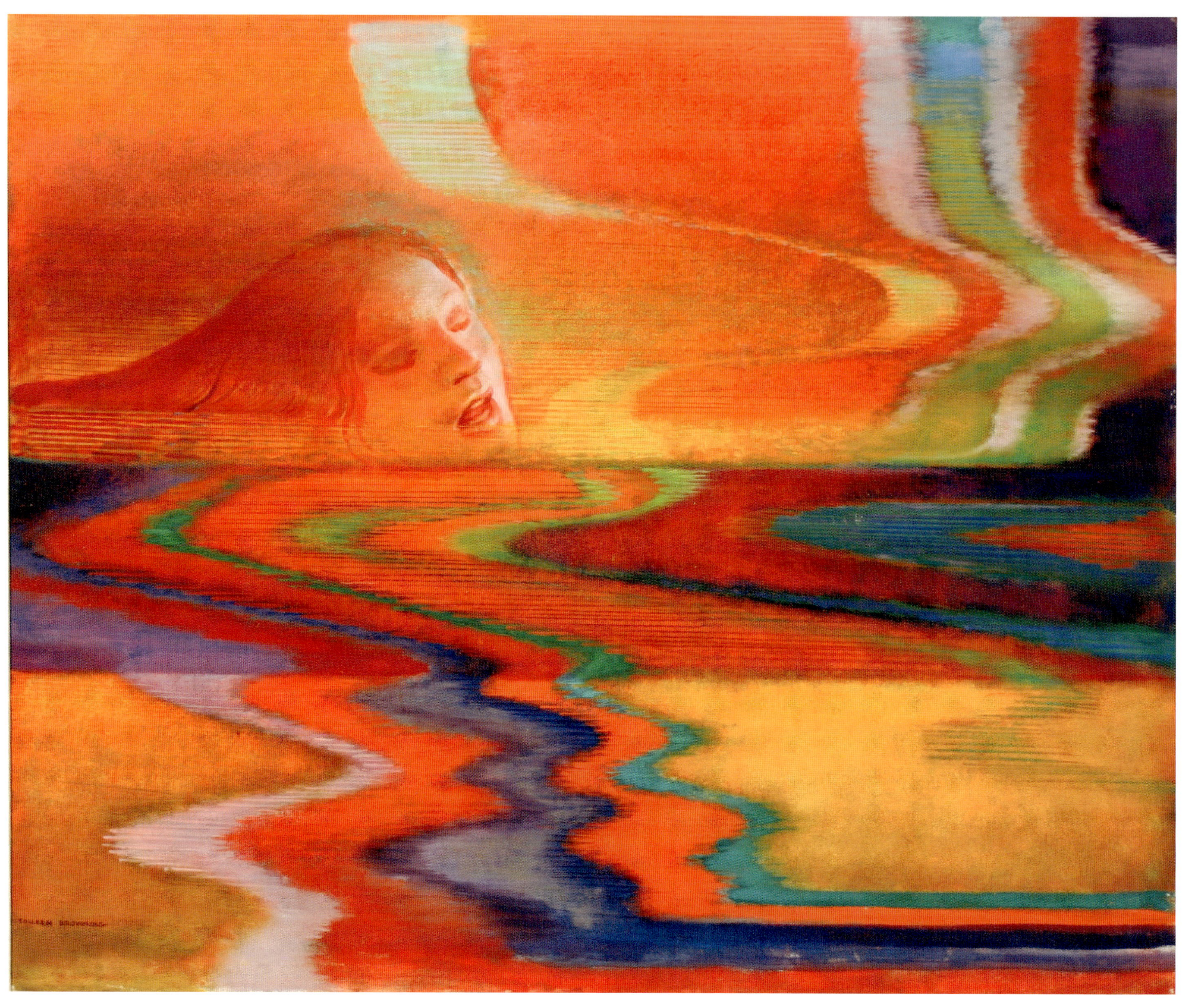

Fig. 8.3. Colleen Browning, Rising Tide,
1994. Oil on canvas, 35½ x 40½ inches.
Gift of the artist.

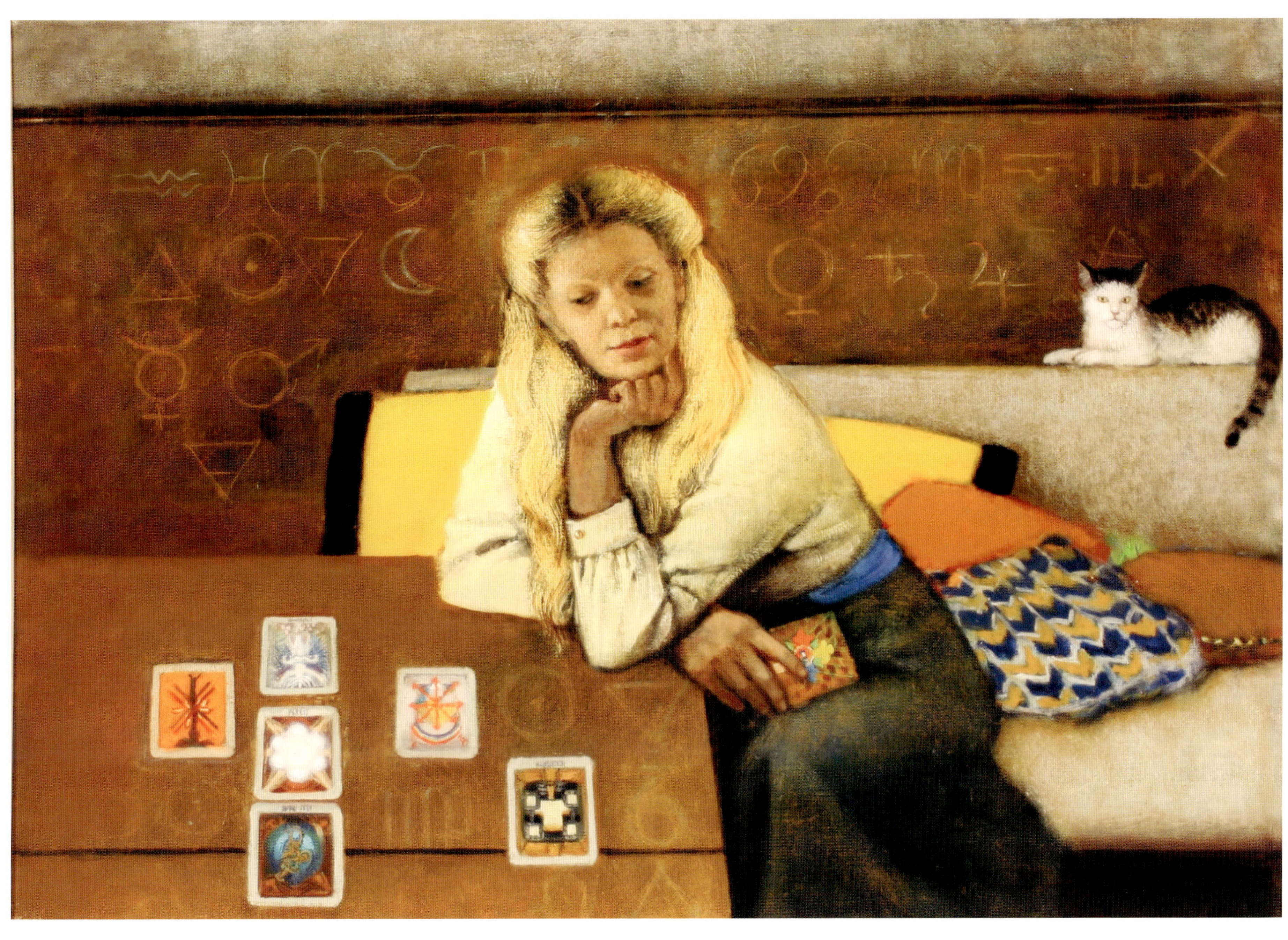

Fig. 8.4. Colleen Browning, The Adept, *1984. Oil on canvas, 27 x 34 inches. Gift of the artist.*

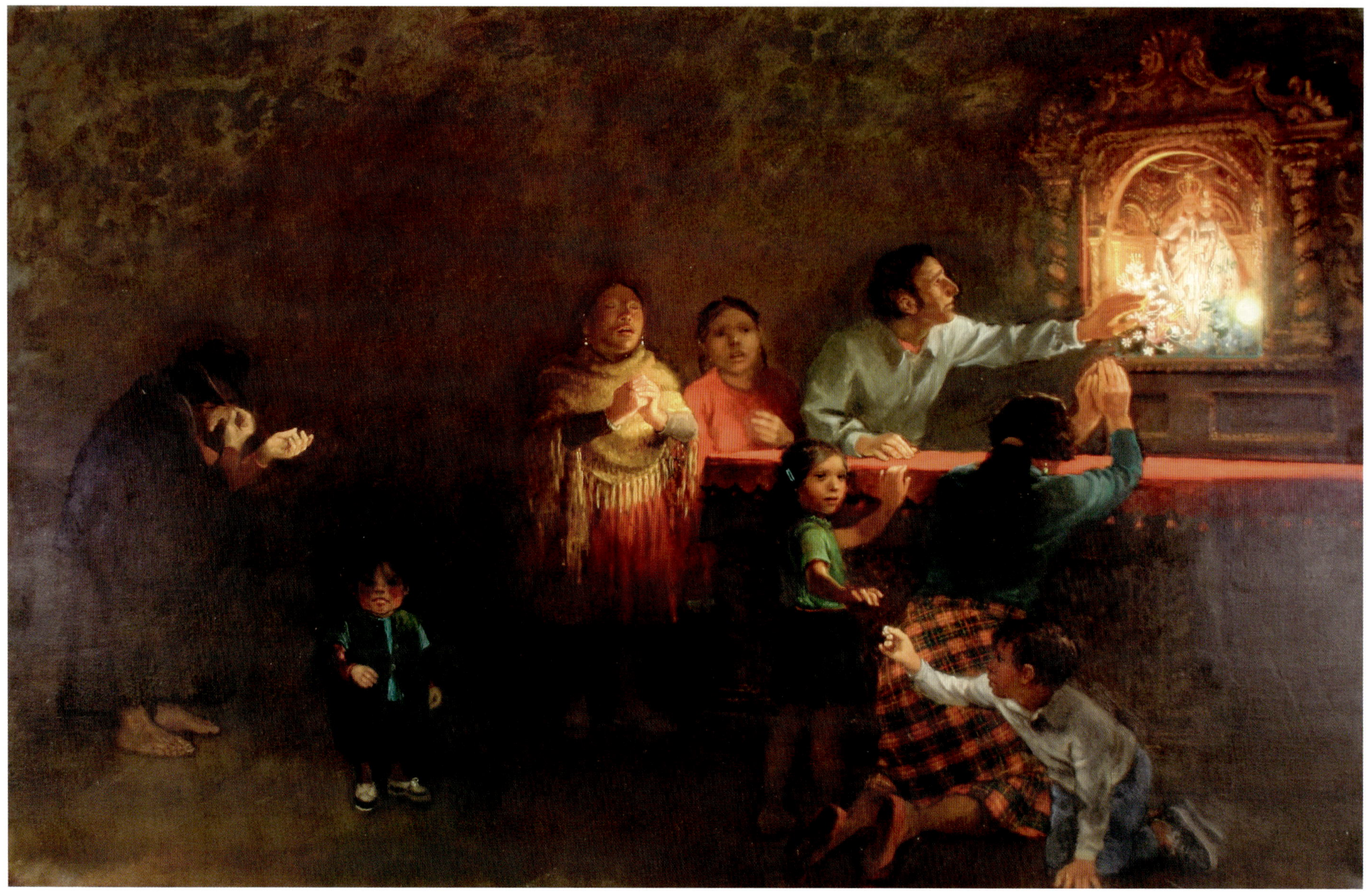

Fig. 8.5. Colleen Browning, Ave Maria, 1987. Oil on canvas, 44½ x 66¾ inches. Gift of the artist.

It is noteworthy that these three paintings, according to the deed, were all "gift of the artist and the Harmon-Meek Gallery" in the summer of 1999, in the aftermath of Browning being diagnosed with a terminal, late-stage intestinal cancer. On the museum's formal stationery with a gift acknowledgment, signed August 4, 1999 from Director Nancy Risque Rohrbach, The National Museum of Women in the Arts, Browning scribbled these cryptic notes about her all-encompassing self-deity image:

> *1. Target for discrimination and injustice; 2. invincible with the bullet holes missing her; 3. saint or sacred figure with the halo; 4. powerful priestess with serpentine bracelets; 5. as the moon goddess Diana, 4 phases of the moon surround the target; 6. fairground performer, exhibitionist and erotic.*

Toward the end of her career, Browning's lifelong rapture with landscape painting rose to the level of the romantic sublime. As if seized with the romantic memories of childhood that rose back to the forefront of her imagination in her twilight years, she created numerous landscapes of exceptional quality and variety.

Finding a clue to Browning's landscape masterpiece *Iguassu III*, 1985 (fig. 8.6), allows us to journey with her over its rainbow and beyond the chasms of an imaginary place. Based on their travels to Iguassu Falls on the border of Brazil and Argentina, she produced copiously prepared preliminary drawings and documentary photographs. For this life-changing project, she summoned up exceptional energies in executing a series of works focusing on the falls. "These falls are the most sublime, overwhelming, transcendent natural phenomena I've ever seen, consisting of five miles of cascades pouring over tiered amphitheatres and curtained with rainbows and clouds of spray," she noted in her unpublished manuscript.

Browning was a kindred spirit along with generations of artist-explorers inspired by Alexander von Humboldt's Latin American travels. In an ongoing travelogue, she was pulled toward the earth mother Gaia's mystical powers. Iguassu Falls is listed as one of the three largest waterfalls on the planet. The falls break into 260 segments in a stair-step pattern along a semicircular escarpment almost 9,000 feet in length. Touring its misty cascades, Browning wrote her impressions: "I wanted to express the ecstasy I felt in an almost all-white painting, an incandescent haze, with the simplest possible compositional structure, yet with a sense of place, but a timeless place, not a 'beauty spot' gush."[2]

Browning's Iguassu series is a group of "mystical, ecstatic masterpieces," commented one critic.[3] "Her use of light almost overwhelms but she draws us in by using small reassurances…cascading waterfalls and a huge rainbow command the large canvas but a minutely detailed palm tree holds fast in the upper left corner, while its counterpoint, another tree, pins down the lower right corner. They are of the earth, as we are, permitting us to share the artist's rapture."[4]

As her last sustained burst of creative activity, she began pondering the existence or possibility of an afterlife and next world. This was manifested by her fascination with psychics, oracles, and soothsayers. Whether she was painting the remote natural wonders of Iguassu Falls or exploring the inner psyche of a gypsy fortune-teller, she seemed preoccupied with visual themes of mysticism. Her later years were dramatically defined in this move toward transcendentalism. Facing the abyss, her pantheistic tendencies emerged with heightened intensity.

A large portion of her late paintings corresponded to a moment dubbed the New Age in the 1980s. She was delving into psychic phenomena as an alternative road less traveled than the exploding digital-microchip worlds of artificial intelligence. Browning was innately anti-technological and easily sympathetic to postmodernist romanticism. Feeling the latest buzz around her students as a studio art instructor at City College and the National Academy, she was ready to flirt with New Age fads gaining traction.

Clairvoyant II, 1984 (fig. 8.7), indicates Browning's exploratory curiosity about the practitioners of occultism. Gathering subject matter for her New Age paintings, she sought out practical knowledge in order to translate mystical secrets into realized images.

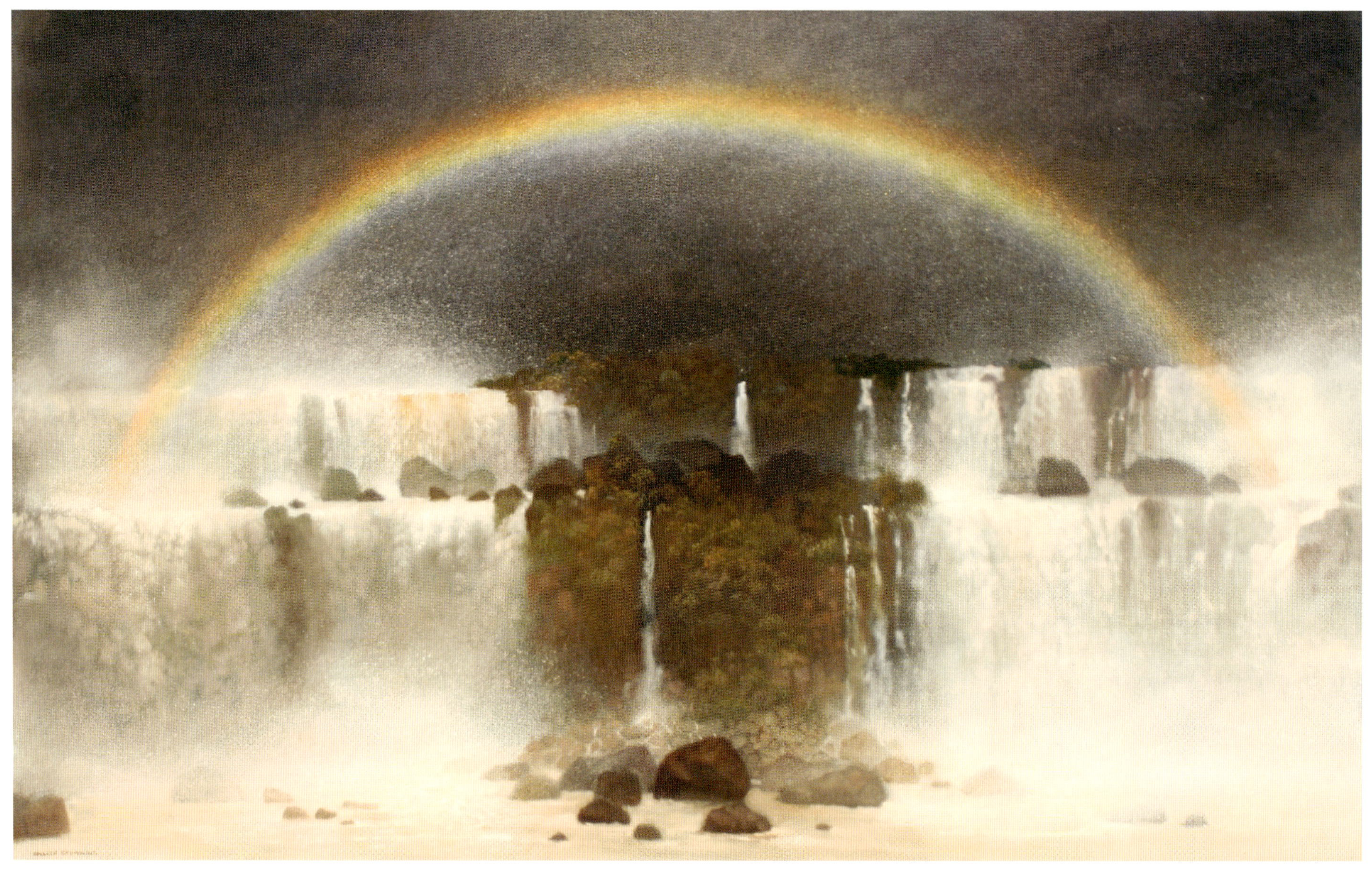

Fig. 8.6. Colleen Browning, Iguassu III,
1985. Oil on canvas, 39 x 60¼ inches.
Gift of the artist.

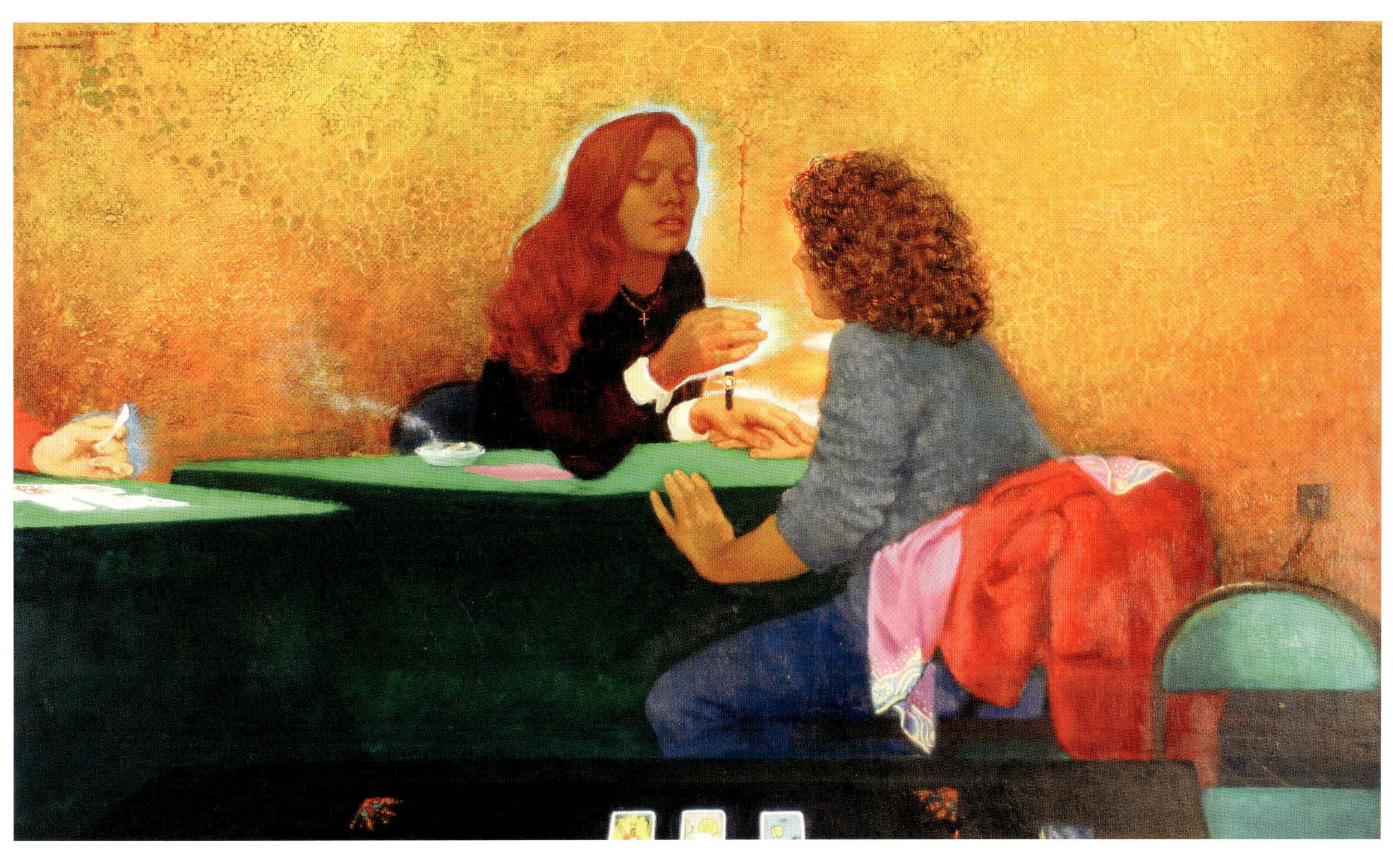

Fig. 8.7. Colleen Browning, Clairvoyant II, *1984. Oil on canvas, 28½ x 46 inches. Gift of the artist.*

Like a closed circuit—note the electrical outlet on the far right side of the image—one needs to be plugged into the universe's voltage to transfer current from mystic to seeker. By using gold leaf in the process, she allows the surface to transport the viewer into the spiritual realms of the Byzantine icon painter. An aura of strangeness invites observers into this imaginative dimension—glowing with the luminosity of Tiffany glass. She intentionally provoked these magical effects:

> *The origin of the painting was that I wanted to do something that had a completely unreal background. Possibly the suggestion of religion in it because some of the paintings of the very early Renaissance had this gold background, which is cracked over the ages. Somebody is dealing with forces that are not everyday.*[5]

The setting is at one of Manhattan's psychic fairs—probably a neighborhood school gymnasium, rented empty storefront building, or sidewalk stand. We observe the left hand of a card-reader on the far left side of the painting, indicating that we are in a public "pay to pray" type of psychic marketplace. The triangular composition pulls the arrangement's focus onto the dangling watch between mystic and client.

Browning points out some pertinent details: "I painted the background thickly with ochres and yellows and then incised it, allowing some of the original red ground to show through, in order to give the effect of the cracking gold backgrounds in fifteenth-century religious paintings. The clairvoyant herself is in clerical black with white cuffs instead of a collar. The cigarette smoke perhaps suggests incense…. The clairvoyant is using psychometry, a method of divination about a third person that employs an object belonging to that person. She is going into a trance while holding her client's hand."[6]

Mastering the practices of reading tarot cards, a deck of 78 cards used for the game of *tarock*, Browning widened her artistic sorcery into the world beyond eyesight. *The Adept* is a psychic self-portrait using a young female tarot card reader whose expertise is unquestioned. The intermediary role of the gypsy fortuneteller is to induce clients into altered states of consciousness. Even her choice of colors—alizarin crimson, thalo green, and auroline glazing—is filtered into the image with marvelous subtlety.

> *This might be compared with the creative experience of an artist or the sense of wonder one can feel when confronted by the beauty of nature or a great work of art. Browning's goal in painting The Adept was to achieve a deeper knowledge and a greater understanding both of herself and of life's natural forces and cycles.*[7]

Capitalizing on the strangely arranged shapes and forms found on their color television set, Browning launched another series, the TV series, in the early 1990s. *Fracture*, 1993 (fig. 8.8), *Disconnections*, 1994 (fig. 8.9), and *Rising Tide*, 1994 (see fig. 8.3), reflect subtle varieties on this inventive theme, each loosening and then tightening in frequencies between pure abstraction and figurative images. They demonstrate her interest in translating interior states of mind using compositional static.

She deciphered their cryptic meanings in a letter to her agent Bill Meek: "These paintings are based on scrambled TV cable images, as a metaphor for social conditions or psychological states. They are realistic paintings of unrealistic phenomena using the arrows and zig-zag ribbons, reversed tonalities and split screens of scrambled TV in general in a sort of symbiosis of contemporary technology and mysticism."

Unexplainable is her use of Wagner's portrait in *Fracture*, which she described as a "deteriorating relationship between a man and a woman."[8] One can safely assume her beloved companion's rugged face is inserted merely as a model, without symbolical indication of marital discord.

Another imaginative sequence of visual experiments is the Fireworks series. Like the Subway series, this dazzling group of paintings tested Browning's tightrope walk between realism and abstraction. *Jubilee*, 1988, is the signature image of this series—a massive canvas in its mural scale and internalized explosive energies. This was her fifth in a series of images that were commenced with the 1983 Brooklyn Bridge Centennial. "I saw the pyrotechnics over the bridge that night from an office high up on Wall Street, with a panorama of the East River and Brooklyn."[9]

The fireworks for *Jubilee* were "based on the Statue of Liberty which I watched from Battery Park, jammed with a huge crowd all looking upwards so that this painting has only the exploding sky as motif."[10] Browning's is a much larger, more exuberant version of an image first made into an art historical icon, James Abbott McNeill Whistler's *Nocturne in Black and Gold, the Falling Rocket*, 1875 (fig. 8.10), in the Detroit Institute of Arts.

Of course, a century later, there would be no sarcastic critic reacting to the purely abstract paint blobs igniting across the sky as multicolored specks streaked across the canvas, as was the case when traditionalist John Ruskin denounced Whistler in 1877 for "flinging a pot of paint in the public's face." He was challenged the next year with a libel suit in a London courthouse. Awarded one farthing in damages, Whistler had been vindicated when he pushed the agenda of modernism and granted a moral victory to artists, ensuring the future of unassailable artistic license.

True to her ever-curious method, Browning demonstrated her due diligence with a fieldwork examination of the history and methods of creating firework displays. Her first step was contacting Fireworks by Grucci, the nation's most respected experts in pyrotechnics. This family business was established in 1850 and the descendants welcomed Browning's artistic inquiries. Over the generations, they have developed innovative techniques and even simulated a mock atomic bomb for the Department of Defense. Today they use computerized technology to light the sky at major events, such as presidential inaugurations, Olympics games, and the openings of world fairs.

> *Before doing this group of paintings I had never seen spectacular fireworks and realized I knew absolutely nothing visually about their changing forms; but I've always loved sparkle—I remember how I admired Christmas tree decorations as a child! So I wrote to the Grucci, the manufacturers of fireworks and stagers of these pyrotechnics, for information.*
>
> *I found it impossible to get that violence and crispness by using a fine brush stroke since the line would expand; and a very thin brush could not hold enough paint…. I discovered that if I cut thick paper and painted the paper's edge, then pressed the edge on the canvas, I got an incredibly vital mark. Jubilee was painted entirely with*

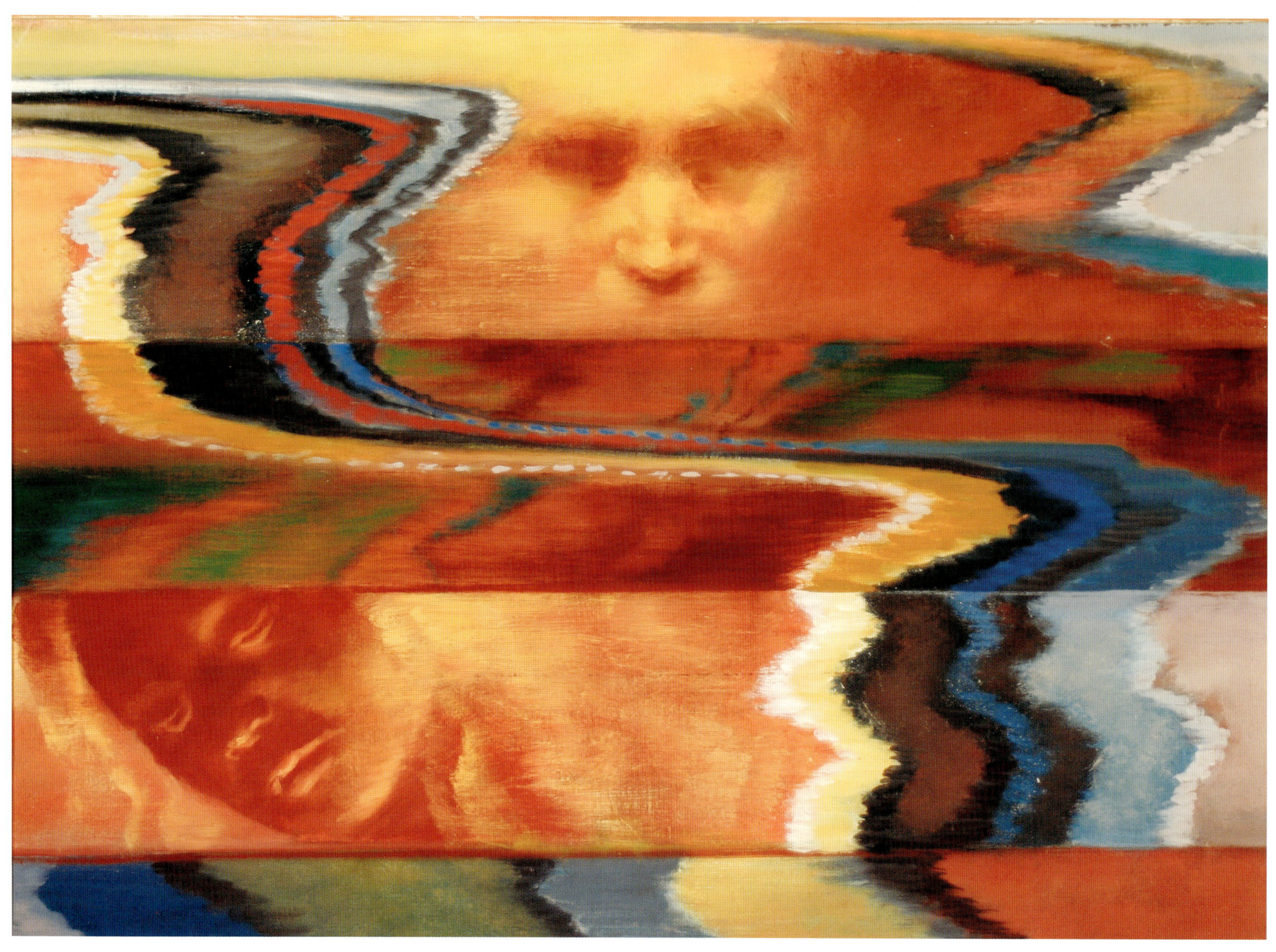

Fig. 8.8. Colleen Browning, Fracture,
*1993. Oil on canvas, 24 x 30 inches. Gift
of the artist.*

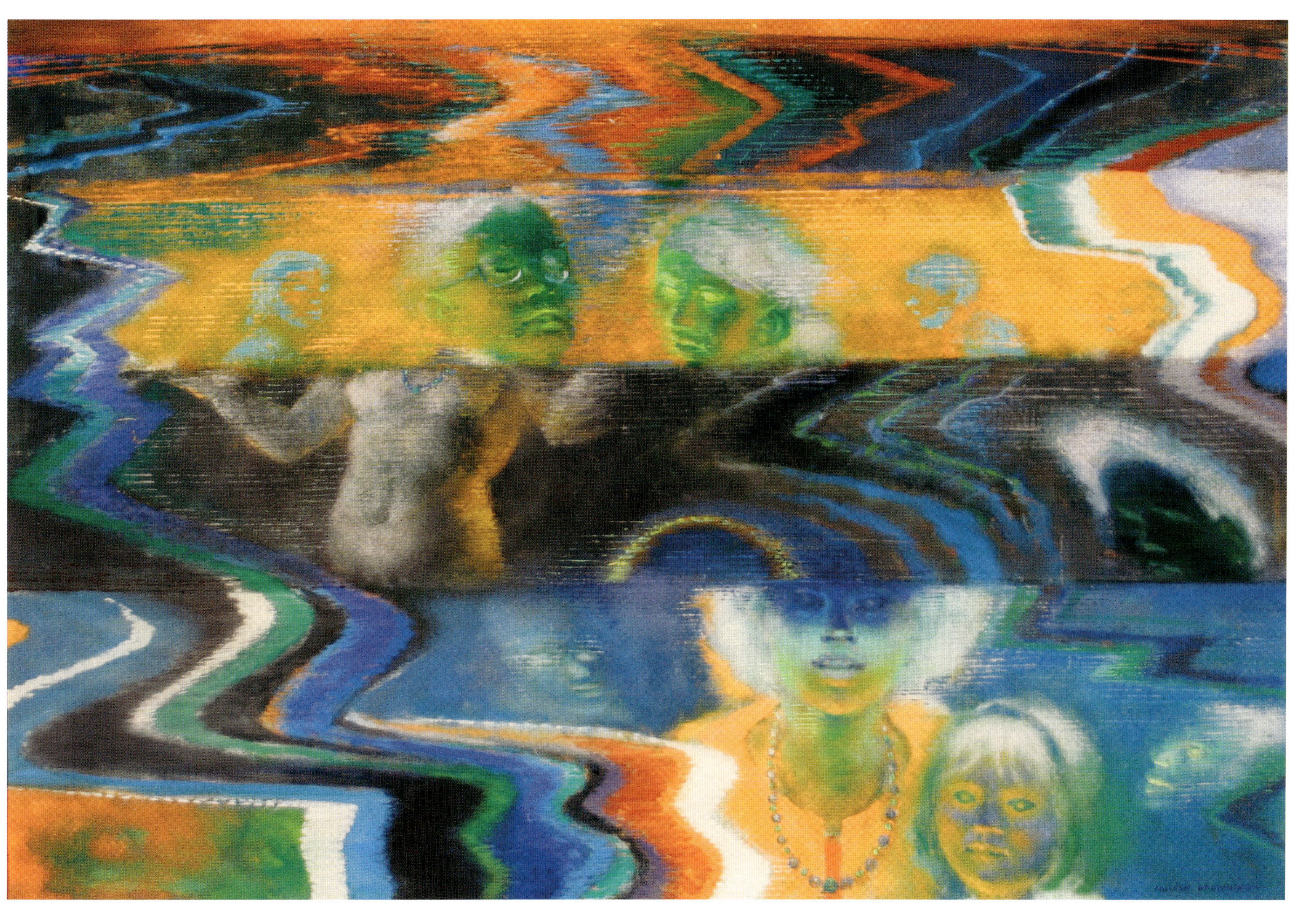

Fig. 8.9. Colleen Browning, Disconnections, *1994. Oil on canvas, 32 x 46 inches. Gift of the artist.*

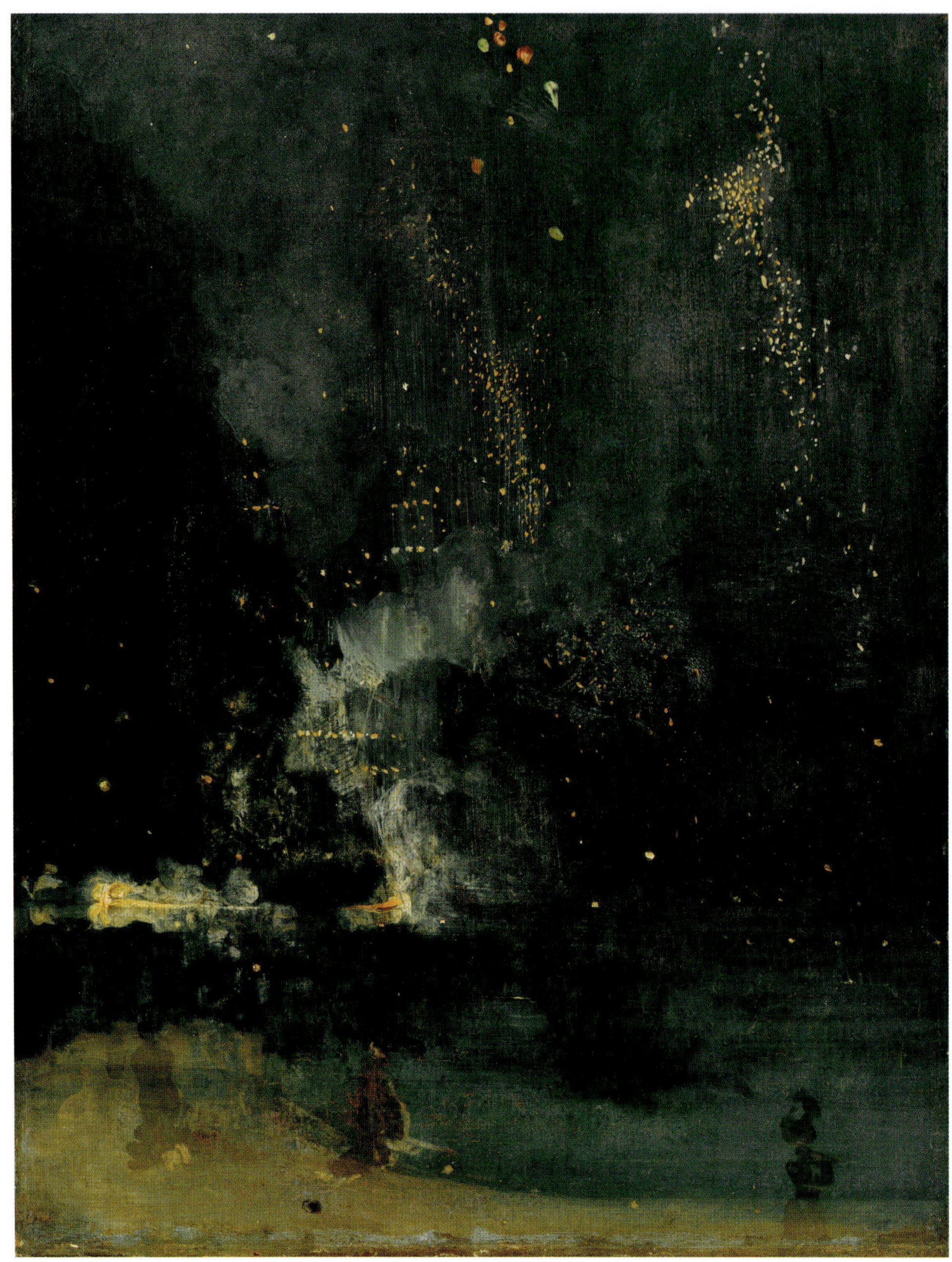

*pressed heavy paper, glazed when dry, flip-sprayed, re-paper-pressed, glazed again and
so on. I had fun![1]*

But the "fun" of vicarious external activities could not replace the prolonged dia‑
logue inside the apartment Browning and Wagner shared for decades. The only sounds
breaking their conversation would have been classical music and news on the radio. The
dial was usually tuned to WQXR, a classical station (now defunct) owned by the *New
York Times*. For dinnertime and evening relaxation they would spin a variety of calypso,
West Indian, and French pop music along with swing band–era jazz selections on a very

modest stereo system. Childless, their entire solar system orbited around each other's career advancement as artist and author. Every correspondence between New York, Grenada, or England (as the couple often returned home for visits with aging parents) included some fawning note of self-encouraging and note of "break a leg," wishing each other success. Praise was showered for Browning's next gallery or museum exhibition, and reciprocally, Wagner's scholarly books, acerbic essays, or creative sideline of churning out erotic potboilers received cheerleading boosts in Browning's tirelessly supportive letters. They were self-validating machines, but only addressed each other.

Browning and Wagner were eccentric loners. But for their own charmed self-embrace, we can visualize these cosmopolitan, globetrotting sophisticates who were essentially in a universe of their own creation and self-definition. In this author's excavation of hundreds of personal documents, letters, telephone books, diaries, and personal memorabilia, there is not one single instance of any documentation of any meaningful friendships. The camera was passed back and forth for photos—but only Browning or Wagner are in the lens.

We are constantly reminded of Browning's incomparable culinary artisanship, as cooking and gardening were her only outlets. But in half a century we do not have one photograph of her ever sharing a meal with any living soul other than Wagner. It would be inaccurate to dismiss them as bashful or socially inept. When seen in public, from video recordings, they were clearly exuberant, even charismatic individuals. They were not shy. They just wanted to be left to themselves.

"I was their closest neighbor here on the 19th floor at 100 LaSalle," commented Dorothy Edmonds, who was 99 years old at the time of this interview. "She's as sharp as a needle," wrote Browning once in a letter giving instructions for men to pick up paintings at Edmonds's apartment. As a friendly neighbor, Edmonds was entrusted with Browning's apartment key when the art shippers would arrive. "I believe I had more contact with Colleen than anyone in the building, but she never once invited me in for a cup of tea or wanted me to even see her artworks." As for Wagner, he was remembered by Edmonds as "quite a hot number who was seen around the building wearing an assortment of flamboyant silk scarves—but always keeping to himself."

The modus operandus of their self-supporting but all-encompassing internalized existence is revealed in a newspaper interview for the popular *New York Post*. Published on March 6, 1976, a quaint domesticity is seen: "At Home with Colleen Browning & Geoffrey Wagner." Author Jerry Tallmer, who was on the founding staff of *The Village Voice* in 1955, contributed to the tabloid daily as veteran cultural affairs correspondent. Writing many behind-the-scenes articles for Broadway's *Playbill*, he enjoyed prying into the personal lives of New York's stage celebrities, writers, and artists.

The story begins with a charming bit of domesticity as he steps through the door at their Morningside Heights residence. "On the kitchen door there were lots of little cards, notations of certain dishes made by Colleen Browning…. 'He grades my meals' said Colleen Browning with a flash of her eyes, a toss of her long copper-colored hair. 'If he likes them he gives them red stars. I really believe fate meant me to meet Geoffrey. I had decided to go to Italy, now that my father wasn't there, and I'd gone all around the Bay of Naples—to Amalfi, Sorrento, Capri—and something told me I had to go to Ischia. There I saw this very good-looking man on the beach. I thought: 'What do I lose if I pick him up? But I couldn't think what to say, so I said: 'Are you Swedish?' 'And I said,' said Wagner: 'Are you a good cook?'"[12]

Brimming with anecdotal details, Tallmer continues his probing house call. "Mr. and Mrs. Wagner were at their ease in sandals, toes free. In the center of the living room there stood an easel: hers. [She] is a highly considerable painter. She was born in Fermoy, County Cork [*sic*], and on March 17, Saint Patrick's Day—'purely by coincidence'—she has a new show opening here at the Kennedy Gallery….'Geoffrey and I have enormous appetites,' she said. 'I like absolute dead silence when I eat. I don't even like to think when I eat.'"[13]

We learn of Wagner's gourmand affection for Browning's "frightfully good home-made strawberry ice cream topped with raspberries; veal goulash with spaetzele; filet of sole bonne femme with two sauces—a white wine sauce and a Hollandaise on top of that with mushrooms all around; pork chops Esterhazy; and ginger silhouette cake," which received four stars.[14]

Strikingly revealing of their indifference for sharing these *grande bouffes* with friends or neighbors, the concluding self-exposing truth of the article comes out: "Entertaining? I entertain Geoffrey every night. It's an absolute catastrophe for him to eat out. Oh entertaining. Well, we don't like a lot of people."[15]

Happily and hopefully transformed by the wisdom of experience as U.S. citizens, both Browning and Wagner developed a profound affection for their adopted country. Decades later, Browning created a series of over-the-top paintings celebrating America. Almost diametrically opposite of Wagner's earlier impression, evidence shows that Browning and Wagner became ardently proud Americans.

From 1972 forward, Browning and Wagner shuttled back and forth from John F. Kennedy Airport on the old Pan-American Airways route between New York and Grenada. On the island, Browning's painting palette became turbo-charged, which she described as a "simmering fizz" of highly saturated colors in the tropical paradise. Successive canvases depicted the bright red and strong greens of the island's exotic flowers and verdant underbrush. The sun-drenched island was a riot of horticultural splendor to the intrepid gardener and painter.

For the reclusive couple, perpetually tanned as obvious sun worshippers, Grenada was their sacred refuge "far from the madding crowd." With its native mixture of African, French, and old British commonwealth cultural heritage where English is spoken, Grenada offered serenity for Browning and Wagner. They quickly mastered Grenadian cuisine, laced with local spices. Wagner was a local celebrity at the tennis club, often chumming along with the premier and lesser governmental ministers. For ex-Brits, Grenada was an ideal home away from home. Their hillside residence, above the Grand Anse Beach at St. George's, ensured perpetual solitude and solace. Browning set up a fully functioning painting studio in the expansive living room area with a breathtaking, panoramic view of the beach and harbor below.

Browning worked with unparalleled intensity; her Grenada-based paintings became luxurious exercises in the fertility of life and living organisms. Nowhere else in her entire oeuvre do we shield our eyes at the bold application of cadmium scarlet—"my favorite color"—in combination with violets, turquoise, and crimson. Featuring her tropical palette, a career landmark article about her in *American Artist* in September 1981, was titled "Colleen Browning: A Rich Tapestry of Color."

She was described as an artist who used colors that showed her extraordinary sense of intensity, which was aptly conveyed in the flamboyantly infused colors of her Grenada paintings. A quiet young woman, often hidden between palm leaves in the sun-dappled jungle, noted the blissful sensuality of the island's ejaculatory flowers. It was Browning. The robust young female, perhaps one-third of Browning's actual age, is the faerie spirit she has depicted as a surrogate of her own decaying figure. Her corporeal degeneration was denied in the midst of these rejuvenating orchids and wisteria—she blooms eternal.

As Monet immersed himself, in his last decades, in the floral universe of his garden at Giverny, Browning's island garden became her earthly palette of myriad shapes and rainbow colors. The asymmetrical arrangement of her flowerbeds, climbing and shooting off varying vines and entwining shrubs, came to represent what she called the "unity of all living things."

Representative images of her Grenada-based works are *Large Group*, 1988 (fig. 8.11); *Shore Four*, 1988 (fig. 8.12); *Siesta I*, 1988 (fig. 8.13); *The Blue Towel*, 1988 (fig. 8.14); and *Walk to the Beach*, 1985 (fig. 8.15). Underlying each of these images is the imaginative way Browning interwove vegetation, water, undulating stripes of beach blankets, accenting patterns on towels, and the hot reds and orange textile patterns on the seminude bathing figures.

Artists devoted to the human form have persistently frequented life classes to remain in tune with their relationship to the figure. They use artificial light in cramped art school studios for the posing sessions. Unwrapping themselves from bathrobes (the nude models are often subsidized by the artists in attendance), they proved that there is no substitute for drawing the nude in the "raw flesh." Grenada's beaches offered Browning endless opportunities to capture the human figure in infinitely arousing and exciting positions of action and rest.

Puncturing their laid-back, West Indies lifestyle, global events in 1983 briefly transformed paradise into a Cold War inferno. "I become upset when I hear the invasion decried," she said, a hint of steel coming into her voice…. "a hard-line Marxist was installed with a an absolutely tyrannous regime…A huge Russian and Cuban contingent was already billeted on the island and a big air base was being built…Castro's speeches and old tangos were played on the loudspeaker all day. I learned Spanish in order to go up and complain. The Cubans were the most sexist group I have ever seen in my life. The trucks would make for me just to keep me jumping."[16]

Just as their English loyalties were tested during the darkest days of the Blitz in London, this conflict brought forth a rush of patriotic fervor to them as American citizens. From their terrace on Grenada, they watched elite commandos of the United States armed forces jumping from helicopters during this late Cold War crisis.

In the most unexpected way, Browning and Wagner were almost in the crosshairs of the United States military intervention and invasion of their tranquil West Indies resort island. At dawn on October 25, 1983, President Reagan ordered a commando-style

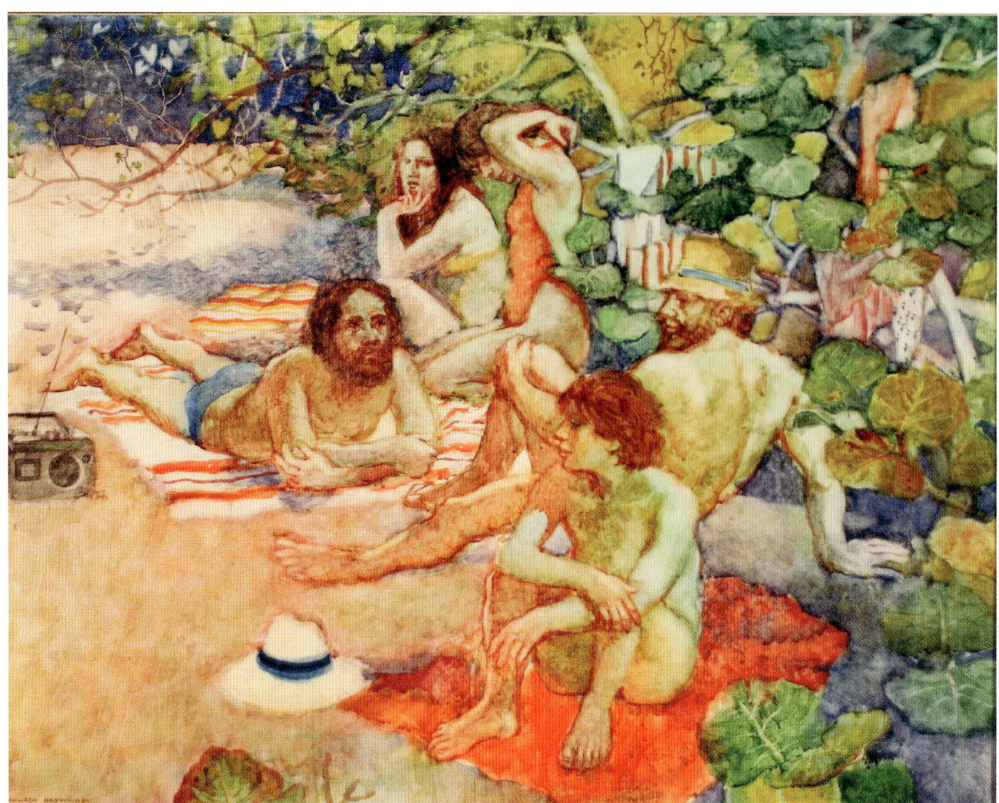

Fig. 8.11. Colleen Browning, Large Group, *1988. Watercolor on paper, 34 x 43½ inches. Gift of the artist.*

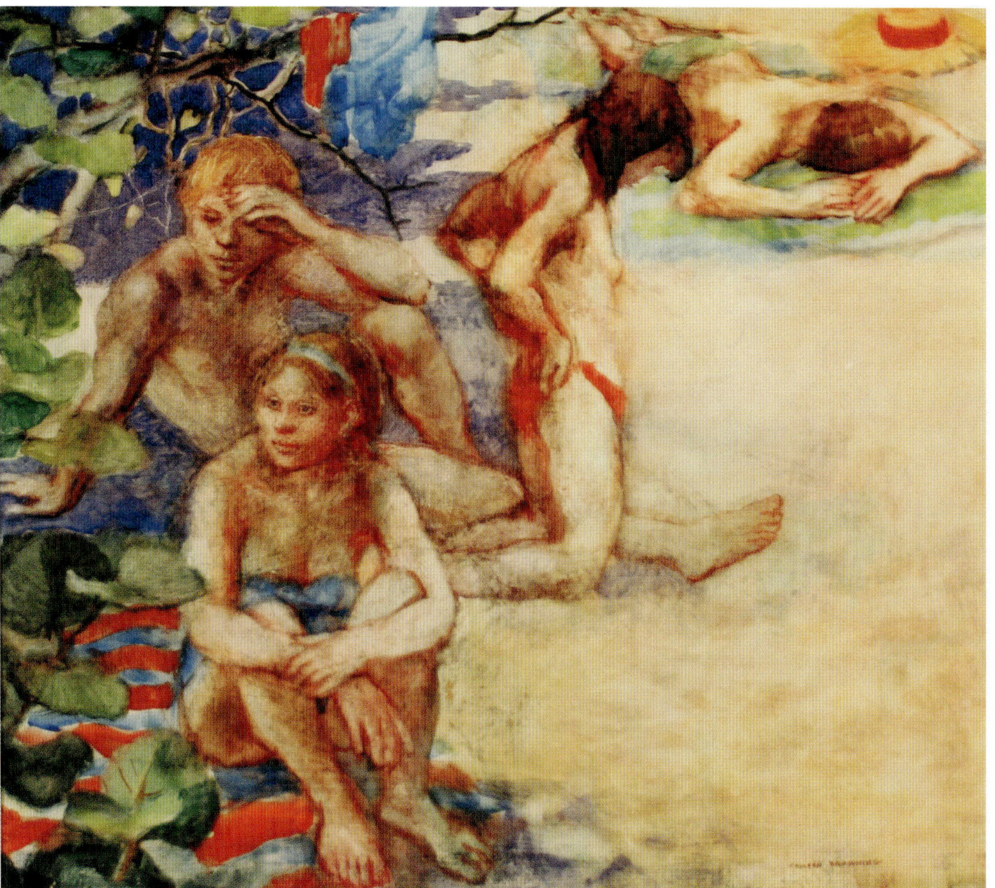

Fig. 8.12. Colleen Browning, Shore Four, *1988. Watercolor on paper, 32½ x 36¼ inches. Gift of the artist.*

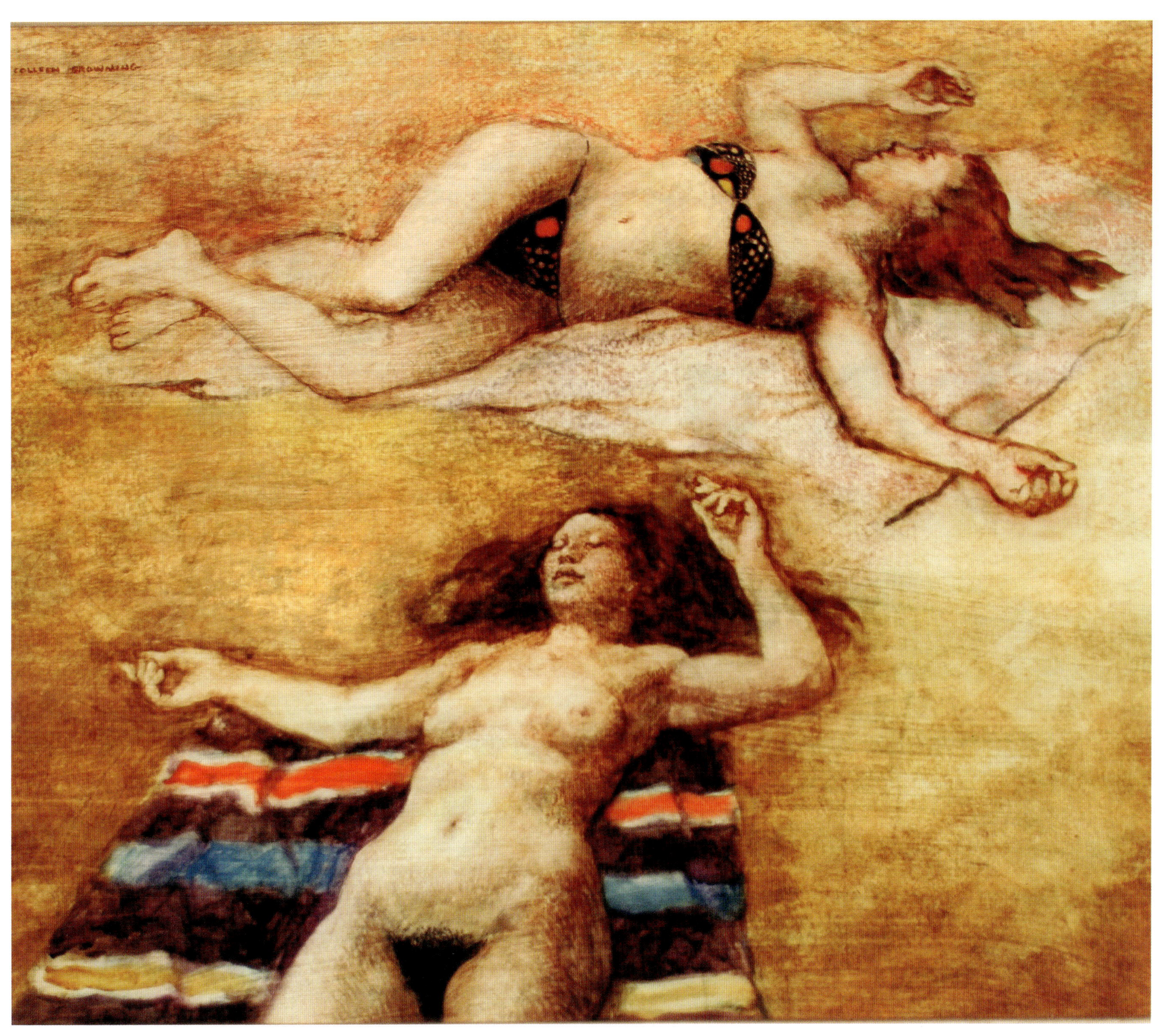

Fig. 8.13. Colleen Browning, Siesta I, 1998. Watercolor on paper, 28½ x 34 inches. Gift of the artist.

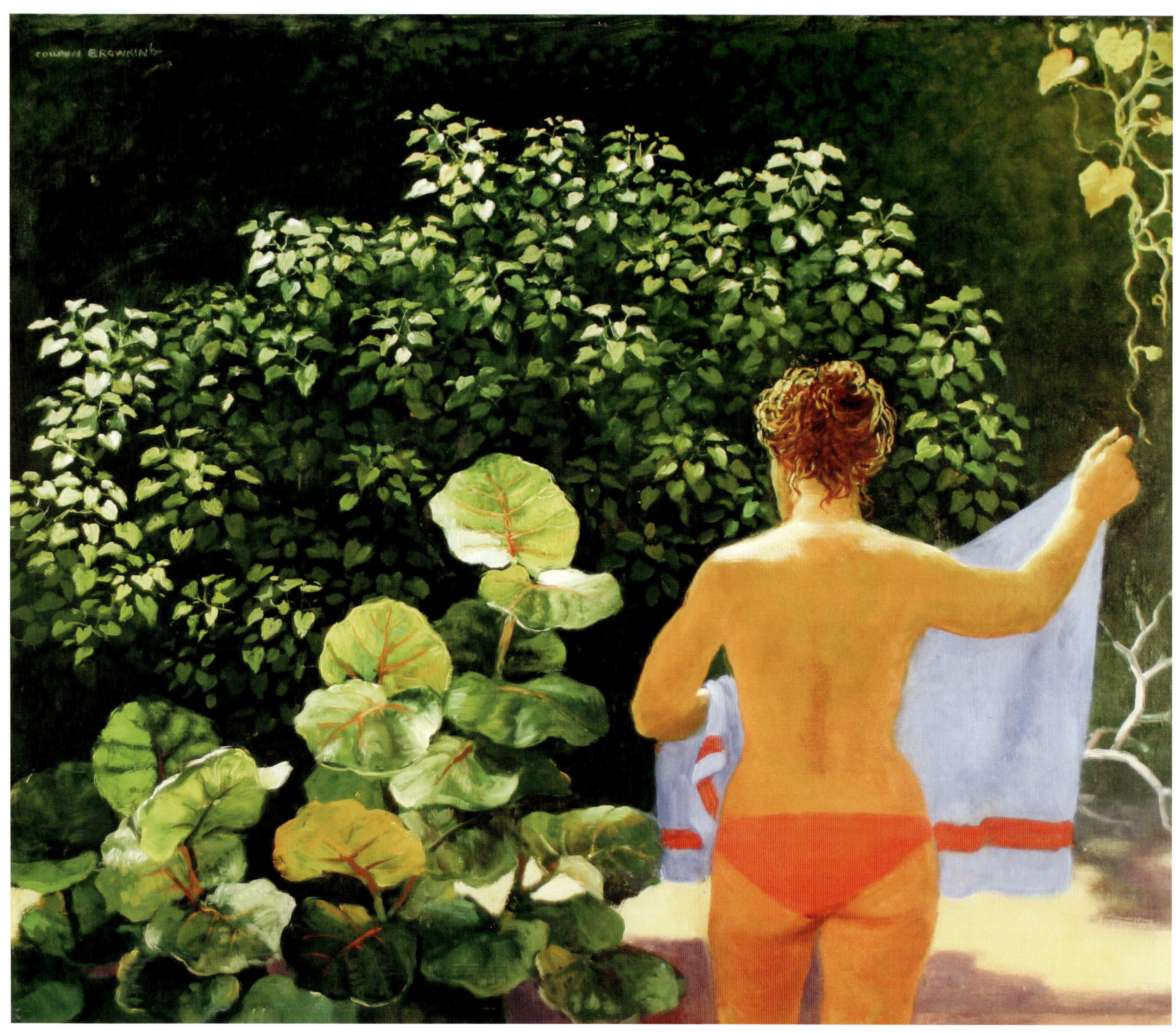

Fig. 8.14. Colleen Browning, The Blue Towel, *1988. Oil on canvas, 35 x 47 inches. Gift of the artist.*

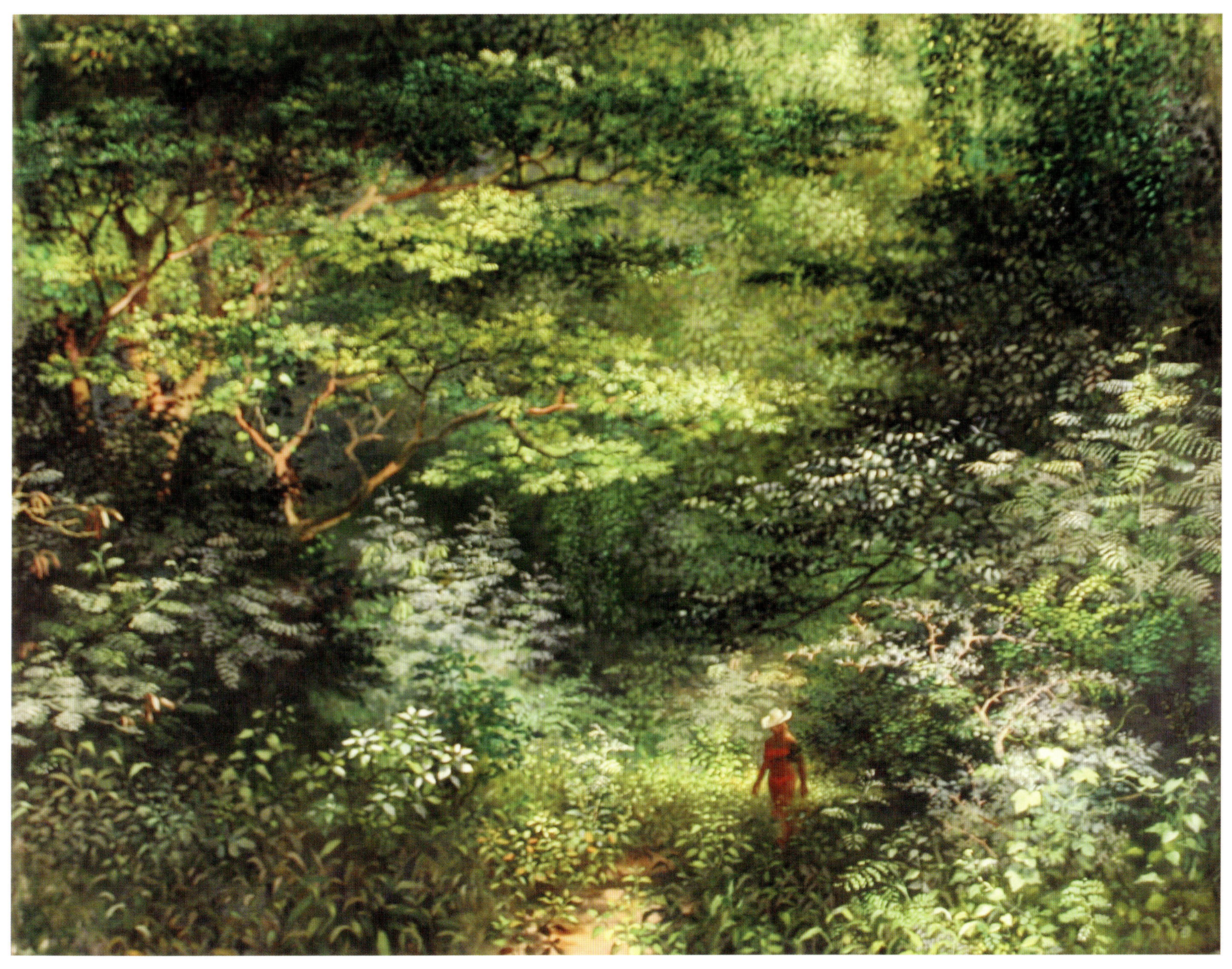

Fig. 8.15. Colleen Browning, Walk to the Beach, *1985. Oil on canvas, 36¼ x 46¼ inches. Gift of the artist.*

invasion of Grenada with a strike force of U.S. Marines, Army Rangers, Navy SEALs, elements of the 82nd Airborne, and a number of Caribbean security forces. Because of insufficient and faulty intelligence, the U.S. military met unexpected resistance as the insurgent force held the island through mid-December. HM Queen Elizabeth II spoke against the U.S. operation and a United Nations motion condemned it as a "flagrant violation of international law."

Code-named Operation Urgent Fury, its purpose was to overthrow a radicalized splinter government that had murdered pro-Marxist Prime Minister Maurice Bishop six days earlier. An assortment of Cubans, Russians, North Koreans, and East Germans had hoped to transform the tiny island into another Cuban-style communist state. American military officials convinced the White House that Grenada could become a refueling and stepping-stone for more Cuban and Soviet influence in the region. To make matters worse, approximately 1,000 Americans were present on the island, mainly medical students at St. George's College.

Browning and Wagner were eyewitnesses to the entire operation. Returning to the brisk military reportage of his WW II classic, *Sands of Valor*, Wagner had a new riveting war story to tell. *Red Calypso: The Grenadian Revolution and its Aftermath* was published in 1988 as a political account of Grenada's failed Marxist regime, along with his sharp criticisms of the liberal media's "myths" surrounding the invasion. "Not nearly enough credit has been given to the [parachute drop] which was the lowest in combat since World War Two, allowing most men only seven seconds of silk—Colleen and I treasure the signature of some of them…. Aerial photographic surveillance had shown four 23 mm anti-aircraft pieces on the hills at the end of the airstrip," thus forcing the AH-64 Apache helicopters to fly in under 500 feet below enemy guns.[17]

The publisher of Wagner's book was Regnery Press, an incubator for many modern classics of American conservatism. Wagner's account took immense pride in America's role in freeing their island home of the Cuban threat and showed his deeply ingrained respect for military sacrifice:

> *The populace responded with GOD BLESS AMERICA signs, USA FOR-EVER adorning what had been Kaunda Square…. The superiority of any men who know their role perfect made it possible for those of the 82nd I met in Grenada to regard the spittle of the liberal press back home with a sort of amused contempt…. Of those post-intervention days Colleen and I treasure memories of General Jack Farris, commander of XVIII Airborne Corps and Fort Bragg, a Vietnam vet all wire and whipcord, sitting on our terrace at sunset reminiscing with Colleen, General Browning's daughter, over the great names of World War Two…Before he left, Jack Farris came round to say goodby to us. Colleen baked him a cake, with stars of rank iced on it.*
>
> *After hostilities ceased, journalists poured into Pointe Salines and by the end of the year Colleen and I totted up that we had hosted (excluding delegations like the Congressional Black Caucus) forty-four journalists from sundry countries, including one girl member of the Japanese Communist Party whose chief virtue was she didn't have a beard…The left press seemed determined to believe its own prefabricated*

Another outcome of Browning's reinvigorated sense of patriotism in the aftermath of the Grenada campaign was an unexpected project featuring Independence Day in a small town in Wisconsin. Browning found herself completely immersed in one of the largest pictorial projects of her career. For the hometown Great Circus Parade capturing the Baraboo High School marching band, the *Milwaukee Journal* wrote about the "artist's trip to Wisconsin for last year's Fourth of July festivities…'I don't know why, but something suddenly clicked in Milwaukee,' she said. 'I guess it was the magic of the circus in everyday surroundings. I was watching the parade…and suddenly something clicked. 'This is Americana' I said to myself. 'This is confidence. It wasn't at all like the anti-Americanism you encounter so often in New York."[19]

It took more than nine weeks to complete her *magnus opus* of sorts, *Picture of a Painting of the Great Circus Parade*, 1988 (fig. 8.16), an oversized canvas 42½ x 66½ inches. Her incredibly imaginative layering of illusions, reflected by mirrors, serves as Browning's theology of the art of painting in many respects. Enormous in scale, bold in conception, and brilliantly executed in terms of its painterly details and passages, this enthralling painting is greater than the sum of its parts.

The genius of the painting simply takes us one step beyond time and space into a vacuum where retinal images, realistic photographs, and floating figures reflected in mirrors magically appear without gravitational relativity in space. Einstein's warped universe is conjured up while the circus wagon reveals clowns, families, balloons, photographs, and a man on stilts projected into our minds but never really attached to the physical world.

"I think the painting sets up an opposition between one type of illusion and another, for it encourages the viewer to ask which is real—the illusionistic circus wagon and clowns in the painting, or the flat surface of the canvas, which has photographs taped to it that destroy the picture's illusions?…I think the paradox is appropriate for this painting since art is magical and astonishing, as is the circus."[20] Only a veteran artist of unequivocal certitude could have reached such a virtuoso achievement. Browning's circus wagon image almost sucks the observer's eyes into a reverberating, pulsating vortex of eye-to-brain activity. As a *summa* of her career, we submit to her magical powers of illusion.

A pendant to this major work is the equally patriotic image *U.S.A. Hooray!*, 1988 (fig. 8.17). The theme of a parade float, with beaming girls dressed in navy togs, explores another of Browning's directional shifts: the thrusting arrangement of three U.S. flags almost directly perpendicular to the picture plane. With deeply arranged shadows set against the morning sunlight that outlined the whirling decorative shapes of the float, Browning created a rococo pastiche of forms.

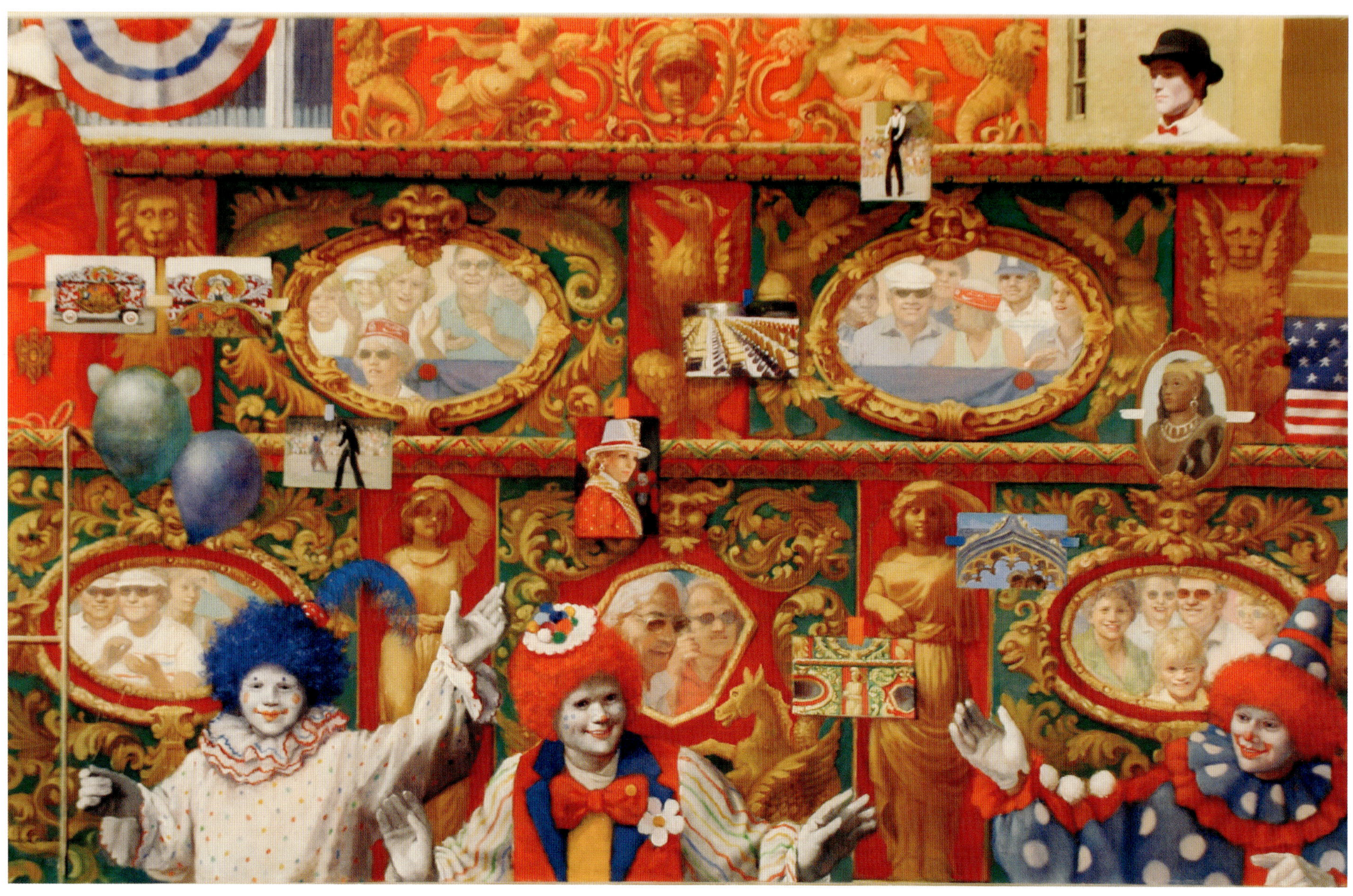

Fig. 8.16. Colleen Browning, Picture of
a Painting of the Great Circus Parade,
*1988. Oil on canvas, 42½ x 66½ inches.
Gift of the Southern Alleghenies Museum
of Art Auxillary, courtesy of Harmon-
Meek Gallery, Naples, FL.*

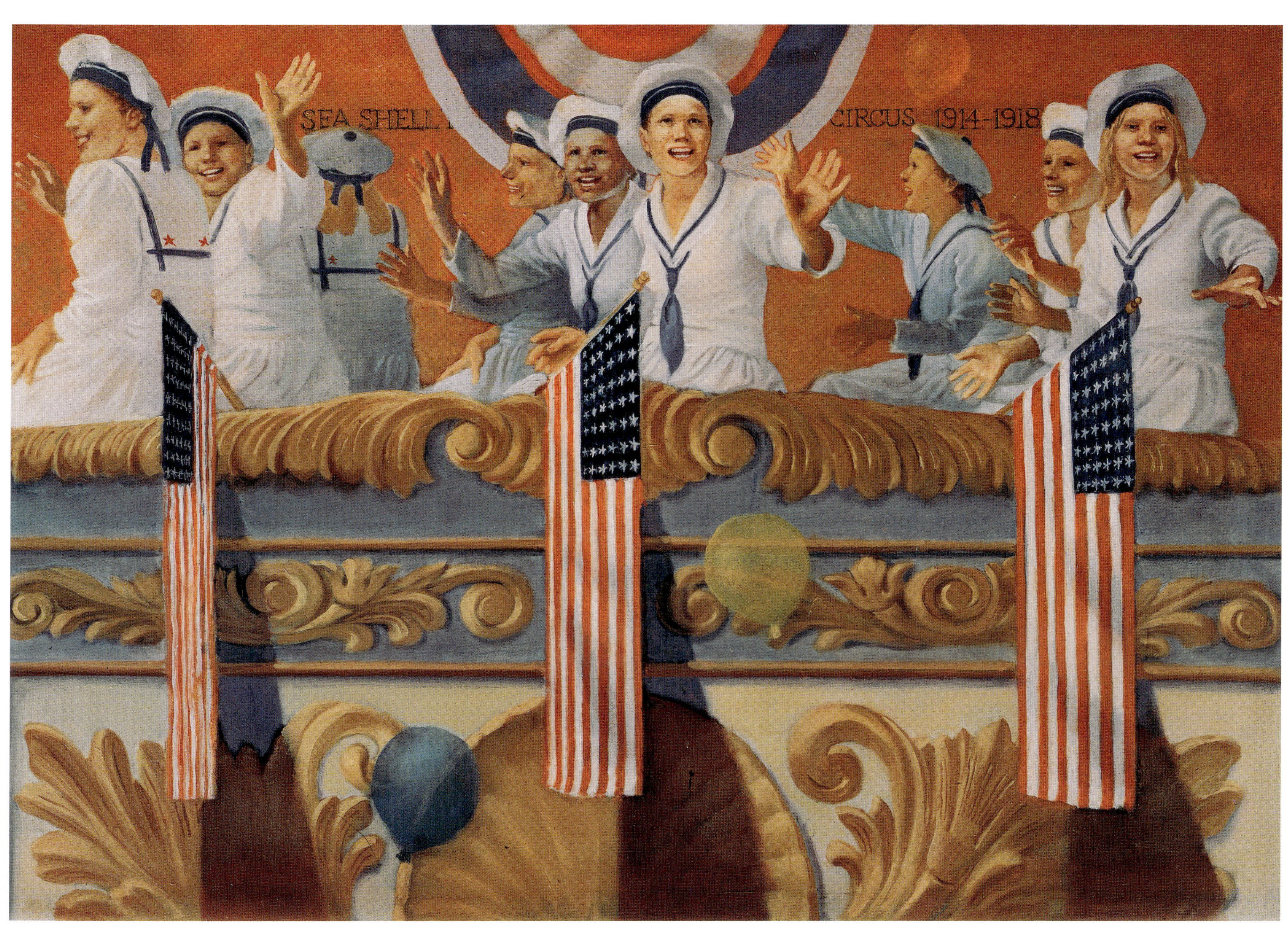

*Fig. 8.17. Colleen Browning, U.S.A.
Hooray!, 1988. Oil on canvas, 39 x 56
inches. Private collection.*

Browning's career reached its pinnacle in her glimpses of the "other side," combining her childhood affection for the faerie world with her updated view of neo-pagan mythologies. An island neighbor and fellow New Yorker was actress Mayo L. Gray, who reviewed the 1986 New York exhibition *Other Worlds* at Kennedy Galleries. Gray had the inside track on Browning's ambitions at this late moment in her career, explaining how Browning's "expansive spirit probes other worlds, taking us with her. Her robust embrace of life has never been stronger, her craft never more finely honed to the subject."[21]

Within Colleen Browning's artistic DNA, a transmissible thread materialized out of her early affiliations to the Magic Realists. It is not by chance or coincidence that links of forged steel connect the Southern Alleghenies Museum of Art (SAMA) to this sturdy chain over the decades. The museum's longstanding commitment and exhibition program promoting the Magic Realist tradition should be duly noted.

In April 1997, the aging painter enjoyed one final victory lap with a capstone retrospective exhibition, *Colleen Browning: A Retrospective*. Perhaps Browning wished for the prestige associated with a national flagship museum for one last hurrah. Tirelessly, she wrote letters to curators and museum directors, and campaigned to have one last burst of validation. Yet she was sagaciously perceptive in coming to terms with her declining artistic fortunes. Rather gallantly she fought against age, obsolescence, and disconcerting irrelevancy.

Striving for rejuvenating attention, Browning was grateful for the attention offered by a developing institution set into the rolling foothills of the Alleghenies in southwestern Pennsylvania. Her career achievement was a major retrospective and full-color catalogue publication at Southern Alleghenies Museum of Art (SAMA), located on the campus of Saint Francis University. Indicative of the institution's devotion and aggressive collecting of American art—with a sympathetic predisposition toward figuration—her art and life were fittingly celebrated. But the befitting supporters and patrons for her nearly marginalized art unpredictably have been found in the most unexpected places. With an almost missionary interest in the all-but-forgotten Magic Realists, Browning's art was given renewed respect and embraced with alacrity among a dedicated community.

Sixty paintings—borrowed from leading public and private collections and spanning five decades of intensive artistic productivity—filled the museum's upper and lower galleries to the rafters. Every period, theme, and stylistic approach of Browning's mercurial career was well represented at her final museum showing (and ultimately the repository of her estate). Who would have imagined that this artist, who lived a bohemian lifestyle as a New Age agnostic in the ultraliberal Upper West Side of Manhattan, would have her destiny entwined with an unassuming art museum set on a Catholic college campus in the heartland of America?

One man who was inspired by the Magic Realists' struggles as they attempted to visualize the complexities of modern humanism and their interior struggles along spiritual paths was Father Sean M. Sullivan, T.O.R. As the visionary president of then Saint Francis College in the tranquil setting of Loretto, Pennsylvania, Father Sullivan was the guiding light to SAMA's mission as a teaching and learning institution. "I became intrigued by the Magic Realists early on in the development of the museum, especially their brush with fantasy. Larry Fleishman, owner of the Kennedy Galleries became a good friend and he helped us with many of our most important early acquisitions including a Bierstadt landscape and Mary Cassatt portrait."[22]

During his productive 23-year tenure as museum director, Michael M. Strueber initiated a landmark event in 1999 devoted to this circle of undervalued artists. He noted that the artists were "visually challenging, presenting with juxtapositions of disparate objects and dream-like situations, that exist out of time,"[23] for SAMA's pioneering 1999 Magic Realist show. SAMA's former curator Michael Tomor highlighted the exhibition's singular achievement: "*Magic Realism: An American Response to Surrealism* is the first exhibition dedicated to this profoundly important movement, perhaps one of the least recognized art movements in 20th century modern realism.... With their extraordinary technique and their evocation of mystery and fantasy, the artists in this exhibition have given us the gift of their dreams."[24] Overall, taking on this heroic project at SAMA was nothing less than a remarkable foray into a heretofore-underappreciated group of artists whose contributions to American painting are only now being fully realized.

Painting of a Painting (White), 1998 (fig. 8.18), a triple-take, arrived close to the end of her self-portrait series, about a year before receiving the diagnosis of terminal intestinal cancer. As such, it is one last hard look at a career that is metaphorically self-analyzed as a jigsaw puzzle of parts, a fragmentary recording of an artist's life deconstructed into segmented elements. Artistic choices are unavoidable, sometimes painfully ironic, especially when the octogenarian depicted has fictitiously implied Milton's ideal: "in the flower of my youth." Like the 1957 film *Three Faces of Eve*, the artist presents three separate facets of her identity.

"As people age, the flesh starts to sag, and loose folds of flesh form wrinkles or bags, giving a very different effect from the smooth, uninterrupted contours of youth," Browning wrote eleven years earlier.[25] The multiple-personality syndrome surely did not afflict her. But it may be suggested that this frame-within-a-frame telescopic set of self-portraits is a series of mirror-like illusions. The actual sitter—the fragile 80-year-old woman—never appears. Instead, we are being asked to play along with this biologically driven artistic deception.

By self-identifying with distant faerie realms of time and place in mythological kingdoms, Browning's final paintings wistfully imagine her own corporeal transcendence. At earlier points in her artistic evolution she merely looked out the window in London, Rochester, Harlem, or in the subways of Manhattan to find her next subject. Toward her final years, she shifted her focus from that which could be visibly seen into imaginary realms of what she hoped to ultimately experience.

An example of her frontal consciousness about the life beyond is *Atlantis Found*, 1986 (fig. 8.19). This painting began when Browning "suddenly noticed in the visible world when elements fused accidentally into a new and unexpected world.... We do have a reef off the beach in front of our house in the Caribbean...the theme that excited me was the idea of a drowned city, an ancient civilization destroyed—perhaps traces of an advanced technology in the abyss that still affects the outside world by radio-activity. A domain now inhabited by primeval monsters!"[26]

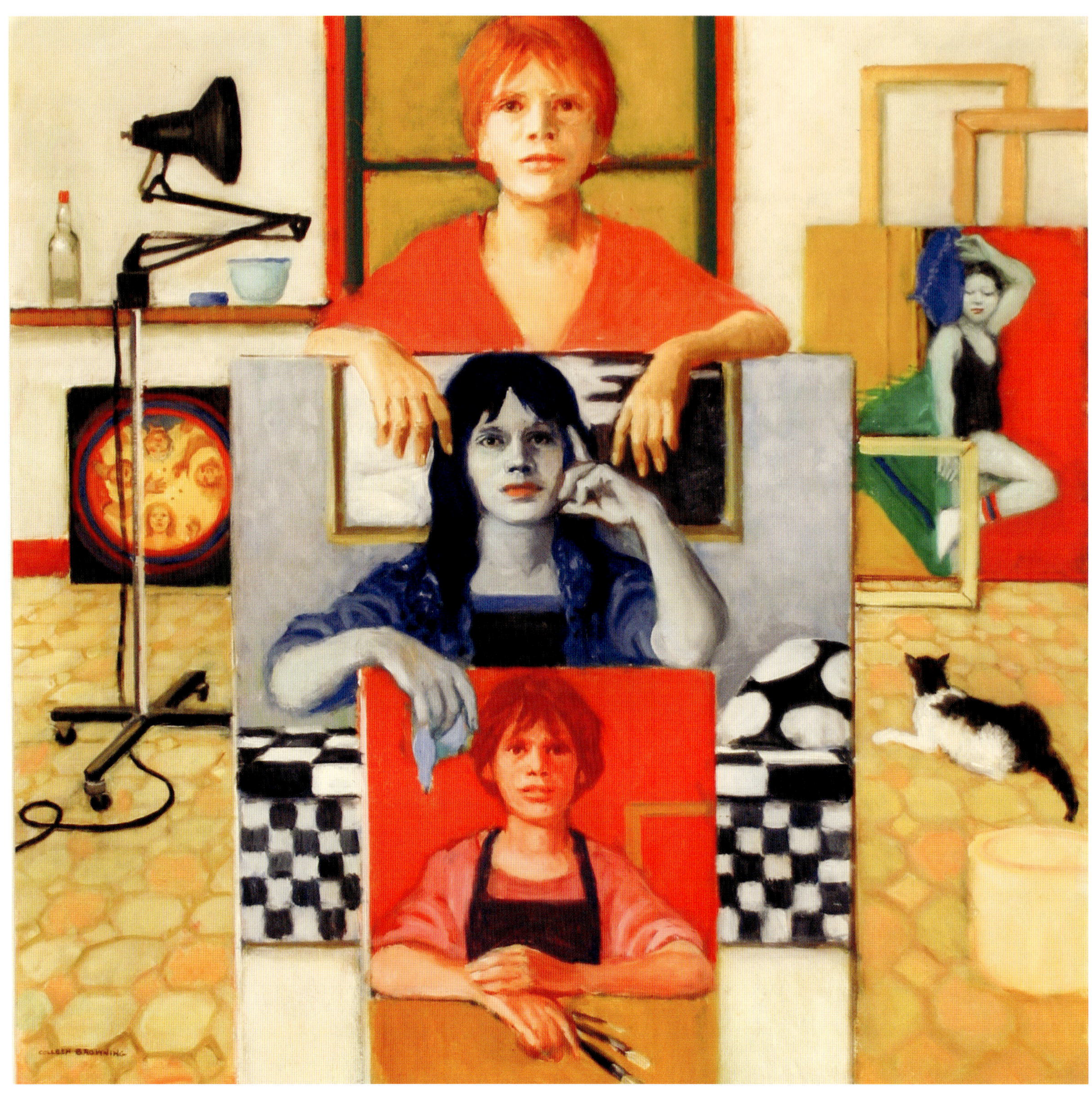

Fig. 8.18. Colleen Browning, Painting of a Painting (White), *1998. Oil on canvas, 24 x 32¼ inches. Gift of the artist.*

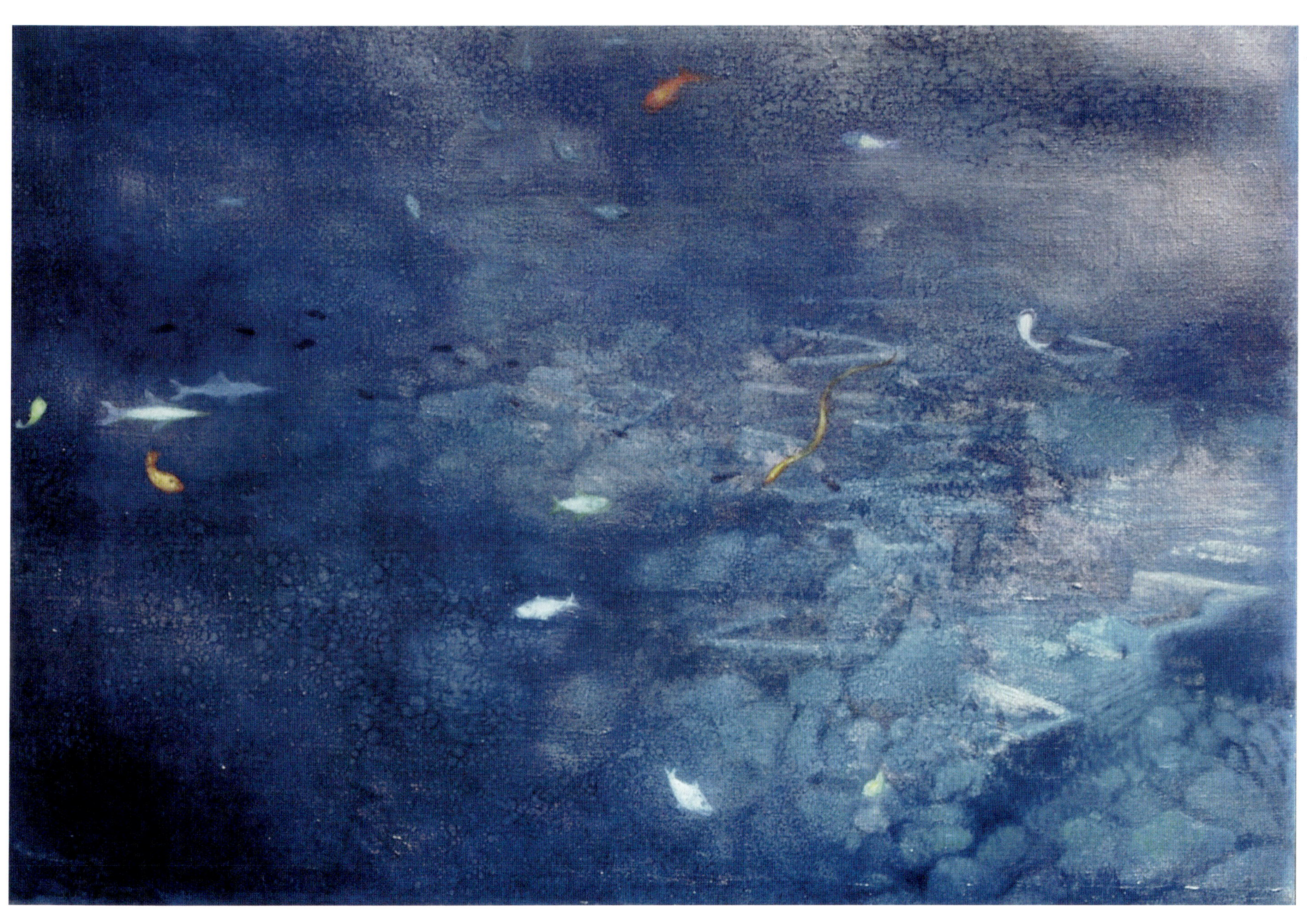

Fig. 8.19. Colleen Browning, Atlantis
Found, 1986. Oil on canvas, 25½ x
36½ inches. Collection of John G. Shedd
Aquarium, Chicago, IL. Gift of the
Geoffrey Wagner Trust.

Browning's late-in-life mysticism reached its crescendo in *La Jablesse I*, 1995 (fig. 8.20). Analyzing her final paintings seems to parallel the desperate attempts of a life-loving person who submits and succumbs to the magic of shamanistic spirit healers. On one particular mission, the afflicted artist departed from the traditional care of her licensed physician to keep hope alive by experimenting with mixtures of "life-healing" potions.

La Jablesse—sometimes known as La Diabless depending on which Caribbean island of the French West Indies you land upon—became Browning's symbolic alter ego. Physically, she was a 75-year-old woman by the time this painting was completed. Worn and weathered, her leathery skin wrinkled into deep folds, enhanced by decades of sun-bathing exposure, she had the startling appearance of a weathered figure. This Caribbean she-devil figure, La Jablesse, was a fatally attractive supernatural woman, a Creole version of ancient Venus luring men into her lair.

A classic myth Browning certainly knew from innumerable classical sculptures and Renaissance paintings she studied during her London years was Ovid's *Metamorphoses*, written 2,000 years ago. The aging goddess Venus attempts to transform herself to lure the virile Adonis into her love nest. Ovid speaks of how the matriarchal Venus, crazed to retain her youthful feminine powers, assumed the appealing disguise of the younger Diana with "her garments girt up to her knees." She even warns Adonis to beware of those creatures in the woods bearing "youth and beauty" as they could disguise "wild beasts." Transferring and transforming the vanity of Venus into her own debilitated fig-ure, Browning sought emotional renewal through the depiction of the Caribbean *femme fatale* legend.

Internally, she retained the youthful passions and libidinal energies of the younger female she had attempted to capture in her fractured, never-truly completed, late self-portraits. But finding an external guise, she selected the fatally attractive figure of La Jablesse, a forest demon who lived in the mountains of the neighboring island of St. Lucia. Stealing men away from their wives and girlfriends, they became hapless victims to a passionate, sexually drenched experience before stealing their souls. As a true nature goddess, Browning depicted the sexual energies stemming from the great mangrove trees that ensnarl men in their twisted vines and dangling branches. Those who submit to the enchanting powers of Jablesse experience momentary pleasures, but are doomed. This was her final life-affirming identity: a bewitching enchantress who could still cap-ture her viewers' hearts and minds.

Without children or a circle of intimate friends, the couple suffered for each other in sickness. Browning's death from intestinal cancer, after three torturous operations, took her at age 85 on August 22, 2003.

Finding the strength to write to Browning's loyal agent Bill and his wife Barbara Meek, Wagner's lachrymal letter conveyed inconsolable grieving. "Dear Bill and Barbara: I have been meaning to summon up courage to write to you ever since a cruel fate took from me the beloved comrade of half a century or more. I can only say you have both been so wonderful to Colleen over the years that we regarded you as family. I was glad you did not see her at the end, a ragdoll half her weight confined to hospitals and nursing homes, unable to speak, to see properly, to eat, lying mute on a vast hospital bed, imported for her,

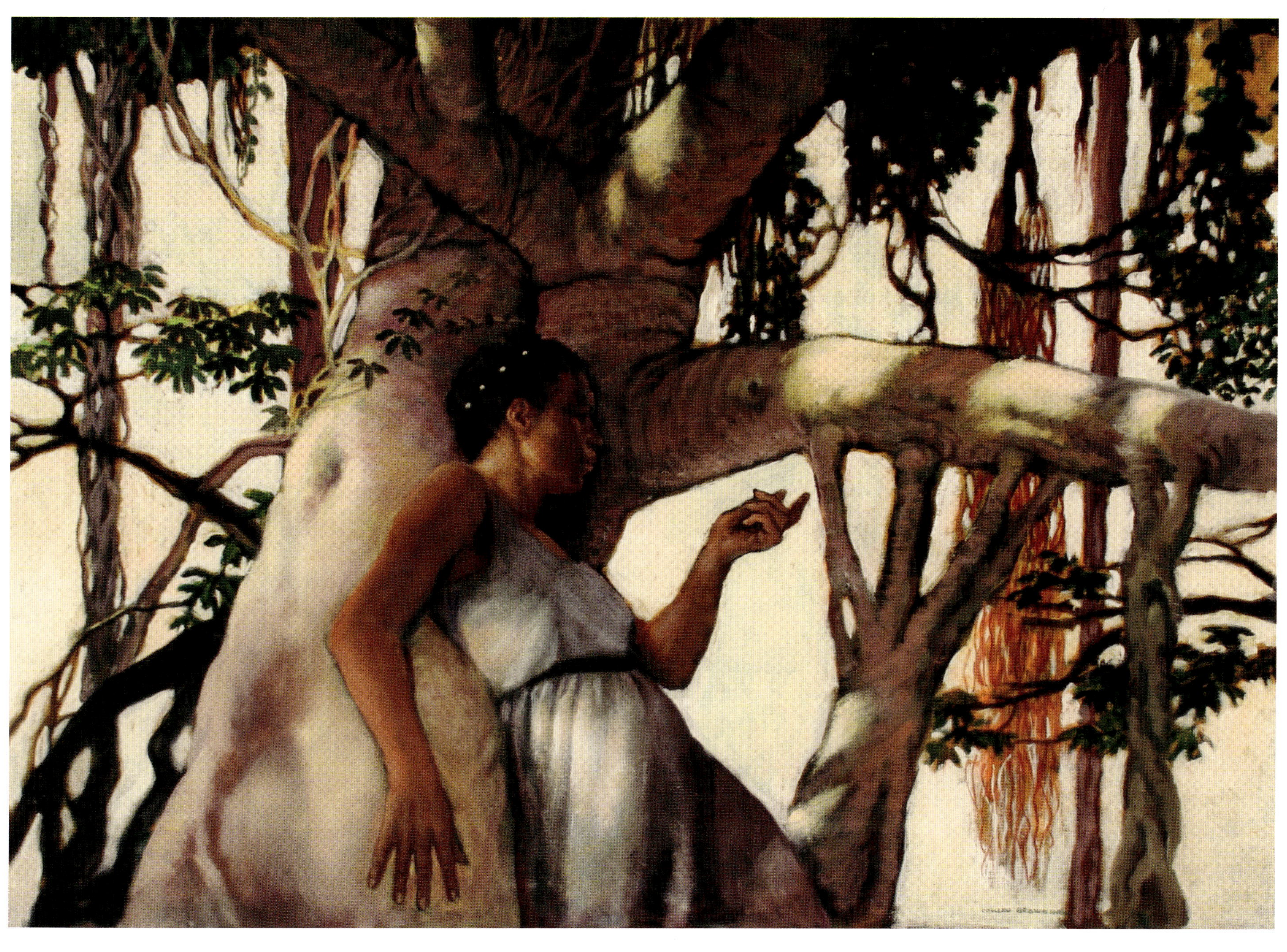

Fig. 8.20. Colleen Browning, La Jablesse I, *1995. Oil on canvas, 36 x 48 inches. Gift of the artist.*

attended by aides at colossal expense with indifferent nurses....To say I shall miss her is a heart-rending under-statement."[27]

Wagner, a tournament-ranked squash and tennis player in his prime, lurched about with writhing physical pain from advancing Parkinson's disease, for another three years. He died on August 21, 2006, in their apartment at 100 La Salle Street, #19, miserably, and alone. This was just one day shy of the third anniversary of Browning's death.

They had lived fully and loved endearingly. But only each other. Devoid of family, caring friends, or even reliable associates, all there is to survey is a remarkable legacy of paintings, scholarly books, essays, poetry, and a trunk full of passionately penned letters promising one another eternal support. So hermetically reclusive in their advancing years, Browning and Wagner were bereft of intimate friends to take care of their affairs. At the time of Wagner's death, it took the intervention of a prominent New York attorney as the named executor to carry out his testamentary wishes. Oddly enough, or perhaps not, their entire estate was handled by a collection of individuals—with the exception of her devoted gallerist Bill Meek—who were peripheral strangers.

Scrupulously this legal team shepherded the process in the absence of immediate family members. They accepted responsibility for an abandoned apartment of scrapbooks, letters, and unsold paintings, sketches, and prints. Their moral compass in unscrambling two lifetimes crammed with personal possessions was directed by the glowing north star of Browning's prolific artistic legacy.

The external art world had spun completely on its axis during Browning's fifty-three years in the United States. Always a competitor, charged with her father's winner-takes-all military discipline, she had triumphed early on, arriving at the zenith of her remarkable career while still in her mid-40s, in 1965, when John Canaday's *New York Times* review sent her reputation soaring into the heavens.

Abstraction, at first the "outsider" movement, had quickly moved from the subject of ridicule to the mainstream focus of contemporary art. Caught by surprise, and to some degree unprepared for their instant obsolescence, were the traditional Realists, such as Wyeth, Koch, Porter, Cadmus, Tooker, Bishop, Marsh, French, and Vickrey. Of lesser fame, Browning felt every bit of this lowering knife on the chopping block.

The Metropolitan Museum of Art's sweeping survey in 1969 convincingly documented the rise and fall of Realism in step and perfectly contrasted with the first half of Browning's career. "By reason of its own achievement and the clear and indisputable effect it has had throughout the world, the art of the New York School stands as the most recent in the grand succession of modern movements from Impressionism through Cubism and Surrealism," declared Henry Geldzahler, curator of contemporary art at The Metropolitan Museum of Art, in his introduction to the landmark exhibition, *New York Painting and Sculpture: 1940–1970*. "After two decades of tremendous energy and inventiveness in abstract painting, the reintroduction of recognizable content (objects, landscape, and figure) appeared at first retardataire and beside the point."[28]

The Dream, 1996 (fig. 8.21), brings Browning's "voyage to romance" to its final destination. She arrived in America filled with boundless ambition, and her artistic talents were almost instantly recognized and prominently exhibited. Discovering unimaginably

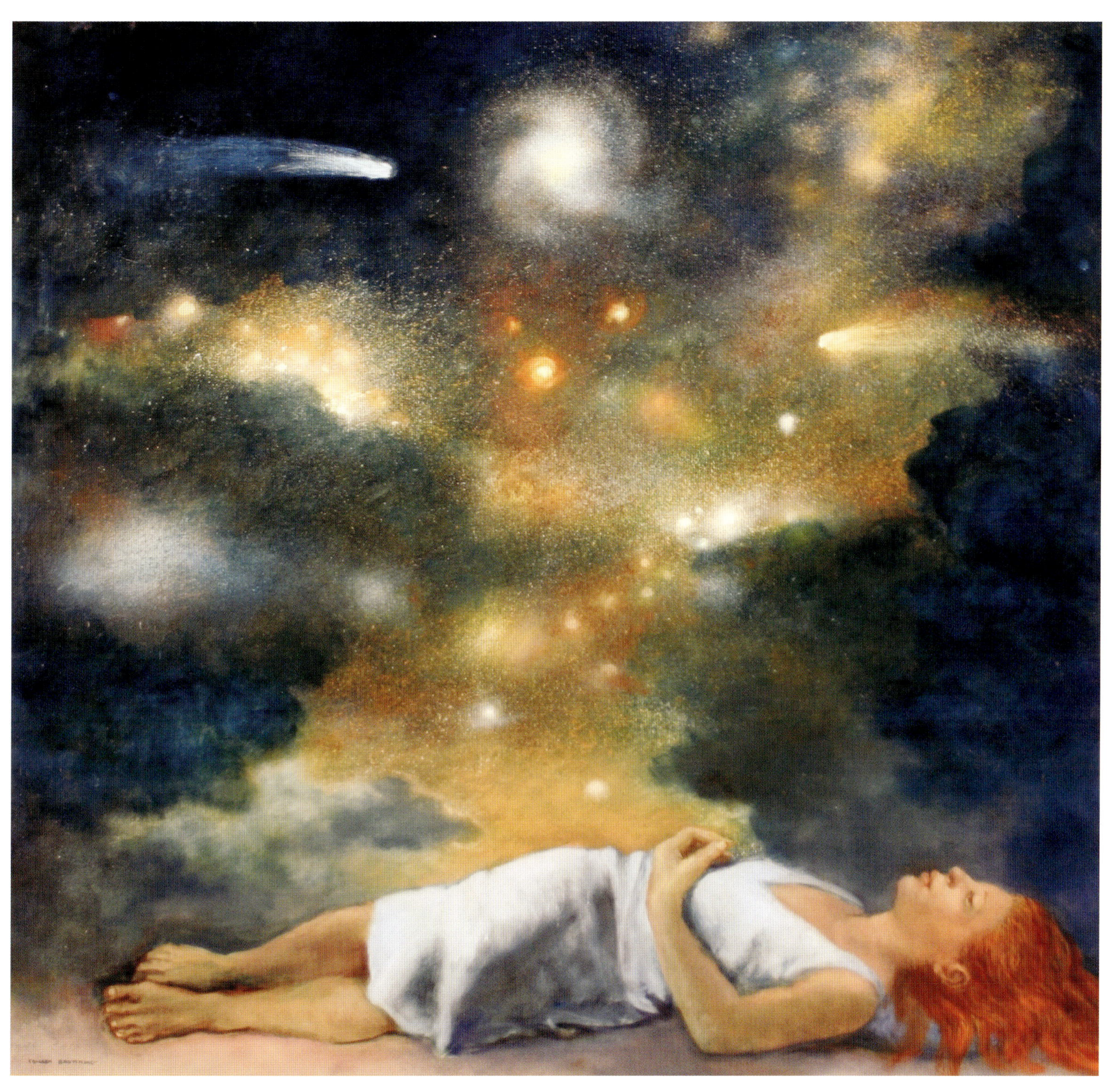

Fig. 8.21. Colleen Browning, The Dream, *1996. Oil on canvas, 44½ x 46½ inches. Gift of the artist.*

rewarding opportunities in the public light, she created, however, a defensive shield that withdrew her inner psyche into an almost cloistered silence. These conundrums—disguising her identity while attempting to truthfully depict the "human condition" pictorial themes of her day—will remain unresolved enigmas.

Her embrace of the universe and its mysteries are forever rendered by that eternally enchanting young woman at rest. A mane of flowing red hair is just close enough in its auburn tint to remind us that this is Browning's avatar peacefully reclining on a sandy beach. In *The Dream* we can now slip onto that cosmic shoreline between the earth, the moon, and the stars. Colleen Browning's voyage has finally come to a perfectly tranquil state of release. She lived—and passed into the hereafter—with an unshakeable commitment to her art.

Browning's death rattle was a gruesome, excruciatingly painful exit. She might have floated in and out of consciousness amid the stark and sterile surroundings of St. Luke's Hospital. She may have dozed into faintly watercolored memories of that gloriously warm summer of 1923 when she was all of five years old. Her father, now recovered from his war wounds, may have taken her down for some wading and trout fishing in the Blackwater River at the family's estate of Cregg Castle. Reduced to a skeletal figure, her emaciated body ravaged by the disease, her last thoughts might have been the poem she wrote back in England. Published proudly by the headmaster of the Camberley School at the end of the spring term in 1930, a tender Browning—a 12-year-old prodigy of an artist and poet—opened her eyes to write:

> ***The Sea on a Summer Morning***
>
> *The whole of Creation is asleep. I alone am awake. The world is still. But, Oh!, the beauty of it at this early hour. Its inestimable loveliness! The wondrous vault of azure haze reaching onward and upward for ever—for who can tell where the heavens end? …And the bosom of the ocean – is but a vast polished turquoise, transparent, lucid and incomparable, the home of shells and pearls and fairy creatures…. The sea is indeed a marvel.*

NOTES

1. Kirsten Swinth, *Painting Professionals: Women Artists & the Development of Modern American Art, 1870–1930* (Chapel Hill: The University of North Carolina Press, 2000), p. 160.

2. Colleen Browning, letter to Howard DaLee Spencer, September 19, 1986.

3. Mayo L. Gray, "Colleen Browning's 'Other Worlds' at Kennedy Galleries," exhibition review, *The New York City Tribune*, May 5, 1986, p. 12.

4. Ibid.

5. SAMA videotape interview, Altoona television studio, 1997.

6. Colleen Browning, *Working Out a Painting* (New York: Watson-Guptill Publications Inc., 1988), p. 131.

7. Howard DaLee Spencer, "Colleen Browning, Recent Paintings," essay and catalogue, Wichita

Art Museum, December 1986, p. 13.

8. Colleen Browning, letter to William Meek (faxed copy), June 28, 1999.

9. Colleen Browning, "A Studio ABC – A Talk with an Imaginary Studio Visitor," unpublished manuscript, circa January 1990, pp. 48–51.

10 Ibid., pp. 48–51.

11. Colleen Browning, "A Studio ABC – A Talk with an Imaginary Studio Visitor," unpublished manuscript, circa January 1990, p. 78.

12. Jerry Tallmer, "At Home with Colleen Browning & Geoffrey Wagner," *The New York Post*, no. 93, March 6, 1976, p. 51.

13. Ibid.

14. Ibid.

15. Ibid.

16. James Auer, "Circus Magic: Parade Impressions Preserved in Oils," *Milwaukee Journal,* July 7, 1989, pp. 1E–10E.

17. Geoffrey Wagner, *Red Calypso: The Grenadian Revolution and its Aftermath* (Washington, DC: Regnery Gateway Press, 1988), p. 169.

18. Ibid., pp. 165–198.

19. James Auer, "Circus Magic: Parade Impressions Preserved in Oils, *Milwaukee Journal*, July 7, 1989, p. E10.

20. Colleen Browning, "The Evolution of a Painting," *American Artist*, July 1989, pp. 54–59.

21. Mayo L. Gray, "Colleen Browning's 'Other Worlds' at Kennedy Galleries," exhibition review, *The New York City Tribune*, May 5, 1986, p. 12.

22. Film interview with Father Sean M. Sullivan, T.O.R., Loretto, PA, October 11, 2009.

23. Michael M. Strueber, "Magic Realism: An American Response to Surrealism," Acknowledgment, exhibition catalogue, Southern Alleghenies Museum of Art, Loretto, PA, June 12–September 16, 1999, unpaginated.

24. Michael A. Tomor, "Magic Realism: An American Response to Surrealism," catalogue essay, Southern Alleghenies Museum of Art, Loretto, PA, June 12–September 16, 1999, unpaginated.

25. Colleen Browning, *Working Out a Painting* (New York: Watson-Guptill Publications Inc., 1988), p. 25.

26. Colleen Browning, unpublished manuscript, 1990.

27. Geoffrey Wagner, letter to Bill and Barbara Meek, Thanksgiving 2003.

28. Henry Geldzahler, *New York Painting and Sculpture: 1940–1970* (New York: E.P. Dutton & Co., 1969), pp. 15–36.

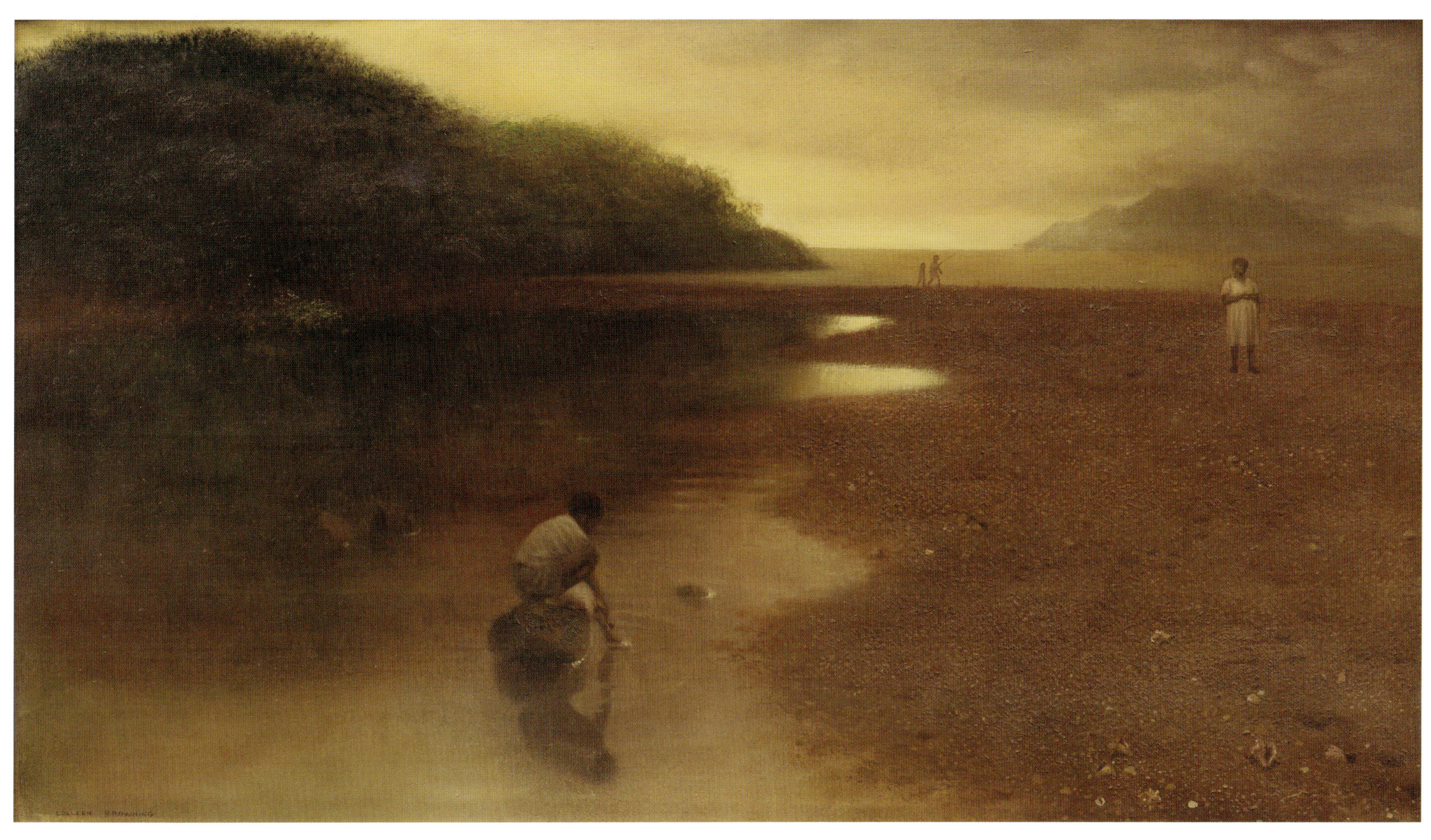

Colleen Browning, Buccament Bay,
1964. Oil on canvas, 20¼ x 35¼ inches.
Collection of the Coleman Barkin Family.

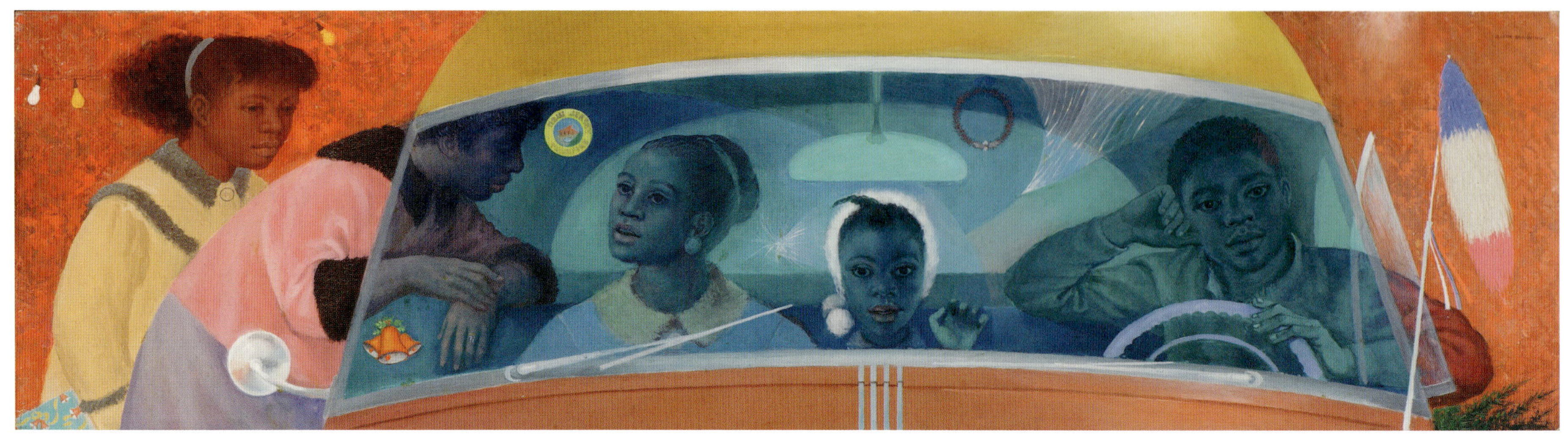

Colleen Browning, Christmas Car, 1954–55. Oil on masonite, 10⅛ x 37½ inches. Collection of Williams College Museum of Art. Gift of the American Academy of Arts and Letters, New York; Hassam, Speicher, Betts and Symons Funds, 1955. 55.8.

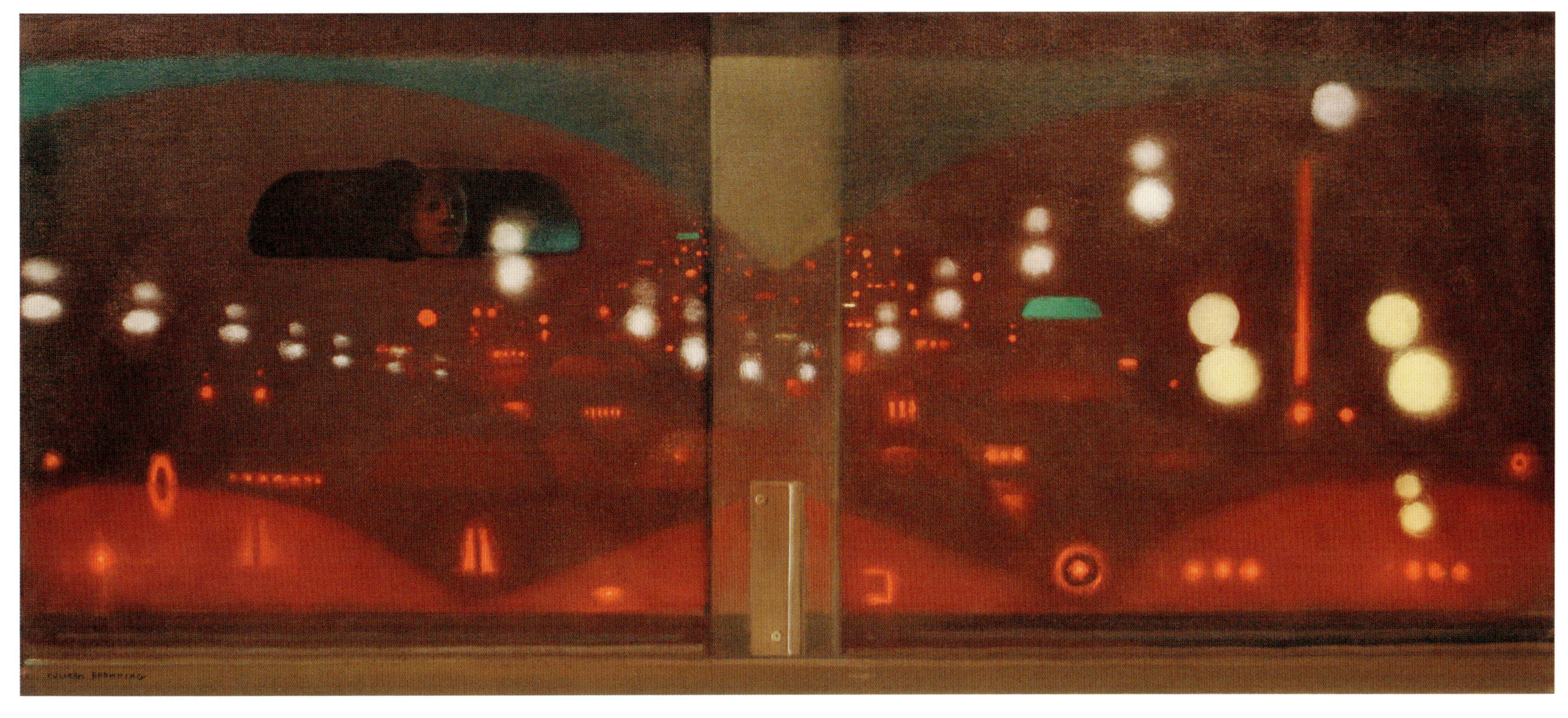

Colleen Browning, Taxi, 1971. Oil on canvas, 17½ x 40 inches. Collection of Nevada Museum of Art, Reno, NV. Gift of Harmon-Meek Gallery, Naples, FL.

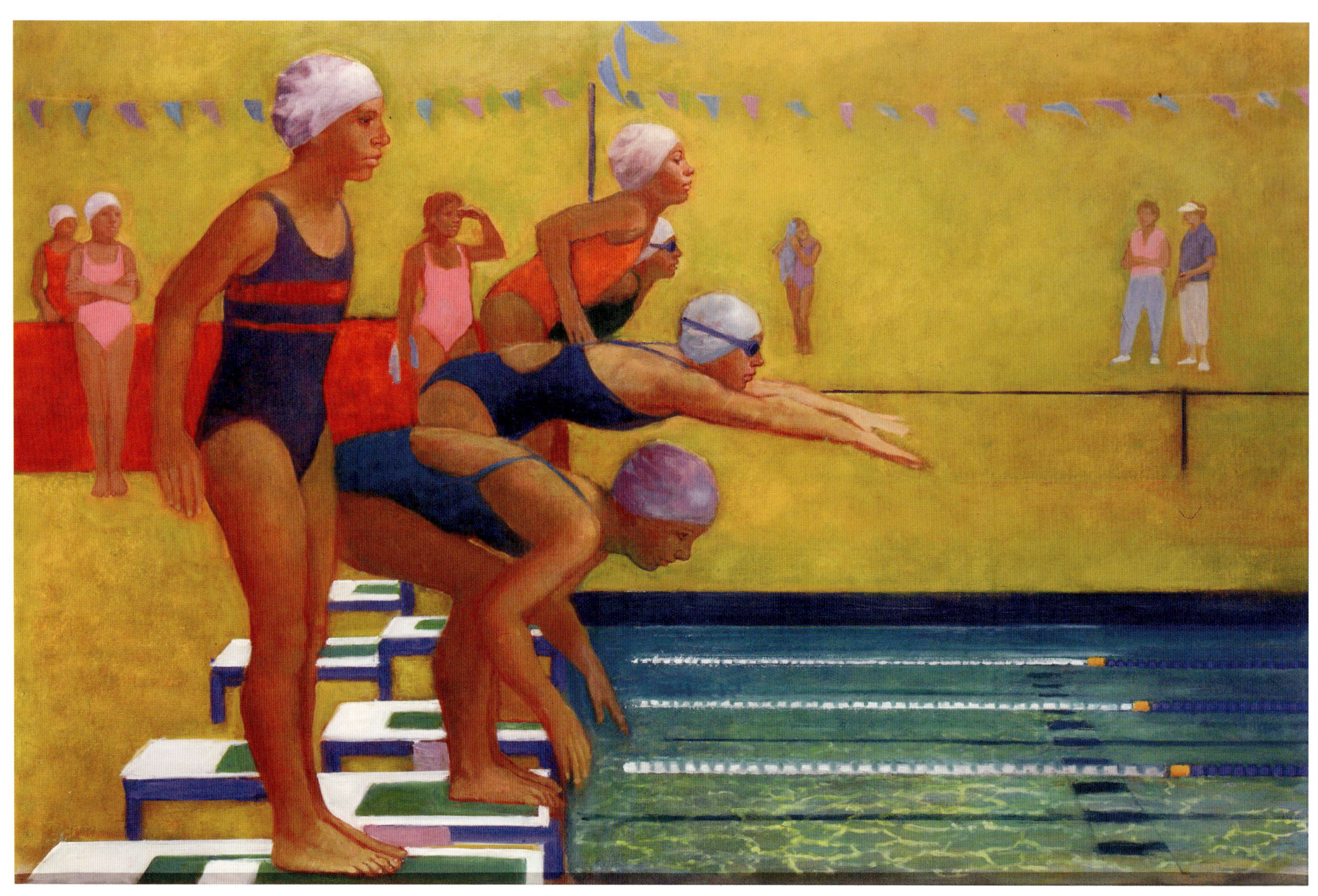

Colleen Browning, Start, 1991. Oil on
canvas, 40½ x 60 inches. The Butler Institute of American Art, Youngstown, OH.
Museum purchase, 1992.

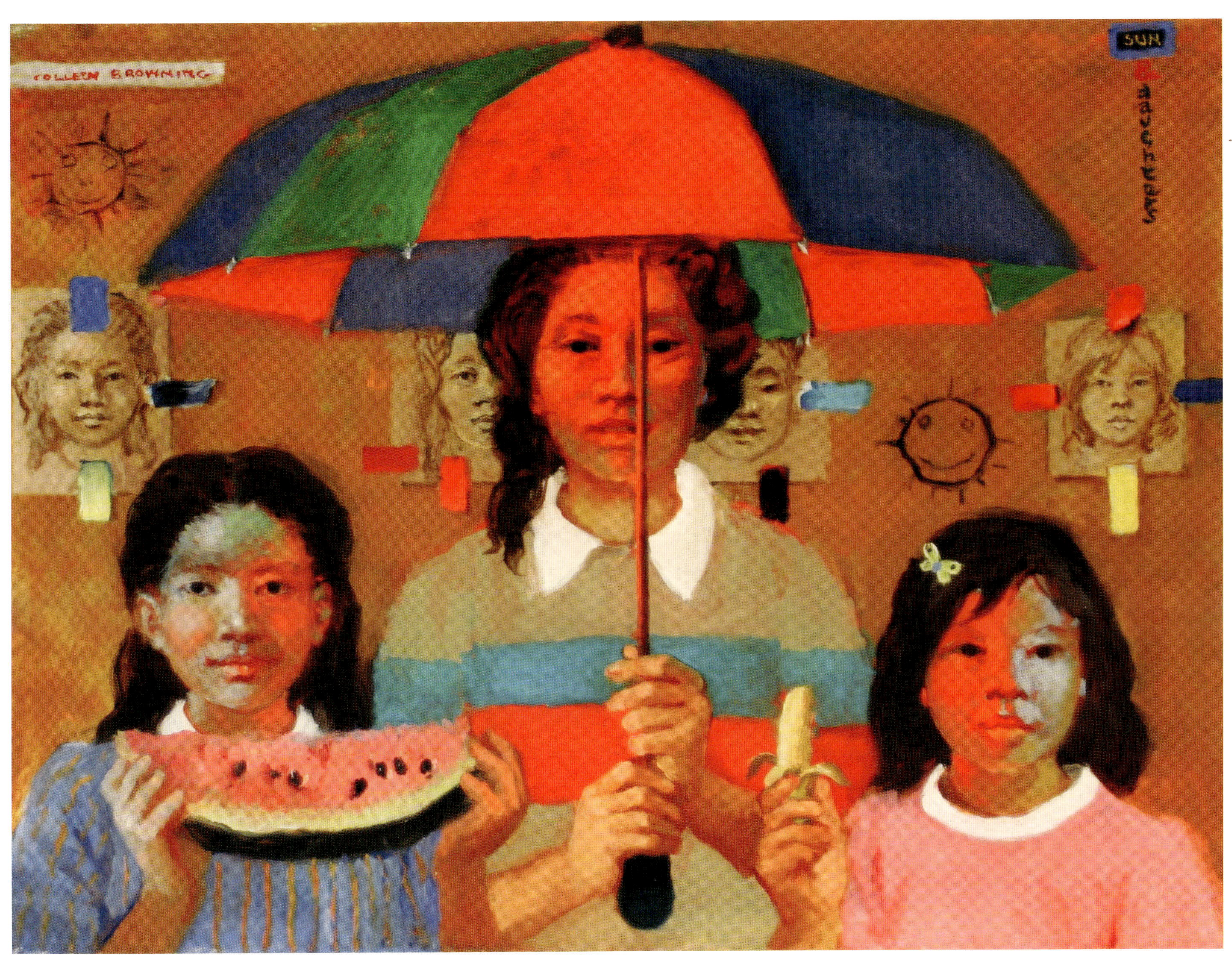

Colleen Browning, Sun and Daughters, *1997. Oil on canvas, 25 x 32½ inches. Gift of the artist.*

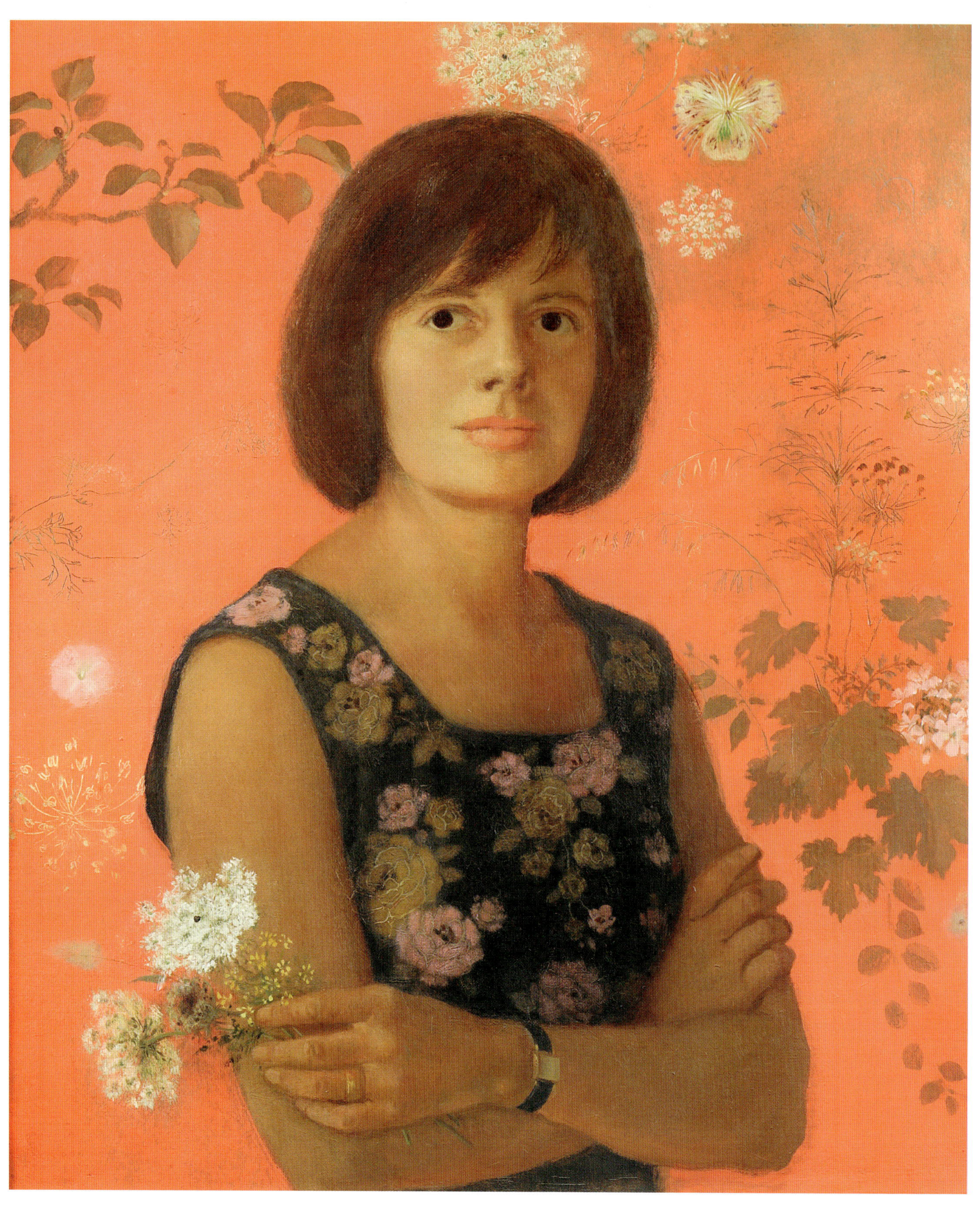

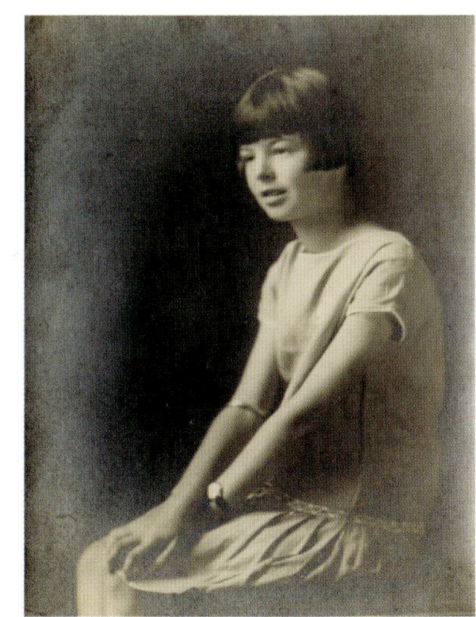

Colleen Browning, c. 1928.

opposite:
Colleen Browning, Self-Portrait *, 1965. Oil on canvas, 24 x 20 inches. National Academy Museum, New York. 1665-P.*

1918   Born on May 16 in Shoeburyness, county borough of Southend-on-Sea, Essex, England. Parents Violet Muriel Cairnes and Captain Langley Browning married on November 29, 1915, before his transfer to WWI battlefields in France and Belgium.

1919–21   Beginning of Irish War of Independence; Colleen spends first three years at family-owned Cregg House, a thirteenth-century castle and newer eighteenth-century manor house on the banks of River Blackwater in Fermoy, County Cork.

1921–24   Captain Browning's brigade transferred to Yorkshire and later assigned to officer duty from 1923–24 in Cologne, Germany. In December 1924, Captain Browning is selected for British Military Staff College in Camberley; family moves to Camberley (Surrey), which becomes Colleen's childhood home.

1925   Brother Shane is born on November 10.

1927   Creates earliest extant art project *The Little Book*, written, illustrated, and printed at age 9¾. Captain Browning departs for India, serving three years in the Punjab; left family behind because "Colleen was too old to be taken to India" and was enrolled in primary school.

1930   Creates illustrations and poetry in *The Fairy Alphabet*, based on Walter Crane's 1899 Art Nouveau-inspired *A Floral Fantasy in an Old English Garden*.

1933   Acknowledging her exceptional artistic potential, Colleen's parents enroll her in the Farnham School of Art, founded in 1866.

1934   Exhibits *Cathedral Wedding*, a watercolor-and-ink fantasy with modernist stylization, at The Society of Women Artists in London. At age 16, she was the youngest artist to showcase her work.

1935 Family moves to Amesbury, Wiltshire. Colleen enrolls in Salisbury School of Art and Crafts. Exhibits watercolors and pen-and-ink sketches at London's Whitechapel Art Gallery. *The Times*, a London newspaper, compliments this "brave show" and "truly remarkable sheets of composition by Colleen Browning."

1936 Urged by her art teachers, Colleen travels to Victoria and Albert Museum to create a copy of Botticelli's *Madonna and Child* as her entry work for the Edwin Austin Abbey Memorial Scholarship, a prize open to aspiring painters from the United States and England.

1937 Colleen earns one of the two Edwin Austin Abbey Memorial Scholarships, which will pay for her attendance at Slade School of Fine Art, University of London for two years. Has watercolor accepted into Exhibition of the Royal Academy of Arts. Begins formal training at Slade School of Fine Art.

1938–39 Completes life-drawing courses and masters classical beaux-arts curriculum at the Slade. Takes 2nd Prize in Decorative Painting. Receives baccalaureate diploma.

1942 Living outside of London, Colleen begins her wartime service drawing aerial maps for the Royal Air Force (RAF). Prepares large-scale topographical maps of Norwegian fjords and land features in Europe. Completes 22' mural of Salisbury's past and present for the Women's Services Club at the military base in Salisbury. Unveiling ceremony attended by Queen Mary.

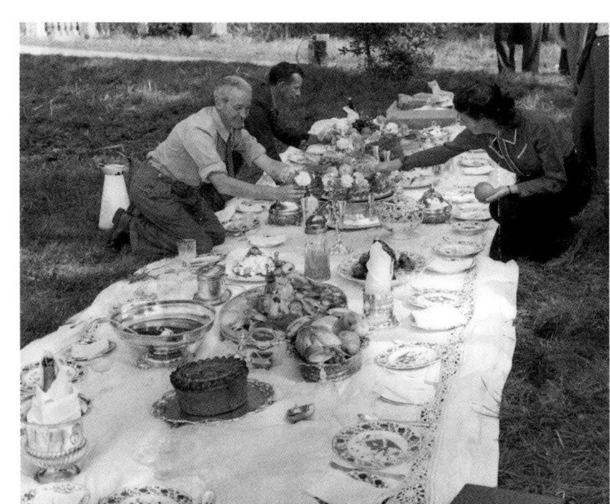

Colleen and crew arrange a picnic for a movie set production scene, J. Arthur Rank Organisation, c. 1948–49.

1945 Travels with parents on a private train through Tuscany and the Italian countryside. As the daughter of occupying army general, Colleen is introduced to many prominent officials and diplomats in Rome and in Vatican City.

1946 Introduced to Filippo Del Giudice, prominent film producer, in London. Offered a position as a set designer at Two Cities Film Studios, critically recognized as a prestigious fine art film studio.

1947–48 Promoted and received film credits as set decorator for avant-garde films produced by J. Arthur Rank Film Organisation (merged with Two Cities), England's premiere film studio. For the classic film noir *Odd Man Out*, her surrealistic paintings are a crucial part of the production. Continus to earn film studio credits, rising to position as set designer on major film projects.

1948 On summer holiday on the island of Ischia, near Naples, Italy, meets Oxford graduate Geoffrey Wagner. Spends the next 72 hours together; Wagner proposes to Browning before departing to the States to teach at University of Rochester. Separation for the next nine months sparks intensive transatlantic correspondence in a literary courtship.

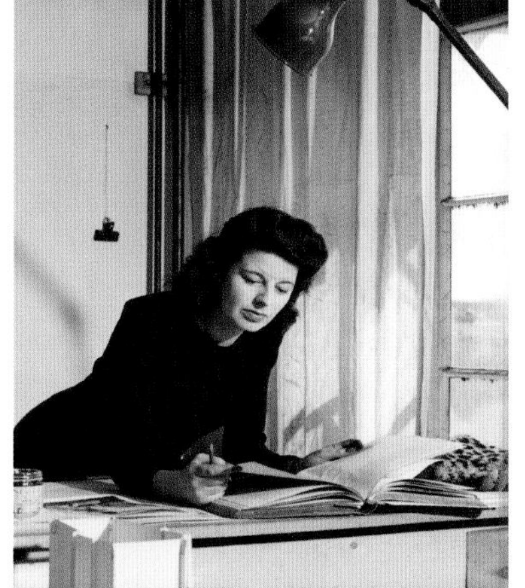

Colleen preparing studio set designs for J. Arthur Rank Organisation, spring 1949.

1949   First solo exhibition opens at The Little Gallery, Piccadilly, London. Departs Southampton on *H.M.S. Queen Elizabeth*, on her "Voyage to romance" (London *Daily Mail* headline) as a young immigrant bride-to-be to the United States.

Married in Manhattan municipal building on June 15. Departs on honeymoon to Mexico. Studies under Diego Rivera at his mural workshop school.

Upon return, lives near University of Rochester campus. Creates mural commission for a new upscale restaurant.

1950   Wins the Juried Art Patrons Award at the 1950 Finger Lakes Exhibition. *Churchgoers* purchased for Memorial Art Gallery, University of Rochester.

Has solo exhibition of *American Scenes* at Rochester Historical Society.

Moves to Manhattan and rents fourth-floor walk-up apartment when Wagner begins doctoral program at Columbia. Begins painting locations and characters depicting the racial and ethnic diversity of their old Italian East Harlem neighborhood.

1951   Accepted into Whitney Museum of American Art annual exhibition, New York.

1952   Invited to join Edwin Hewitt Gallery and given her first solo show. *TIME* and *Newsweek* run favorable articles about her Harlem paintings.

Holiday selected for 3rd place for Popular Choice Award at Carnegie International, Carnegie Institute, Pittsburgh. Part of group exhibition at University of Illinois, Urbana.

During summer vacation on island of Ibiza, paints *Mother and Child*, which is sold to the San Francisco Palace of the Legion of Honor.

1953   Shows work in annual group exhibitions at National Academy of Design, New York (received Joseph S. Isador medal); The Butler Institute of American Art, Youngstown, Ohio; American Watercolor Society, New York (Ida Wells Stroud award).

Lenox and Mondrian featured in *New York Times*, Sunday magazine, comparing her Harlem painting to works by John Marin, Stuart Davis, Joseph Stella, and Piet Mondrian.

Sidewalk purchased by Nelson Rockefeller.

1954   Exhibits in annual group shows at National Institute of Arts and Letters (American Academy of Arts and Letters); The Art Institute of Chicago; Walker Art Center, Minneapolis; The Butler Institute of American Art, Youngstown, Ohio (second prize and honorable mention); Brandeis University, Waltham, Massachusetts. Edwin Hewitt Gallery, New York, holds a solo exhibition of her work.

Telephones purchased by The Butler Institute of American Art, Youngstown, Ohio.

Jungle Gym acquired by Lincoln Kirstein.

Receives Yaddo artist fellowship.

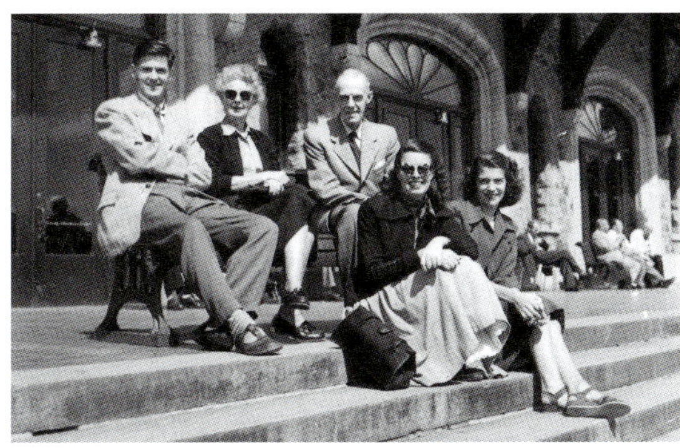

Shane, parents Violet and Captain Langley Browning, Colleen, unidentified friend, c. late 1940s.

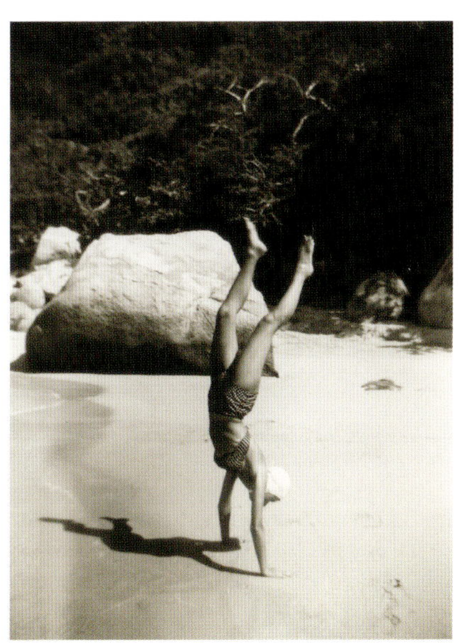

Colleen, c. early 1950s.

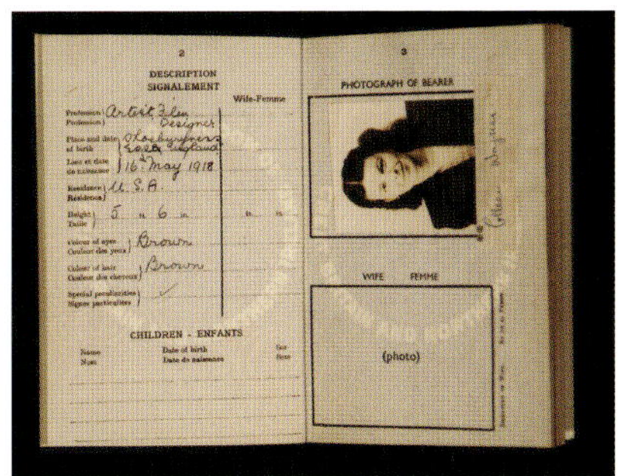

Colleen Browning's passport.

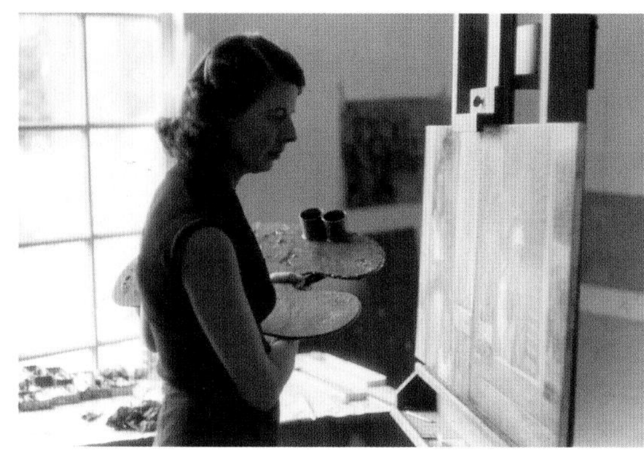

Colleen at work on At Micaud *in her studio, 1956.*

1955   Shows art in group exhibition at Carnegie International, Carnegie Institute, Pittsburgh. Spoleto Festival. Wins McDowell Colony Fellowship.

1956   Exhibits in group shows at Whitney Museum of American Art, Whitney Biennial, New York; Los Angeles County Fair, *Contemporary Art, United States* (Juror's Award); Stanford University, California (Browning is among artists Avery, Rothko, and Hopper. Wins special award for figure painting).

Begins summering on island of Corsica.

1957   Exhibits in group exhibitions at Whitney Museum of American Art, New York; National Academy of Design, New York (Julius Hallgarten Prize); Columbia Museum of Art, South Carolina (Popular Award; purchase of *Green Afternoon*). Has solo exhibition at Edwin Hewitt Gallery, New York.

Featured in *American Artist* magazine.

1958   Participates in annual group exhibition at The Butler Institute of American Art, Youngstown, Ohio.

1959   Exhibits at University of Illinois, Urbana.

1960   Shows work in a group exhibition at National Academy of Design, New York, and in a solo exhibition at Robert Isaacson Gallery, New York.

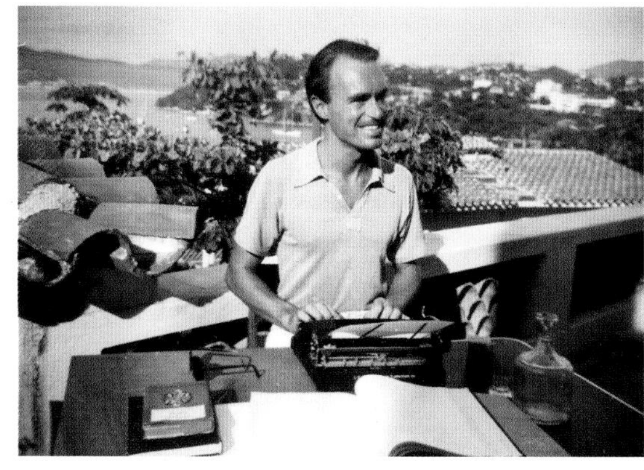

Geoffrey Wagner working in Grenada, c. early 1960s.

1961   Exhibits in Biennial Interamericana, Mexico City. Mentioned in *Cosmopolitan* magazine in "Amazing Inventiveness of Women Painters," along with Isabel Bishop, Georgia O'Keeffe, and Louise Bourgeoise.

Moves to 100 LaSalle Street in brand-new, owner-occupied apartment-studio in Morningside Heights.

1962   Shows in group exhibitions at Pennsylvania Academy of the Fine Arts, Philadelphia, and Milwaukee Art Museum.

1963   Exhibits in group exhibitions at Whitney Museum of American Art, New York, and San Diego Fine Arts Festival (*20th Century Realists*), and in a solo exhibition at Robert Isaacson Gallery, New York.

Receives National Academy of Design Purchase Award, Henry Ward Ranger Fund.

1964   Featured in "People of Our Time," a *New York Times* Sunday magazine preview of New York World's Fair; *Telephones*, a Harlem scene, is prominently placed next to works by John Koch, Ruth Gikow, and Robert Vickrey.

1965   Participates in group exhibition, *Women Artists of America*, at Newark Museum, New Jersey, and in a solo exhibition at Kurt Seligman Gallery, New York.

Elected Associate of the National Academy of Design, New York.

1966   Exhibits in a solo exhibition at Lehigh University, Bethlehem, Pennsylvania, and in a group exhibition at Virginia State College.

Elected Academician of the National Academy of Design, New York.

Begins summering in Grenada, West Indies.

1967   Wagner has sabbatical leave, allowing Browning to travel with him to Morocco and Corsica.

1968   Participates in group exhibitions at The Museum of Modern Art, New York, and Detroit Institute of Arts.

1969   Joins Kennedy Galleries, New York (with a solo exhibition), the beginning of a 20-year relationship with the distinguished midtown gallery.

1970   Shows work in a group exhibition at National Academy of Design (Adolph and Clara Obrig Prize).

1972   Exhibits in solo shows at Kennedy Galleries, New York; Columbus Museum of Arts and Sciences, Georgia; Columbia Museum of Art, South Carolina; Florence Museum, South Carolina.

Builds house in Grenada, West Indies. Browning is assaulted in her kitchen and suffers disfiguring scar on forehead. Transforms her *Umbrella* series with symbolic themes.

1973   Diagnosed with early stage of cancer and undergoes difficult surgery and recovery.

1974   Shows in group exhibition at The Butler Institute of American Art, Youngstown, Ohio (Today's Art Medal of Merit).

Commissioned to produce lithographic poster for United States Olympics Committee.

1975   Shows work in group exhibition, *Twelve American Realists*, at The Cleveland Museum of Art.

Participates in Kent Bicentennial Portfolio, *Spirit of Independence* (sponsor Lorillard Company commissioned works of 12 artists).

1976   Exhibits work in group exhibition, *Painting Today*, at Indianapolis Museum of Art and in a solo exhibition at Kennedy Galleries, New York.

1977   Participates in group exhibitions at Philbrook Museum of Art, Tulsa, Oklahoma (*Contemporary Landscape Painting*), and at Oklahoma Art Center, Oklahoma City.

1978   Shows in solo exhibition at Towson University, Maryland.

Receives portrait commission of His Eminence Terence Cardinal Cooke from New York Archdiocese.

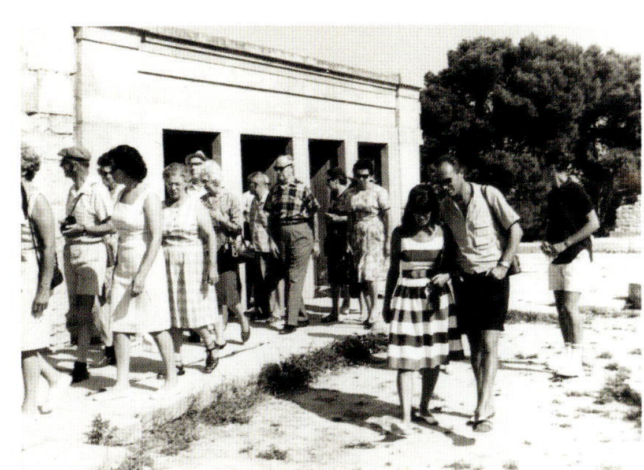

Colleen and Geoffrey on the island of Crete, c. mid-1960s.

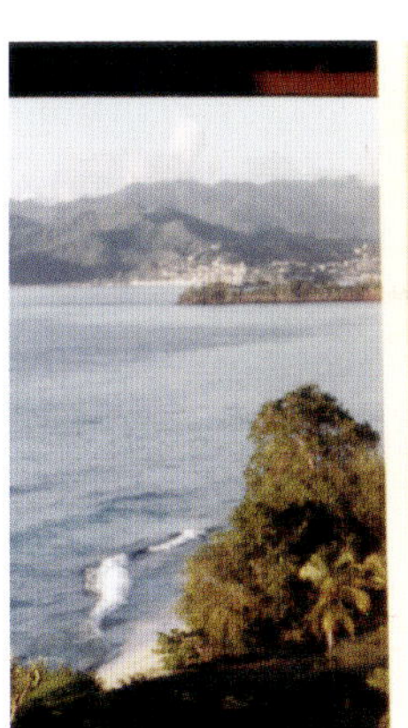
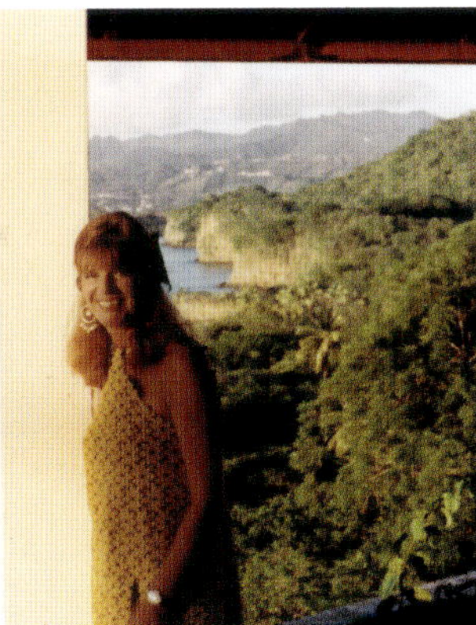

Colleen in Grenada home, 1973.

1979   Exhibits in group shows at MacNider Art Museum, Mason City, Iowa, and Texas Tech University, Lubbock, and in a solo exhibition at Kennedy Galleries, New York.

"Colleen Browning" article published in *Arts Magazine*.

1980–81   Shows in annual group exhibition at National Academy of Design, New York.

"Colleen Browning: A Rich Tapestry of Color" featured in *American Artist*. "Art: Reflections of Infinity" appears in *Architectural Digest*.

1982   Exhibits in national group tour *Realism and Realities: The Other Side of American Painting, 1940–1960*, a landmark exhibition and text by Greta Berman and Jeffrey Wechsler, Rutgers University Art Gallery, New Brunswick, New Jersey, and in a solo exhibition at Kennedy Galleries, New York.

1983   Browning and Wagner, awakened by helicopters landing joint forces of U.S. Marines, Rangers, Navy SEALs, and the 82nd Airborne, are eyewitnesses from their hilltop home to U.S. military invasion of Grenada at dawn on October 25.

Exhibits in *Art and the Law*, a national group tour, and in an annual group exhibition at National Academy of Design, New York.

1984   "Colleen Browning and the Texture of Life" appears in *Art International* magazine.

1985   Exhibits in *Art and the Law*, a national group tour.

1986   Shows work in group exhibition, *Pyrotechnics in American Art*, at The Butler Institute of American Art, Youngstown, Ohio, and in a solo exhibition at Kennedy Galleries, New York.

Receives Pollock-Krasner fellowship grant.

1987   Shows work in retrospective exhibition at Wichita Art Museum, Kansas.

Publishes full-color how-to book *Working Out a Painting*, printed by Watson-Guptill Publications Inc.

1989   Shows in solo exhibition at Kennedy Galleries, New York.

Writes "Evolution of a Painting" for *American Artist* magazine.

1990   Takes part in group exhibition at Terra Museum of American Art, Chicago.

1991   Exhibits in a retrospective exhibition at The Butler Institute of American Art, Youngstown, Ohio, and in an annual group exhibition at National Academy of Design, New York.

Target is accessioned into The National Museum of Women in the Arts in Washington, DC.

1993   Shows work in a solo exhibition at Melvin Gallery, Florida Southern College, Lakeland. First exhibition (a solo show) at Harmon-Meek Gallery, Naples, Florida.

1994   Has retrospective exhibition at E.L. Wiegand Gallery, Nevada Museum of Art, Reno, and a solo exhibition at Harmon-Meek Gallery, Naples, Florida.

1995   Shows work in group exhibitions at Boca Raton Museum of Art, Florida, and at The Barnum Museum, Bridgeport, Connecticut, as well as in a solo exhibition at Harmon-Meek Gallery, Naples, Florida.

Red Umbrella featured on the cover of *Journal of the American Medical Association.*

1996   Artwork highlighted on the cover of *Journal of the American Medical Association.*

Has solo exhibition at Harmon-Meek Gallery, Naples, Florida.

1997   Exhibits work in *Colleen Browning: A Retrospective* at Southern Alleghenies Museum of Art in Loretto, Pennsylvania, and was honored for lifetime achievement.

1999   Learns of her diagnosis of intestinal cancer.

Shows work in solo exhibition at Harmon-Meek Gallery, Naples, Florida.

2003   Passes away at St. Luke's Hospital, New York, on August 22.

Arkansas Arts Center, Little Rock, AR

Ave Maria University, Ave Maria, FL

Boca Raton Museum of Art, Boca Raton, FL

The Butler Institute of American Art, Youngstown, OH

The Cleveland Museum of Art, OH

Columbia Museum of Art, SC

Corcoran Gallery of Art, Washington, DC

Detroit Institute of Arts, MI

Drury University, Springfield, MO

Eastman School of Music, University of Rochester, NY

Fairfield University, CT

Fort Wayne Museum of Art, IN

Goddard Center for the Visual and Performing Arts, Ardmore, OK

Golisano Children's Museum of Naples, FL

John G. Shedd Aquarium, Chicago, IL

Kalamazoo Institute of Arts, MI

Lancing College, Lancing, West Sussex, England

Los Angeles County Museum of Art, CA

Lowe Art Museum, Coral Gables, FL

Maier Museum of Art at Randolph College, Lynchburg, VA

Memorial Art Gallery, University of Rochester, NY

Midwest Museum of American Art, Elkhart, IN

Milwaukee Art Museum, WI

Missouri State University, Springfield, MO

The Museum of Modern Art, New York, NY

Naples Museum of Art, Naples, FL

National Academy of Design, New York, NY

Nelson-Atkins Museum of Art, Kansas City, MO

Neuberger Museum of Art, State University of New York, Purchase, NY

Nevada Museum of Art, Reno, NV

New Britain Museum of American Art, CT

New York State Museum, Albany, NY

Ohio Wesleyan University, Delaware, OH

Oklahoma City Museum of Art, OK

Orlando Museum of Art, FL

Philadelphia Museum of Art, PA

Rhodes College, Memphis, TN

Saint Louis Art Museum, MO

The San Diego Museum of Art, CA

San Francisco Palace of the Legion of Honor (de-accessioned, 2010), CA

Southern Alleghenies Museum of Art, Loretto, PA

Springfield Museum of Art, MO

State Museum of Pennsylvania, Harrisburg, PA

Swope Art Museum, Terre Haute, IN

Syracuse University Art Galleries, NY

University of Missouri, Columbia, MO

Walker Art Center, Minneapolis, MN

Wichita Art Museum, KS

Williams College Museum of Art, Williamstown, MA

1949 The Little Gallery, London, England

1951 Edwin Hewitt Gallery, New York, NY

1954 Edwin Hewitt Gallery, New York, NY

1957 Edwin Hewitt Gallery, New York, NY

1960 Robert Isaacson Gallery, New York, NY

1965 Kurt Seligman Gallery, New York, NY

1969 Kennedy Galleries, Inc., New York, NY

1972 Kennedy Galleries, Inc., New York, NY

1972 Columbus Museum of Arts and Sciences, Columbus, GA

1972 Columbia Museum of Art and Science, Columbia, SC

1972 Florence Museum of Art, Science, and History, Florence, SC

1976 Kennedy Galleries, Inc., New York, NY

1979 Kennedy Galleries, Inc., New York, NY

1982 Kennedy Galleries, Inc., New York, NY

1986 Kennedy Galleries, Inc., New York, NY

1987 Wichita Art Museum, Wichita, KS (solo retrospective)

1989 Kennedy Galleries, Inc., New York, NY

1991 The Butler Institute of American Art, Youngstown, OH (solo retrospective)

1993 Melvin Gallery, Florida Southern College, Lakeland, FL

1993 Harmon–Meek Gallery, Naples, FL

1994 E.L. Wiegand Gallery, Nevada Museum of Art, Reno, NV

1994 Harmon–Meek Gallery, Naples, FL

1995 Harmon–Meek Gallery, Naples, FL

1996 Harmon–Meek Gallery, Naples, FL

1997 Southern Alleghenies Museum of Art, Loretto, PA (solo retrospective)

1999 Harmon–Meek Gallery, Naples, FL

2008 Harmon–Meek Gallery, Naples, FL (solo memorial exhibition)

2009 Southern Alleghenies Museum of Art, Loretto, PA (solo retrospective)

1950 Memorial Gallery, University of Rochester, Rochester, NY

1951 Whitney Museum of American Art, New York, NY

1952 Carnegie International, Carnegie Institute, Pittsburgh, PA

1952 University of Illinois, Urbana, IL

1953 National Academy of Design, New York, NY

1953 The Butler Institute of American Art, Youngstown, OH

1953 American Watercolor Society, New York, NY

1954 National Institute of Arts and Letters (American Academy of Arts and Letters), New York, NY

SELECTED GROUP EXHIBITIONS

1954 61st American Exhibition, Art Institute of Chicago, Chicago, IL

1954 Reality and Fantasy 1900–1954, Walker Art Center, Minneapolis, MN

1954 The Butler Institute of American Art, Youngstown, OH

1954 Brandeis University, Waltham, MA

1955 Carnegie International, Carnegie Institute, Pittsburgh, PA

1956 Whitney Biennial, Whitney Museum of American Art, New York, NY

1956 Contemporary Art, Los Angeles County Fair, Pomona, CA

1956 Stanford University, Palo Alto, CA

1957 Whitney Museum of American Art, New York, NY

1957 National Academy of Design, New York, NY

1957 Columbia Museum of Art and Science, Columbia, SC

1958 The Butler Institute of American Art, Youngstown, OH

1960 National Academy of Design, New York, NY

1961 Biennial Interamericana, Mexico City, Mexico

1962 Pennsylvania Academy of the Fine Arts, Philadelphia, PA

1962 Milwaukee Art Center, Milwaukee, WI

1963 Whitney Museum of American Art, New York, NY

1963 20th Century Realists, San Diego Fine Arts Festival, San Diego, CA

1963 Robert Isaacson Gallery, New York, NY

1965 Women Artists of America, Newark Museum, Newark, NJ

1966 Lehigh University, Bethlehem, PA

1966 Virginia State University, Petersburg, VA

1968 The Museum of Modern Art, New York, NY

1968 Detroit Institute of Arts, Detroit, MI

1970 National Academy of Design, New York, NY

1974 The Butler Institute of American Art, Youngstown, OH

1975 Twelve American Realists, The Cleveland Museum of Art, Cleveland, OH

1976 Painting Today, Indianapolis Museum of Art, Indianapolis, IN

1977 Contemporary Landscape Painting, Philbrook Museum of Art, Tulsa, OK

1977 Oklahoma Art Center, Oklahoma City, OK

1978 Towson University, Towson, MD

1979 MacNider Art Museum, Mason City, IA

1979 Texas Tech University, Lubbock, TX

1980 National Academy of Design, New York, NY

1982 Realism and Realities: The Other Side of American Painting, 1940–1960, Rutgers University Art Gallery, New Brunswick, NJ (traveling exhibition)

1983 Art and the Law (traveling exhibition), West Publishing Company

1983 National Academy of Design, New York, NY

1985 Art and the Law (traveling exhibition), West Publishing Company

1986 Pyrotechnics in American Art, The Butler Institute of American Art,
Youngstown, OH

1990 Terra Museum of American Art, Chicago, IL

1991 National Academy of Design, New York, NY

1995 Boca Raton Museum of Art, Boca Raton, FL

1995 Barnum Museum, Bridgeport, CT

1999 Southern Alleghenies Museum of Art, Loretto, PA

The Antioch Review, vol. 14, no. 1, spring 1954.

Auer, James. "Circus Magic: Parade Impressions Preserved in Oils." *Milwaukee Journal*, July 7, 1989.

Barrett, Mary Ellen and Marvin Barrett. "Colleen Browning's Young Career." *Glamour*, June 1954.

Berman, Greta. "Colleen Browning and the Texture of Life." *Arts International*, August 1984, vol. 27/3.

Berman, Greta and Jeffrey Wechsler. *Realism and Realities: The Other Side of American Painting 1940–1960*. New Brunswick, NJ: Rutgers University Art Gallery, 1981.

Browning, Colleen. *A Studio ABC – A Talk with an Imaginary Studio Visitor*. Unpublished manuscript, c. January 1990. Browning-Wagner Archive, gift of the Estate of Geoffrey Wagner to Southern Alleghenies Museum of Art, Loretto, PA.

———. "A Visit with Colleen Browning," videotape interview with Southern Alleghenies Museum of Art, education program, Altoona, PA, April 1997.

———. "By the Artist." Catalogue statement, *Colleen Browning: Recent Paintings*, Kennedy Galleries, January 31–February 17, 1979.

———. Script for a videotape (never produced), c. 1972. Browning-Wagner Archive, gift of the Estate of Geoffrey Wagner to Southern Alleghenies Museum of Art, Loretto, PA.

———. "The Evolution of a Painting." *American Artist*, July 1989.

———. Video-recorded interview of the artist reminiscing, Harmon-Meek Gallery, Naples, FL, March 1993.

———. *Working Out a Painting*. New York: Watson-Guptill Publications Inc., 1988.

Browning, Major General Langley. "Irish Gunner." Unpublished manuscript. Browning-Wagner Archive, gift of the Estate of Geoffrey Wagner to Southern Alleghenies Museum of Art, Loretto, PA.

Broyard, Anatole. "Book Review: I'm Majoring in Me." *New York Times*, December 2, 1976.

Camp, Richard with Father Sean M. Sullivan, T.O.R, film interview, Southern Alleghenies Museum of Art, Loretto, PA, October 11, 2009. Producer: San Francisco: Camp Creative Media.

Camp, Richard with Michael M. Strueber, film interview, Southern Alleghenies Museum of Art, Loretto, PA, October 11, 2009. Producer: San Francisco: Camp Creative Media.

Canaday, John. "Art: Against the Currents of Fashion." *The New York Times*, March 27, 1965.

———. "Art Review: Wood Carvings of Puerto Rico." *The New York Times*, March 22, 1969.

———. "The People of Our Town." *New York Times Magazine*, April 19, 1964.

Challis, Georgina Ellen. "Colleen Browning: A Rich Tapestry of Color." *American Artist*, September 1981.

Chew, Paul A. "The Popular Prize." *Carnegie Magazine*, Carnegie Institute, Pittsburgh, PA, January 1953.

Clune, Henry W. "Seen and Heard," society column, "She Can Cook, Too." *The Rochester Democrat Chronicle*, December 8, 1949.

Colleen Browning. Exhibition catalogue, Kennedy Galleries, NY, March 5–29, 1969.

"Colleen in Harlem." *TIME*, January 28, 1952, vol. 59, no. 4.

Corn, Wanda M. *The Art of Andrew Wyeth*. California: The Fine Arts Museums of San Francisco, 1973.

Cozzolino, Robert. *With Friends: Six Magic Realists*. Exhibition catalogue, Elvehjem Museum of Art, University of Wisconsin-Madison, 2005.

Craft, John Richard. "Colleen Browning: The Recent Paintings." Exhibition catalogue foreword, Kennedy Galleries, NY, and Columbia Museum of Art, Columbia, SC, March 1972.

Craven, Wayne. *American Art: History and Culture*. New York: Brown and Benchmark, 1994.

Dondero, Congressman George A. "Modern Art Shackled to Communism." Speech, U.S. House of Representatives, August 16, 1949, published in the Congressional Record, First Session, 81st Congress; reproduced in Herschel B. Chipp, *Theories of Modern Art*. Berkeley: University of California Press, 1968.

Dorante. *Art News and Review*, May 21, 1949, vol. 1, no. 8.

Eliasoph, Philip. Telephone interview with George Tooker, August 25, 2010.

———. Telephone interview with Robert Vickrey, January 24, 2011.

Fields, Sidney. "Only Human" column, "The Wagners: Harlem Without Tears." *Daily Mirror*, March 27, 1953.

"Firing Line." Transcript taped in NYC on April 25, 1977, telecast on PBS, April 29, 1977. A production of Southern Educational Communications Association (SECA), Columbia, SC, Leland Stanford Jr. University.

Frankenstein, Alfred. "A Word of Warning – Take the Pittsburgh Art Show Slowly." *San Francisco Chronicle*, February 1, 1953.

Frankenstein, Alfred. *The Reality of Appearance: The Trompe l'Oeil, A History of Pictorial Illusionism.* Berkeley, CA: University of California Art Museum, 1970.

Geldzahler, Henry. *New York Painting and Sculpture, 1940–1970.* New York: E.P. Dutton & Co., 1969.

"General's Daughter Is Academy Entrant." *Evening Standard*, London, May 28, 1940.

Getlein, Frank. *Colleen Browning.* Exhibition catalogue, Kennedy Galleries, March 5–29, 1969.

Gombrich, E.H. *Art and Illusion, A Study in the Psychology of Pictorial Representation.* Bollingen Series, 25, no. 5, Princeton, NJ: Princeton University Press, 1961.

Gorer, Geoffrey. "American Symbolic Realism." *The Listener,* August 3, 1950.

Gray, Mayo L. "Exhibition Review: Colleen Browning's 'Other Worlds' at Kennedy Galleries." *The New York City Tribune*, May 5, 1986.

Greer, Germaine. *The Obstacle Race: The Fortunes of Women Painters and Their Work.* New York: St. Martin's Press, 1979.

Hills, Patricia and Roberta K. Tarbell. *The Figurative Tradition and the Whitney Museum of American Art.* Exhibition catalogue, Whitney Museum of American Art, New York, 1980.

Kent, Norman. "Colleen Browning." *American Artist*, February 1957.

Kirstein, Lincoln. "Symbolic Realism." Exhibition catalogue foreword, Edwin Hewitt Gallery, New York, April 3–22, 1950.

Kloss, William. *Modern American Realism.* Washington, DC: Smithsonian Institution, National Museum of American Art, 1987.

Kramer, Hilton. "Art Review: Avery's Mastery in Paintings on Paper." *The New York Times*, January 8, 1972.

Kriegel, Leonard. "Colleen Browning." *ARTS* magazine, February 1979, vol. 53, no. 6.

Lucie-Smith, Edward. *American Realism.* New York: Harry N. Abrams, 1994.

Lucie-Smith, Edward. *Art Now, from Abstract Expressionism to Superrealism*. New York: William Morrow & Co., 1977.

Lynes, Russell. "Highbrow, Lowbrow, Middlebrow." *Harper's Magazine*, February 1949.

MacAdam, Barbara. "Where the Great Women Artists Are Now." *ARTnews*, February 2007, vol. 106, no. 2.

McShine, Kynaston, ed. *The Natural Paradise: Painting in America, 1800–1950*. Exhibition catalogue, The Museum of Modern Art, New York, 1976.

Mecklenburg, Virginia M. *American Abstraction at Mid-Century*. Washington DC: Smithsonian Institution, 2008.

Miller, Dorothy C. and Alfred H. Barr, Jr. *American Realists and Magic Realists.* New York: The Museum of Modern Art, 1943.

National Academy Museum & School of Fine Arts, New York, press release, June 23, 2010.

Nochlin, Linda. "Why Have There Been No Great Women Artists?" In *Women, Art and Power and Other Essays.* Boulder, CO: Westview Press, 1988.

185 Years of Women as a Subject in American Art (1820–2005). Naples, FL: Harmon-Meek Gallery, 2005.

Orsi, Robert A. *The Madonna of 115th Street: Faith and Community in Italian Harlem, 1880–1950*. New Haven: Yale University Press, 1985.

"Palace Hut for Service Women," *The Salisbury and Winchester Journal*, July 24, 1942.

Preston, Stuart. "About Art and Artists: The Edwin Hewitt Gallery Reopens." *The New York Times*, October 9, 1954.

"Public Ignores Abstract Art in Picking Winners at Show: Conservative Paintings Cop Top Prizes as Pittsburghers Disagree with Experts." *The Pittsburgh Post-Gazette*, December 9, 1952.

"Quick Decision Woman," *Variety*, London, May 2, 1949.

"Realism Without Tears." *Newsweek*, January 28, 1952, vol. 39, no. 4.

Rosenberg, Harold. "Old Song and Dance." *The Antioch Review*, vol. 14, no. 2, summer 1954.

Southgate, M. Therese. *Journal of the American Medical Association*, cover, April 26, 1995, vol. 273, no. 16.

Spencer, Howard DaLee. *Colleen Browning: Recent Paintings*. Exhibition catalogue, Wichita Art Museum, Kansas, December 6, 1986–January 11, 1987.

"Stray Notes: From the Shrine of the Little Flower." Parish newsletter, St. Peter Claver's Church, Brooklyn, NY.

Strueber, Michael M. *Colleen Browning: A Retrospective*. Exhibition catalogue, Southern Alleghenies Museum of Art, Loretto, PA, 1997.

Tallmer, Jerry. "At Home with Colleen Browning & Geoffrey Wagner." *The New York Post*, March 6, 1976, no. 93.

The New York School: The Painters and Sculptors of the Fifties. New York: Harper and Row, Icon Editions, 1978.

Tomor, Michael A. *Magic Realism: An American Response to Surrealism.* Catalogue essay, Southern Alleghenies Museum of Art, Loretto, PA, June 12–September 16, 1999.

Tomor, Michael A. "Magic Realism: An American Response to Surrealism." *American Art Review*, 1999, vol. 2, no. 4.

Wagner, Geoffrey. "The New American Painting," *The Antioch Review,* vol. 14, no. 1, Spring 1954.

———. "Slashing and Sloshing." *Truth.* October 4, 1957, vol. 157, no. 4228.

Weissman, Julian. "New York Reviews." *ARTnews*, April 1976, vol. 75, no. 4.